SILK IN INDIA

SOME ACCOUNT OF SILK IN INDIA,

ESPECIALLY OF

THE VARIOUS ATTEMPTS TO ENCOURAGE AND
EXTEND SERICULTURE IN THAT COUNTRY

SILK IN INDIA

SOME ACCOUNT OF SILK IN INDIA,

ESPECIALLY OF

THE VARIOUS ATTEMPTS TO ENCOURAGE AND EXTEND SERICULTURE IN THAT COUNTRY

BY

J. GEOGHEGAN

GYAN

Published by

Gyan Publishing House
5, Ansari Road
Daryaganj, New Delhi-110002
Phone: 011-47034999, 9811692060
E-mail: books@gyanbooks.com

Distribution Network
gyanbooks.com
India, USA, Canada, UK, Australia

ISBN: 978-93-6433-146-3 (PB)
First Published, 1872

2nd Impression 2024

Printed at: Gyan Press, Delhi.

SILK IN INDIA: SOME ACCOUNT OF SILK IN INDIA, ESPECIALLY OF THE VARIOUS ATTEMPTS TO ENCOURAGE AND EXTEND SERICULTURE IN THAT COUNTRY

AUTHOR: J GEOGHEGAN

Silk in India.

SOME ACCOUNT OF SILK IN INDIA,

ESPECIALLY OF

THE VARIOUS ATTEMPTS TO ENCOURAGE AND EXTEND SERICULTURE IN THAT COUNTRY.

COMPILED BY

J. GEOGHEGAN,

UNDER-SECRETARY TO THE GOVERNMENT OF INDIA, DEPARTMENT OF AGRICULTURE, REVENUE, AND COMMERCE.

CALCUTTA:

OFFICE OF THE SUPERINTENDENT OF GOVERNMENT PRINTING.

1872.

CONTENTS.

INTRODUCTORY.

SECTION I.—SILK IN BENGAL.

SECTION II.—SILK IN BOMBAY.

SECTION III.—SILK IN MADRAS.

SECTION IV.—SILK IN THE PUNJAB.

INTRODUCTORY.

THE ravages of the disease, or complication of diseases, which has been devastating the silkworm-rearing countries of Europe, and the practical remedy for which, notwithstanding M. Pasteur's researches, does not, as yet, seem to have been discovered, have naturally roused attention to the possibility of rearing healthy broods in regions hitherto untried, or of extending the productive powers of silk-producing countries still unaffected by the taint. In furtherance of these objects, the Silk Supply Association was formed in England; and India was the quarter to which the Association first turned. The advantage of a further development of the silk industry in provinces where it already exists, or of its extension to other provinces where it is not yet established, was obvious, and Government expressed its willingness to do what might be possible. The first thing needful seemed to be to collect such information as was attainable in regard to past attempts to foster sericulture in India, the degree of their success, if successful, and the causes of their failure, if the reverse; together with materials for a general review of the present position of all industries connected with silk in India.

Object of the compilation.

2. Accordingly, all available records have been got together, and a circular was addressed to Local Governments and Administrations, in which the following points were noted as those on which information was desired:—

Scope of the enquiries instituted.

"Places where silk culture has been pursued, with particulars of climate;
Extent of land under cultivation in mulberry, or other food for silkworms;
Quantity of silk produced;
Quality and price of ditto;
Kinds of silkworms kept, with their scientific names;
Method of rearing the worms;
Method of reeling the silk adopted;
Particulars as to extent of European enterprise;
Amount of silk woven on the spot, and nature of fabrics;
Quantity and value of silk exported (1) by sea, (2) by land;
Full particulars of any attempts or experiments made during the past 30 years, or by private persons, with a view to improve or extend the culture;
Opinions of qualified persons, official and non-official (whether in regard to stock of worms, their food, mode of rearing, manipulation of silk, or on any other point), and improvements recommended."

3. Replies, of more or less value,* have been received to this call, and from them and such other records as could be obtained from any quarter, the following account has been compiled.

Materials obtained.

4. The plan followed has been to take each province in succession, and trace, as far as the materials would allow, the efforts made by the British Government to encourage and improve the manufacture of silk within its limits.

Plan followed in compiling them.

In tracing the history of these efforts, opportunity has been taken to cite the opinions of the authorities consulted, and to give a general view of the industry in its present state, as well as of any changes which it may have undergone within the last 30 or 40 years. In all these aspects, I cannot but admit that the narrative is very imperfect, but I have, for the most part, had to deal with very imperfect materials.

As it was desirable to bring together the information from various provinces about the habits of the tusser and other non-domesticated silk-producers, I have done this in a separate chapter, instead of distributing the information province by province. On this subject, Captain Hutton's monograph will be referred to. I have reproduced it entire, in the form of an Appendix.

5. But before proceeding to the more detailed account of the progress of silk culture in India, a slight sketch of the spread of this industry throughout the world may not be out of place. The introduction to M. Léon de Rosny's translation of the Japanese

Brief sketch of general spread of silk culture.

* I wish particularly to acknowledge the completeness of the information supplied by the Government of Madras. In the 3rd Section I have reproduced, with a few slight additions and a few as slight omissions, the excellent summary prepared by the Madras Board of Revenue, and forwarded by the Local Government.

treatise of Sirakawa, of Sendaï, on silkworm breeding in Japan, contains an interesting sketch of the spread of sericulture in Asia. For other countries I have had to trust to such scattered notices as were attainable, and I fear the account may not be altogether accurate; it does not pretend to be exhaustive.

China the cradle of the silkworm.

6. There seems to be no doubt that China is the country where the product of the silkworm was first used as a material for textile fabrics, and that the industry has gradually radiated from China as a centre, till it covers, at the present day, a number of very widely distributed areas of very diverse climatic conditions. The Chinese historians carry back the cultivation of the mulberry and the breeding of silkworms to the period of myths. If they are to be believed, the art of silk reeling was known in China in the time of Fouh-hī, a century before the date usually assigned to the biblical deluge, and the Empress Sī-lîng-chí, wife of the celebrated Hôang-ti (2602 years before the Christian era) did not disdain to share in the labours attending the care of the insect, as well as in those of the loom, the invention of which seems to be attributed to her, and to have raised her to the position of a tutelary genius, with special altars of her own. But whatever the precise date of the discovery, it appears there can be no question of the very high antiquity of the knowledge of the worm and its product in China. A series of imperial edicts, and a voluminous literature of practical treatises, testify to the importance of the industry and the care that was taken to foster an art which was considered, according to M. de Rosny, 'best fitted to promote the morality of the people and extinguish pauperism in the Empire.' The original cradle of sericulture in China, if we are to depend on the 'very respectable authority' of the Sacred Book of the annals, included the country of 'Yēn, lying south-west of the present province of Shantoung; the country of Ts'īng, answering to the north-west region of the same province, the country of Sîu, covering the south of Shantoung and the northern portion of Kiangsou; and lastly the country of Kīng, which now constitutes the province of Houkouang.' The industry now extends to the whole of China except the extreme northern provinces. Not even an approximate estimate can be made of the amount of silk produced, but, besides exporting some 10 million pounds annually by sea, the yield is sufficient to clothe in silk all but the lowest classes of a population alleged to number 400,000,000. According to Captain Bowers, of Sladen's Expedition, the silk trade in the west of China is now nearly suspended. Large quantities used to be raised in Yunnan and Szechuen, but the industry has suffered from the Panthay revolt and consequent disturbances.

Silk in the Corea.

7. The region indicated above, as the cradle of the silkworm in China, lies over against the peninsula of the Corea and the Japanese Island of Kiou Siou, where the civilisation of Niphon seems to have first taken root six or seven centuries before the Christian era. The jealousy of the Chinese Government appears, for some centuries, to have kept the secret from spreading even to the Corea. But, according to a Chinese authority, the art of silk reeling was introduced into that peninsula in the 12th century before Christ, and spread rapidly throughout the whole region; this account is confirmed by the narrative of an embassy from China to the Corea in the years 1119—1120 B. C., which describes the nobles and the chief officers of the court, with their wives, as dressed in the same kinds of silk fabrics as are still to be found in this extreme eastern peninsula.

Passage of the silk-worm southwards to Annam;

8. It was not till a much later epoch, nor, we may presume, till the industry had spread southward in China far beyond its original limits, that, still following the same direction, it reached the Annamite kingdoms. M. de Rosny dates its introduction there from the third century before our era. In Tonquin and Cochin China the manufacture of silk has taken considerable hold, and in the 17th century there appears to have been a large export of silk from these countries. At the present day I gather that the silk is mostly used for home consumption; it is said to be markedly inferior to that of China.

and to Siam.

9. The Siamese appear to have learnt the art in the beginning of the 7th century B. C., but the manufacture made no great progress till the 18th century, when the opening of more frequent communication with China gave a certain stimulus to the traffic in

silk. At the present day, according to Crawfurd, the industry has again fallen into disfavour, and the few places where it still maintains an existence, only produce a small quantity of a coarse fabric inferior to the manufactures of Java and Celebes. Some Siamese silk now finds its way to the looms of Ahmedabad.

Silk in the Malay Archipelago.

10. Of the success of silk in these last-named islands, or in others of the Malay Archipelago, I do not find any distinct records. It appears, however, from an article in the "Technologist" for 1865 (seemingly from a Dutch source) that the Government of Netherlands India, has, at considerable expense, made several attempts to introduce the *Bombyx Mori* into Java. In 1838 we find, among the list of emigrants from India, four "silk-winders" bound for Batavia. In 1862 a trial was made with the *Siamese* silkworm at Buitenzorg, Samarang and Malang, and with some success, the silk fetching 44 florins the kilogram in France. The Government was said, in 1863, to be endeavoring to push the cultivation of the mulberry, and experiments were also being made with some wild species. No decided results had, however, been obtained. From the above it would appear that the Siamese had introduced one of the Chinese multivoltines. In Labuan silk was produced, also from a multivoltine worm, in 1869 and 1870. The then Governor was sanguine of success, and a report by Mr. Cobb, on the silk and cocoons sent from Labuan in 1870, is favourable.

In Indo-Chinese regions.

11. Into the Indo-Chinese tracts there seems to be reason to believe that the knowledge of silk passed from the Western Provinces of China. The breeding of silkworms is now practised in the modern kingdom of Ava and the provinces of British Burmah. Of the industry in the latter, a fuller account will be found in a separate chapter.

In India.

12. The date of the introduction of silk into India is probably not to be ascertained. A word *Kauseya* occurs in the Rámáyana, the Mahábhárata and the Laws of Manu, but whether it means silk; whether, if so, the silk was what is now known as tusser silk, or silk of a domesticated bombyx; and whether, in the latter case, the silk was imported, either raw or in fabrics, or produced in India, are questions on which the learned are not yet decided. Whatever may be the date of the introduction of the worm, its geographical distribution at the present day, and the fact that the species first introduced was a multivoltine, seem to me to lead to the conclusion that the insect was first introduced into India from the north-east. The history of the various other attempts to naturalise the worm, in the several provinces of India, will be found at full length further on. On these points the narrative has nothing conjectural about it.

Passage of the silkworm westward.

13. The emigrations of the worm already noticed seem generally to have included, if they did not altogether consist of, multivoltine species. In the passage of the industry westward to the north of the Himalaya the univoltine *Bombyx Mori* alone played a part. This is readily accounted for. Looking at a map shewing the distribution of silk culture, we should see a great blank between China proper and what is now the country of the Atálik Ghází. The great Thibetan table-land has, apparently, never been the seat of silk manufacture; probably because its climate is inimical to the mulberry. Only the annual worm, in the egg stage, could endure the tedious transit of this inhospitable region.

To Khotan.

Passing westwards, we find the worm re-appear in Khotan. Its introduction into that province was not later than the year 419 A.D. The Buddhist pilgrim, Hiouen-tsang, describes how a woman baffled the Chinese monopolists, and how the seeds of the mulberry and the eggs of the silkworm were carried across the frontier by a Chinese princess in the lining of her head-dress (la ouate de son bonnet), as she went to join her betrothed husband the king of Kiu-sa-ta-na. According to the same authority the worms emerged before the mulberry had come into leaf, and it became necessary to feed the young brood on the leaves of various other plants.

To the Khanates.

From Khotan we may presume the art to have passed to Bokhara, Khiva, Samarkand, and the Khanates generally. In the section on silk in the Punjab some notices of the industry in those regions will also be found. We may suppose that the silk of Kashmere has the same origin.

Silk in Persia.

14. The introduction of the Bombyx into Persia cannot be dated with exactitude. But M. de Rosny believes it followed shortly after the naturalisation of the insect in Khotan. Long before this, however, the Persians had been conversant with silk; and had in fact held complete control of the supply of the commodity to Constantinople. They had in their hands the route by India and the Persian Gulf, as well as the overland traffic, and Gibbon cites from Procopius the almost fabulous rates to which the monopoly of the carrying trade ran up the price of what was then a luxury. By the 7th century of the Christian era, the breeding of the worm and the manufacture of silk fabrics had firmly established themselves in Persia, and probably, where sericulture has taken root in Afghanistan, it is an offshoot of the Persian industry. At the present day the mulberry grows almost throughout Persia; but the true silk region lies on the south shore of the Caspian, between the mouths of the Araxes and Gurgan, or, in other words, the provinces of Shirwan, Ghilan and Mazenderan.* The first is a Russian province. The industry is also carried on in the Persian provinces of Kachan, Meshed and Yezd. A paper in the "Technologist" for 1865 states that the worms are very carelessly treated and the silk very variable in quality. England, Russia and France import raw silk from Persia. But its quality is low, it being ill-reeled and irregular. The Persian silk crop of 1863-64 is said to have yielded 1,129,536 lbs., valued at £734,198. The average price was 12*s.* to 16*s.*: for the best quality 18*s.* Of this produce 400,000 lbs. were shipped to Great Britain, 30,000 lbs. to France, and 141,600 lbs. to Russia. Within the last few years the yield has much diminished. Indeed Sir H. Rawlinson speaks of the silk crop as an entire failure. It is probably from Persia that silk culture spread into the Caucasus and Mingrelia, where, however, it does not seem to have attained any great development.†

In Asia Minor.

15. I have been able to find very little about silk in Syria and Asia Minor. In 1836 the former province produced 856,000 lbs. of raw silk, and the annual outturn of Asia Minor is said to be about 1,200,000 lbs. The Broussa or Brutia silk has now a very high reputation, and ranks with the best Italian silk. The improvement is due to better reeling.

In Japan.

16. To return again to the extreme east. The date of the introduction of the silkworm into Japan seems somewhat obscure. But, commencing with the 5th century of the Christian era, the industry has rapidly spread. In fact the people addicted themselves to the pursuit with such ardour that, in fear lest other branches of agriculture should be altogether abandoned, the Japanese Government has, at times, forbidden the extension of mulberry cultivation, or attempted, by sumptuary laws, to restrict the use of silk garments to certain classes. Sericulture has spread to almost all the islands of the Japanese Archipelago. But the northern isles are somewhat too cold, and the southern too hot, to be a favorable field for the enterprise. According to a report by Mr. Adams, Secretary of Legation, "the silk districts are confined to the principal island, and may be divided into three groups; the northern designated under the general name of Oshiu; the south-western, including those of Echizen, Sodai, Mashita, &c.; and the central, which produces the Mayebashi, Shinshiu and other varieties of hank silks, as well as the silks of the Koshiu and Hachoji." The opening of the ports has considerably increased the growth of mulberry in Japan. There are no statistics as to the internal consumption of silk: the Consul at Kanagawa estimated the total yield at 135,000 bales. In 1862-63 the exports rose to 25,800 bales (of a little over 100 lbs.) This year was exceptional. But the average exports of the four following years were about 15,000 bales. Cocoons and eggs are also largely exported. The following are

---

* Of this very tract, Marco Polo writes:—"It is from the country on this sea, also, that the silk called Ghellé is brought." Colonel Yule notes thereon:—"The province of Gíl gave name to the silk for which it was and is still famous. * * * This *seta ghella* is mentioned also by Pegolotti and by Uzzano, with an odd transposition, as seta *leggi*, along with seta *masandroni, i. e.*, from the adjoining province of Mezenderán."—*Yule's Marco Polo, Bk. I., Chap. IV.*

† Marco Polo, however, speaks of silk being produced "in great abundance" in "Georgiania," a region which, as laid down by Colonel Yule, would include these countries.

given as the values, in *dollars*, of raw silk, cocoons and eggs, respectively, exported in 1868 and 1869:—

	1868.	1869.
Silk	10,638,041	4,864,990
Cocoons	123,040	177,805
Eggs	4,199,138	2,728,500

17. It was not till the middle of the 6th century of our era that the silkworm was introduced into Europe. After an unsuccessful attempt to stimulate to competition "his Christian allies the Æthiopians of Abyssinia, who had recently acquired the arts of navigation, the spirit of trade and the seaport of Adulis, still decorated with the trophies of a Grecian conqueror," the Emperor Justinian found by a lucky chance the means of gratifying his wish to defeat the monopoly of silk hitherto held by the Persians. This chance was the advent of the "two Persian monks" who had been long resident in China, and who now offered to import the eggs of the silkworm. They were liberally encouraged by Justinian, and Gibbon relates (not without a scholarly sigh at the thought that they did not rather bring another Chinese art, and so preserve to us "the comedies of Menander and the entire decads of Livy") how they "again entered China, deceived a jealous people by concealing the eggs of the silkworm in a hollow cane, and returned in triumph with the spoils of the east." "Under their direction," he continues, "the eggs were hatched at the proper season by the artificial heat of dung; the worms were fed with mulberry leaves; they lived and laboured in a foreign climate; a sufficient number of butterflies was saved to propagate the race, and trees were planted to supply the nourishment of the rising generations. Experience and reflexion corrected the errors of a new attempt, and the Sogdoite ambassadors acknowledged, in the succeeding reign, that the Romans were not inferior to the natives of China in the education of the insect and the manufacture of silk."

Introduction of silk into Europe.

18. The industry rapidly took root in Greece, as is apparent from Gibbon's account of the manufactures of Corinth, Thebes and Argos in the 10th century, and as the modern name of the Peloponnesus shews. Silk is still produced in the Morea and in the islands of Cyprus and Crete. But the total outturn does not seem to exceed 150,000 lbs. per annum, and the silk is of inferior quality.

Silk in Greece.

19. Spain seems to have been the next country of Europe to see the silkworm introduced. "The secret," says Gibbon, "had been stolen by the dexterity and diligence of the Arabs; the Caliphs of the East and West scorned to borrow from the unbelievers their furniture and apparel, and two cities of Spain, Almeria and Lisbon, were famous for the manufacture, the use, and perhaps the exportation of silk." The industry still survives. I have not found any very recent notices, but in 1842 Spain produced about 2,000,000 lbs., of which Valencia yielded three-fifths and Murcia and Grenada each one-fifth. The cocoons are said to be excellent,* but the silk, reeled by the peasantry, is irregular. In Portugal the industry has within the present century attained a considerable development. According to a report from Consul Crawford, the silkworm of the province of Traz-os-Montes alone in Europe has escaped infection. The same authority gives the average annual export of cocoons at 7,500 cwt. The industry is more generally in the hands of small producers than in other parts of Europe. The tree used was the black mulberry, which attains the dimensions of a forest tree; but of late many plants of the best varieties of French and Italian white mulberry had been planted. At the Exhibition at Oporto in 1867 ten provinces competed, and beautiful cocoons and manufactures are said to have been exhibited. A throwing factory had been established and three new reeling machines invented.

In Spain and Portugal.

20. The worm was first introduced into Sicily by the Normans, and (again to quote Gibbon) "this emigration of trade distinguishes the victory of Roger from the uniform and fruitless hostilities of every age. After the sack† of Corinth, Athens and Thebes,

In Sicily.

* A paper from South Australia, which I have recently seen, describes the Spanish cocoon as "large, fawn-coloured, and as hard as a walnut nearly," and slightly pinched in the middle.

† 1147 A. D.

his lieutenant embarked with a captive train of weavers and artificers of both sexes, a trophy glorious to their master and disgraceful to the Greek Emperor. The King of Sicily was not insensible of the value of the present; and in the restitution of the prisoners he excepted only the male and female manufacturers of Thebes and Corinth, who labour, says the Byzantine historian, under a barbarous lord, like the old Eretrians in the service of Darius. A stately edifice, in the palace of Palermo, was erected for the use of this industrious colony, and the art was propagated by their children and disciples, to satisfy the increasing demand of the western world. The decay of the looms of Sicily may be ascribed to the troubles of the island and the competition of the Italian cities. In the year 1314, Lucca alone, among her sister republics, enjoyed the lucrative monopoly. A domestic revolution dispersed the manufacturers to Florence, Bologna, Venice, Milan and even the countries beyond the Alps, and thirteen years after this event the statutes of Modena enjoin the planting of mulberry trees and regulate the duties on raw silk."

In Italy.

21. In Italy, till the outbreak of the modern epizoic, the insect seems to have found a most congenial habitat, and sericulture has spread more or less all over the peninsula. The estimates of the total produce of Italian silk vary exceedingly. The report of the Turin Chamber of Commerce for 1870 estimates the outturn of the preceding season at the value of 77½ millions of francs, representing about 13 million kilos of cocoons. It is not clear whether this is for the whole Italian kingdom; but at any rate it seems to include the northern provinces down to Tuscany, Umbria, and the Marches. Mr. Winkworth in the "Technologist," on the other hand, estimates the yield of Italy at upwards of 100 million pounds of cocoons, or more than three times the estimate of the Turin Chamber of Commerce. The British Trade Journal, too, puts the value of Italian cocoons at 11¼ millions sterling, or between three or four times the value estimated by the Italian authority cited above.* The epizoic disease has made great havoc in Italy, which is now largely dependent on imported seed.

In France.

22. The culture of silk does not seem to have taken any hold in France till the commencement of the 16th century, when Francis I.† introduced silkworms from Milan to Lyons, and the rearing of the worm was simultaneously commenced in the Valley of the Rhone. This tract still continues the head-quarters of the industry in France, the Cevennes silk bearing the highest reputation. But sericulture had up to the year 1857 been also much extended towards the north and west. In 1789 France produced 1,000,000 lbs. of raw silk, and in 1853 the outturn of cocoons reached to 26 million kilos (corresponding to about 5 million English pounds of raw silk). In 1857, however, the fatal epizoic broke out, and the yield of cocoons had fallen to 13 million kilos in 1867. France carried the industry to Algeria, and in 1861 that province produced 4,206 kilos of cocoons. A Government bounty was offered to encourage the pursuit, and about £1,000 paid in rewards in the same year. In 1869 the produce had risen to 22,754 lbs. (English) of cocoons. But the cocoons had carried disease with them.

In Algeria.

Attempts to grow silk in the British Islands.

23. The manufacture of silk in England dates from the year 1585, when the sack of Antwerp by the Spaniards drove many Flemish artisans to England. The industry received a further impetus from the revocation of the edict of Nantes, just a century later, when a large body of French weavers crossed the channel and settled themselves in Spitalfields. The manufacture has always been fostered by Government, though not perhaps in the most judicious way, and now consumes some 12 million pounds of raw silk annually. Several efforts have been made to establish the breeding of the silkworm in the United Kingdom, and so render the silk-spinners and weavers independent of foreign countries for the material of their operations. But none of these efforts have been successful. James I. in 1608 issued circular

* The lower or Italian estimates are confirmed by the reports of Consul Colnaghi and Mr. Herries, Secretary of Legation, *apud* McCulloch's Commercial Dictionary.

† Henry IV. and Sully also encouraged the industry, and patents of nobility were bestowed on those who persevered in the pursuit for 12 years.

letters to persons of influence recommending the subject to their attention, and arrangements were made for the distribution of the mulberry. Some old trees still exist dating from the time of this attempt, which did not, however, succeed in naturalising the worm in England. In the year 1699 the Sieur de la Forêt travelled through the midland and eastern countries and distributed some 100,000 mulberry plants. In 1718 a company obtained a lease of Chelsea Park for 122 years; mulberries were planted and buildings erected, but the enterprise ended in failure. In 1825 (or 1835?) another attempt was made in the county of Cork in Ireland, and 80 acres were planted with 400,000 mulberry plants; buildings were erected and rearing commenced on Dandolo's plan. But wages were found to be too high, and the company transferred its operations to Malta. In the period 1836-1846 a small experiment was carried on by a Mrs. Whitley at Lymington in Hampshire. This lady appears to have cultivated the *Morus multicaulis* or Philippine mulberry with success. Recently attempts on a small scale have been made in many parts of England, and in May 1870 the Silk Supply Association commenced experiments in breeding worms, in rooms assigned for the purpose by the Science and Art Department, Kensington. Eggs were obtained from China, Japan, Russia, Mongolia, Natal, Tuscany, and England. The Tuscan, Chinese, and Japanese cocoons were pronounced excellent, the first indeed remarkably fine; the "Mongolian" breed yielded inferior cocoons, long, narrow, and pointed. The cold of the early nights of July 1870 had proved fatal to many worms. These recent efforts have not done much to illustrate the possibility of rearing worms in England *as a successful commercial enterprise*. The possibility of doing so, apart from this condition, hardly requires further proof.

In the parts of Europe.

24. In Bavaria and in Sweden the worm was in the year 1841 being reared as a commercial speculation. In Russia, Peter the Great and Catherine both encouraged sericulture, and their policy has been handed down to their successors. In 1841, persons engaged in the pursuit enjoyed important privileges, and the southern provinces now produce a certain quantity of silk. Some particulars of the export to the Khanates will be found in the section on silk in the Punjab. Hungary also produces silk. An article in the "Encyclopædia Britannica," Ed. 1860, says the yield of Hungary was "lately" 200,000 lbs. from $1\frac{1}{2}$ million trees in 40 localities. Some silk is also produced in European Turkey, including the principalities. The British Trade Journal estimates the total yield of European countries, except Italy, France, and Spain, at nearly one million pounds worth of cocoons.

In America.

25. The attempts to naturalize the silkworm in America date from the reign of James I., who encouraged the enterprise in the "plantations" of the New World as well as in England. Again, when the Chelsea Park scheme above noticed failed, an attempt was made to establish sericulture in Georgia and Carolina; the importation of silk free of duty was permitted, and direct bounties were offered in encouragement; the quality of the silk, however, proved indifferent, and the experiment had no permanent success. In 1789 another trial was made, but failed owing to the high rate of wages. Again a scheme was organized in 1831, and a large quantity of excellent silk was produced. But the enterprise was made the basis of a monstrous stock-exchange speculation, and ultimately collapsed.

In 1854 M. Prevost, a Frenchman, introduced the mulberry into California. The plants throve well, and four years later he imported silkworms' eggs from China and France. Those from the latter country succeeded, producing good cocoons. In the following years the attention of the State Government was drawn to the matter, and in 1866 the legislature of California passed "an Act for the encouragement of silk culture," which offered a reward of $250 for each plantation of 5,000 two-year old mulberries, and of $300 for "each one thousand silk cocoons" produced within four years. The latter reward seems enormous, but I have quoted correctly from the paper by Mr. W. Baldwin in the "Silk Supply Journal," which is my authority on this subject.

The growth of mulberry was in this way largely stimulated, and at the end of 1869 it was calculated that there were upward of four million trees in the State, belonging in almost equal proportions to three species, *viz.*, *Morus multicaulis*, *M. Alba*, and *M. Moretti*. The last is described as like *M. Alba*, but with a purple berry. The worms introduced are also of three species, one annual, the second bivoltine, the third trivoltine. But the first is the species by far most common, and is indeed said to pay better than the others. Mr. Baldwin appends an account of a visit to the "Davisville silkworm nursery," near Sacramento. Upwards of a hundred acres were planted with three kinds of mulberry, the trees numbering about 700,000. There were two "cocooneries," one being rented to four Frenchmen, who were supplied with eggs and mulberry on condition of their paying one-half the gross proceeds. The other, managed by the proprietors, contained upwards of three million worms at the time of Mr. Baldwin's visit. The most noticeable point in his account is the free ventilation allowed. "The windows were all open, and are so left during the whole time the operations are carried on, unless when very cold or wet, the sun's rays being prevented from penetrating by coarse canvas screens placed against the windows." This is quite opposed to Count Dandolo's theories. No cocoons had been exported, the industry being confined to the production of eggs* which fetched $4 per oz.; but it was expected that some 20,000,000 cocoons would be exported in 1870. The manager of the Davisville concern was trying experiments in crossing the "Californian" annual with the French and Japanese. The California worm is itself, however, a recent importation, the paper does not say whence.

I have also seen brief entries of experiments in Kansas, Iowa, and Utah. An American paper (seemingly) quoted in the "Silk Supply Journal" says that 'the Marquis de Boissière, reputed to be worth four million francs, has undertaken the culture of silk in Franklin county, Kansas, on a large scale, and has brought out a colony of sericulturists.' At a meeting of the Silk Supply Association in February 1870, the Hon'ble H. D. Kilbourne stated that he had in 1857 undertaken to grow mulberry in Iowa, and had in two years raised 10,000 plants by layers. The plants grew readily. An American official report recently received says that accounts of success with silkworms in Utah are increasingly frequent, upwards of 50 families in one neighbourhood having engaged in the pursuit. "Samuel Carnaby," of Spanish Fork, reports that he has worms fed upon "osage orange," and that a successful experience of four years has led him to use that plant exclusively.

In British Colonies.

St. Helena.

Labuan.

Jamaica.

Mauritius.

26. The failure of the worm in Europe has drawn attention to the possibility of raising healthy stock in several of the British Colonies. In St. Helena sericulture used to be carried on by the East India Company till they gave up their charter. The experiment in Labuan has already been noticed. In Jamaica an attempt was made in Lord Metcalfe's time, but failed, apparently from extravagant expenditure, at the outset. In Mauritius two gentlemen MM. Descroizelles and d'Unienville have "spent several years of their lives in laudable efforts to implant the culture of silk in Mauritius," and it has been lately reported that they have produced 14 lbs. of silk of good quality and colour. A previous smaller sample had been valued at 28*s.* to 30*s.* per lb. The mulberry is said to thrive on the island.

In Australia.

In Australia, most of the colonies have taken up the question more or less seriously. New South Wales, South Australia, Victoria, and Queensland have all produced silk, and some excellent practical papers have been written, especially by Mr. Brady at Sydney, and Mr. Francis at Adelaide. Mr. Brady commenced a series of experiments in acclimatization in 1862, and has imported mulberries of every country, and the most celebrated and choicest breeds of silkworms. All these, he says, he has naturalised; among them some of the Bengal multivoltines. Near Adelaide, Mr. Francis has bred several kinds of univoltines and made some interesting experiments in crossing. Cocoons have also been produced in Queensland and Victoria. But the possibility of *commercial success* has not yet been demonstrated.†

* But an extract from the "Daily News," quoted in the "Silk Supply Journal" for February 1870, says that silk-weaving had been attempted at San Francisco.

† A report by the Melbourne Acclimatization Society (recently quoted in the "Pall Mall Gazette") complains that it is found difficult to promote sericulture in Victoria "in a real practical manner, so as to be of benefit to the colony."

The question of the price of labour has not, perhaps, been sufficiently considered. The Ailanthus worm has been bred at Sydney, and both that breed and the *Bombyx Mori* seem to have been tried in Van Diemen's Land so long ago as 1862. But I have not found any record of the success of the experiment in Tasmania.

In Tasmania.

In New Zealand experiments have been made with the Ailanthus worm *(Attacus Cynthia)*, and with Japanese (seemingly) trivoltines. But not with much success hitherto.

In New Zealand.

Vigorous efforts have been made by the South African colonies to take advantage of the opportunity afforded by the failure of the European crops and enrol South Africa among silk-producing regions. In Cape Colony a species of mulberry already flourishes. It is generally believed to be indigenous, but more probably is a Japanese mulberry imported by the Dutch. In 1868 the Colonial Government imported from Japan and distributed gratis some thousands of silkworms' eggs. In the following year cuttings and seed of the *Morus alba* were imported, and small rewards offered for every plantation of 100 trees maintained. The worm, however, is reported to thrive better on the so-called wild or indigenous mulberry than on the plants introduced from France. A Company has been set on foot at Stellingbosch, and "very beautiful silk" from the Cape was received by the Silk Supply Association. The same body speaks most favourably of cocoons produced in Natal in 1870 or 1871, from seed obtained from a "high class Japanese breed" acclimatised in Egypt. The same colony had also reared with success some Japanese trivoltines obtained direct from Japan. The mulberry used seems to have been the same as the Cape "wild" mulberry, which grows luxuriantly in Natal.

In South Africa.

27. Though Madagascar is not a British colony, I may here jot down the brief notice I have found of silk in that island. There is said to be an indigenous silkworm of great size, fed in the open fields on the pigeon-pea (Ambiravatry) and yielding very large cocoons. Little attention, however, is paid to it by the natives. This is probably the silk of which Mr. Consul Pakenham writes :—"There is another silk in Madagascar much esteemed on account of its strength, which I am told is collected in a state of floss in the interior, and afterwards treated much the same as cotton." (Compare the carding of the Eria silk in Assam.) Mr. Pakenham states that "the notorious M. deLastelle" imported Bombyx eggs from China, introduced the mulberry and set up a regular magnanerie at Tamatave, which produced "several thousand pounds" of fine silk. The letter containing these particulars is dated the 11th August 1869.

In Madagascar.

28. The "British Trade Journal" gives an estimate of the silk yielded by the Pacific Islands (£24,000 worth of cocoons). I have traced nothing more detailed on that point.

In the Pacific Islands.

29. Tripoli seems to yield some silk, but I have no figures more recent than 1842, in which year that country is said to have produced 126,000 lbs. of raw silk.

In Tripoli.

30. The experiment does not appear to have been tried in Egypt till quite recently. The Khedive has now started a mulberry plantation of about 1,000 acres, some 25 miles from Alexandria, and placed it in charge of a European Superintendent. Plants to the number of 90,000 have been put down, and meanwhile experiments have been made in rearing, by feeding the worms on the mulberry grown in His Highness' private gardens. The cocoons are said to have been excellent, and "several private cultivations" are also reported successful. A paragraph in the "Egyptian Messenger" (June 1871) is the only authority for the above statements.

In Egypt.

SILK IN INDIA.

SECTION I.

SILK IN BENGAL.

First introduction of the silkworm into India.

THE date of the introduction of the silkworm into India is, as already noticed, still an open question. Indeed, the very name (desi, or indigenous), applied to the oldest species, shews that even the tradition of a foreign origin for the insect has died out. But the distribution of the worm, both within the continent of India, where it first occupied the valley of the Brahmaputra and a portion of the tract lying between that river and the Ganges, and in the regions beyond the eastern frontier, points, with tolerable certainty, to a primary introduction by land from the eastward. This was the opinion of Mr. Atkinson, Commercial Resident at Jungypore, at the end of the last century.

Early attention of East India Company to the silk trade.

2. The value of silk, as an article of trade, was appreciated by the East India Company at an early period of its existence. The Calendar of State Papers, for the years 1617—1621, teems with extracts on the subject. But Chinese, Japanese, Siamese, Cochin Chinese, and above all Persian silk, seem to have been at first held in more estimation than the silk of Bengal. There is a long and interesting account of negotiations carried on in 1617 and the following year between Sir Thomas Roe and the "Sophy" of Persia, with a view to secure to the English Company the monopoly of Persian silk. The export was estimated at from 2,000 to 3,000 bales, and in 1619 Persian silk sold in London for 26*s.* 10*d.* per lb. The only specific notice of Bengal silk, on the other hand, in these earlier years, is an order of 1621 countermanding the buying of the commodity.

Early notices of Bengal silk.

3. But the treaty with the Shah fell through, and as the settlements in Bengal spread, Indian silk seems to have attracted more attention. The earliest of the Madras records, "a letter to our Agent and Council in Fort St. George," dated 9th November 1670, notifies the despatch of four factors on £25, and seven writers on £10 per annum, of whom one factor and one writer, "well skilled in silk," were destined for Cossimbazar. Again, in September 1679, we find Mr. Vincent taken to task in regard to two Englishmen who had caused trouble and probable loss by trading in silk at Cossimbazar; and in the same year the Chief of the Factory at Fort St. George made a tour through the Bengal Settlements, in the course of which he paid special attention to the subject of silk. Thus, under date 18th and 19th November 1679, he writes: "white silk bought at Serpore and tannee (thání?) silk examined: to be packed with coarse silk ropes, which may be sold in England at good profit, without paying freight or customs in the country."

Introduction of the *Bombyx textor*.

4. Early in the eighteenth century,—in 1710, according to Captain Speed,—a new species of worm was introduced. This was the so-called bara palu, or large worm—Captain Hutton's *Bombyx textor*. Mr. Atkinson of Jungypore believed that this species came either from China or some country bordering thereon. It was first cultivated, he writes, at a village in the neighbourhood of Jungypore, having, according to the consistent common report there, been brought by a dealer in elephants from Tipperah or Sylhet. He had learnt from cultivators, whose fathers had reared the first breed of the worms, that it had, when he wrote (1796), "so much degenerated as not to bear any comparison with what it formerly was. They even assure me that the cocoons do not yield much more than one-half the quantity of silk that they in their youth remember them to have done."

5. The trade of the East India Company in Indian silk was, however, inconsiderable till about the middle of the last century. At that time the cultivation of the domesticated kinds of silkworms seems to have prevailed in very much the same regions of Bengal Proper as at the present day. It was to be found in the districts of Rungpore, Dinagepore, Purneah (these two including what is now Maldah), Rajshahye, Moorshedabad, Beerbhoom, and parts of Hooghly, Midnapore, and Howrah. Buchanan, writing, however, at the beginning of the present century, mentions Bhaugulpore also as producing *Bombyx* silk to a small extent. The eria or arindi worm (of which more hereafter) was also bred in Rungpore and Dinagepore; and in the western jungles of Midnapore and Ramgurh, Bhaugulpore and Monghyr, the manufacture of tusser silk was already, and had probably been for ages, on foot. The industries connected with the production of marketable raw silk from the domestic worms were then, as now, triple, *viz*:, (1) that of the growers of mulberry; (2) that of the rearers of the worm; and (3) that of the reelers of the silk. The worms reared seem to have been of three kinds: (1) the bara palu, an annual worm (*Bombyx textor* according to Hutton); (2) the desi palu, or indigenous worm (*Bombyx fortunatus*, Hutton), a multivoltine; and (3) the nistri (*Bombyx Crœsi*, Hutton), a species of uncertain origin, and apparently less widely distributed than the other two. Of the nistri, there seem to have been three varieties. All these worms were fed for the most part on the *Morus Indica*, kept down to the size of a shrub by continual lopping, and their silk was wound from the cocoons in a rude and primitive fashion.

Silk industry in the middle of the eighteenth century.

6. The causes of the small demand for Bengal silk were not far to seek. The most obvious was the defective reeling of the so-called country-wound silk, which, in the absence of filatures under the Company's own control, was all that could be obtained for export. The main fault of the Bengal raw silk was inequality in the same skein. 'It was common to find part single, part double, treble, and in many instances even quadruple. The mode of assortment was also much neglected, and the article had fallen into disrepute.'

Defects of Bengal silk.

7. To remedy this defect, then, the Company first addressed itself, and in 1757 sent out to Bengal "Mr. Richard Wilder, a gentleman who had the reputation of being perfectly acquainted with the culture and preparation of silk in every stage,"* but whose attention was mainly directed to one branch of the subject; for we read that he "continued in India till the time of his death in the year 1761, and laid the foundation of great improvements in *winding*." In 1765-66 Mr. Joseph Pouchon "was engaged by Government to carry on at Cossimbazar the improvements begun by Mr. Wilder." It does not, however, appear that any considerable quantity of silk, wound by the improved method, was exported.

The Company takes steps to remedy them.

8. On the acquisition of the dewanee, efforts were made to extend the cultivation of silk. The planting of mulberry was urged upon zemindars and landholders, and encouragement given for the clearing of lands suited to this purpose. Apparently something stronger than persuasion was at this time brought into play in promoting the spread of sericulture, for the Court of Directors felt themselves constrained to warn the Government of Bengal that, "though there was no branch of this trade which they more ardently wished to extend than that of raw silk, yet they could not think of effecting so desirable an object by any measures that might be oppressive to the natives, or attended by any infringement of that freedom, security, and felicity which it was desired they should enjoy under the Company's government and protection." It was in the same despatch suggested that it should be made worth while to silk-*weavers* to forsake that occupation and to take to silk-*winding*. In conformity with the instructions of the Court, an advertisement was published in 1772, inviting ryots to cultivate mulberry in addition to their actual holdings, and declaring that new or waste lands, laid out or reclaimed for this purpose, should be held

Measures for the extension of silk cultivation;

* As the letter notifying his despatch puts it: "he has been conversant in raw silk during his whole life, and is a perfect judge of it from the worm to its being made fit for the weaver."

rent-free for two years, and at half the pergunnah rates for the third year. This measure resulted in a large increase of exportations, but the silk being still badly reeled, the market became overstocked. Nevertheless, this point had not been overlooked by the Directors, for they had in 1769 decided "to introduce into Bengal the exact mode of winding practised in the filatures of Italy and other parts of the Continent," and for this purpose had sent out three gentlemen, Messrs. Wiss, Robinson, and Aubert, assisted by a staff of reelers and mechanics chosen from Italy and France, and provided with tools, implements, and models to enable them to set on foot in the Bengal filatures the system pursued at Novi. Mr. Aubert died on the way out. But Messrs. Robinson and Wiss had arrived in Bengal in 1770, had erected buildings, with arrangements on the Novi pattern, at Cossimbazar, Bauleah, Comercolly, and Rungpore, and had reported favorably on the docility and expertness of the natives in adopting the improved method (the main principle of which was the crossing of threads on the same reel). And, indeed, the first silks prepared on the Italian method reached England in 1772, and were reported to be a great improvement.

and for improvement in reeling.

9. The efforts towards amelioration of the breed of worms and of their food, which were made about the same time, were not so vigorous. No attempt seems to have been made to carry out a suggestion laid before the Directors for the introduction into India of the seed of the Italian worm. But in 1771 the Bengal Government obtained from China "a quantity of the China worm, it being supposed that they produced stronger silk and in larger quantity. These worms were distributed throughout the silk districts, and," says the report from which I quote, "may have been the means of improving the breed in Bengal." Mr. Speed, however, says the breed rapidly degenerated from carelessness and improper management, and that further supplies had to be subsequently obtained by Mr. Frushard and Captain Kyd; the stock introduced by the latter forming the origin of the present China breed. There is, however, as we shall see further on, some confusion between the names of the various breeds, which I have not been able to clear up satisfactorily.

Efforts to improve the stock of worms;

10. About 1771 also "mulberry plants were brought from China and planted in the Governor General's garden, but from some prejudice of the natives, they were never generally cultivated." Hon. A. Ramsay, too, in his evidence given in 1830, speaks of the obstructiveness of the people's habits. He says:—"The Court of Directors wished the natives to use the old leaves in preference to young leaves, but the natives were averse to it, and it could never be carried into effect."

and the mulberry.

11. In 1773 the importance of encouraging the cultivators of mulberry and the winders of silk was again urged on the Bengal Government by the Court of Directors, and it was suggested that the country to the east of the Puddah should be chosen for the extension of sericulture, as best protected against the Mahrattas.* The supply of skilled superintendents was also carefully kept up, Messrs. Platell, Baumgartner, Frushard,† and Brigante being among the number appointed. On the whole, it was not till 1775 that the new method of winding really came into operation, and from 1772 to 1775 the exports of raw silk, including the filature assortment, did not exceed an average of 187,494 "small pounds" per annum. The new mode of winding, however, being once established, considerable exportations of filature silk took place, and the consignments of all sorts of silk, from 1776 to 1785, averaged upwards of 500,000 "small pounds," or nearly twice the English importations from "Italy, Turkey, &c." In fact, the Bengal silk drove all competitors, except Italian and China silks, out of the English market.

Further injunctions of the Court of Directors.

---

* A letter from Cossimbazar in December 1751 says:—"The dearness of raw silk and silk piecegoods for some years past is owing to the Mahrattas constantly entering Bengal, plundering and burning the people's houses, and destroying the chief aurungs, from whence the workmen have fled to distant parts, and not to any malpractices in the gentlemen there."

† I cannot make sure whether this was the Frushard who afterwards became a sort of unattached Superintendent of Filatures in Beerbhoom, and of whose struggles Mr. Hunter gives a graphic account. It seems probable it was the same man.

The trade in raw silk thrown open in 1783.

12. In 1781, military exigencies "had absorbed" the provision made for investment in silk, and in order to keep up the factories and prevent the dispersion of the new trained workmen, it was resolved to throw open the trade in raw silk, and to offer the Company's filatures on lease to "adventurers." The measure was not carried out till 1783, and in 1785 the exclusive trade was resumed, and a yearly provision of 540,000 "small pounds" ordered. Owing, however, to calamities of season, this amount was in no year reached till 1793. In that year the consignment amounted to 677,988 lbs. *plus* 91,885 lbs. exported by private individuals and warehoused by the Company.

Exports of silk from 1793 to 1808.

13. From 1793 to 1808 the supply of silk from Bengal fluctuated within wide limits, as will be seen from the following table:—

YEAR.		Company's Bengal raw silk imported.	Private Bengal raw silk imported warehoused by Company.	TOTAL.
		lbs.	lbs.	lbs.
1793	...	677,988	91,885	769,873
1794	...	494,487	......	494,487
1795	...	379,543	12,984	392,527
1796	...	340,060	21,046	361,106
1797	...	88,219	......	88,219
1798	...	352,780	......	352,780
1799	...	643,803	1,618	645,421
1800	...	454,600	......	454,600
1801	...	310,368	......	310,368
1802	...	78,950	35,794	114,744
1803	...	336,189	68,904	405,093
1804	...	415,917	205,793	621,710
1805	...	460,303	375,601	335,904
1806	...	235,215	173,308	408,523
1807	...	225,984	267,601	493,585
1808	...	325,243	53,225	378,498

The Directors urge an increase in the supply.

14. In 1808 "the systematic rigour with which the decrees of the enemy interdicting all commercial intercourse between Great Britain and the Continent were enforced, having occasioned an active cessation of the customary importations of Italian raw silk" into England, and great distress having resulted among English silk-weavers, the Directors urged the Government of Bengal to take all possible means for increasing the supply of Indian filature-wound silk. The result, however, does not seem to have been what was anticipated, the consignments for the years 1809—1811 being as follows:—

YEAR.		Company's silk.	Private silk.	TOTAL.
		lbs.	lbs.	lbs.
1809	...	116,124	46,623	162,747
1810	...	373,598	211,120	584,718
1811	...	258,953	145,803	404,756

Further steps in the same direction.

15. "In 1812 great disappointment was experienced from the deficiency of the consignments of raw silk. The supply from Italy being simultaneously diminished, the prices of the article in the home market rose to an unprecedented height. To alleviate this evil, the Court directed the local Government to purchase private filatures, or to take them on long leases, or, if more economical, to erect filatures, so that they should be equal to the preparation of a considerably augmented supply, not short, it was hoped, of 8,000q laes."

Government mulberry plantations ordered to be set on foot.

16. In conveying these orders, the Court of Directors added a suggestion as to the practicability of establishing mulberry plantations on account of Government. They pointed out that the existing plan not only exposed the Company to "all the inconveniences of competition by which the price is enhanced," but deprived its agents of all control over the selection either "of the insect, or of the species of mulberry on which it is fed, on both of which points the quality of the silk must ultimately depend." And they desired "that the China insect and plant might receive particular consideration."

Views of the Board of Trade.

17. These orders of the Court of Directors were forwarded to all Silk Residents by the Bengal Board of Trade, with the following comment:—

"That mulberry plantations can be established on account of the Company, so as in time to render the public investment in a considerable degree independent of other sources of supply for cocoons, is not, we conceive, to be expected, considering that, for the accomplishment of such an end, lands to so great an extent must be cultivated, and servants so numerous must be employed, as well as buildings be erected for the rearing of cocoons, comprehending altogether such a field of care and superintendence as no Resident could be competent to, in addition to the minute and constant attention requisite to the peculiar and important duty of manufacturing silk. Such a plan, even if it were found to be practicable, would, in all probability, from the greatness of the expense attending it, prove decidedly objectionable.

"To improve the breed of the silkworm throughout the districts where they are produced, and also to introduce a superior description of the plant used for their food, or at least to substitute a better mode of cultivating the Bengal mulberry plant than that at present employed, are objects unquestionably much to be desired, with a view to procure a greater degree of firmness and consistence to the thread of the cocoon, on which the excellency of the silk depends. But we are of opinion that the only mode of effecting these grand and distinguishing points is in the way of inducement with the present cultivators of the mulberry plant and present rearers of the silkworm. In these respects, great exertion, assiduity, and perseverance on the part of the respective Residents would, we are disposed to believe, be capable of effecting no small degree of improvement, notwithstanding there would evidently, from the well-known habits and prejudices of the natives, be no inconsiderable obstacles to be overcome. It might be desirable that an attempt should be made to introduce the China mulberry into general use, and to this end that a small plantation should at first be made by two or three of the Residents contiguous to their factories, from the cuttings to be supplied from the Botanic Garden, with a view to ascertain by experiment the property of this plant to nourish the silkworm, compared with the plant of Bengal. The Residents might also be able to induce some of the cultivators to allow a little more space to the plants, and thus make trial of the improvement suggested by Dr. Roxburgh, whereby he conceives that the leaves, by having a more abundant supply of light and air administered to them, would be rendered better food.

"With regard to an improvement in the breed of cocoons, the most effectual way, we conceive, would be by an interchange of communication between the several Residents, and by an endeavour to import from China the most esteemed breed of that country. Previously, however, to our giving any orders on the points above-mentioned, we desire to receive your sentiments respecting them with reference to the 17th, 18th, and 19th paragraphs of the letter from the Hon'ble Court of Directors.

"There is another circumstance to which we feel disposed to attribute the inferiority of the cocoons, namely, the worms being stinted in their food, from a well-grounded apprehension that the rearers, particularly when the bund is unfavourable and the supply of mulberry leaves scanty, and consequently dear, give the worms no more food than is indispensably requisite and necessary for their support, and we cannot but think that, if the worms were better fed, the cocoons would be much superior to what they are at present, and that the staple of the silk would be considerably stronger."

Dr. Roxburgh on the mulberry.

18. I also extract in full, as shewing that Government was alive to the importance of the question of the worms' food, a letter from Dr. Roxburgh, which belongs to the same period, and which was circulated to Commercial Residents by the Board of Trade:—

"I have received your letter of the 6th instant, together with an extract of the general letter from the Hon'ble Court of Directors, under date 15th May 1811, together with the copy of the Minute of the Board of Trade on the 1st of October 1796, and beg you will inform the President and Members of the Board that it would afford me much real satisfaction to be able to render even the smallest assistance in the important enquiry under their consideration; but unfortunately I have no practical knowledge of the management of silkworms, nor do I think I can suggest anything useful that is not already better known to the Board than to me.

"The observation in the Minute, 'improper food:' this I think may be the sole cause of degeneracy, if such has really been the case, and I think it corresponds with the habits of the natives, who bestow as little labour on their husbandry as they possibly can; and without much care, constant attention, and labour, the Indian mulberry plant, as well as that of China, soon becomes stunted, and though not absolutely diseased, yet unfit to yield leaves of the best quality. I would, therefore, recommend that much attention may be paid to the mulberry plantations, let the species or sort be what it may, for I well know that few trees degenerate so fast as the various species of this useful family.

"Accompanying this, I send you my ideas on what I think the best mode of rearing the plant in general use for feeding silkworms in Bengal, chiefly taken from the natives themselves, and only requiring to be faithfully followed to ensure a constant supply of wholesome food for the worms.

"Another consideration of much real importance must be attention to freshness of the leaves when given to the insects, for though our domestic quadrupeds draw the best of nourishment from dry food, yet I believe the caterpillar of the silk moth will thrive best when fed with the freshest leaves, gathered at a proper age, so as to suit the digestive organs of the little animals through their various stages. All these matters are perfectly known to the people employed in the work; but I know from long experience that to avoid trouble the great body of the natives will forfeit many of their comforts.

"I doubt if standard trees would yield so many or such good leaves as in the cut state in which the natives keep their plantations. I rather think not, and believe no better method can be thought of than what is in general practice, if liberally conducted. A little more space to the plants is the only improvement I can suggest. A more abundant supply of light and air to the leaves would, I think, render them better food. However, this is only my own idea, and may not stand the test of experiment.

"Like improving the various sorts of our domestic animals, as well as vegetables, there cannot be a doubt that the utmost attention should be paid to pick out and reserve the very best cocoons for breeding from, while present advantage to the breeders may induce them to pursue a different practice.

"Meteorological knowledge would operate but slowly in the improvements the Board have at heart; yet it is highly proper that this useful branch of philosophical research should be more cultivated over India than at present. Permit me, therefore, to suggest that the medical gentlemen at the various stations might be encouraged to keep a register of the weather, which could at all times be applied to various useful purposes, even our own health.

"I have no knowledge of the China mulberry being cultivated in any of these provinces for the silkworm, which is rather surprising, as it is more luxuriant and of quicker growth than the common sort, the leaves greatly larger, and every way more substantial. At present there are but few trees in the Botanic Garden; but as it grows readily from cuttings, I will venture to assure the Board that in a very short space of time hundreds of the plants and their cuttings will be ready for distribution should they be wanted."

"*Observations on the Indian Mulberry tree* (*Morus Indica, Linn. sp. ed. Willd., Vol. iv., p.* 370).

"For the cultivation of this plant over Bengal for feeding silkworms, a light, rich, elevated soil is made choice of; for the Hindoo cultivators say clayey* ground or such as allows the water to settle about the roots of the bushes will not do; the plantations, they say, require to be renewed once in three or four years to insure a constant succession of the best leaves. Cuttings are employed and planted about the close of the rains in rows three feet asunder, and about half that distance in the rows.

"A plantation once formed requires no great labor to keep it in order, as the close luxuriant growth of the plants keeps the weeds pretty well under; however, it is necessary to dress the ground now and then, and to earth up the plants while young, or when the rain washes away the earth from their roots. The ground is generally so moist at all times of the year in Bengal as to render irrigation almost unnecessary,—an advantage the Coast of Coromandel cannot boast of, and will ever render it impossible for that country to cultivate silk at as low a rate as in Bengal.

"The plant is usually cut four times in the year, and stripped of its leaves twice. The latter mode is practised during the rains, when cutting the plants would injure them by the water penetrating the cut parts; besides, by leaving the branches at this season at their full length, there is less danger of their being overflowed during the inundation of the Ganges.

"The ryots who cultivate the mulberry bush do not always rear the worm. When they do not, they cut and sell the leaves upon the tender twigs to those who breed the animal but do not cultivate the plant, by the basketful, in some parts called a *coopie*, and which is said to weigh on an average about one hundred pounds avoirdupois. The average price is about three *coopies* for the rupee. While the worms are very young, they not only strip the leaves from the twigs, but cut them small; afterwards when the worms are larger, the whole leaves upon twigs are given, and they remove the sticks when the leaves are consumed. The annual value of the

* Buchanan, however, distinctly mentions the fact of mulberry being grown in a clay soil in the south-east of Dinagepore. At the same time he admits that the produce is less than in a "free" soil. Experience everywhere from Italy to Japan seems to confirm Dr. Roxburgh's observations as to the best soil for mulberry.—J. G.

crop per beegah (the third of an English acre), taking the general average of markets and also the general average of lands in point of quality of the soil, may be about Rs. 8; deducting for the rent of the land Rs. 2, it leaves a profit of Rs. 6 to the ryot for his labor, &c."

Views of Mr. Atkinson, Resident at Jungypore.

19. I here introduce, though of somewhat earlier date (1796), the substance of a valuable paper by Mr. Atkinson, Resident at Jungypore, and an authority upon silk.

The causes of degeneracy are various :—

1. Improper food, the worms being nurtured on "the dwindling kind of mulberry leaf generally appropriated to that purpose in India."

2. Improper management of the worms. Under this head Mr. Atkinson names the absurd and superstitious practices in use among the natives, which he is certain are prejudicial; the situation of their houses "surrounded with trees and jungle," and exposed to "noisome smells arising from stagnant water and other nuisances."

3. The present mode of conducting the Company's silk investments in the aurungs :—

"Advances being made for an article, the valuable part whereof bears so small a part to the invaluable part as a given weight or number of cocoons, no argument is necessary to prove that the quantity and not the quality must prove productive of present advantage to the cultivator. For, though he may pay some attention to a portion of his cocoons, for the purpose of delivering the same as a sample for fixing the factory prices for a silk-harvest, yet no sooner are their prices established and published than it becomes his immediate interest to distribute the mulberry plants he can command to as many silkworms as the same can possibly keep alive. And if more care and a larger proportion of food are bestowed on a part of his worms, the cocoons thereof are invariably designed for private trade, and the inferior are only delivered in liquidation of his balances. Although it is very certain that the existence of the whole crop originated in the previous advances made to him on account of the Company, yet the Resident has no means of preventing the practice. It is true that the evil will, in some degree, revert on the cocoon-cultivator, because the silk agent must necessarily lower his prices as he finds the cocoons decrease in value; but few or none of the lower order of natives being capable of sacrificing present interest to any prospect of future gain, the silkworms of these provinces have been for many years gradually declining, and I am afraid will continue to decline until some remedy can be applied to correct the evils above-mentioned. Previous to the introduction of the filatures, the profits of the silk cultivators depended immediately on the excellence of the cocoons, as they must be reeled into silk before the harvest could be carried to market. In this case it was the special interest of the owners to produce the best cocoons in their power, and to guard the breed of silkworms from degenerating. But since the establishment of filatures has enabled them to put off very bad cocoons, they have become remiss and negligent, and the more minute, but still essential, precautions and attentions necessary to attain perfection in cocoons have, from disuse, it seems, been entirely forgotten. It being very certain that the above cocoons do not afford silk agents any room for hoping to meet the expectation of the Hon'ble the Court of Directors on an extensive scale, the improvement, therefore, of the breed of silkworms becomes a consideration of importance, which I am afraid cannot be effected but by the introduction from other countries of a more perfect race than we at this time have in Bengal. Supposing it practicable to procure a breed of silkworms superior to those we at present possess, the mode which most obviously occurs to establish a general culture thereof is to distribute the same throughout the cocoon villages in the different aurungs. But I greatly fear that the carelessness and improper management of the natives would render this mode ineffectual, as indeed is evident in the case of the China cocoons. The method which next presents itself is the establishment of breeding-houses or nurseries under the inspection of silk agents for the purpose of rearing cocoons for supplying the filatures. From attending to the subject for several years I am convinced that this method might be carried to a considerable extent. Yet still the expense requisite for constructing breeding-houses equal to the furnishing an extensive filature with cocoons renders this mode exceptionable, and, moreover, the circumstance of insuring sufficiency of food for the worms would create a necessity of distributing the breeding-houses throughout the aurungs, and consequently remove the greater number of them from the personal care of the agents, in which case, although healthy situations might be chosen, yet I apprehend it would be equally difficult to guard against imposition and prevent the quality of the cocoons from being impaired by want of care and judicious treatment of the worms especially. They must necessarily be fed upon such mulberry plant as the natives are in the habit of cultivating. Under the presumption that it is very possible to obtain a renovation of our breed of silkworms, I take the liberty of offering my opinion on the mode of conducting the business that appears to me the least objectionable. The method I would propose is the introduction of breeding-houses for the purpose of producing 'lunch' or silkworms' eggs alone; these to be distributed to the cocoon cultivators at lower rates than the market prices, or, in other words, that it be made more to the advantage of the bussoonah to deliver the whole of his harvest of cocoons than to reserve any part thereof for seed. By this mode and by due care and attention to the breeding-house, I think the quality of the original cocoons might be preserved and even improved; and, under the above circumstances, as the bussoonah could have no motive for reserving 'lunch,' the cocoons would never pass beyond the first stage to degenerate. I am further of opinion that the expense of an establishment of this nature would be very trifling. I think that the price to be paid for 'lunch' by the cocoon cultivator considerably below the market rates, aided by silk from inferior cocoons which it might not be eligible to retain for breeding, would nearly, if not quite, defray the charge of the breeding-house to which the use that might be made of the cocoons which the moth had perforated would also contribute."

He recommends importation of a North China breed probably through the North-East Frontier. The previous season he had received *Italian* eggs, but they all perished. But he speaks most highly of the Italian cocoons.

Experiment at Santipore in 1826.

20. It does not appear that any definite proposals for the improvement either of the breed of worms or of the mulberry arose from the correspondence between the Board of Trade and the Residents. In 1826, however, the Resident at Santipore was allowed to incur an expenditure of 25,000 sicca rupees in a trial of "neez" cultivation. "The entire process of planting the mulberry, of rearing the silkworms, and of winding off the silk, was to be conducted under the personal inspection and direction of the Commercial Resident and factory servants, the necessary buildings erected, the proper instruments provided, and the workmen paid by him, the object being to ensure that the silkworms should have a full supply of food, and be managed with the greatest care and attention, and thereby afford silk of a superior quality to that made from cocoons supplied by the pykars, and at a cost considerably less than the common rates of the factory." The experiment, which was carried on till 1830, unfortunately failed entirely in producing a supply of silk, and not only so, but entailed considerable pecuniary loss; outstanding balances of a dubiously recoverable sort having been allowed to accumulate to a large extent, the plan was therefore abandoned.

Experiment with Heathcote's reel.

21. In the years 1827 and 1828, an experiment was made at two of the Company's filatures with Messrs. Heathcote & Co.'s silk-reel. The patent is thus described:—

"Mr. Heathcote's method of reeling a silk of 15 cocoons is to divide into 3 sets of 5 cocoons each. The filaments from these sets are separately connected into three ends, or strands, at guides placed at proper distances from each other. The three distinct ends thus converge to a common eye or guide, and are united into one compact thread by the *croisée*. This *croisée* is formed by passing the thread round two small and light pulleys, and then crossing the thread upon itself, and attaching it to the reel. By these arrangements the eye of the *fileur* can readily distinguish between 5 cocoons or 4 or 6, so as to always throw on a fresh cocoon as the ends singly fail. This single *croisée* of the thread upon itself renders it unnecessary to have two skeins running upon the reel from the same basin. It also entirely prevents the 'marriage,' a very prejudicial union of the two threads, which occurs so frequently on the common plan, when the *croisée* is formed by two threads crossed over each other. If, however, an expert *fileur* can attend to more than 3 sets of 5 cocoons each in the same basin, a second skein may be wound upon the reel, as the second thread would also pass round a similar but distinct set of pulleys, and this *croisée* be made upon itself. In this manner the *fileur* could attend to 30 cocoons in 6 sets of 5 each, and if one thread break it is repaired without deranging the other, and without passing a double thread or 'marriage' upon the reel. The example thus stated of Mr. Heathcote's method of reeling a 15-cocoon silk, with the following table, will shew their applicability to all sizes of silk exceeding 5 cocoons:—

6	cocoons ought to be divided into	2	sets of	3	each.
8	ditto	2	,,	4	,,
9	ditto	3	,,	3	,,
12	ditto	3	,,	4	,,
16	ditto	4	,,	4	,,
20	ditto	5	,,	4	,,

and so on to any desired number, never exceeding 4 cocoons in each set when the number exceeds two sets."

(I have accurately quoted the last clause, though it seems inconsistent with the explanation of the reeling of a 15-cocoon silk in 3 sets of 5 cocoons each.) The silk reeled on this principle was reported by the Directors to be in no way superior to the ordinary filature silk, and Mr. Heathcote's patent was not adopted.

Prizes offered for good silk.

22. In 1829, the sum of Rs. 20,000 was placed at the disposal of the Horticultural Society, Calcutta, for the improvement of staples generally. Of this sum, Rs. 2,200 was allotted by the Society to providing prizes for good silk.

Experimental filature at Howrah.

23. In 1831, an experimental filature was established at Howrah for the purpose of testing the absolute and comparative merits of certain proposed improvements in reeling machinery, including furnaces and basins. The inventions tested were (1) Mr. Becher's quadruple copper basins, set in masonry with water-pipes,

cocks, &c.; (2) Captain Somerville's furnaces with four copper basins and iron doors; (3) Mr. Shakespear's pottery ghyes of four basins, with chimneys, &c. The result of the trial was that the furnace and basin invented by Mr. Shakespear were declared the best. Captain Somerville's reel being, however, superior, Government ordered the gradual adoption of these improvements. But it is not apparent how far their orders were acted on in the interval which elapsed before the cessation of the Company's trade.

Experiments with foreign mulberry and worms.

24. It was also suggested that the ground attached to the filature might be used as a nursery for the Italian worms and white mulberry plants about this time received from Bombay. The experiment, however, seems to have been tried at Beauleah and Sonamookhee instead. I briefly note the results.

On the 15th September 1832, the Bombay Government forwarded to Bengal eggs of the "Italian silkworm bred at St. Helena." These, with some other subsequent supplies, were distributed to the Commercial Residents of Beauleah, Sonamookhee, Hurripal, and Comercolly, and a portion sent to the Horticultural Society for trial at their farm at Akra. At Sonamookhee, the Resident, on 2nd April 1833, reported as follows:—"Of the three papers of Italian eggs sent me, a considerable proportion have successfully hatched, and the silkworms have spun white cocoons, such as I have described to Dr. Lush, *viz.*, not so large as the Bengal annual, and with a tinge of green, owing perhaps to the change of plant on which they were fed, yet the small specimens of silk obtained, as far as I can judge, evince tenacity of fibre and softness approaching to the silk of our annuals, which bears the closest affinity to the best Italian silk." Mr. Shakespear had also obtained a considerable quantity of eggs with which to prosecute the experiment in the following year. Owing probably to the retirement of the Company from trade in 1834, no such experiment seems to have been made. At any rate its results are not on record. At Beauleah the Resident reported that, owing to the habit of the St. Helena eggs to hatch at intervals, and the inconvenience and difficulties it caused, he had, "although worms sufficient to produce a maund of cocoons of forty kahans were hatched, been able to mature but one kahan and six puns (1,760) cocoons fit for winding off into silk. These, moreover, were of a very indifferent description, and not having been fit for letter A, had been spun into B." The season, from drought and excessive heat, is stated to have been very unfavorable to the experiment; but in the opinion of the Resident, "there was nothing from what had been seen to induce the belief that the Bombay eggs were in any way better than the annual worm of Bengal, or that, under any circumstances, their produce would have realized better in quantity or quality." I have not been able to find any record of the experiments with the St. Helena eggs at the other places to which they were distributed. The mulberries sent by the Bombay Government were two varieties of the Italian white mulberry received from St. Helena, one variety being named the *doppia foglia*. Experiments were tried at the Sonamookhee Residency and the Akra farm, and the larger kind was successfully reared; but neither it nor the *doppia foglia* seems to have been to any extent naturalized in Bengal.

Cessation of Company's trade.

25. "The Court's letter, dated 23rd July 1833, informed the Government of Bengal that, under the provisions of the Bill then in progress through Parliament, the Company's trade with India and China would cease, but that the purchase of silk was to be continued for 1834," and it was subsequently intimated that "the provision of silk should also be carried on in 1835 at such filatures as should remain in the Company's possession. But Government was directed to take measures for the disposal of the silk factories as speedily as consistent with prudence; the injunction to use prudence being understood to refer less to the pecuniary gain or loss of the Company, than to the interests of the people, and to the keeping up the supply of silk." It was declared that the silk-growers should not be suddenly deserted, unless there were capitalists ready to carry on the filatures, even though some loss should be incurred in protecting them. In consequence of these instructions, attempts were made in 1835 to dispose of the filatures by public auction, but up to 1836, at any rate, most of them remained in the Company's hands. The hired native filatures were, however, given up, and the

purchase of silk, by contract, discontinued, from which two sources a portion of the investment had always been derived. In 1837 the severance was completed.

Exports of Bengal silk from 1812 to 1835, with average price from 1817 to 1835.

26. I append a statement of the imports into England of Bengal silk for the years 1812 to 1835:—

Raw Silk imported from Bengal.

YEARS.		Company's Bengal raw silk imported.	Private Bengal raw silk imported warehoused by the Company.	Total Company's import and private import warehoused by the Company.
		lbs.	lbs.	lbs.
1812	...	558,862	423,565	982,427
1813	...	831,891	252,459	1,084,350
1814	...	722,727	114,239	836,966
1815	...	522,810	279,476	802,286
1816	...	381,215	398,549	779,764
1817	...	373,459	128,876	502,335
1818	...	758,116	420,860	1,160,976
1819	...	553,105	197,922	751,027
1820	...	811,875	259,572	1,071,447
1821	...	817,625	172,838	990,463
1822	...	845,382	197,235	1,042,617
1823	...	850,668	310,518	1,161,186
1824	...	660,012	271,637	931,649
1825	...	699,230	220,206	919,436
1826	...	898,388	338,635	1,237,023
1827	...	926,678	99,361	1,026,039
1828	...	1,039,623	96,686	1,136,309
1829	...	1,129,710	258,044	1,387,754
1830	...	1,096,071	90,092	1,186,163
1831	...	1,030,280	64,597	1,094,877
1832	...	750,828	205,625	956,453
1833	...	698,851	52,129	750,980
1834	...	757,517	53,124	810,641
1835	...	721,509	6,026	727,535

General view of the system in Bengal during period of the Company's trade.

27. We have thus reached the stage when Government retired from business, the narrative having been, so far, almost entirely taken from the "Report of the proceedings of the East India Company in regard to the trade, culture, and manufacture of raw silk" submitted in 1836. It may be useful at this point to give a sketch of the system as it existed at its most flourishing epoch. We find, then, that in March 1832 there were distributed throughout the silk-producing districts eleven head factories, *viz.*, those of Beauleah, Comercolly, Cossimbazar, Hurripal, Jungypore, Maldah, Radnagore, Rungpore, Santipore, Sonamookhee, and Surdah. At each of these head factories was a Commercial Resident, established in a handsome, in some cases even palatial,* "residency," and having commercial jurisdiction (so to speak) throughout a surrounding tract of country. Part of the Resident's duty was the supply of the "provision" of silk. To enable him to produce the whole or a part of this "provision," he had a certain number of filatures at his disposal—some Company's property, others hired (the proportions varying in the different circles), scattered throughout his jurisdiction, and to these filatures the cocoons were, as a rule, brought by the pykars or middlemen, who purchased them from the rearers of silkworms, who again made their own arrangements with the growers of mulberry. The latter two classes were, as a rule, distinct, but sometimes the silkworm rearers grew their own mulberry. Advances of cash were made

* For an account of the Residency at Soorool, in the days of Cheap the Magnificent, see Mr. Hunter's "Annals of Rural Bengal," Vol. I., page 353. Soorool seems to have been abandoned afterwards, and the Commercial Resident's head-quarters removed to Gonatea, the factory of the 'adventurer' Frushard, at the time of which Mr. Hunter writes. At that period [*circ.* 1780], there were three head factories and twelve subordinate factories in the tract described as "the western principalities," and the total mercantile investment of Beerbhoom is said to have varied from £45,000 to £65,000 a year. Mr. Hunter's sixth chapter contains an interesting account of the Company's system of commercial management.

to the pykars, and they were paid, sometimes by the weight of "green" cocoons, but more generally according to the outturn of silk. Sometimes advances were made direct to the rearers of the worms; and those who took such advances were, at any rate till the year 1829, granted peculiar privileges. For instance, they could not be summoned by the civil courts except "when the investment was at a stand," and they were "protected from the oppressions of the natives more than those who were not employed under the Company." The prices fixed in 1833 were the following:—

	Rs.	A.	
March bund (or crop) large ...	8	8	Per seer (of *silk*, to wit) with certain additional remuneration for superior colour or fineness.
" " small ...	7	0	
April " "	7	0	
Rainy " "	6	2	
October and November	7	2	

Extent of the filatures.

28. The total number of basins in the filatures, owned or occupied by the Company in 1831-32, is given at 15,723; thus, Company's basins 12,039, hired ditto 3,684, total 15,723.

Other means of provision.

29. Such portion of the provision as could not be produced by the filatures was obtained, by purchase, in the form of raw silk, either direct from native spinners, or through brokers. These brokers were sometimes European 'adventurers',—*e. g.*, the Mr. Frushard in Beerbhoom, of whom Mr. Hunter gives an interesting sketch. He "founded little tributary filatures throughout the whole north-east jungle of Beerbhoom," and his head factory (Gonatea) "rebuilt several times, now forms the most imposing mercantile edifice in the district." From the year 1826, however, the country-wound silk ceased to form any part of the "investment." At the Cossimbazar, Maldah, and Santipore factories silk goods were *manufactured*, but from the country-reeled or "putney" silk. All filature silk was exported "raw."

Private traders.

30. In some districts, notably that of Rajshahye, the Company had not a monopoly of the trade in silk, though the Residents evidently looked with jealousy on the outsiders; and as the former had the means, to a certain extent, of running up the price of cocoons, the private traders do not seem to have been very successful, and only got the inferior sorts of silk. In fact, the Directors at one time complained that the prices were run up so high that no private speculator could enter the market, which was, moreover, often overstocked by the operations of the Company. An instance of this is given in the following extract from the evidence of Hon. A. Ramsay before a Select Committee of the House of Lords in 1830:—

"I can speak from my own knowledge of one speculation I made in silk in the year 1805, when Marquis Cornwallis went to India. He arrived in the month of July, and immediately put a stop to the Company's investments. There was a great scarcity of money, at the time, in the market, and the silk people came to me to know what was to be done with their silk. I told them I could not take their silk, and they must sell it to individuals. Their answer was that there were no individual purchasers in the market, and they could not sell it. There was a discount on bills at that time of 15 per cent. between Calcutta and Moorshedabad. They, the brokers, came in a body and offered me their silk and to take the loss of the 15 per cent. on themselves, which I agreed to. I sent the silk to England, and I lost, I think, about £2,000 on it.

Question.—Upon what quantity? *Answer.*—I think there was about £20,000 (? 20,000lbs), and I never traded in silk again."

Species of worms.

31. The cocoons seem to have been the produce of worms of four species. Three of these I have noticed above as having, probably, been existent in Bengal in the middle of the last century. Four kinds are distinctly mentioned as in existence in 1819, and we know when two of these, the China worm and the bara palu, were first introduced. The first kind was the large or annual worm (*B. textor*), yielding its yearly supply in March, its silk being of a high quality. This worm predominated in the Cossimbazar circle, where it yielded the greater part of the March crop of silk, but was found also in Hurripal, Jungypore, Radnagore, and Sonamookhee. The Jungypore Resident in 1819 complains of the cultivation of this worm having become "extremely precarious and uncertain," and attributes

this to degeneracy in the stock. The second kind (*B. fortunatus*) was the desi or indigenous worm, doubtless the first domestic species naturalized in India. It afforded five harvests in the year, called, respectively, the October, November, March, April, and June—July bunds. The two last bunds were the weakest, but the March bund also was precarious, depending on the weather and yield of mulberry. In Hurripal the desi worm had in 1819 only just been introduced, and it was then unknown in the Radnagore circle. This worm was generally ranked next to the bara palu (*B. textor*). The third species or China worm (*B. Sinensis*, Hutton) was, as we have seen, introduced at various times between 1771 and 1790. In 1819 it was said to have degenerated. There was large intermixture between it and the desi species in the Cossimbazar circle. As a pure breed, it seems to have chiefly prevailed in Jungypore and Hurripal. Mr. Speed, in a paper which I shall presently quote at greater length, writes of the China worm :—"It cocoons monthly between November and June if attention be paid, but more generally from January to May. Rate of breeding much the same as the desi, than which it is of a somewhat larger size, and is perhaps the most profitable kind of worm, being of shorter life; will feed on indifferent leaf, and is of hardier constitution, that is, less liable to be affected by the vicissitudes so injurious to other worms." It is to be noticed, however, that Mr. Speed calls this the "*Madrasee* or China worm." Now, the report of the Board of Trade gives the Madrasee as one of the kinds of *nistri*, (see below), and at the present day Madrasee is a synonym for nistri. The description given by Mr. Speed seems, moreover, to agree better with that of the nistri as given by the Board of Trade. On the other hand, Mr. Speed distinctly speaks of a cross between his "China or Madrasee" and the desi moth. No such cross between nistri and desi is mentioned by the Board. The subject is somewhat obscure. The fourth species or tribe was called the nistri or sometimes the Madrasee, the *B. Crœsi* of Captain Hutton. The Board of Trade express themselves doubtfully as to the origin of this tribe or species. It is said to include three species or varieties, but on this point, too, the report is confused. It seems to have prevailed chiefly in Beauleah, Comercolly, and Maldah. It was a multivoltine, yielding apparently six harvests, of which, however, the April, June, July and September bunds were the most abundant.

According to Mr. Atkinson the "desi" worm had also degenerated. Mr. Atkinson recognizes only the three breeds, large annual, "desi," and China *or* Madrasee. He classes them in the above order as regards quality of silk. From the history he gives of its introduction from 1781—1788, his third species is the China species, and not the nistri. Under careful breeding he says he obtained good silk from it, but in the hands of the natives, who crossed it with the country breed, it had so degenerated that he had tried to persuade them to give it up. But they clung to it for three reasons: (1) it was more rapid in its evolutions; (2) it was hardier; and (3) it was less squeamish as to its food than the worms of country stock.

Yield of silk.

32. Dr. Buchanan estimates the yield as follows:—In Dinagepore, on the Mahanunda (*i. e.*, in the portion of what is now Maldah lying east of that river) $2\frac{1}{2}$ seers (of 88 sicca) of cocoons produced 15 sicca weight of silk, or 6·8 per cent. More to the eastward, on the Korotoya, the yield was said by the ryots to be $2\frac{9}{16}$ seers to 28 seers of cocoons, or just 4 per cent. "Mr. Monkton," however, put it at one-eighth the weight of cocoons, or 12·5 per cent. In the then district of Purneah, now western Maldah, and only separated by the Mahanunda from the first tract, the yield is given by Buchanan as 1 in $17\frac{1}{2}$, or 5·7 per cent. The papers published with the report of 1836 do not give any very full information as to the yield of silk from the several species of cocoons. The Sonamookhee Resident, however, calculates the yield of 103,500 kahans of cocoons of the annual species at 150 factory maunds of silk, a kahan being 1,280. This would shew that it took 903,200 cocoons to yield a factory maund of silk. Mr. Shakespear also furnishes the following figures:—48 kahans (= 61,440) of cocoons of the October, November, or January bunds yielded 2 seers 12 chittacks of silk; 24 kahans (= 30,720) of the annual cocoons yielded 2 seers 4 chittacks. In the March bund, 45 kahans (= 58,620) of the small cocoons yielded 2 seers 2 chittacks of silk. These figures, assuming Mr. Speed's calculations as to weight of cocoon (see below),

would give a yield of 8·3 per cent. on weight of cocoons for the small size, and 9·4 per cent. for the annuals. Mr. Speed gives the following figures on the subject: he thus puts down the number of cocoons *on the fifth day* required to make a "seer of 80 sicca weight;" of desi 2,080; of *his* Madrasee 1,760; of annual 1,280: 256,000 desi cocoons will therefore weigh 123 sicca seers. The yield of these 123 seers he sets down at 11 seers 1½ chittacks "by customary limit," and 13 seers 11 chittacks "by private accomplishment." So for the annual cocoons he gives a yield of 8 seers 13 chittacks by "customary limit," and 10 seers 8½ chittacks "by private accomplishment," from 157,000 cocoons, weighing 122 seers. The case of the Madrasee cocoons cannot be clearly made out. These figures would give as the percentage of silk to weight of cocoons,—desi, "by customary limit," 9 per cent.; by "private accomplishment," 11·1 per cent.; annual, "by customary limit," 7·2 per cent.; "by private accomplishment," 8·6 per cent. The Hon. A. Ramsay, however, in his examination before the Select Committee of the House of Lords in 1830, stated the amount of spun silk obtained from Bengal cocoons to be only 5 per cent., while Mr. W. Prinsep in 1832 gives the following figures:—"annual worm,—1 maund of 80 sicca to the seer yields about 3 seers of good silk (=7·5 per cent.); small (desi) worm,—1 maund will yield 2¼ seers of good silk (=5·625 per cent)." Mr. Turnbull of Ghattal, in a more recent paper, estimates the yield of cocoons of each of the four kinds as follows:—annual, 5·625 to 6·875; Madrasee, 5· to 6·25; desi, 5·625 to 6·25; China, 5·375 to 6·25 per cent.; and in a letter lately communicated by the Government of Bengal, this gentleman expresses a distinct opinion that the "yield per cocoon has not diminished." These different sets of figures are hard to reconcile. I may note here that some silk which won the Horticultural Society's medal in 1839 was reeled from annual cocoons, yielding 14·3 per cent.

Food of the worms.

33. The food of the worms consisted, for the most part, of the common desi tút, or indigenous mulberry. There was also a so-called bidesi, or foreign mulberry. Mr. Shakespear, Resident at Sonamookhee, describes them and their mode of cultivation as follows:—

"There are two species of mulberry plant in the aurungs of the Sonamookhee Residency, west of the Bhaugirutty river. One is the desi (indigenous), called 'Kajlah,' the other bidesi (exotic); both bear fruit, which begins to set towards the end of October, and ripens in about two months.

"The sati is supposed to be the Madrasee or foreign: its bark is of a pale grey colour, that of the 'Kajlah' is darker. I cannot speak to the culture of plants and usage at other silk aurungs, having never been at any of them.

"With reference to the culture of the desi plant, it is to be observed that the ground is generally so moist at all times of the year in Bengal as to render irrigation almost unnecessary. The plant is usually cut four times in the year, and stripped of its leaves twice. The latter mode is practised during the rains, when cutting the plants would tend to injure them, by the water penetrating the cut part, or eventually by the overflowing of the Ganges.

"But this apparent local fertility is unfortunately combined with great humidity, and sudden transitions of temperature from heat to raw cold, and cold to heat, which are the great evils the manufacturer of our silk has to contend with in Bengal, opposed to the superior advantages possessed by the Italians, of a pure, mild, and regular temperature, specially on the borders of a mountainous country, such as the northern provinces of Italy, Piedmont, Milanese, and the Tyrol approaching the Alps."

Mr. DeVerinne, Superintendent of the Akra Farm, wrote: "The kind of mulberry preferred by the silkworm has a small leaf of dark colour, rather thick, called double leaf, and difficult to pick. Its botanic name is *Morus alba.* The kinds that will thrive best as standard trees are called *morus alba*, of a white berry, and *morus rubia*, of a black berry, with upright large trunks, rising 20 feet high or more. Mr. DeVerinne, however, thought the "common dessy (*morus Indica*) best adapted for cultivation on the Bengal plan." Mr. Storm describes four kinds as used in the "districts of Calcutta. The native names are *saw*,* *bhore*,† *desi*, and *China*. The two first produce fruit (black), but the last two have no fruit. The leaves of the *saw* are very large, but they are not given to the worms till they have passed two *goome*.‡ The leaf of the *bhore* is small and

* Probably eccentric spelling for "sháh."
† Probably eccentric spelling for "bara," *i. e.*, large mulberry.
‡ Bengalee "ghum," meaning "sleep."

jagged; the leaf of the *desi* is small and plain; and the *China* is also small, but jagged at the stem. The leaves are considered all equally good for feeding the worm. The mulberry tree is not cut down for five years; it is then allowed to grow for five years more, when it is rooted out."

Mr. Hyde, Resident at Beauleah, reported:—

"In the Beauleah aurungs the mulberry cultivation is entirely accomplished from cuttings of five or six inches in length; and in the course of five or six months after plantation they become sufficiently rooted in the ground to admit of the shrubs being cut. The cuttings are set three or four together, with six inches space between each cluster, and in rows, leaving sufficient width between the rows to admit of the ground being turned up by the khodali, and the small plough used in Bengal. The fields are never irrigated; but if the weather be favorable, with a seasonable supply of rain, five or six crops may be obtained throughout the year, but never fewer than four, unless the season should be unusually droughty. If the mulberry plants be originally planted in good land, well attended, and kept well weeded, the plant will last ten or fifteen years. In that case it is necessary to supply fresh earth annually, as manure, after the first two or three years. The time, however, which one set of cuttings will take to produce the leaf, with nutrition, depends much on the quality of the soil, and the attention paid to render it fertile. Some fields will not last more than four or five years. The height to which it grows before it is cut varies as the weather may be favorable or otherwise. It may be stated from two to four feet. The plant, when required, is cut three or four inches from the ground, except in the rainy season, when the stumps are allowed to be eight or ten inches in length. After the plant has been used for the worm in July, it is allowed to grow to waste in order that the rains or inundations may not destroy or injure it. The rains having subsided, the plant is cut down, the land ploughed and dressed as may be requisite for the grand bund of the year called the November bund. * * * In the Beauleah aurungs not a worm is reared from the leaf of the *tree*; but the large or annual worm prefers the leaf of the shrub which is well matured to that which is young and tender. Hence it is inferable that the annual worm would thrive better with the tree leaf than the shrub leaf. The tree, though never used in this district, is said to be cultivated in part of the Rungpore and Radnagore districts. The mulberry shrub, notwithstanding it occasions more labour and expense, is more profitable than the tree, from its yielding four or five crops in the year, and thereby is more suited to the *desi* and *nistri* worm."

The following is an extract from a letter from Mr. Richardson, Resident of Comercolly:—

"The kind of mulberry used in these aurungs is called *desi tút*. The season for planting mulberry is the month of Kartik (October), although I have planted it with success all the year round. The cuttings are about five inches long, and are planted in rows about seven inches apart. In my opinion, it would be better a little further apart, and in a diamond shape. The leaves of the first cuttings of new planted mulberries are reckoned poisonous, and, if given to the worms, kill them. After this the plant will be fit for cutting about every two months. After each cutting the field should be weeded and dressed with a little manure, and in the month of Kartik, every year, the mulberry should be cut and the field undergo eight or ten ploughings, and be well manured. Cultivated in this way, it will flourish for seven or eight years. After this period the ground should have a fallow, or be appropriated to other less exhausting crops for two years, when it may be planted with mulberry again. Mulberry I planted last year round my house was cut this year on the 10th March, height 2 feet 6 inches and 3 feet; and again cut on the 10th May, height 3 feet and 3 feet 6 inches; and it is now (30th June) 2 feet and 2 feet 6 inches. On the 30th April 1832, I sowed some mulberry seed which came up on the 20th May, and was 1 foot 6 inches high, and ready for cutting, on the 25th August. The leaves of this mulberry are preferred by the rearers of cocoons. The mulberry is never permitted to grow into trees in this part of the country, though I have tried it, and it will grow into a tree upwards of 10 or 12 feet high; but the wood is liable to be attacked with worms, and the tree soon decays. I should consider this mode of cultivating mulberry very expensive and ruinous to the chásás."

Mr. Grant, Resident of Hurripal, writes thus:—

"There are two varieties of the mulberry here, one of which, the *desi*, is generally cultivated for feeding silkworms, the other, called simply, by the natives, the large mulberry, bears a purple fruit and is cultivated in gardens. Although the large mulberry yields more leaves, the *desi* is preferred, as agreeing best with the worms. It appears that those fed with the garden mulberry yield an inferior cocoon. The *desi*, I believe, gives a white berry, but is not allowed to produce fruit. The method of cultivation differs from that in use about Beauleah and Maldah, the leaves only being here gathered from standards. Slips are planted in October, and leaves are gathered from the plants in the following June. Between three or four years from the first gathering of the leaves the plants are cut down close to the ground. This is done in February, and leaves are again plucked from the new sprouts in June. In good soil the trees last upwards of fifteen years, and in bad, not less than six or seven; but whatever may be the time a tree lasts, it is a rule to cut it down close to the ground every three years, so as to keep the standard of a height which enables a man to pluck the leaves without climbing. The earth is dug up and the trees manured in October, and at this time they are also watered. Fresh earth is put round them in February, and they are watered two or three times more during the year. Whenever grass appears, the earth is dug up to destroy it. The reason given by the natives to preferring the standard trees to cultivating the same way as at Beauleah is, that the soil is too dry down here to answer in any other way than with the standard."

Method of rearing worms.

34. The method of rearing adopted will appear from the following extracts:—

The stock on first establishment. 1*st, receiving houses.*—The best size is about 24 feet long, 15 feet broad, and 9 feet high, including a raised floor of 3 feet; the walls to be of earth about a cubit thick, and roof of thick compact thatch, the ridge being 14½ feet from the ground; or 8¼ perpendicular feet higher than the upper part of the wall, with doorways to the southward (most preferable) or eastward, and two small windows at nearly the top of the walls on the same sides. Such a house is equal to 200 kahans or 256,000 worms, that is, 5 ghurrahs or machans, each having 16 dalas or shelves of 5½ × 4½ feet, with a raised rim of 2 or 3 inches, well leeped or plastered with cow or buffalo's dung; the last being the most esteemed by the natives, with good appearance of reason, as the odour is more congenial to the worms, and each of these shelves is sufficient space for 2½ kahans or 3,200 worms.

The ghurrahs are supported by four corner bamboos resting on soraces or small earthen saucers, to contain water for the purpose of obstructing the passage of ants and other insects.

To each house there should be 10 chundrukees, pheengs or spinning mats of 3½ × 4 feet, with the raised work of three inches. The remainder of the fittings-up are a close bamboo chick for the door, another for each window, a few baskets of large size for the carriage of leaf, a knife, or bytunee, for cutting the same during the early stages of the worm; three or four gunnies for purdahs and spreading on the floor, with a small number of earthen pots or kulsies for sundry purposes, the whole costing from 50 to 65 rupees per house, according to the locality and the facility of procuring labor and cheap material. *Extra expense.*—To every 12 houses there should be an extra building of thatch and mat 20 feet long, 12 feet broad, and 8 feet high, with mud floor, serving to put away material not in use, but more especially to afford protection to the chundrukees or spinning mats during the night in spinning time; the worm being inclined to relax its operations during darkness and the changed air of the night, to consequent deterioration of the cocoons: while by the influence of light and protection from night air, the animal continues unremittingly its labour, and hence an improved cocoon; the cost of the building may be from Rs. 4-8 to Rs. 6-8 per rearing house.

* * * * *

Of the mulberry about ⅜ths is actual leaf and ⅝ths wood and waste. During the 1st stage or kullup (kalpa), the leaf must be very finely cut up; for the second, quartered; and for the 3rd and 4th, it is given whole on the stick as cut from the field; most carefully cleaning out every morning of the last two stages, the worms being easily removed for this purpose after they have ascended on to the fresh supplies. The supplies of food are given twice a day during the 1st and 2nd, and every six or eight hours of the two last stages, and even oftener if the worms are observed to eat with avidity, which is generally the case for two or three days in each of the latter stages. As soon as the worms are ready to spin, they turn from a greenish-cream to a mellow light orange colour, not unlike the pulp of a ripe papaya, imagined with a bloom on it, with a transparent streak down the back, passing, as is observed, the emission from tail to head, which forms the silk. They are then put into the chundrukees, placed in the open air facing the sun, when not too powerful, or turning aside a little in such case, but under no shade, and all night under cover, with a lamp burning till past midnight as well as just before day-break. The worms work with activity for 36, and gradually relaxing, continue their operations for 56, hours. About four or five days afterwards the cocoons are ready for reeling, except during the rains or two last bunds, when they will be ready the third day, and not keeping sound for many days should be run off as quickly as possible; while at other periods killing the grub either by exposure to the sun for about four or five hours during the cold weather, or heating in an oven at a moderate temperature for about three hours in the hot weather preserves the perfection of the cocoons."—*Mr. Speed's paper in Vol. III. of Transactions of Agricultural and Horticultural Society of India.*

The practices and prejudices of the Hindoo breeder of the silkworm in these districts may not be uninteresting. They pretend to hold the insect in a degree of religious awe, and thus, as sacred, impose on themselves penances for its salvation, handed down from one generation to another through time immemorial, which are strictly abided by. In the progress of feeding the worm, more especially during the critical periods of the four ages, or sickness while moulting, during which the worm has reached two-thirds of its full growth, and until it ultimately closes itself in its pod, the intercourse of the sexes is forbidden. Girls and women, whether in their courses or parturient, are excluded. Men do not shave or perform their ablutions, or oil their bodies, but remain clad in their dirty clothes. Fish, turmeric, garlic, onions, snuff, and tobacco are prohibited, though they smoke outside their houses.* Surely the proscribed have the best of it. To crown the whole conjuration, as a charm against evil spirits, an old shoe, with a bundle of thorns, is hung upon the *chick* (lattice screen) at the door of the breeding-house.—*Letter from W. Shakespear, Resident of Sonamookhee.*

Method of reeling; (1) among natives;

35. The method of reeling pursued by the natives is thus described in the report already so largely quoted:—

The *chásás* or rearers of the silkworm wind off the cocoons in earthen basins (with the aid of cow-dung as fuel instead of wood) upon the common Bengal *nuttahs*, or reels made of

* "In Italy and France the breeders are particular in keeping their hands and clothes free from the taint of tobacco, snuff, garlic, onions, and oil, as being all dangerous poisons to the worm, precautions which the wily Hindoo perverts to mysterious prohibitions, and the exclusion of others not initiated in the sanctity of his rites."

bamboo, the thread so reeled being called *putney*. Fine and coarse threads are wound in the same skein indiscriminately, and parts of the husk frequently introduced to increase the weight; it is hence necessary to have the *putney* re-wound. This is first done on bobbins, in order to preserve the different degrees of fineness. The silk is then wound from these bobbins upon a large reel to separate and distinguish the colours of each assortment, and is taken off as soon as dry to be twisted into skeins.

But Dr. Buchanan, writing somewhere in the period 1807—1814, says that, in the tract of country which now forms the district of Maldah, the natives had almost entirely abandoned "the original Hindoo manner of winding the silk from the cocoons by means of a small reel (laya) about 8 inches in diameter, which is fastened to a spindle that the workman twists round with his hand, and a larger reel (gayi), moved by a winch after the European fashion, is generally employed. Several people in the district have huts in which there are one or two reels, each provided with a small furnace and vessel for containing hot water," and the instrument was let out by the day. The defect was the want of any method of imparting a twist to the thread. The reeling machines used in the filatures were based on the best European models, and the greatest pains were taken to secure a firm, even, well-crossed thread.

(2) at the Company's filatures.

36. As to the extent of silk manufacture I have not been able to obtain much information. We have seen that the Company manufactured silk stuffs at three of its Residencies, but from country-wound silk. The stuffs seem to have been chiefly undyed piece-goods, known as corahs, and bandannas. There was doubtless a good deal of silk made for home consumption also, but I have not found any figures to shew either the exports* or the total production for the period of the Company's trade. Buchanan gives an elaborate account of the silk manufacture in Maldah and the neighbourhood. The cloths made were almost all mixed, the warp being silk and the woof cotton. The warp was generally disposed in stripes, the woof being of one colour. The patterns did not display much taste. There were said to be about 11,000 looms in this region, but not one-half of them constantly employed. Buchanan estimates the value of the stuffs exported annually to the westward, to Moorshedabad, and Calcutta, at not less than 10 lakhs annually.

Silk manufacture.

The industry still exists about Maldah and English Bazar, but in a languishing condition. The aspect of the town of old Maldah is that of the dreariest decay.

37. Whether the domesticated silkworm was introduced into Assam from Bengal or, as I believe, *vice versâ*, the method of treatment found to prevail in the former province, when we first obtained possession of it, and which still continues to be followed, seems to have closely resembled that pursued in Bengal. Two sorts of *Bombyx*, the bara palu (*B. textor*), and the chota palu (*B. fortunatus*) were reared. The following notice is extracted from Buchanan, and includes some particulars as to the munga and eria, of which fuller details will be found further on:—

Silk in Assam.

The native women of all castes, from the queens downwards, weave the four kinds of silk that are produced in the country, and with which three-fourths of the people are clothed. Considerable quantities of the two coarser kinds are also exported. There may be one loom for every two women, and in great families there are eight or ten, which are wrought by the slave girls. The raw material is seldom purchased; each family spins and weaves the silk which it rears, and petty dealers go round and purchase for ready money whatever can be spared for exportation, or for the use of the few persons who rear none of their own. The silk cloth serves generally for that which is wrapped round the waists of both sexes, and is made of different sizes, according to the purpose to which it is to be applied—

1st.—Dhuti, from 8 to 16 cubits long and from 2 to 2½ wide. One end is wrapped round the waist, the other end is thrown round the shoulders. They are used both by men and women.

2nd.—The Rihe is wrapped round the waist of women, but being short does not admit of passing round the shoulders. The pieces are 6 cubits long by 1½ wide.

3rd.—Mekla seems to be the original female dress of Kamrup, and is the same with what I have described as the dress of the Koch women in Rungpore, and with the female dress in Ava, and of the shepherd tribe in Mysore.

4th.—The Chhelang is a piece for wrapping round the shoulders of men in cold weather; it is 6 cubits long by 3 wide.

* Mr. Holwell, writing in 1759, mentions six kinds of cloth and raw silk as being exported from Nattore (in Rajshahye) both to Europe and to the markets of "Bussora, Mocha, Judda, Pegu, Acheen, and Malacca." From the passage as quoted by Mr. Skrine (to whom I am indebted for the reference) it is not quite clear whether the cloths were all of silk.

5*th*.—Jhardar or Mongjuri is a piece used by women for the same purpose. It is from 4 to 5 cubits long and from 2 to 2½ wide. The Jhardar is of a flowered pattern, the Mongjuris plain.

6*th*.—Mosaris are pieces 30 cubits long by 1¾ or 2 cubits wide, and are intended for curtains. They are of a very thin fabric, and are flowered. The proper silk, or Pata, as it is called in Assam, is only used for the dhutis of the great. Each costs from Re. 1 to Rs. 8.

The Medanggori silk, which constitutes the dress of the higher ranks, is wrought into dhutis, most of which are dyed red with lac, but some are white. They cost from Rs. 2½ to 6, chiefly owing to a difference of size, being all nearly of the same fineness. Rihes cost from Re. 1 to Rs. 4. The Muga silk is the dress of the middle ranks. Dhutis, which are mostly undyed, sell from Re. 1 to Rs. 4. Meklas from Re. 1 to Rs. 3; the Jhardars from Rs. 2½ to Rs. 4; the curtains from Re. 1 to Rs 6. Rihes from 8 annas to Rs. 3.

The Erendi silk serves as clothing for the poor. Rihes cost from 4 to 6 annas; Chhelangs from 8 annas to Rs. 2. Meklas from 8 annas to Re. 1. Mongjuris 8 annas.

The small proportion of the silk that is dyed has this operation performed on it by the women, by whom it is woven.

I extract Mr. Hugon's description of the Assam reel as exhibiting the implement in its simplest expression :—"One person winds off the silk with an instrument made of three pieces of stick joined together, two lying parallel, and the third crossing them at right angles; the perpendicular one is held at one end with the right hand, and the left directs the thread on the crossbars, taking care in doing this to make it rub against the forearm to twist it, whilst another person attends to the fire and the putting on of new cocoons."

Attempt to establish a filature at Durrung.

38. Some time about 1834 or 1835 an attempt seems to have been made to improve the system of sericulture in Assam, for Mr. Hugon, writing in 1837, says:—"Mr. Scott, a few years ago, introduced from Rungpore reelers, reels, and plants of the *Morus alba*, and established a factory at Durrung, with a view to extend the culture of mulberry silk and improve the reeling of the munga. Several causes rendered the experiment abortive, the want of European superintendence and Mr. Scott's untimely death being the principal ones." In a note the late General (then Captain) Jenkins remarked that he believed Assam excellently adapted for the culture of silk. Nothing, however, seems to have been done, and the following abstract of Colonel Agnew's paper of 1869 agrees in all essentials with Mr. Hugon's account of 1837.

Present state of sericulture in Assam.

39. The pât is identified by Colonel Agnew with *B. Mori*, but Captain Hutton says it is *B. Textor*. It is a purely domestic breed, yielding a white silk, highly prized, the privilege of wearing which used to be restricted to royalty. The cocoons chosen for breeding are kept in a loosely-tied cloth, and put in a quiet place. In from 20 to 25 days the moths emerge, and after being left with the males for a short time, the females are removed to pieces of cloth or slender sticks of bamboo, on which they deposit their eggs. These are kept about ten months till the hatching season, which in Upper Assam is generally the end of December, and in Lower Assam the end of January. The eggs are then taken out and exposed to the air. When the young worms appear they are placed in bamboo trays, sometimes lined with cloth, and fed with tender leaves of the mulberry ("noonee"). The size of the leaves supplied is increased with the growth of the worms. Great attention is paid to cleanliness. In from 30 to 40 days they commence to build their cocoons, being placed for the purpose either on bundles of leaves or in bamboo trays divided off. The breed is *annual*. Before spinning, the cocoons are placed in the sun for three or four days, and boiled in a solution of potash obtained from the stalks of rice. The silk is fine and white, the fabric resembles tusser silk. The silk fetches from Rs. 20 to 25 per seer. The kind called chota pât is reared in the same way, but the silk is not so good. Captain Hutton says it is *B. crœsi*, the nistri or Madrasee worm. Mr. Hugon says there were no large plantations of mulberry; a few men of rank have small patches sufficient to produce silk for their own use: the few ryots that sell the silk generally have not more than a seer to dispose of in the year—the produce of a few plants round their huts or in the hedges of their fields. And I believe this to be true at the present day. The cultivation and manufacture of munga and eria silk, however, as we shall see further on, are industries of considerable vitality in Assam.

The tusser industry in Bengal.

40. The existence of the tusser industry has already been mentioned in paragraph 5. Leaving for another place such notices as I have collected of the habits of the insect or insects known under this name, and the mode of dealing with it adopted in the different provinces, I shall merely put down here such scanty information as I have been able to discover as to the extent of the industry in Bengal from a commercial point of view. The tusser cocoons, then, seem to have been for centuries an article of trade throughout the great forest-covered high land tract which rises everywhere on the south and west behind the alluvial plain of the Ganges and the strip of coast that forms the province of Orissa. The Bengal Board of Trade in a minute of 1819 speak of the tusser as reared "in all the western forests from Ramgurh to Midnapore." The quantity of cocoons yielded or cloth made is not estimated. The product of these tracts seems mostly to have found its way to the looms of Bancoorah and Bishenpore, of Bhaugulpore and of Futwa, Gaya and Nawada. Buchanan gives a sketch of the industry at the three last-named places, estimating the value of the out-turn of mixed cotton and tusser cloths at Futwa at 3¼ lakhs of rupees. At Gaya and Nawada, the fabric most in vogue seems to have been the Manpuri dhoti, a favourite with Mahratta pilgrims. It was a cotton sheet with a tusser silk border, such as is now made in the Central Provinces. Buchanan gives an account of the worm and its treatment in Bhaugulpore, where it was (and is) to be found in "the part of the district situated east from the Chandan and between that and the Rajmehal hills." The same authority estimates the annual export from the Bhaugulpore district of tusser cocoons at the value of about one lakh of rupees. But besides the cocoons exported, cloth of mixed tusser silk and cotton to the value of about two lakhs was among the exports of the district; 3,275 looms were said to be engaged in the manufacture. The better kinds, known as dariyahs, namunahs, baftahs and chaharkhanahs, were mostly exported; coarser pieces, called khariasris, being woven for use in the district. "Two moguls," writes Buchanan, "make advances to about the value of Rs. 1,00,000, mostly for dariyahs and namunahs, to be sent to the west of India. The commercial Resident at Maldah advances about Rs. 10,000, mostly for baftahs and namunahs, and about Rs. 90,000 worth is sent by different smaller traders to Calcutta."

According to Mr. Brownlow (in Journal of Agri-Horticultural Society, vol. xiii], "some few villagers in Cachar make use of the tusser cocoons, which are spun yearly by the wild worms on the *zizyphus* trees in their compounds, but they go no further than this, and will take no trouble to rear a brood of wild worms and place them on the trees, nor to keep watch."

And in the Sunderbuns the worms were gathered and the silk woven into dhotis.

The jungles of the hill tracts of Orissa produced a considerable supply of tusser which was reeled in the villages, and exported both to Calcutta and parts of the Madras Presidency.

The tusser silk was mostly woven into fabrics in the country; but for a few years* small quantities were exported in a raw state. The following passage is extracted from Dr. Royle's work on the Resources of India:—

"The tusser silk is still better known, having also afforded the natives in Bengal, &c., a coarse, durable silk which is much esteemed in India, both for ladies' and children's dresses, for the latter especially on account of its cheapness and durability. This silk will probably become an extensive article of commerce, as some of it having been sent on speculation to Paris in its unbleached state, was there employed as a covering for parasols, and was found to answer so well that an instantaneous demand for it sprung up. The price advanced, and the quantity imported has greatly increased. In 1835, only 158 pieces; in 1836, 830; in 1837, 2,647; and in 1838 no less than 4,249 pieces were imported. Other uses will probably be found for it when it is better known, and from the extensive tracts over which the tusser silkworm is distributed, we know that this commerce is susceptible of great extension."

Owing, however, to the spread of cultivation, the production of tusser is said to be diminishing in the Lower Provinces.

The industry in "eria" silk.

41. The history of the eria silk in a commercial point of view is meagre, probably because it is mostly used for home consumption. The worm *(Attacus ricini)* seems to have been

* I notice, however, in the "Technologist" for 1863, the statement [cited from a French source] that tusser silk was beginning to be thrown in England with some success. The export of *raw* tusser must therefore have again begun.

reared in Rungpore, Dinagepore, parts of Bhaugulpore and Purneah, and in Assam. The Fort St. George Agent in 1679 writes of "vast quantitys" being produced in the "country about Gooraghaut." But, according to Buchanan, the total area under castor-oil plant in the four Bengal districts above-named was not more than 5,000 bighas. The Madras Agent ordered some of the silk to be dyed various colours and sent home for trial, and in his journal for December 1679, we find an entry—"ordered that 600 pieces of arundee and 4 bales of arundee yarn be provided at Maldah factory to be sent home next year." The result of this experiment is not apparent. Attention was again drawn to the product by Sir W. Jones in 1791 and by Dr. Roxburgh in 1804. Buchanan also suggested that it would do to mix with wool, and that a few hundredweights should be sent home to test its usefulness in this respect. He says it was very seldom sold, the people who kept the insect rearing only enough to make cloths for their family, and Mr. Benthall, writing from Dinagepore in 1837, says:—"They seldom take it to the markets, and I believe it is never exported from the district." It is not mentioned by the Board of Trade in 1819, but Mr. Glass of Bhaugulpore seems early in the century to have sent home some of the silk, and he wrote:—"I understand that some manufacturers to whom it was shewn seem to think that we have been deceiving them by our accounts of the shawls being made from the wool of a goat, and that this silk, if sent home, would be made into shawls equal to any manufactured in India." It is still said to be made in Dinagepore, "in some quantities, for wear by the Mahomedans and low-caste Hindoos."

Of the eria in Assam, Mr. Hugon writes as follows:—

"These cloths are mostly used for home consumption; a few are bartered with the Bhootias and other hill-tribes. Large quantities were formerly exported to Lhassa by merchants known in Durrung as the Kampa Bhootias. The quantity they used to take away was very considerable, but in the latter years of the Assam Rajas' rule, from the disorganized state of the country, the number of merchants gradually decreased. Three years ago only two came after a long interval,—one of them died, and I believe the trade has not again been revived. These two merchants complained that they could no longer procure the cloths suited to their markets. No exports of it are mentioned in the returns of the Hydra chowkey. The quantity the country is capable of exporting under an improved management would be very large, for it forms at present the dress of the poorer classes at all seasons, and is used by the highest for winter wear."

Mr. Hugon estimates the annual production* of eria silk at 1,000 maunds, most of which could be exported and replaced by cotton were it so improved as that there should be any demand for it. He particularly directs attention to the possibility of finding some solvent for the gum which prevented the reeling of this silk. Mr. Brownlow, already quoted, states that in Cachar "the Eria or Renri worm is trained by Cacharees, a hill people resembling the Munipoorees and Assamese in their features, in isolated villages in the hills; but the total extent of this cultivation is very small, and it seems to have no tendency to spread among the people of the plains." The cocoons are, after being softened in a mixture of cow-dung and water, carded off to a spindle by the women of the tribe.

Particulars of the habits and treatment of this worm will be found in another chapter.

The mungá industry in Assam.

42. The mungá silk industry is confined† to Assam. Mr. Hugon, in 1834, estimated the quantity of land planted with food for the mungá at 5,000 acres, capable of yielding 1,500 maunds of silk.

"The mungá," says Mr. Hugon, "forms one of the principal exports of Assam. The average quantity passed at Gowalpara during the last two years that duties were levied was 257 maunds, valued at Rs. 56,054. It leaves the country principally in the shape of thread, most of it going to Berhampore. It is probable that the cloths made from it pass under the name of tusser; the latter, as far as I recollect, appears to have less gloss. The Hydra chowkey returns comprise only the products exported by water. The total quantity that leaves the province may, I think, be estimated at upwards of 300 maunds, for mungá also forms a portion

* The present Deputy Commissioner of Durrung puts the annual yield of eria in that district alone at 1,000 maunds, of which one-third is exported either in the form of *cocoons* or woven into heavy cloths (bor kapor).

† I have, however, recently seen it stated that there is in Hill Tipperah a village of Assamese immigrants who, some 40 or 50 years ago, accompanied an Assam Chief's daughter, on the occasion of her marriage to the Tipperah Rajah, into her adopted country and carried with them the "tusser." If this story be true, the worm is probably the mungá. It is said to be bred by the little colony for sale among the neighbouring Tipperah villages, among which there are 20 or 25 families of weavers.

of the traffic with Sylhet (across the hills), the Cossyahs, Bhootiahs, and other hill-tribes. The Assamese generally keeping more for their own use than they sell, the total quantity produced in the province may be reckoned at 600 or 700 maunds. It has been in great demand in Bengal, for, within the last few years, although the production has been greater, from the more settled state of the country, the price has risen 20 per cent. When I first arrived in this district it would be obtained without difficulty from the ryots at Rs. 3½ or 4 a seer. The competition is so great that the traders pay for it in advance, not, as with other products, to get it at a lower rate, but merely to secure their getting it. This competition is also owing to the greater number of small traders who resort to the province since the abolition of chowkies, which may have caused a rise in the price of the product in Assam without a corresponding increase in the exports."

Mr. Hugon advocates the use of mungá in coloured fabrics, it being easily dyed. In its natural fawn colour it stands washing much better than ordinary silk, keeping gloss and colour to the last. The cocoons sent by Mr. Hugon were pronounced by Mr. W. Prinsep "very fine, particularly those fed from the soom and the sonhaloo trees, which are superior to the produce of the jungles about Bancoorah." The thread was declared by the same authority "quite equal to that which is used in the best *China* tusser cloths." The cloth, however, was considered "not equal either to the Bengal tusser cloth, or to the China cloth of the same description." The Silk Committee of the Agri-Horticultural Society reported favorably on some mungá silk sent down by Captain Jenkins in 1839, and expressed their opinion that the article was "calculated to become of extensive and valuable use to our home manufactures."

A recent letter from Colonel Hopkinson, the Commissioner of Assam, gives more modern figures. It thence appears that the soom forests (on which the worm is chiefly fed) cover an area of about 34,000 acres, of which about 18,000 are assessed, yielding a revenue of nearly Rs. 28,000. By far the greater portion of the assessed area lies in the district of Sibsaugor. The production of the silk is said to employ some 48,000 persons, but it is not their sole calling. The outturn of silk is estimated at upwards of 100,000lbs. But as it is admitted that the greater part of the silk is reserved for home manufacture, this estimate cannot be regarded as absolutely trustworthy. The price of the yarn per seer varies from Rs. 5 to Rs. 9 in the several districts. The small portion exported goes to Calcutta and Dacca. From the former place it is said to find its way, to some extent, to Bhaugulpore and Bombay.

An account of the mode of rearing the mungá and dealing with the product will be found elsewhere.

General result of the Company's management of the silk-trade.

43. The general result of the Company's connexion with the silk culture of Bengal may be very briefly stated. The only direction in which any effective improvements had been introduced was that of reeling and drying. The method of cultivating the mulberry and the kinds cultivated were in 1835 just what they were a century before; attempts had been made to introduce new stocks of worms; but the worms introduced from China had not thriven, and in respect to other breeds the attempts do not seem to have been made with energy enough to have warranted any expectation of success. The breeding and rearing of the worms were left to the natives, and as shewn by Mr. Atkinson in the paper quoted in para. 19, the system of the Company was such as in every way to encourage the very vices of management which the character of the people had at first engendered. The evidence both of Company's servants and of London silk-brokers, taken before the Select Committee of the House of Lords in 1830, is very distinct as to the fact of degeneration of Bengal silk. In reeling, the Company had no doubt effected most important improvements, as Mr. Wiss' elaborate instructions, compared with the account of the country reel, shew. Indeed, it was only in this way that Bengal silk held its place in the European market at all. The natives, too, were alive to this fact, for Mr. Ramsay tells us "many natives reeled silk in the same way as the Company, according to the Italian mode."

Subsequent history of silk in Bengal but meagre.

44. Since the silk trade passed into private hands in Bengal, Government has not taken any active measures for the promotion of the industry, which indeed may have been thought to possess sufficient vitality to stand alone. Except, therefore, such figures as

the tables of exports may afford, there is little to illustrate the history of silk in Bengal from 1834 onwards. I give such meagre gleanings as I have been able to make.

Attempt to introduce Morus multicaulis.

45. In December 1839 the Government of Bengal forwarded to the Agri-Horticultural Society a letter from Colonel Sykes to the Court of Directors, in which that gentleman drew attention to a work entitled "The Silk Culturist's Manual," published at Philadelphia, U. S. A., by one John D'Homergue, which shewed that a mania for silk cultivation prevailed in America, and brought to notice the "very important fact of the recent introduction and rapid extension of the cultivation in Europe and America of a new species of mulberry, the consumption of the leaves of which by the silkworms materially improves the quality of the silk they spin," and which was alleged to be "otherwise highly valuable for its hardiness and the facility with which it is propagated." This was the *Morus multicaulis* from the Philippines, first introduced into France in 1820 by M. Perottet. The advantages of the *Morus multicaulis* are thus summarized :—

1. That it does not require any particular soil.
2. That it yields very little fruit, so that the leaves are more easily cleaned, and less matter of a fermenting nature is introduced in the body of the silkworm.
3. That it does not rise too high, and yields a greater quantity of leaves, which can be easily gathered by women and children.
4. That it puts forth its thin, tender and soft leaves earlier than other mulberries, which permits the period of hatching the silkworms to be anticipated some days.
5. That the roots possess the remarkable property of throwing up numerous small flexible stalks without forming properly a principal trunk.
6. That these stalks assume in a very short time a great length.
7. That the leaves speedily acquire a remarkable development, and are promptly renewed.
8. That these stalks or branches strike root, as cuttings, with extraordinary facility without particular care, even before they have acquired a ligneous consistence.

Thirty-two plants of the *Morus multicaulis* were afterwards received by the Society from the American Consul at Singapore, and were probably distributed by the Society; for we find some at Lucknow and Lahore. I cannot discover that the new species to any extent took the place of the kinds ordinarily used in the Lower Provinces.

Mr. Bashford's experiments in crossing.

46. In the years from 1854 onwards, Mr. Bashford, Superintendent of the Surdah filature, made some experiments in crossing, of which he gave an account to the Agri-Horticultural Society.

The following is an abstract of the papers on the subject :—

In February 1854 Mr. Bashford received a consignment of French seed which in about 15 days began hatching, and continued to hatch irregularly for about three months. The worms were treated as the country worms, and "the healthy few of the early incubations, astonishingly large and strong compared to our country stock, were placed to spin in the usual mat-frames, and gave very beautiful cocoons, some quite equal in size and firmness to the samples received with the eggs. * * The later worms, having to bear extremely hot weather, did not succeed so well."

Mr. Bashford now allowed the moths to eat out and paired French male moths with females of the desi and Madrasee stock, and French females with indigenous males. "The disparity of size was immense; however, impregnation was effectual, and both pairings alike gave eggs of a yellow colour when deposited, the French female a darker colour than the country female; but after three days those from the French female and Bengalee male turned dark and remained unhatched till next year." The eggs from French males and country females on the contrary hatched about the tenth day. These worms yielded "cocoons more flossy and less firm than the original." * * "Still there was a vast improvement on the Bengalee stock. The worms from hatching to spinning occupied about 34 days." These moths were for the most part paired among themselves, but the eggs yielded *at once reverted to the annual type.* Those of females paired with the indigenous male also reverted. The cross male with country female, however, hatched, but owing to bad weather none of the progeny reached the chrysalis stage. Mr. Bashford "reeled off a few of both the pure and cross cocoons, and the silk was quite equal to the best French; the cross cocoons, though changed in shape, gave nearly as good produce as the pure and as strong a fibre." The same results were presented by a cross of Italian and China (annual) moths with country stock. Mr. Bashford continues:—"I commenced the year 1855 with the first cross French, Italian and China females on Madrasee and desi stock, and second cross French, Italian and China male produce on indigenous females, which had gone back to annuals, and about the time these eggs began to hatch in January 1855 I received another large supply of French eggs. I had now such a quantity of eggs of different sorts that it was difficult to keep them separate; however, they had as much care bestowed on them as possible. Incubation of all the crosses went on as irregularly as with the first importation, and it was several months before any one batch had finished hatching." The result of the experiments is not very clearly stated, but it seems that the produce proved all annual. "There was very little difference in the cocoons over last year's; the offspring of the China female retained its original white colour, although crossed upon yellow cocoons, but the shape altered to a point at both ends; the cocoon was larger and the fibre seemed as strong as the parent cocoon, as was the case with the fibre of all the other crosses. This was a very unfavorable year for experiments, and many thousands of the worms died." In 1856 Mr. Bashford continued his experiments and hoped to have produced a breed which, if left to itself, would combine some of the superiority of the French, Italian and China cocoons with the multivoltine nature of the country worms. But to his astonishment, all the crosses when paired among themselves reverted in one, two, or three generations to the annual habit, the cocoons, too, though superior to Bengal cocoons, being inferior to those of France, Italy and China. Mr. Bashford concludes his paper by a description of the native happy-go-lucky method of silk culture, and expresses a doubt whether the worm might not be much improved by greater attention to the essentials of its health. The points in which he suggests improvement are: more careful cultivation of the mulberry; a fuller supply of leaf to the worms; more attention to selection in breeding, to ventilation and equable temperature of rearing-houses, and to the proper drying of the cocoons.

In a subsequent paper Mr. Bashford gave the sequel of his experiments. Owing to a break in the rains, he got a very fair crop of cocoons in the autumn of 1856, and the applicants for seed were numerous and had very fair success with their worms, which escaped the disease then prevalent among native worms. The cocoons were a great improvement on the native ones, and Mr. Bashford reeled six bales of silk of very superior quality. A large quantity was also sold for seed and spread widely over the district. But "the crop this time was a great failure, the worms deteriorated, from being treated as natives rear their country species, became reduced in strength and size considerably, and the cocoons were light, flimsy, and a perfect disappointment." The general conclusion arrived at by Mr. Bashford was as given above. An anonymous correspondent cited by Mr. Bashford also insists upon "light, equal warmth, pure air, room, cleanliness, and fresh-gathered leaves;" but expects some advantage from a slight infusion of European stock. This correspondent also urges selection in breeding, *viz.*, the choosing of the healthiest moths and only the first 50 or 100 eggs laid. Captain Hutton in certain observations on Mr. Bashford's paper expressed his opinion that crossing would be of no use; that doubtless greater attention to the food and health of the worm would even in Bengal tend to improve the cocoons yielded; but that the real difficulty in Bengal was an inimical climate. Captain Hutton here puts forward the theory, which he has worked out in other papers at greater length, that Mussoorie was the proper climate for the silkworm.

Mr. C. E. Blechynden writes a paper confirming the view, suggested by Mr. Bashford, that the fault really lies in the evil effect of the native system of rearing. More light, more air, more food, and the employment of the leaf of the *standard* mulberry are the changes for which Mr. Blechynden contends.

Signor Lotteri's proposals.

47. In 1859 a Signor Lotteri drew the attention of the Government of Bengal to the Assam mungá worm as capable, with care and better reeling, of yielding a silk that would compete with Chinese. The specimens he sent were pronounced to be similar to tusser silk, though better reeled than usual. The Agri-Horticultural Society

shewed that attention had already been drawn to the subject in 1839, but nothing had come of it. Beyond a request to the Government of Bengal to afford Signor Lotteri what assistance was possible in his further enquiries, no action was taken by the Government of India, and the matter seems to have dropped in 1860.

In 1870 Signor Lotteri renewed his proposal and asked for the grant of 10,000 acres in Assam rent-free for the prosecution of an attempt to improve and increase the products of the mungá and eria worms. The offer was, however, declined by Sir W. Grey.

Alipore and Rajshahye Agricultural Exhibitions.

48. At the Alipore Agricultural Exhibition in 1864, silk, both wild and domestic, was exhibited, and prizes to the amount of Rs. 200 were awarded to certain specimens of tusser silk, Rs. 385 being allotted to domestic silk. No silk-reeling machinery seems to have been exhibited.

Experiments with Japanese worms.

49. In 1866 experiments were tried by Captain Hutton at Mussoorie and by M. Lagarde in the Moorshedabad district with so-called Japan bivoltine and multivoltine seed. But the experiments were in neither case a success, and Captain Hutton declared the eggs to be the produce of a cross between *B. Mori* and *B. Sinensis* and liable to revert to an annual form, as he had found in his attempts to cross *B. Mori* and *B. Cræsi*, and as Mr. Bashford had found in his experiments. In 1870 M. de Cristoferis of Jungypore also made a trial of Japanese bivoltine seed. The eggs hatched very irregularly. The worms were five weeks before beginning to spin. Most of the cocoons were kept for seed. The eggs hatched again "before they had thoroughly changed their colour into brown." From this M. de Cristoferis infers that they had become, from bivoltine, multivoltine. The worms shewed no signs of disease, but the yield of silk was not greater than that of the nistri or of the bara palu, *viz.*, one factory seer of silk from 14 kahans of cocoons. The silk was pronounced very good in quality; worth Rs. 27 per seer.

Experiment in Behar.

50. In 1867, Mr. Fox and some other gentlemen began an experiment in sericulture at Biheea in the Shahabad district, which is interesting as apparently the only attempt hitherto made in Behar. They found that the mulberry grew well, and in the course of the three years over which the trial extended they produced 20 seers of silk from one of the Bengal multivoltine species. The value of the silk is not stated in the report. After three years these gentlemen abandoned the experiment, having spent upwards of £200, and not being willing to incur further expense. The difficulties they had to contend with were the difficulty of getting good seed and the occurrence of sudden mortality among their worms, sweeping off apparently the whole stock and compelling them to indent on Bengal for a fresh supply. I much doubt, though they speak hopefully, whether the dry hot weather of Arrah would not be fatal to any multivoltine. It might be possible to rear some breeds in the year by the annual importation of Bengal seed (a practice followed in the district of Maunbhoom where *bombyx* silk is thus raised on a small scale); but an industry thus conducted would not be able to compete with that of Bengal proper.

History of Bengal silk exports.

Period.	*Average exports in lbs.*
1838-39 to 1841-42	... 1,384,242
1842-43 to 1845-46	... 1,555,130
1846-47 to 1850-51	... 1,290,024
1851-52 to 1855-56	... 1,511,506
1856-57 to 1860-61	... 1,511,768
1861-62 to 1865-66	... 1,485,763
1866-67 to 1870-71	... 1,558,246

51. The figures supplied by the Collector of Customs, Calcutta, shew that the total quantity of raw silk exported by sea has not varied much during the last thirty-three years. I have grouped the results in the margin in seven periods. To this must be added for three last periods respectively, 41,552, 616,138, and 740,398 pounds of chussums or waste silk; and in 1870-71, 164,164 lbs. of cocoons were, apparently for the first time, exported. The decline of the Bengal silk trade is rather comparative than absolute. While the exports from Bengal have been almost stationary, those of China have, since 1841 when the treaty ports were thrown open, increased enormously, and in 1859 Japan silk began to come into the market. The imports into London of the latter alone ran up to $2\frac{1}{2}$ million pounds avoirdupois in 1863, but of late years Japan silk is falling into disfavour on account of its

careless reeling, and the excessive exportation of silkworms' eggs has also injuriously affected the production. Again, though the amount of Bengal raw silk exported by sea has not increased, the price, at any rate of the better kinds, has steadily risen. The Agri-Horticultural Society indeed give the very remarkable figures in the margin as the prices of raw silk for the 12 years ending with 1870. But I doubt if these can be accepted as authoritative. In fact, it is very difficult to obtain a fair estimate of average price when the fluctuations are so frequent as they seem to be in the case of silk. The rise is undoubtedly to a great extent due to the introduction of the European improvements in the system of reeling, for which I believe the silk trade has chiefly to thank Mr. Bashford, Superintendent of Messrs. Watson and Company's Surdah filatures, whose efforts to better the quality of Bengal silk were rewarded with the gold medal of the Society of Arts, and whose example was followed by most of the European firms engaged in the manufacture.

	Per seer. Rs. As.		Rs. As.
1858 ...	8 0	to	16 0
1859 ...	9 8	„	16 12
1860 ...	10 0	„	21 0
1861 ...	9 8	„	19 0
1862 ...	7 0	„	15 8
1863 ...	9 8	„	19 8
1864 ...	11 0	„	17 0
1865 ...	11 0	„	19 0
1866 ...	14 0	„	26 0
1867 ...	12 0	„	25 4
1868 ...	11 0	„	26 0
1869 ...	15 0	„	27 0
1870 ...	16 0	„	25 8

Still the prices of Bengal silk undoubtedly rule below those of China and Japan and *à fortiori* below the better Italian and Bruttia silks.

The exports of country-made silk piece-goods have greatly declined. Baboo Kissen Mohun Mullick, in his "Brief History of Bengal Commerce," makes the following pertinent remarks on this subject:—

"Choppas, bandannas and corahs come under this head. In the time of the East India Company, choppas and bandannas were printed at Cossimbazar of various colors and choice patterns, supplied by the Company's agent, and were in those days favorite articles with the English and foreigners, used as handkerchiefs and neckcloths. Their exports were heavy, and would find a ready market in England. But a taste for novelty so common in Europe as well as in other countries, which from time to time influences change of fashions, materially interfered with our printed goods, and printers, both in England and France, were busy in their designs, and printing there was thus stimulated to an enormous degree, upon plain cloths called corahs, imported to a large extent from this country for that purpose. Unfortunately, however, for our native manufacturers, the weavers in Europe stood in their way as regards the silk corahs with which they took upon themselves to supply the markets of Europe for printing purposes. Although their make and texture are far inferior to ours, specially in point of durability, yet preference is given to them by the mass of the people there, for the sake of cheapness, resulting from the cloths being made of *chussum* or waste silk, the exports of which, both from here and China, of late have materially augmented, and hence our exports to Great Britain of choppas and bandannas as well as of corahs have dwindled down to mere trifles, as the following comparative statement will shew—

	1849-50.	Value in Rs.	1869-70.	Value in Rs.
Corahs in pieces ...	633,729	34,63,000	80,373	6,21,164
Choppas and bandannas in pieces	69,764	4,01,700	2,167	18,198

"On the other hand, the exports of *chussum* to Great Britain have materially increased. In all 1861—953, and in 1869 14,000 maunds. This refuse in earlier days was as worthless as jute cuttings were, but now both are treated as important articles of merchandize."

The following extracts from the report on the administration of the Customs Department, Lower Provinces, for 1870-71, will shew in a general way the present position of the Bengal silk trade as far as the sea-exports illustrate it. No statistics of the inland exports of bombyx silk, nor of the present yield of tusser silk, are available:—

"In silk, raw or chussum, there has been an export of 17,684 cwt., valued at Rs. 1,22,83,377, being a decrease of 2,216 cwt. in quantity, and Rs. 13,09,707 in value. Of raw silk 8,410 cwt., valued at Rs. 93,82,092, have gone to Great Britain; 1,455 cwt., value Rs. 18,95,002, to France; and to Italy 135 cwt., value Rs. 1,92,996. Great Britain has taken more than in 1869-70, but France only half of what she took in that year. Of chussum, 6,175 cwt., valued at Rs. 5,21,396, have gone to Great Britain, but France has taken more than double of the quantity in 1869-70, *viz.*, 879 cwt., valued at Rs. 87,997." * * *

"Silk piece-goods have been exported to the value of Rs. 10,35,938. Of this, Great Britain has taken Rs. 6,98,972 worth in corahs, and Rs. 1,00,019 in tussers and Rs. 17,214 worth in choppas. Of this latter description, Mauritius has taken Rs. 10,180, and Bourbon

Rs. 11,170. Of other silk manufactures, France has taken Rs. 12,408, Ceylon Rs. 17,312, Penang and Singapore Rs. 17,073, the Persian Gulf Rs. 4,395, and America Rs. 11,345."

Present state of sericulture in Bengal.

52. At present the production of bombyx silk in the Lower Provinces (excluding Assam) seems to be confined to the districts of Rajshahye, Maldah, Moorshedabad, Midnapore, Beerbhoom, Hooghly, Burdwan, Bograh, Howrah, Nuddea, Jessore, and the 24-Pergunnahs.* The five first are the great silk-producing districts. In the rest the industry is of much less importance. Indeed, in Nuddea and Jessore there seems to be but one filature in each district; in both cases towards the northern boundary. The area over which the industry now extends is probably less than it was fifty years ago, when it seems to have spread further to the east and north into Dinagepore, Rungpore, Bograh, and Pubna.

Mr. Skrine, Assistant Magistrate, has supplied an interesting account of the industry in the district of Rajshahye. There are 34 filatures owned by Europeans and 63 owned by natives, or 97 in all, containing 5,760 basins and employing between 11,000 and 12,000 hands. Mr. Skrine estimates the yielding of raw silk at 5,000 maunds, *communibus annis*, and believes that no less an area than 150 square miles is under mulberry, while a quarter of a million of people derive their support from the trade in one or other of its branches in this one district alone. In Maldah, the Collector estimates the value of the trade in raw silk and cocoons carried on at the weekly market held at Amaneegunj at two lakhs of rupees a week. I think this estimate (from which, be it remembered, is excluded the value of the cocoons supplied to the European filatures, which are obtained by private contract and not in the open market) must be very greatly exaggerated. Mr. Hunter (Annals of Rural Bengal) estimates that the silk industry in Beerbhoom supports 15,000 persons, and puts the yearly value of the silk manufactures of the district at 16 lakhs of rupees. For other districts even conjectural estimates are not forthcoming.

Question of degeneracy of the Bengal worms.

53. The assertion of the degeneracy of the worm dates as we have seen from many years back. Mr. Atkinson's natives declared that the yield of the bara palu had diminished 50 per cent. The preponderance of authority is certainly in favour of the view that the Bengal species have degenerated; but the subject does not seem to have been very carefully investigated, and Mr. Turnbull of Ghattal maintains that the fact of degeneracy has yet to be proved. Most of those engaged in silk manufacture assume this point and confine themselves to discussing the remedies. These are various. It seems generally admitted that the attempts to introduce exotic breeds have not of late years succeeded. It would also appear that though there has sometimes been a large mortality among silkworms, no epizoic such as the "muscardine" and the "pébrine," which have devastated France and Italy, has as yet appeared in India. M. Gallois of Midnapore appears to think the cause of degeneracy may be in the mulberry being too long cultivated in one spot. M. Perrin of Berhampore on the other hand extols the native mulberry cultivation as careful and judicious. Mr. Marshall urges an attempt to improve the stock by offering prizes for the best bred cocoons, and the distribution of tracts in the vernacular on the best method of selection. Most authorities agree that the natives stint the worms, and Mr. Atkinson long ago saw the difficulty of dealing with this tendency on their part. Mr. Malcolm, of Ramnugger, in the Kandhee sub-division of Moorshedabad, maintains that the worm has been injured by being forced into unduly rapid reproduction of itself; that whereas "20 or 25 years ago" there were but four breeds or "bunds" in the year, there are now from six to eight. It may be that the worm has been forced in this direction, but I do not find that the "bunds" are anywhere given as less than five, even so long as 50 years ago.

Present state of silk manufacture in Bengal.

54. I have not been able to obtain much information on the present state of silk *manufacture* in Bengal. The exports shew that the industry still survives, but in a languishing condition. The Maldiki cloths, described by Buchanan, are still

* Some sixteen years ago a native erected some large factories in the Baraset Sub-division of this last-named district. But the attempt failed, it is alleged, because it came in collision with the rising and highly remunerative jute industry.

woven in the decayed old town, and the "corahs" of Baloochur and Moorshedabad are still well known. In Bancoorah, Bishenpore, sundry towns in the Burdwan and Hooghly districts and Bhaugulpore weavers are still to be found, and some of the patterns in bright and boldly contrasted colours are striking enough. Dr. Forbes Watson's illustrative list contains but four samples from Bengal of fabrics employing silk in their construction, *viz.*, two of silk piece-goods from Bhaugulpore and Berhampore, a specimen of gold embroidery on silk from Moorshedabad, and one of the tasteful silk embroidery on muslin from Dacca.

SECTION II.

SILK IN BOMBAY.

First attempt at sericulture in Bombay.

THE earliest attempt* to introduce the culture of silk into Bombay is said to have been that of Dr. H. Scott in 1795, of which, however, I have not been able to obtain any details. We may presume that it had no permanent results.

Mr. Baber at Dharwar.

2. In 1823† Mr. Baber, the Collector, introduced worms from Mysore into the Southern Mahratta Country, first at the Dharwar Jail, and thence among a few Mussulmans about Dharwar, Hooblee, and other towns in the province. These persons had leases of seven years and advances of cash, and were reported by Dr. Lush in 1833 to be "then cultivating one or two acres each of *desi* mulberry, producing a few maunds of silk, merely for local consumption, which are sold in the bazaar at Hooblee at from Rs. 3½ to Rs. 4 the seer of 8 oz. avoirdupois." A package of silk was also sent from Dharwar to England, apparently in 1827, but the ship in which it was carried was wrecked and the sample damaged. The Court of Directors reported that, "had the parcel been in a sound state, the raw silk would have produced about 12 shillings a pound." The cultivation seems, at any rate for a time, to have taken some little root in Dharwar. In 1842 about 400 lbs. weight of a very inferior silk was made, partly in the Jail and partly by free natives. Even now the Collector reports that (besides the jail experiment as to which see paragraph 30) "one Bundoobye has a small mulberry plantation, and yearly turns out a fair supply of cocoons." But cotton has for the most part driven out silk in Dharwar, and Mr. Robertson is of opinion that water is too far below the surface for irrigated mulberry cultivation to pay.

Experiments in Khandeish and at Poonah.

3. The following extracts from a letter from Mr. Ashburner, Collector of Khandeish, to the Government of Bombay, supplemented from other sources, give an account of some further attempts to foster sericulture in the Western Presidency:—

"Silk was first introduced into Khandeish in the year 1826 by the then Collector, Mr. Giberne. It does not appear where he procured the worms from, or what species they were, but I gather from the correspondence that they were not the indigenous tusser silkworm. In 1827 a small establishment was sanctioned by Government for a mulberry garden, and a sample of silk was produced which was reported by a Committee of silk brokers in Bombay to be of inferior sort, not suited to the China or English market, but valued, for local manufacture, at from Rs. 7 to Rs. 9 per seer. The Collector felt confident that, as soon as the mulberry trees began to yield better food for the worms, the silk would improve. In 1831 Khandeish silk was valued at from Rs. 7-2-0 to Rs. 10-2-0, and classed as equal to 3rd or 4th class Canton silk. It was sold in the Dhoolia Bazaar at Rs. 9 per seer. In 1837 M. Mutti, who had then been temporarily employed as Superintendent of Silk Culture, was sent to inspect the Khandeish Silk Factory. He reported that the worms and mulberry trees throve well at Dhoolia, but they were in the charge of three peons, who were entirely ignorant of the proper mode of treating the worms or winding the silk, so that, considering the neglect and improper treatment they had received, he was surprised to find the silk so good. It was then selling in the bazaar at Rs. 12 or Rs. 13 per seer. M. Mutti particularly noticed the luxuriant growth of the mulberry at Dhoolia, but complained that instead of planting the trees in rows, close together, they should have been grown as standards 25 feet apart. In 1838 the silk factory at Dhoolia seems to have been transferred to a Borah named Nooroodeen, who, after a few years, became bankrupt, from speculations unconnected with silk, and the culture was abandoned, Government having determined to concentrate all its efforts in the experiment then in progress at Poona under the superintendence of M. Mutti.

---

* It is, however, stated by Dr. Kennedy (as quoted by Mr. Williamson, Revenue Commissioner, in a paper of 1837) that "two centuries ago" silk had been one of the products of Guzerat, Champaneer being then the principal seat of silk manufacture, and that he (Dr. K.) had, in 1829, seen families of silk-weavers among the ruins of that city. And in the calendar of State papers relating to the East Indies, 1617-1621, I find mention of a cargo of silk brought home by one Laurence Walldo from *Surat*. Some of this was "to be dyed for better experience" and was therefore probably *raw* silk. But it may have come from Bengal, for in 1679 the Governor of Fort St. George notes in his diary of a tour of inspection "at the head of the Bay", that on 5th December in that year, on his way down from Cossimbazaar to Hooghly, he "lay to at Puttalee, where some Guzeratee merchants live and buy considerable quantities of silk for sale at Ahmedabad." Dr. Kennedy perhaps confounded the manufacture of silk fabrics with the production of the raw material. I also find allusion to a "casual experiment" in silkworm breeding by the Portuguese, in Colaba apparently. The date is not given.

† In his evidence (as reported) before the Select Committee of the House of Lords in 1830, Mr. Baber says his experiments were during the years 1815, 1816, and 1817. But I think there is some mistake about it, for this statement is not consistent with certain letters of his own.

"The above is a very brief history of the rise, progress, and fall of silk culture in Khandeish. The facts elicited after twelve years' experience are, that the mulberry grows luxuriantly, and that, notwithstanding the improper manner in which the worms were kept, and the ignorance and neglect of the men who had charge of them, the worms throve, and produced silk which sold in the bazaar at Rs. 12 per seer. The failure of the experiment appears to have been owing to the want of special knowledge and experience of the persons who had charge of it. Mr. Giberne, the originator of the experiment, admits that his information on the subject was entirely theoretical, and, from first to last, no one who had ever had any practical experience in silk-culture had any share in the management. Had Mr. Giberne remained at Khandeish, the result might have been different. But he appears to have been transferred at a very early period of the experiment. His successor was probably without even his theoretical knowledge, and taking no particular interest in the subject, it was neglected. * * * *

"In the year 1829, Mr. Giberne's experiment having attracted the attention of Government, the Bengal Government was requested to send to Bombay five convicts, with their families, who were skilled in the management of silkworms and the winding of silk. These men brought with them a quantity of eggs. They were attached to the Jail at Poonah."

But, from want of careful supervision, they appear to have done little, either in the way of producing silk, or of teaching the process to others.

Trial at Ahmednugger.

4. Another attempt was made at Ahmednugger, where Dr. Graham, the Civil Surgeon, was allowed land yielding Rs. 602 per annum, rent-free for 25 years, and was given an advance of Rs. 3,000.* Dr. Graham reports progress in a letter, dated 31st December 1831, from which the following are excerpts:—

"My labours, since obtaining the grant of the Furrah Bagh lands in July 1830, have, till lately, been directed to planting the small mulberry, which is, I believe, the *Morus Indica*. It has a small berry, and, in favourable soils, throws out a pretty good sized leaf, which is sometimes indented and sometimes not, and is the same, as far as I can understand, as that used in Bengal, where it rises, as in this country, from 6 to 10 feet high. This was planted in close hedgerows, as in Bengal, and when it had attained the height of 4 or 5 feet, every alternate row was taken up by the roots and carefully planted at regular distances of 12 feet square on other spots of ground. This was thought to be favourable for ploughing and harrowing in every direction round the trees, and to be a great saving of manual labour, which could not be avoided in the close rows. About 12,000 or 15,000 trees were removed in this way. It was found, however, that while trees were placed at such distances, there was a useless expenditure of water by flowing over the vacant ground between each tree. This vacancy was, therefore, filled in with cuttings, so as again to form them into hedgerows at 12 feet distance, the intermediate space being well ploughed, but now only in one direction, and sown with gram (or other low grains which do not rise high to injure the trees), so as to leave 2 or 3 feet on each side of the row perfectly clean. This was intended to make the ground pay, and was, at the same time, the most economical plan of watering and keeping the trees clean. The reason for persevering with this kind of mulberry was that the leaf seemed better adapted for producing a fine kind of silk, having more of the resinous and saccharine, and less of the fibrous, part than the *Morus rubia* which has a long fruit with a large, coarse, deeply indented leaf; and thus, in proportion to the weight of the leaf, the small mulberry would hold a greater quantity of silk than the large, and also of a superior quality. I am sorry to say that this kind, I now find, is not adapted to this soil, which, in most parts, is of a black and hard nature, into which the roots of the small tree cannot penetrate with facility. I have, therefore, lately directed my attention to a kind of mulberry intermediate between the large and the small, and which, my head Chinaman informs me, is the best in the country. It grows into a pretty large tree. Within the last fifteen days, 800 trees have been transplanted of this kind, and to give them every chance, large holes have been dug and filled with white earth and manure, so that the roots may acquire strength and nourishment enough from the rich light soil to enable them to penetrate the black and denser soil. One field of this kind is laid out in hedgerows with 12 feet distance, and as these acquire sufficient height they are transplanted, and in the course of two or three years may grow into trees.

"There are also about 60 trees of this kind coming on, which have been budded upon the small and also about 10 of the large coarse-leafed on the small, which were tried to ascertain what alteration it might make in the leaf. Some cuttings of the *Morus alba* were obtained from the village of Jamgaum, where there are four or five trees growing luxuriantly and of a great size upon a variety of the black soil. One plant of this kind and a species of the *Morus Indica* growing at St. Helena, together with the *doppia foglia* of the Italians, are growing very well. These were received from Dr. Lush at Dapooree. About 60 beegahs are under mulberry cultivation, but being mostly of the small kind, for which the soil is not so favourable, the leaf is not very large.

"The disadvantages under which I labour are these: the adhesive and hard nature of the soil, consisting of a very great proportion of alumina without any silicious earth to keep it open, and consequently its great absorption and retention of water, which by evaporating from the surface, causes a sudden contraction in bulk, when the soil splits into fissures and exposes the

* He seems also to have been given the services of some Chinese and Bengalee convicts conversant with silk-winding.

roots of the trees; the exhausted powers of the land in consequence of continued irrigation by the Koonbees, who formerly cultivated the lands, and its abounding with spontaneous grasses called *Hurrialee* and *Roonda*, which give us incessant trouble. They run under the ground in every direction, to the depth of four feet or more, and have roots about the size of a writing quill, and joints from which other roots strike out. These often form a complete basket-work round the roots of the trees, and bind them so that they cannot expand. Scarcely has one piece of ground been well cleaned, before another, from the frequent watering, is overrun with these grasses, which are continually re-appearing, being supplied from the roots at a great depth.

"These are the peculiar disadvantages which I have to combat in regard to the rearing of trees, on which almost entirely the success of my undertaking depends. I am endeavouring to overcome them by every means in my power, so that the natives may perceive the possibility and advantages of raising silk in the Deccan. I am happy to be able to state that several natives have begun to form plantations.

"The palace of the Furrah Bagh has been repaired at considerable expense; a passage has been made across the tank; and feeding rooms fitted up exactly on the plan recommended by Count Dandolo. This extensive building, from its coolness, being surrounded with water, and the large accommodation it affords, is admirably adapted for feeding-rooms for a large tract of country. * * * * * * * *

"The reeling of the silk is conducted by two Chinamen, one on Rs. 48, and the other on Rs. 16 per mensem. They have a most simple winding machine, which they brought secretly with them from China. The most approved English machine that could be procured in London has been sent to me, and the one used by the Italians; but neither of them is adapted to make the reeling a domestic operation like the simple China one, which requires only one person to manage the whole, and may be used by the Hindoo or Mussulman women in any of the corners of their huts or houses. The silk throwsters have brought their women and sons and learnt under the Chinamen, and would not receive any wages from me until they were expert enough to be regularly employed: so desirous are the natives of acquiring the art of reeling. The quantity of pure silk from my cocoons* is $\frac{1}{11}$th of their weight, the same proportion as in Italy and much greater than in Bengal. There will be no necessity for my entering into the mode of feeding and reeling, as the former is so well laid down by Count Dandolo, and the latter can be acquired by practice. I may, however, mention the China tattee, on which the worm spins, which is two feet broad, about four feet long, and is formed of bamboo twisted into loops. The worms are thickly placed among these loops and exposed freely to the open air, which renders the cocoon harder and dries the watery or serous fluid which the worm throws out in such quantities as it is spinning.

"The first crop of worms in November last yielded about 4 lbs. of silk. There was a great mistake made in having calculated too small a quantity of leaves for the crop. The consequence was that the worms having been badly fed in the later stage, the cocoons were soft and small. One could judge of the quantity of leaf consumed to the silk obtained. * * * The natives offer me the same price as for the China silk, Rs. 14 to Rs. 18 per bazaar seer. * * * Probably I may hereafter find it advantageous to give out the cocoons and have them reeled in the native houses at so much the seer, and by having the very simple native throwsting machines erected in the palace, I may save the profit which the Borahs have on the raw material passing through their hands before it reaches the throwster and weaver."

The sequel of Dr. Graham's experiment seems to have been as follows:—He continued planting standards till he had some 1,500 trees of the 'Madras' mulberry, when he was compelled by sickness to go home. In his absence Dr. Straker conducted the experiment for about three years, but without much success, the worms being badly reared and yielding small cocoons and little silk. Dr. Graham, on his return, seems to have repaid his advance to Government, and made over the establishment to Lieutenant Shortrede, who took Major Byne, a retired officer, into partnership. The latter proceeded to substitute St. Helena standard mulberry for what Dr. Graham had planted. In 1838 the original lease was extended for 19 years more. From Major Byne it passed to a Captain or Mr. Fenwick, and was working in 1842, when 52 lbs of silk were produced; but by July 1845, "the whole speculation" had, according to the then Collector, "turned out a complete failure."

Experiment on the Island of Bombay.

5. A Parsee, Framjee Cowasjee by name, seems to have tried sericulture on the Island of Bombay.

Opinions on silk produced.

6. Of the quality of silk produced, Dr. Lush writes as follows:—

"Of the samples of silk laid before the Society, valuations have been made at Poonah, Ahmednuggur, and Bombay, from which it appears that the silk now produced by Mr. Graham, and by Sorabjee Patell, reeled by the China reel, is precisely adapted to the consumption of the country. If the article be made finer, it would not, for native manufactures, fetch a higher price. If finer silk is reeled, it must be sent to Bombay for exportation. These Poonah

* According to Mr. D'Oyly, the present Collector of Ahmednuggur, Dr. Graham reared the Bengal annual worm.

and Ahmednuggur samples are classed in Bombay with the China silk called *Taysaam*, which sells at Rs. 12½ and Rs. 13 the pucka seer (2 lbs). Thus from mulberries planted in all manner of ways, with the sorts mixed, and by the simple Chinese reel, one great step has at least been made *to produce that which will sell the best at the nearest market.* If we expect to see the production of silk extend among the natives, we should at first propose the use of the Chinese reel only. It is worked by one man. The Italian reel requires three, one at the basin, one to turn the handle or winch, and one to keep up the fire. The Chinese reel requires a very small quantity of fuel,—another *Deccan* argument in its favour. The Italian reel, in return for the labour of three persons and larger expense of fuel, reels double the quantity of silk in a given time. Italian reeling would require an extensive factory, and its machinery is not portable. Any reeler may carry about the Chinese apparatus and work it where he pleases. I need not enlarge upon the extensive market there is in India for coarse raw silk. I will just allude to the article of spun silk, which is made from the damaged cocoons, those which are deformed, abortive, or have been perforated by the moth. These, in Mr. Graham's establishment, are turned to good account. They are spun into a coarse thread, after being soaked for a night with some lentil seed. They are pulled out and twisted around a bamboo skewer, exactly as twine is made in this place for fishing nets. This spun silk brings Rs. 6 the pucka seer at present, and when made a little finer it is expected to sell at Rs. 8."

Breeds used.

7. With regard to the breeds used in the experiments of this period, it would seem that at first the experimenters worked with the breed introduced into Dharwar from Mysore; that Italian eggs from St. Helena were afterwards tried, and when both these stocks failed from disease, Dr. Lush at last obtained a supply of the annual worm (*bara palu*) from Bengal.

Experiment at Kaira.

8. An experiment, though at a somewhat later date (1837), was sanctioned at Kaira in Guzerat, under the superintendence of Dr. Burn, the Civil Surgeon. Land for a mulberry garden was given him, and the use of an empty barrack as a rearing house, and an initial outlay of Rs. 400, with a monthly expenditure of Rs. 40 for two years, was permitted. In January 1838 Dr. Burn reported that he had planted some 800 mulberries, of the St. Helena species, obtained from the Deccan, and that they were thriving. He contemplated pursuing the standard method of cultivation. He was allowed to extend his cultivation, and the monthly grant of Rs. 40 was doubled. In 1840 Dr. Burn reported his plantation flourishing. It had afforded food for 60,000 worms, and some silk had been reeled, though rudely. Allowances, of Rs. 15 a month each, were therefore sanctioned for three Guzeratee youths to go and learn reeling under Signor Mutti. Dr. Burn was continuing the trial in 1842 (or even in 1849, if a newspaper letter hereafter quoted is to be trusted for accurate dates) and seemingly with some success. The Bombay Government can give no further information.

The most important trial, that made under superintendence of Signor Mutti.

9. But these and one or two other attempts, of which a brief notice by Signor Mutti (extracted further on) is all the account I have been able to trace, were only desultory and unconnected efforts in comparison with the experiment made under the immediate auspices of Government during the years 1837—1847.

First dealings of Government with Signor Mutti.

10. In October 1829, Signor Mutti, a native of Italy, offered his services to Government as Superintendent of any establishment that might be formed for the cultivation of silk; but as no such intention was then entertained by Government, his offer was declined. He was, however, given to understand that the most liberal encouragement would be extended to scientific and enterprising persons who might wish to engage in the speculation on their own account. Encouraged by this assurance of aid, Signor Mutti resolved to undertake the manufacture of silk, and, on his application, the Collector of Poonah was directed (April 1830) to make over to him the Kutroor Bagh, at that place, free of rent for 15 years, on condition that the ground should only be applied to the growth of mulberry. To this, in the course of 1830, 1831, and 1832, several plots were added; Lord Clare, the then Governor, taking a strong interest in the subject, and urging the desirableness of supporting Signor Mutti, to whom, moreover, an advance of Rs. 6,000 was made. The Collector of Poonah was, at the same time, authorized to remit the rent for six years on land cultivated with mulberry, and to make tuccavee advances for wells. In consequence, however, of some disagreement between Signor Mutti and his partner, Sorabjee Patell, most of the lands

assigned to the former had to be resumed; but he was left in possession of the Kutroor and Dhundhuree Gardens.

Proposal to appoint him Superintendent of Silk Culture.

11. Till 1837 no further aid seems to have been given Signor Mutti. But on the 21st January of that year the Right Hon'ble Sir R. Grant, then President, recorded a minute expressing his high opinion of the system introduced by Signor Mutti, and proposing that he should be appointed Superintendent of Silk Culture in the Deccan, his travelling expenses being paid, and Rs. 100 a month being granted for the payment of an assistant and certain gardeners, and should, if his exertions were successful, be suitably rewarded at the end of two or three years.

Difference of opinion between the Government of Bombay and the Government of India on the subject.

12. The Government of India, when asked to sanction this scheme, demurred. "All cultivation of silk," it was said, "on the part of Government, is in course of abandonment, and the object proposed can only be that of giving encouragement to private enterprise. But unless the circumstances of the Deccan should be exceedingly different from those of Bengal, His Lordship in Council is at a loss to imagine how any person, with whatever skill and genius he may be endowed, can be expected to establish, with an Indian population, by mere precept and instruction, extensive improvements in a branch of industry in which there is no new experiment to be tried, no mystery to be resolved, but in which, particularly, the large application of capital has been found necessary."

The Government of Bombay replied, forwarding papers giving the views of Signor Mutti and others on the prospects of silk in the Deccan, and proposed an experiment at an estimated cost of Rs. 35,000 spread over four years, the principal item in the estimate being the salary of the Superintendent, which was fixed at Rs. 500 a month. The method to be pursued was thus described: "It forms no part of M. Mutti's plan that, in order to effect the object in view, Government should establish silk manufactories or be in any way connected with the manufacture. All that he proposes is the appointment of a properly qualified person, whose duty it shall be to establish nurseries at Poonah, Ahmednuggur, and Yowla (at which place a community of silk-weavers has been established for many years past); to convert a number of *Kooruns* (or tracts of grazing land) into mulberry gardens; to move about the country with the view to encourage the ryots and others, by the offer of premiums, to plant the mulberry tree; to teach them how they are to be reared, and to exercise, at the outset, a general superintendence over all such mulberry plantations." The Government of India, however, still viewed the project as doubtful, and advised a reference to the Court of Directors.

The question referred to the Court of Directors and temporary arrangements made.

13. This reference was accordingly made by the Government of Bombay, Signor Mutti being in the meanwhile appointed temporarily on a salary of Rs. 250 per mensem, with a native supervisor on Rs. 50, and license to spend a sum not exceeding Rs. 100 a month, in setting on foot mulberry plantations; the arrangement to be subject to report at the end of six months. The reply of the Court of Directors, addressed to the Government of India, may be here extracted, as shewing the views then entertained on the general question of the encouragement to be given by Government to the introduction of new products. "We have already," wrote the Hon'ble Court, "expressed our opinion that the carrying out of measures of this nature should generally be left to individual capital and enterprise, but that Government may fitly lend its assistance for the introduction of new products that give a fair promise of being beneficial to the country, or for the improvement of old products, or for their extension to different parts of the country, when, without such assistance, there would be little probability of their being so introduced or extended, strictly limiting that assistance, however, to determining the feasibility and probable advantages of the proposed measure, and to practically demonstrating the means of its successful establishment. We therefore approve of the arrangements which have been sanctioned by you, and if the progress of these arrangements should fully satisfy you of the propriety of an outlay to the extent proposed by the Bombay Government, we authorize you to sanction it."

Signor Mutti's first reports, 1838.

14. Meantime, Signor Mutti had commenced operations on the temporary footing sanctioned by the Government of India, and on the 21st July 1838 he submitted his first report as Superintendent of Silk Culture in the Deccan.

In a second report dated October 1838, he thus recapitulated results :—

Mulberry trees have been planted as follows, *viz.*—

	33	villages in the Deccan.
	6	,, in Bombay.
	1	,, in Concan.
TOTAL ...	40	

	213	individuals have been induced to plant them in the Deccan.
	24	,, ,, ,, in Bombay.
	1	individual has ,, ,, in Concan.
TOTAL ...	238	

Of those in the Deccan—

110 take the greatest possible care of their plantation.
54 tolerably so.
49 very little or no care whatever.

I beg to annex the following abstract of slips planted, and description of people who have undertaken to plant them—

Deccan, by the ryots, slips	439,481
,, besides, in the Government Nursery Garden at Sassoor ...	49,850
Bombay	125,100
Concan	2,500
TOTAL SLIPS ...	616,931

Deccan, planted by—

1 Nawab,
2 Shetts,
24 Patells,
8 Koolkurnees,
30 Brahmins,
4 Goldsmiths,
3 Blacksmiths,
1 Tailor,
72 Malees,
50 Koonbees,
8 Mussulmans,
2 Gosains,
1 Fakir,
2 Desmookhs,
2 Gooroos of the temple,
1 Moar,
1 Aral,
1 Jemadar,

TOTAL ... 213 in the Deccan,

and all these things have been effected without annoyance to any of the parties concerned.

In the same report Signor Mutti gives an account "of 4,252 mulberry plants, of several species, transplanted and reared as standard trees." They seem to have belonged to the "St. Helena" species, to the *doppia foglia*, the Philippine *(Morus Multicaulis)*, and three other "red" species. Signor Mutti also states that he had "kept at Kutroor an establishment of several persons, whom he had instructed in all the branches of silk-making to the best of his ability, and had succeeded in rendering them smart, intelligent, and active." He had also received the "most satisfactory reports" of his silk from London, Glasgow, and Manchester, where "it had been valued as high as 23*s*., 26*s*., 29*s*., though reeled quite independently by natives." Upwards of twenty natives were reported to be acquainted with the winding of silk, and the people to be ready, of their own accord, to adopt the system generally. Signor Mutti was at this period so sanguine as to write: "Government will have no occasion to keep up the silk culture establishment longer than two or three years at the utmost.

In 1838, moreover, a sample of silk produced by M. Mutti was sent for report to Mr. Joseph Ewart, silk broker of Manchester, who reported as follows :—"The thread is very good, being clean and even, and in every way shews excellent management on the part of the cultivator. In answer to the question as to which quality is most saleable, I can only say that they are all equally good for the several manufactures to which they may be applied. The No. 3 size is particularly so, owing to its being comparatively a very even thread and free from dirt. The consumption and relative prices both depend so much on the description of goods in demand, that a precise answer to this question would probably mislead M. Mutti. Suffice it to say, that silks of the quality which he has produced would always be saleable, more or less, as they would command a decided preference over the Bengal silks now imported, at the same time coming into closer competition with the Italian silks."

Progress of the experiment in 1839.

15. The report of July 1839 is not so flourishing, but perhaps equally shews Signor Mutti's confident temperament. Drought, the incursions of cattle, and neglect had much injured the plantations, but the Superintendent was still sanguine. He thus sums up :—

"*1st.*—The prejudices of the natives have been overcome regarding planting mulberries, rearing worms, and winding silk.

"*2nd.*—In the Deccan, Bombay, and Concan, we have several natives engaged in making properly mulberry nurseries; transplanting and pruning the trees correctly.

"*3rd.*—The system introduced of transplanting the mulberry plant, without earth, has been proved to succeed very well, and their transplantation is found to be very economical, as instead of a man removing one tree at a time, with earth, he can remove those without earth in hundreds. The natives were astonished to see this mode of plantation so successful; and I was myself surprised to see the buds shoot out, with leaves, four days after being transplanted.

"*4th.*—The quantity of eggs produced by the butterflies have increased.

"*5th.*—The white cocoons, that were before small, are now increased to just the same size as the yellow and sulphur, and the eggs are regularly hatched.

"*6th.*—Experience has now shewn that it was not only at Kutroor Bagh we had cocoons of a quality that 10,000 would suffice to produce a pucka seer of silk, instead of 13 and 18,000 cocoons as stated in my Guide; but we have that quantity also at other places, by which saving of leaves, wages, labourers, and room required for the rearing of worms are effected, and the result of product increased.

"*7th.*—The capability of the natives to wind silk of a superior quality has been established beyond doubt.

"*8th.*—The value of a mulberry plantation, in the sale of the leaves, has been shewn. The leaves bought for feeding the worms at Wargaum have been purchased by Goondgal, from the ryots, at 1½ pice the pucka seer, and the greater part from pruning their young mulberry plants, under one year of age, in the villages of Chinchooree, Wargaum, Sawargaum, Narangaum, Goonjoolwaree, and Malligaum. I attended myself as a mediator, on this the first occasion of the kind, to point out the value to them, and to give them a few observations. I had the satisfaction to see those natives very much satisfied, and, moreover, to hear the natives at Narangaum, a people, by-the-bye, very difficult to satisfy, call me their 'Danea;' that God had sent me to them—adding, that during other years at this period (March) in which they have no products, they generally had recourse to their *Sowkars* to get some money to go on with, but now they are assisted by the mulberry.

"*9th.*—From an experiment made at Naigao, near Bombay, at Mr. F. de Ramos' Estate, it has been found that the consumption of leaves, of the St. Helena species, for the worms, from the day they were hatched until they began to spin, has been proved to be 12 pucka seers (of 80 tolas) for 1,000 worms.

"The very 'Mutti worms,' that require 31 days in Poonah to begin to spin, have spun in Bombay in 24 to 26 days."

In the year 1839 the advance of Rs. 6,000 granted to M. Mutti was written off 'in consideration of the benefit his exertions were calculated to confer on the country, and of the losses to which he was subjected by ineffectual attempts to introduce the bush system,' a system now abandoned by him in favour of the 'standard' plan of cultivation.

1840.

16. In 1840 Signor Mutti was allowed to proceed to Egypt on sick leave, and an honorarium of Rs. 2,000 was given him; and in the same year an advance of Rs. 4,000 was given to Mr. Ramos, his assistant. The Bombay Government, in forwarding to the Government of India copy of Mr. Ramos' report, again

urged their previous scheme; but the Governor General in Council thought the proposals went far beyond what the principles laid down by the Court of Directors would warrant, and confined himself to sanctioning an increase of Rs. 50 a month to Signor Mutti's pay. In June 1840 that gentleman returned to India. Of his operations for the next three years I have not been able to obtain distinct accounts. But the Government seems to have been satisfied with his proceedings.

17. In November 1843, however, Sir G. Arthur, then President, recorded a minute strongly advocating perseverance in the experiment; and as his views seem to have been in a great degree based upon certain reports of Signor Mutti's in 1843, I will summarise the facts contained in them.

1843.

In Poonah itself, Sorabjee Patell had "extensive plantations of several thousand mulberry trees of from 2 to 10 years of age" and made "a small quantity of silk." There were besides in the station of Poonah some 1,400 mulberry trees of the age of 3 to 7 years. In 36 villages of the Poonah Collectorate there were 50,806 trees from 1 to 5 years old, belonging to 317 individuals. This was exclusive of "mulberry hedgerows." In two villages independent persons had begun to rear worms. Both (singularly enough) were Brahmins; one had "clandestinely taken a few thousand eggs," had "reared worms and made good cocoons." The latter had "been rearing 61,000 worms with favourable success and a profitable result." In this Collectorate, moreover, Signor Mutti mentions six breeding places which he had under his own superintendence. But except as to Sawargaum, where 35,000 worms are said to have been reared, no details are given. Reeling was carried on at Wargaum.

In the Furrah Bagh at Ahmednuggur Dr. Graham's experiment had fallen into the hands of a Mr. Fenwick. He had "15,000 trees mostly from 2½ to 5 years old, an establishment of very good pruners, rearers of worms, and winders of silk. Only 52 lbs of silk were made last year (1842), owing to the trees having been neglected when young, and requiring very mild treatment." At Mulligaum there were "about 1,000" trees, one year old: at Dhoolia "several hundreds from 6 to 14 years of age;" at Kunnur "about 8,000 flourishing trees from 3 to 6 years old;" at Nassick 300 trees: but at none of these places was any sericulture going on. In Kattywar the Civil Surgeon had taken up the subject, and in 1842 had obtained eggs of some multivoltine species, and obtained some 90 seers of cocoons, of which however more than half "became bad in the rains." Trees, to the number of "2,000 or 3,000," had been planted and "flourished astonishingly." Many of the natives too had begun to plant mulberry. At Kaira Dr. Burn was continuing his experiment, and had "made several specimens of silk, some of it of a superior quality." At Ahmedabad there were "some mulberry trees," and a successful experiment had been made there. At Bassein "Messrs. Brownrigg" had "about 400 trees and a great quantity of hedgerows of mulberry;" and contemplated a silk manufactory. At Kaman, a "wealthy banian" had "got a small plantation of mulberries," and had "been rearing worms." At Dharwar there were 200 trees and 25,000 shrubs, besides 10,820 shrubs in the Jail garden: 272 lbs. of silk of the value of Rs. 500, had been made by natives, while the prisoners had made 144 lbs., which sold at Rs. 2·55 per lb. At Mahim one person had "2,500 trees and hedgerows of from one to three years old" and made "a small quantity of silk." Of the experiment in Bombay and Salsette Signor Mutti writes as follows:—

"The wonderful progress the mulberry tree is making in Bombay and Salsette is astonishing. The rearing of the worms is a secondary consideration in Bombay; they thrive, more or less, throughout the year, without any necessity for precautions and care to guard against extremes of temperature as in Europe; but what is still more satisfactory and important to the object of producing silk, the worms of four stages or changes of skins form the cocoons in from only 22 to 27 days, according to the season, instead of from 30 to 40, as is usual in Europe and elsewhere. The eggs hatch, regularly throughout the year, in nine days, without having recourse to artificial apparatus, which is generally required in Italy.

"The silk, though wound by inexperienced hands and young lads, has been pronounced to be very superior." The number of trees is shewn at 21,825 (standards), owned by about 50 persons.

Bombay Government recommends perseverance in the attempt.

18. The despatch to the Court of Directors was framed, almost word for word, on Sir G. Arthur's minute. Dividing the process of producing silk into the three branches of "growth of leaves, rearing of worms, and winding," the Government of Bombay held it established not only that the mulberry tree would thrive and reach an early maturity in the Western Presidency, but that the native cultivators were willing to grow it "in sufficient quantity to afford an ample supply of leaves within circles not too extensive to admit of the leaves within each being brought in good order to the same central establishment for rearing worms." Under this head the multiplication of such circles was all that was necessary.

Equally sanguine was the view expressed as to rearing the worms. It was asserted that the worms could be reared with less risk, and in a shorter period than in Europe, and that the worms were as good as required for the higher qualities of Italian silk. In fact the Bombay Government regarded Signor Mutti's services, in this branch of the industry, as required rather to repress injudicious haste in plunging into the enterprise, than to encourage the people to undertake it.

The introduction of the art of winding, it was thought, also wanted only careful supervision at the outset. "The case," said the despatch, "is simply this:—M. Mutti finds the people ready and anxious to embark in the new branch of industry, and apt to learn all the various processes which he offers to teach them; if left to themselves, they will inevitably fail through ignorance or precipitation, and M. Mutti has to exert himself to prevent this, by selecting from among the people, who are generally willing to follow his advice, those who are best qualified for conducting each process, assigning them their several departments, and by his *advice* only, regulating and controlling their operations, till all shall have thoroughly learnt the parts which it is desirable they should fill, and be able to carry on correctly each process on the most approved principles by *custom*, instead of being compelled to draw deductions from an extended experience by which M. Mutti has, after repeated failures, arrived at *his* conclusions, a course in which it would be quite out of the question to expect any native to follow him."

Specific measures proposed.

19. The Government of Bombay, therefore, recommended the following measures:—

"*1st.*—The office of the Superintendent of Silk Cultivation should be continued for five years longer, from the date of the receipt of the sanction of the Court of Directors to that measure. The success which may attend the labors of the Superintendent, as shewn at the end of these five years, will enable Government to judge of the propriety of continuing to employ him for any further period.

"*2nd.*—Four buildings for rearing worms, and one for 12 reels to wind silk, should be erected by Government in the Jooneer or Paubul District, at a cost not exceeding Rs. 5,000; these buildings to be public property.

"*3rd.*—The breeding of worms, &c., should be conducted on account of M. Mutti himself, or some private individual, and *not* of Government.

"*4th.*—The cost of any building already built by M. Mutti with money lent him by Government, or from his own private means, and anything spent by him, on permanent fixtures substantially put up, may be allowed for, out of the above Rs. 5,000, on inspection by the Collector, who should visit the establishment for the purpose.

"*5th.*—The sum allowed for establishment to the Superintendent, should be continued as long as his own salary is allowed, and an addition of Rs. 50 per mensem granted to the present amount, Rs. 150.

"*6th.*—The Collector may be authorised to advance Rs. 2,000 as a loan, without interest, to M. Mutti, to be repaid by instalments of Rs. 100 per mensem, as long as his salary is on its present scale.

"*7th.*—For three years Rs. 3,000 per annum may be held, by the Collector, at the disposal of the Superintendent, to be advanced by him at his discretion as tuccavee, on the usual terms, he rendering to the Collector an account of why, and to whom, the advance has been made, and furnishing receipts, &c., in the ordinary form.

"*8th.*—All silk must be made entirely at the expense and risk, and be the sole property, of private individuals. The only aid afforded by Government will be in the shape of tuccavee, and such instruction as the Superintendent may afford.

"9*th.*—The Superintendent should submit, through the Collector and Revenue Commissioner, an annual report of the progress he has made."

The Collector of Poonah was directed to carry into effect all the above propositions, except the point which was referred for the orders of the Court of Directors. And to give the "first impulse to the industry" in the island of Bombay and its neighbourhood, a region, so the Government had persuaded itself, superior in natural capabilities "even to the Deccan," it was proposed to appoint an Assistant Superintendent. The particular attention of the local authorities was also directed to the subject of silk in districts such as Khandeish, Dharwar, Kaira, Ahmedabad, and Kattywar, where desultory experiments had been made, "sufficient," however, "to prove the adaptation of these districts, even in a higher degree than the Deccan, both for the mulberry tree and silk-worms." As far as the Ahmedabad experiment is concerned, a recent letter assigns it to the year 1841, and expressly says it was *unsuccessful*.

The Directors sanction these proposals.

20. The Directors sanctioned the proposed measures, requesting that specimens of the silk produced might be forwarded to them with an account of the work and cost of production, and a report as to the spread of cultivation among the natives. The despatch, according this sanction, was received on the 13th January 1845. Very shortly afterwards Signor Mutti fell ill, and though his leave was not sanctioned till November of that year, he seems to have been capable of little work during the interval, and Mr. Ramos was appointed to do the duty of Superintendent.

Collapse of the experiment.

21. In this same year doubts seem to have arisen as to the real success of the experiment. But it was not till 1847 that a Committee was appointed to report on the subject.

The two members of the Committee, Dr. Gibson and Mr. Davidson, recorded their experience separately, but joined in offering their opinion that any further attempts by Government to cultivate the mulberry with a view to silk in the Deccan were not likely to be attended with success. Dr. Gibson, from personal inspection of standard mulberry plantations, from the experience of Dr. Graham and others in bush cultivation, expressed the most decided opinion that neither bush nor standard could be profitably grown in the Deccan, and that the results exhibited by Signor Mutti had been due to an artificial stimulation, thus deceiving both Government and himself. Some small experiments in the Dharwar Jail and Dapooree, led Dr. Gibson to the same conclusion. I extract the last three paragraphs of his report:—

"14. Seeing that the climate of the Deccan is mild, generally so favorable to the worm (save in the height of the dry season, and so eminently favorable to the quality of the silk), it may be asked, why the trials hitherto made have all ended in loss? To this I would answer that the causes may be looked for—

1*st.*—In the very limited extent of garden ground, or of ground sufficiently moist for trees to grow without irrigation.

2*nd.*—The general poverty of the soil, producing a tree poor in leaf and comparatively stunted in growth.

3*rd.*—In a few patches of superior soil, such as a small spot of Government garden at Neergoora (*vide* my report of 1840 or 1841), the tree is luxuriant and would pay, but such spots are very rare, and are eagerly sought after, for superior products, at the rate even of Rs. 20 per acre, annual rent.

4*th.*—In that the limited extent of garden land leaves little to spare beyond what is necessary for the supply of the people with vegetable food, and for the export of the same to the coast, and that even this limited extent is so sub-divided among families, that mulberry cultivation, at once extended and continuous, cannot be looked for.

5*th.*—In the fact that the mulberry growth interferes with the rotation of crops, and that no products can be profitably grown between the rows of trees or bushes.

6*th.*—In the dryness of the climate which also tends to produce a leaf at once scanty and harsh.

7*th.*—In the comparative thinness of population and consequent dearness of labour.

"15. I can readily see why in a country so thickly peopled as is Bengal, with a climate comparatively moist, and immense tracts of new river alluvial land, the mulberry should pay well. I can also see why the same causes (though operating in a slighter degree) should render the mulberry an article of profit in Mysore, as it is said now to be, and I am not sure that in the district of Hungul (Collectorate of Dharwar), and situated on the Mysore border, were the extensive tanks, &c., now so dilapidated, brought back to their pristine state (*vide* my report of 1844-45), that there might not be profit in the cultivation, but I have not been able to see that in any district, save that above-mentioned, we could enter on the cultivation with a probability of profit.

"16. The plantations formed in Guzerat some 12 years ago I have not had an opportunity of examining, as they were formed after I had left that province. Therefore I do not intend that any of the present remarks should be applied to these."

Mr. Davidson's opinion is much to the same effect.

Remarks of the Court of Directors.

22. The following extract from a Revenue despatch from the Hon'ble Court of Directors, to Government of Bombay, No. 10, dated 2nd August 1848, briefly sums up the case:—

"It is much to be regretted that this experiment, which has now been proved to have resulted in utter failure, should have been allowed to continue so long in progress at a total outlay of upwards of a lakh of rupees. If an investigation, similar to that which has recently been made, had been instituted at an earlier period, the hopelessness of success in the attempt would have been demonstrated, and a large amount of public money, which has now been uselessly expended, might have been saved. We entirely approve your having directed the immediate abandonment of the experiments."

Mr. Ashburner's opinion on the cause of the failure.

23. I append Mr. Ashburner's remarks on the causes of this disaster:—

"It is difficult to state exactly what were the causes of failure, but I have learnt enough, in the voluminous records I have read, to account for the probable causes of want of success. In the first place, M. Mutti appears to have been a man very unsuited to superintend an experiment requiring persevering hard work. His system appears to have been to hatch the eggs in a nursery at Poonah, and to distribute the worms to persons in the villages, in which there were mulberry gardens, within 15 or 20 miles of Poonah. The worms require feeding six times during the day and four times during the night. M. Mutti was a weak, delicate man, in constant ill-health. It is easy to understand what would happen to worms entrusted to natives under these circumstances, when the Superintendent could exercise so little supervision over them. M. Mutti was, apparently, quite honest, but an enthusiast, entirely wanting in habits of business. During the eight years he was employed he spent Rs. 47,000 of Government money, and it was at last discovered that he had kept no accounts whatever.

"The want of permanence in his appointment must have had a very injurious effect on his operations. He could never make arrangements in advance, which are absolutely necessary in a protracted undertaking of this kind. This appears to have struck the Government at last, for just before M. Mutti left, he was appointed for five years certain. Another cause of failure was the attempt to work the experiment on what may be called the Public Works system. A sum of money was sanctioned, and, on its expenditure, a few months'c orrespondence was necessary in order to procure a fresh grant. This system is disastrous enough with bridges when left in an unfinished state; but when it is applied to insects, whose very existence depends on their getting a supply of mulberry leaves at a certain hour, its mischievous effect may be imagined. On at least one occasion, the Collector took the responsibility of advancing the money necessary to save the whole crop from destruction, and on another M. Mutti raised a loan in his own name.

"At a very early period of his appointment, M. Mutti reported that the breed of worms had deteriorated, and he asked for fresh seed from Bengal and China. Many attempts were made to procure fresh seed from both places. A small quantity was procured from China; but the next supply failed, and each successive consignment from Bengal failed from one cause or another. Some were sent at the wrong season, some were improperly packed, others hatched while in transit, &c. Finally, M. Mutti reports that one of his subordinates having mixed two species of worms, which ought to have been carefully kept separate, the breed was quite spoilt. This appears to have been the deathblow of the undertaking; the worms rapidly died after this, and no fresh seed being procured, they gradually became extinct."

Lessons of the experiment.

24. The experiment in Bombay is mainly instructive on the question of the mulberry and its cultivation, and I now go back to give the history of the case, in this aspect, with somewhat fuller detail. In the first attempts at silk-growing the worms were fed on shrub mulberries of the *desi* kind, cultivated and cut on the Bengal plan. And on this system Signor Mutti at first began to work. He had, however, convinced himself before he became a Government servant that this system was unsuited to the Deccan, and his whole career then became a propagandism of the "standard" theory. Dr. Lush, on the other hand, seems to have inclined to the Bengal system; at any rate he did not wish to condemn it unheard, and he obtained from Mr. Shakespear, of the Sonamookhee Residency in Bengal, an

opinion on certain questions connected with the subject. These questions, with Mr. Shakespear's answers, I here extract:—

1st query by Dr. Lush.—What kind of mulberry do the worms prefer?

Answer.—Decidedly the indigenous (*desi* or *kajla*) cut plant, the leaves being closely set, and more abundant in the proportion of two and a half to one. It is the *morus alba* or white mulberry, not allowed to fruit.

2nd.—What kinds will grow best as standard trees, and what are best adapted for cultivation on the Bengal plan?

Answer.—Worms fed on the standard (*sâti* or *bidesi*), or foreign, do not thrive. It is therefore only cultivated for fruit, and that sparingly. It arrives at maturity or fruit-bearing in about three years. It is the *morus rubra*, or red mulberry, approaching to black, *morus nigra*, a poor fruit, about an inch long, cylindrical, bears twice in the year, about October and March.

Remarks.—The cut plant flourishes in the low lands about Rangamatti, where the soil is sandy, which keeps the roots cool: and irrigation is not so necessary, or, indeed, used here, as it quickly loses itself in the sand; but in the high tenacious loamy soil, where water will pass over the surface quickly, irrigation is had recourse to, and a more abundant crop is produced. But too much watery matter, though eaten voraciously by the insect, is hurtful, from its comparative want of solid nutritive matter. The nature of the plant itself being sufficiently succulent without artificial means, a rich soil is by no means so proper as that with an admixture of sand.

Dr. Lush further desires information from Bengal on the following points:—

1. Has the Italian plan, now following at Poonah, of setting cuttings from the standard 8 or 12 feet apart to be trained up as standard trees, the leaves of which it is proposed not to gather for four years, been tried in Bengal, and if it has, with what success?

Answer.—Not in the aurungs of the Sonamookhee Residency.

2. Will the leaves be improved, or otherwise, as food for the worms in this climate by being produced from old trees?

Answer.—The established practice, already fully explained, seems to prove the contrary.

3. Provided the trees and leaves be improved by age and produce a large crop as they grow older, still will it be possible, with any supposable rate of profit, to compensate for the capital of a silk farm lying dead for four years, and in a country where labour is dearer than in Bengal, and irrigation necessary?

Answer.—With reference to the 1st and 2nd queries, I think I may safely add that certain disappointment and loss of capital would attend such speculations, contrary to the existing nature of things in these aurungs.

25. The reference to Bengal also called forth the following remarks by Dr. Wallich, dated 12th April 1833:—

Dr. Wallich on the mulberry.

"I am not acquainted with any plant, of agricultural or commercial interest, of which the natural history is involved in greater doubt and obscurity than the mulberry. The cultivated species are scarcely to be distinguished from each other by the ordinary characters employed for the purpose in other plants. At least all attempts of the sort have proved abortive; recourse is, therefore, had to marks derived from the size of the tree, place of growth, colour of the fruit, and the like, all which are vague and unsatisfactory. In point of fact the real species of mulberry are very few in number, and plants which have hitherto been considered as species, are in all probability nothing but varieties, and those varieties eternally changing according to soil, climate, and mode of cultivation. It is chiefly aided by the labors of Dr. Roxburgh, in his valuable Flora Indica, and of Dr. Hamilton, in his matchless Statistical Surveys, that I am able to offer the following sketch of the different Indian mulberries, without, however, pretending to fix these, as yet, by any specific character or distinction.

"*1st.*—*Morus Indica* of Linnæus, the common *Toot* of Bengal. This is a native of India, and undoubtedly a distinct species. There exist two varieties, which may perhaps be different species, but which it is best for practical purposes to consider as varieties only. One of these varieties is never allowed to grow large, but constantly cut down to a stunted twiggy shrub, in order to induce it to produce an abundant supply of tender shoots and leaves: of all the plants that yield food for the silk-worm in India, that is by far the most important, on account of the extreme facility of its cultivation and the productiveness and luxurious juiciness of the leaves which are the favorite food of the worm. The climate of Bengal is above all others favorable to the cultivation of this shrub, owing probably to the comparative moisture, both of its soil and atmosphere, conditions which are peculiarly favorable to its growth, and the absence of which is, probably, the leading cause of the incapacity of the peninsula to compete with our part of India in this branch of husbandry. A plantation of the *Toot* will last several years, and may be renewed from cuttings with perfect ease, and this process must be performed every fourth or fifth year if a full and sufficient crop of leaves is desired. A moderately rich light soil, not too much mixed with clay, sufficiently elevated to secure the plantation from flooding either from rivers or rains, and occasional ploughing and weeding and a slight manuring, constitute the chief points of attention which this sort of mulberry demands, and if the patient and industrious Indian cultivator could only be made to prefer this method to the miserable plan usually adopted, he would reap a far more secure and ample reward from his labours than the scanty and precarious returns which he generally derives. There would be no such failures of the crops of leaves, nor would such a vast proportion of worms perish annually, for want of food, as frequently happens to the planters and breeders.

"The other variety is a tree of considerable size bearing white fruit, whereas the preceding sort has them purple. It is called *morus alba* by Linnæus, and is perhaps a really distinct species. It is cultivated, though in a trifling degree, as food for the worm.

"*2nd.*—*Morus atropurpurea*, of Dr. Roxburgh, introduced from China into this garden and now to be found in most private gardens. It is a native of that country as well as Cochin China, and is employed there as food for silk-worms. Dr. Roxburgh informs us that it has not been found to answer that purpose in Bengal. It forms a smallish tree with long straggling branches, dark foliage, and deep purple, large fruit.

"*3rd.*—*Morus leptostachya*, so called by me on account of its long and very slender fruit, which is white and exceedingly sweet. This large tree is met with in most parts of Hindoostan to the west, where it is generally called *Shah Toot*. I am not aware that the leaves are much used for rearing the worm. It is perhaps the *morus latifolia* mentioned by Dr. Lush in his very able and interesting letter, and also contained among the dried specimens now returned, although I must confess my doubt as to its being Lamarck's identical tree of Bourbon.

"*4th.*—A very marked mulberry tree with strongly serrated leaves, and therefore called by Dr. Roxburgh *morus serrata*. It was found by Major General Hardwick in the Alpine regions of North Hindoostan, and the late Mr. Moorcroft sent plants of it from thence to this garden, where they thrive tolerably well. I am not aware that the leaves are used."

Signor Mutti's views.

26. Signor Mutti's views, on the mulberry question, will be seen from the following extract from his remarks on the silk culture of Bengal :—

"In Bengal several prejudiced opinions exist regarding the method of training the mulberry as a standard, *viz.* :—

"*1st.*—It is said that by feeding the worm with the leaf of the tree, the silk becomes coarse.

"This is plainly contradicted by the fact that in Italy, where the finest silk in the world is made, the worms are fed only with the standard leaf. I myself here find that by following the same Italian plan I get the cocoons and finer silk.

"*2nd.*—It is said that the leaf of the tree being hard, the worms do not eat it.

"This clearly shows that as the worms are not properly reared they become weak, and therefore have not strength enough to subsist upon hard leaves. In Italy not only are the worms fed with the leaf of the tree, but we make there also a difference and distinction in the leaves, paying more for those of an older tree and hard ones ; and it is also to be borne in mind that, in this climate, this insect, for a part of the year, ought to be more healthy and stronger than there, where only by artificial means and precautions, we are able to keep it up.

"*3rd.*—It is said that the standard mulberry does not succeed in Bengal, it having been tried, but without success.

"The very same thing was said here some years ago regarding the Concan and Deccan, but experience has now proved the contrary. It was just for the sake of removing the prejudice which was excited on the subject, that I undertook to train 14 varieties of mulberries as standards ; among which there were several of very bad descriptions and bushy, including the China divided leaf, and every one has astonishingly succeeded, fine standard trees, with large stems, branches, &c. The only inconvenience I had was that they gave me a great deal more to do than the good species.

"They succeeded not only in the Deccan but in Bombay and Salsette, where the climate, in some places, is approaching to that of Bengal, but with this disadvantage that it is not so moist and damp as in Bengal, which is a very grand thing.

"*4th.*—It is said that, with the bush system, silk can be made five and six times a year, whereas with the tree only three or four.

"True it is, but it is also a fact, that—

"*1st.*—The result of the worms fed with the bush leaf will not produce as much as that fed with the standard leaf.

"*2nd.*—With the bush system a person is engaged all the year round in rearing worms and winding silk, and, after all, does not make so much silk as the other who uses the tree.

"*3rd.*—The bush occupies a great extent of land and gives fewer leaves as compared with the tree.

"*4th.*—The leaf of the bush has little substance, and cannot be expected, nor is it possible, to produce as good cocoons as from worms fed with the leaf of the tree.

"*5th.*—The bush requires for ever expense and trouble, which is not the case with the tree, as, after a few years, nothing is required for the latter except pruning and thinning, which labor is amply repaid by the wood obtained, and this certainly is a very great object; saving money and labor.

"*6th.*—For the proprietor of the land having standards in his ground the place is a valuable one, it is actually a capital that he has got, and the income which he yearly derives from such estate is far superior than if it is planted with bush.

"But what is also a very great object is that with the leaf of the tree, if the worms are properly reared, we may always have splendid cocoons, which not only is a great advantage from the greater quantity of silk that would result, but also that we may easily have fine, even and clean silk; and it is quite a mistake to expect to have perfect silk from bad cocoons, and notwithstanding the ability of the workman, the work is tedious and the result unsatisfactory. Let an experiment be made of one beegah or 100 plants of the St. Helena species, following my directions given in the Guide to the Silk Culture, regarding the planting and rearing the standard, and I have no hesitation to say that the result will be, that not the bush, but the standard tree, system will be found to be the one that should be followed even in Bengal.

"If the same extent of land now occupied with bushes were substituted with standards, a very much greater quantity of silk would be obtained, and more easily, would result of better quality, besides the other advantages I have already mentioned; and in conclusion I doubt not that the cultivators of the mulberry, the proprietors of the land, those rearing silkworms and winding silk, will be a great deal more satisfied."

Sir G. Arthur states that Signor Mutti converted Dr. Lush and others to his views; on the other hand, it is to be remarked that Mr. Ramos, Signor Mutti's successor, attributed the failure of the experiment mainly to the adoption of the standard, instead of the bush, system of cultivation.

Trial in Sind, 1847.

27. According to the Bombay Horticultural Society an experiment was made in Sind in 1847, but without success. No details are given. I should suppose that the intense dry heat of Sind proved fatal to the silkworm.

At Broach, circ: 1849.

28. A correspondent of the *Bombay Gazette*, writing in October 1871, mentions an experiment at Broach "about 22 years ago." The attempt was made by a Parsee gentleman named Sheriarjee Pestonjee, who brought worms from Kaira and planted "hundreds of mulberry trees in a place called the Borah Baree." The silk was, according to the writer, found "equal if not superior to Chinese stuffs," but the enterprise was not a commercial success, as Mr. Pestonjee ultimately "found himself compelled to resign the trade, under the burden of some thousands of rupees of debt." The Commissioner of the Northern Division also briefly mentions this attempt.

Dr. Birdwood's proposal in 1858.

29. From the period of the failure of the experiments under Signor Mutti and his successor, nothing seems to have been done, till, in 1858, the question of silk was again brought to notice by Dr. Birdwood. That gentleman advocated an attempt being made to utilize the wild worms which were to be found in many of the districts of the Bombay Presidency. But, beyond calling for reports, which shewed that the tusser moth was to be found in more or less abundance in most districts, no steps were taken. I find, however, notice of an attempt with Bombyx silk at Gokak, in Belgaum. Mr. Havelock says he saw silk made there more than 13 years ago. The trial seems to have been persevered in for 9 years. And in Sattara, in 1859, "the mamlutdars were ordered to try an experiment in sericulture, but it seems to have entirely failed."

Further experiments at Dharwar.

30. The next silk experiment in the Bombay Presidency seems to have been made in 1865 by Dr. Mackenzie, Superintendent of the Dharwar Jail. The results, at the early stage, are not forthcoming, but in the 16 months from June 1868 to September 1869 * inclusive, the jail produced 10 lbs. 14½ oz. of raw silk, valued at Rs. 8 a pound, from 145 lbs. 10½ oz. of cocoons. A comparison of the results of the last six with the first ten months of this period shewed marked improvement in the weight of the cocoons, and the percentage of silk to total weight. In the last six months the proportion was about 8·7 per cent., as contrasted with 6·7 for the preceding ten months. This improvement Dr. Mackenzie attributes to increased attention paid to the (1) food of the worms, (2) regularity in feeding,

* From a recent report by the Collector it appears that the experiment is still being carried on.

(3) ventilation and lightsomeness of rooms, (4) equable temperature, kept from 85°—90°, and exclusion of damp. The worms were fed on shrub mulberry, cut down at the commencement of each monsoon, and not allowed to grow more than 3 or 4 feet high. The worm bred is not specified by Dr. Mackenzie, who indeed seems at a loss to identify it. But, from the description, it seems to have been one of the Bengal multivoltines; its total course is given at 55½ days.

Proposed renewal of the experiment in Khandeish.

31. In 1867 the subject was attacked by Mr. Ashburner, then Collector of Khandeish. He applied for a grant of Rs. 1,500 a year to enable him to attempt the introduction of silk into his Collectorate. After giving a summary of the earlier experiments, Mr. Ashburner observes :—"Notwithstanding this failure, the fact remains that both in Khandeish and Poonah very excellent silk was produced, and there is no reason to doubt that, under proper management, it can be produced again. Silk culture was only introduced into Bengal after years of perseverance and repeated failures. I do not think the experiment has had a fair trial in Bombay. If it were again sanctioned, it would be conducted on more favorable terms than was possible 35 years ago. The silk districts of Bengal are connected by rail with Khandeish, with the exception of the distance between Nagpore and Jubbulpore. The steamers from China will land seed for Bombay in 20 days. The people have in great measure conquered their prejudices against the destruction of animal life, and are now more enterprizing and ready to take up any speculation that seems likely to be profitable." Mr. Ashburner's proposal was sanctioned; but about the same time he left the country on furlough, and under his successor the experiment did not make much immediate progress. It was then amalgamated with the agricultural experiments under trial at the Khandeish farm, and Mr. Fretwell, who was appointed Superintendent, visited Mysore, to study sericulture there. The disease among the worms in Mysore, however, prevented the experiment being immediately entered upon, and in April 1869 Mr. Sheppard reported that he was going to push on mulberry cultivation during the monsoon, and hoped to begin the trial of sericulture in the following cold weather. But the farm was reduced to a cotton farm by the Bombay Government, and the silk experiment went to the ground. Dr. Bainbridge, however, Superintendent of the Dhoolia Jail, began an experiment in November 1870, with "some 400 to 500 eggs of a variety which ran through all its stages in about 60 days." The seed was obtained from Dr. Mackenzie of the Dharwar Jail. The first brood was successfully fed on *Morus Indica*, but appeared, though healthy, stunted in size. About 8,000 worms resulted, of which 1,000 died at an early stage. The worms of this breed seemed larger and stronger, and 300 moths yielded 50,000 eggs, the hatching of which fell due in the beginning of June. Three-fifths hatched; but the worms all died within a fortnight. Dr. Bainbridge attributes this misfortune either to the excessive heat or to effluviun from a latrine. 5,100 cocoons weighed on an average 2·4 grains after destruction of chrysalis by immersion in hot water.

Experiment now being made.

32. An experiment is now being made at Panchgunee with seed obtained from Bangalore. No definite results have as yet been attained.

Present state of silk industry in Bombay.

33. At the Broach Exhibition of 1868-69 prizes were offered *(a)* for a silk-reeling machine, *(b)* for raw silk, and *(c)* for manufactured silk. For the first there was no competitor, but a prize of Rs. 30 was given for dyed silk thread; and four competitors, among them an English firm, obtained prizes under the head (*c*). And at the Akola Exhibition, of 1868, I find that the Bombay *Government* obtained the first prize for the "finest specimen of pure silk." Dr. Forbes Watson's "Textile Fabrics of India" includes silk piece-goods, and "loongees" and "sarees" of cotton and silk used conjointly from *Surat;* embroidery of gold and silver on silk from *Sattara;* silk piece-goods from *Ahmednuggur;* silk piece-goods and silk and cotton "sarrees" from *Belgaum;* silk and cotton "loongees" from *Bombay;* and silk and cotton "sarees" from *Dharwar.* Burhanpore near Khandeish also manufactures silk, and there are small colonies of weavers at Jinjeera, Yeola, Tanna and Revdanda (in Colaba). The establishment of the manufacture at the two last places seems to be due to

the Portuguese. The Bombay Chamber of Commerce, writing under date the 28th December 1871, says that there is "no production of silk in any portion of the Bombay Presidency." At any rate there is no export trade. The raw silk used in Bombay manufactures is, according to the same authority, mostly imported from China. Very little Bengal silk is used. The Chamber seems to have overlooked the imports from Mysore. There is a considerable import both of China and Bengal manufactured silks. The China silk imported is chiefly "punjum" (? 5th class), a very inferior sort, worth from Re. 1-4 to Re. 1-12 per lb. A better variety is, however, imported in small quantities, and some fine raw silk is imported from the Persian Gulf, and is in great request at Ahmedabad for fine kincobs. The imports of China silk into Bombay seem to be gradually increasing. For the years 1861-62 to 1865-66 they averaged about 1,200,000lbs. In 1870-71 they had risen to 2,043,631lbs; the average price also having risen from Rs. 3 to Rs. 4. Bombay also imports some Bengal silk by sea; an average of about 100,000lbs was thus annually imported during the five years ending 1870-71. About 300,000lbs of China silk and a small proportion of Bengal silk is re-exported to Kurrachee. The importation of Persian silk seems to have fluctuated greatly. In 1861-62 86,303lbs of this silk were imported into Bombay: in 1865-66 the amount fell suddenly to 23,000lbs and in the following year to 10,000lbs. It has now again risen, and in 1870-71, 42,558lbs were imported, valued at Rs. 2,12,449. As in regard to China silk so here, the price seems to have risen, if the custom house valuation is to be trusted. The recent increase in the quantity imported is somewhat remarkable, as of late the silk crop in Persia has been short. Indeed, Sir H. Rawlinson (in his recent evidence on the Euphrates valley scheme) speaks of "a total failure." This must not be understood literally, it would seem. There is nothing to show accurately the quanity of silk exported by rail from the Bombay Presidency.

I append an account of the silk industry in Guzerat, especially at Ahmedabad, just received from the Government of Bombay:—

In respect to silk manufactures, Ahmedabad has long held a prominent place as a manufacturing city in India. Its Kincobs and Brocades, though not quite so rich as those of Benares, are much sought after in consequence of their durability and non-fading qualities of their gold tissues. Its Mushroos are supposed to be the best in India, and the ordinary silk cloths are also in good demand. But the trade now is not what it used to be in former times. The improvement of machinery in Europe and the extensive traffic in cotton and woollen goods, which flows into this country from England and the Continent, and which places within the reach of the Indians cloths at comparatively accommodating prices, have affected it to a considerable extent.

But the trade still gives occupation to a very large section of the population of this city, whose means of support depend wholly upon it, and the exports of Kincobs, Mushroos and other silk goods maintain even now a very fair position. Bombay, Kattywar Rajpootana, Central India, Nagpore territory and the Nizam's dominions are among the provinces where these goods find a sale. The various processes in their manufacture, from the assorting of silk to the last touches of finish, are all conducted in the city itself.

Raw silk is imported from China, Bengal, Bussora, and Bokhara *viâ* Bombay, and the quantity brought averages about 2,500 Indian maunds, the value of which may be estimated at Rs. 15,00,000.

The imports of Bokhara silk are of recent origin; it was first brought three or four years ago, and the quantity imported is small. The silk is ready spun, and is used only for woof in a loom.

Of China silk the consumption is large, and both descriptions are imported—white and yellow. The hanks or skeins are first reeled off on a circular bamboo frame, and the thread is then assorted according to quality. It is well known that the entire length of a hank is not of one uniform fineness. The assorting is made with particular reference to the degree of fineness or coarseness of thread, and the process, which is carried on also by reeling (a separate reel being assigned for each quality), depends entirely upon the feel or touch of the silk on the finger of the person manipulating it. A hank is divided into five different sorts—

1. Tumbolia,
2. Serika,
3. Takra,
4. Wana,
5. Koree,

and the value of the silk varies from Rs. 24 per Indian seer for the superior sort to Rs. 19 or 20 for the inferior description. Nos. 1 and 3 are used almost invariably for the woof, while

No. 4 supplies the warp, and No. 5 is sold to the Putwas who make cords, tassels, &c., of it. When cloths of a superior texture have to be turned out, both the woof and warp are taken from Nos. 1 to 3.

The best Bussora silk is valued at Rs. 18 or 19 per Indian seer. It comes in a raw state, and does not yield any Tumbolia.

The Bengal silk stands in the same estimation as the Bussora, and commands the same value. Two descriptions are imported, *viz.*, Radhanugree, which yields chiefly Tumbolia and Jadee or coarse-yielding Takra and Wana.

A new trade has sprung up very lately in Siam silk, which is known here as Singaporee, from the fact of its coming from Singapore. It is very inferior in quality, and sells at Rs. 8 to 6 per Indian seer. It is used for warp in coarse manufactures.

Manufactures in silk are carried on also at Baroda and Surat, though not to the extent obtaining in Ahmedabad.

If, then, silk were raised in Guzerat it is impossible to say to what extent the trade in the articles manufactured from it might not be developed from the impetus it would receive from a reduction in the prices of the raw material, not to speak of the means of livelihood the industry would give to hundreds of people who now fritter away their time in idleness and have no fixed occupation of any kind; and if the produce were large enough we might also have an export trade in the raw material itself to the positive benefit of the Province.

SECTION III.

SILK IN MADRAS.

Earliest mention of silk-cultivation in the records of the Government of Madras (1791).

THE records of the Madras Government prior to 1791 contain no direct mention of silk-cultivation.

Silk-cultivation not, however, a new thing in the Peninsula at that date (1791).

2. There are, however, scattered notices which show that the industry was no new thing in the Peninsula: the mulberry was growing at Hyderabad in the Deccan; skilled silk-weavers could be got from Bangalore; at Warriore in the Trichinopoly District there was a colony of silk-weavers, and at Warrapollien in the same district two silk-weavers were found, who said they, among many others, had been employed in rearing and feeding silkworms and in weaving silk under the orders of Hyder, by whom they were carried away prisoners to the country of that leader. In 1791 it was understood that Tippoo Sultan had lately supplied the interior of the Peninsula with silk made at Seringapatam. There was also employed at Trichinopoly a native who had been sent to Bengal by Tippoo Sultan to learn the silk-trade.

In 1793, a present made to an Englishman at Madras consisted of a beautiful "Kincob" made of silk produced and worked up at Trichinopoly on the estate of the sons of the Nawab; and in 1795 several pounds of fine silk were sent as a present from Abdul Wahab Khan, son of the Wallajah. It is also mentioned that the Nawab's camels were dressed on gala days in trappings and cloths of silk of home-manufacture.

The silkworm supposed to be not indigenous to India.

3. That the silkworm is not indigenous to Southern India appears to be taken for granted by those best informed on the subject.

From whence imported, and by whom, into the Peninsula; mulberry trees whence obtained; A.D. 1790 (Circ.)

4. It was from Bengal apparently that the silkworms were imported, and from Hyderabad in the Deccan, that the mulberry trees were obtained by Dr. James Anderson, Physician-General at Madras, the successful culture of which by that officer on his own account led to the establishment of mulberry plantations at the Company's expense, and to the direct encouragement given to silk-cultivation by the Governor in Council during the last decade of the 18th century.

Dr. James Anderson, Physician-General.

His eventual success in rearing silkworms.

5. An enthusiast of great energy, having considerable knowledge apparently of botanical and industrial enterprises, Dr. Anderson had been successful in the introduction and rearing of the Nopál or cochineal insect, and had twenty years previously [or in 1771] introduced and planted mulberry trees in a large garden or farm belonging to him in Nungumbaukum, a suburb of Madras. These trees throve so well as to induce him to obtain at various times silkworms from Bengal which eventually succeeded to his satisfaction in December 1790. Several of his friends, too, had been induced to make like experiments, both in planting mulberry trees and taking charge of silkworms in various places on the coast.

Other persons also interested in silk. Experiment by Dr. Anderson.

A. D. 1791.
The Governor in Council urged to take direct management in introducing this industry among the people of the country.

6. Dr. Anderson, therefore, urged upon the Governor in Council that he should not let slip the opportunity of establishing this industry as an object of public utility and a certain source of gain both to the commerce of the Company and the good of the people.

Dr. Anderson's arguments in favour of this measure.

Not only was the cultivation of silk in Bengal confined to a limited tract of country compared to that available in the Peninsula, but Dr. Anderson was convinced that not only is a tropical country better suited to silk-culture than the more temperate climes of Europe, but that the Peninsula, owing to its more equable temperature, had great advantages even over Bengal. In Europe, too, the worm undergoes but one evolution in a year; his, he said, had completed three evolutions within the past six months. Further, it was an industry well adapted to the tastes and habits of the people; it would be an incentive to them to take up and plant the lands desolated and laid waste in the late wars; it would give employment to numbers of children and women who would otherwise be idle.

The immediate measures proposed by Dr. Anderson for the above object.

7. The immediate measures he urged upon the Governor in Council were that the mulberry plantations already made by private individuals should be encouraged and superintended by officers responsible to the Governor; and that fresh plantations should be started in the various circars, districts, or divisions, under the Collectors or nearest Paymasters, all expenses of planting, watering, and fencing, being defrayed by the Company.

His proposals adopted by the Governor in Council.

8. These proposals were adopted as the first step towards establishing silk-culture as a national and permanent industry; it being thought that the advantages of the system of feeding and rearing silkworms and reeling silk could not be generally made known, except under the patronage of the Company.

More details of the experiments mentioned in paragraph 5.

9. Before stating the manner in which these proposals were carried out, it may be as well to show what had hitherto been done in the way of planting mulberries and reeling silk, apparently entirely under private enterprise. The (white) mulberry had, as before stated, been imported from Hyderabad; 5,000 trees were then thrivng in Dr. Anderson's garden. At Vepery and St. Thomé there were small plantations, and in the Nawab's grounds called "Old Mackay's Gardens," Messrs. Chase, Hall, Stewart, and Mr. Popham at Valore were rearing silkworms. At the Cantonments of Sheveram,* Cheveremerdu and Jemeconda there were mulberry trees in existence, as well as in the fort at Chingleput and at Palaveram. There were plantations at Arcot in the Cavalry Cantonment and at Vellore; at Arnee, too, in the same district, a Captain Mackay, who had considerable success, was engaged in the industry; and at Ganjam there were said to be enough mulberries in the gardens of Messrs. Wynch and Richardson to supply cuttings to the whole district. The cheapness of labour and distance from the seat of war rendered the Northern Circars generally more favourable for the experiment. At Nellore Mr. Dighton (Collector), and at Madapollam (on the Godavery) Mr. Chamier (Collector), had planted mulberries. What had been done by natives of the country has been briefly mentioned.† Further, Dr. Anderson had already wound silk from silkworms reared in his own garden on a reel the construction of which had been improved by him, and in the use of which he was prepared to instruct any one. There was also then at Madras a Mr. Corbett who had had considerable experience of the industry in various countries in Europe, and Dr. Anderson was in communication with officials and friends all over India ready to assist him; a Mr. Glass at Boglipore in Bengal could send him the China mulberry which was superior to that of Bengal, as well as the China white silkworm and tusser-worm.

Instructions to the Board of Revenue to carry out the resolution of Government; lands in suitable situations to be appropriated for mulberry plantations, and proper encouragement to be given to its cultivation.

10. The Governor in Council fully entering into the spirit of the undertaking, accordingly instructed the Board of Revenue "to give orders to the Collectors to appropriate, at first, small portions of land in suitable situations, and to afford every proper encouragement to the cultivation of the mulberry tree;" informing Collectors that they would be supplied with cuttings from Dr. Anderson's garden, he being requested to afford the benefit of his opinion and advice to promote the object in view.

Places where mulberry plantations were either in existence or made by Government.

11. In addition to the plantations already mentioned, the mulberry appears to have been planted at Ellore, Rajahmundry, Ongole, Tanjore, Trichinopoly, and Palamcottah; also subsequently at Madapollam (on the Godavery), Waltair near Vizagapatam, and Masulipatam. Where private individuals were not ready to

---

* On the banks of the Paleru, between Conjeveram and Chingleput.

† Supra, paragraph 2.

undertake the experiment, Collectors, Surgeons, and Paymasters were placed in charge as Superintendents, all charges being defrayed by the Government.

Cocoons raised and two skeins of silk sent to Government by Dr. Anderson.

12. Shortly afterwards Dr. Anderson was able to report that twelve cocoons, raised in his garden from Bengal eggs, produced ten and a half grains of silk against six grains, the average outturn in Bengal; and on the 12th July 1791 he forwarded to the Government "two small skeins of silk wound off cocoons in his garden, the first wound on the Piedmontese reel."

"The first crop of silk after the arrival of the worms from Bengal" was, he says, "of a dull straw colour, but now of a brilliant white."

Suggestions made by the Governor in Council for erection of a filature at Madras.

13. In the month of June this year the Governor in Council suggested that it might be desirable to start a filature, and approved a suggestion of Dr. Anderson's that the young women in the Asylum should be employed in winding silk from the cocoons, as the nucleus of a sufficient filature for Madras and its environs. Nothing more, however, is heard of this latter proposal.

Report on Silk Factories in Bengal, by Mr. Spencer Corbett of Madras.

14. Towards the close of the year Mr. Spencer Corbett, before mentioned, went to Calcutta at his own expense, as the Government did not consider the time had yet come for them to incur the expense of his voyage, to learn the method of silk-culture pursued there, and being introduced to the Superintendents of the silk agencies, in the following February, he submitted an exhaustive report on the subject.

1792.

15. The records of 1792 are full of correspondence between the Board of Revenue and Collectors and Dr. Anderson, relating to the laying out, watering and fencing of the plantations at the places named, the details of which do not seem to be of importance now.

Specimens of cocoons and silk from Madras sent to Calcutta. Favorable report thereon.

16. Early in the year specimens of the cocoons and silk produced in Madras were sent to Calcutta, and a statement of the cost of production called for; this Dr. Anderson was unable to give. The report of the Superintendent and Silk Committee at Calcutta was, on the whole, favorable. They say, "the white, No. 1, is very excellent. No. 2 not so good, but by no means bad, both considerably finer than the Company's regulating muster. The yellow, being thrown silk, cannot be received in England." Two skeins sent by Dr. Anderson for transmission to England were pronounced good, but badly reeled.

100 skeins of silk sent by Dr. Anderson forwarded to England.

17. On the 25th July 1792, 100 skeins wound by Dr. Anderson in May were sent to England by the ship *Dutton*, and that gentleman stated that he had received a report from one of the first brokers in London, speaking most favourably of two skeins sent by him for report. This silk was reported superior to Bengal silk.

Disappointment of Dr. Anderson at success being not so speedily attained as he expected.

18. So far there appeared to be every reason for confidence in the success of the undertaking, but further experience showed that Dr. Anderson had been perhaps a little too sanguine. Before long his complaints against the Board of Revenue and all officials with whom he had to deal, became neither few nor temperate. But in most cases it is clear that the difficulties to be contended against were the real causes of delay and want of success, and not the apathy of those entrusted with the experiment. It is evident from the letter of the Chief and Council at Masulipatam in which they report the measures taken by them to carry out the wishes of Government that the country under their management was in such a disturbed state, owing to disputes among the Zemindars, that neither the Governors nor the governed could have either time or inclination for the peaceable pursuit of rearing silkworms; nor was land suited to the growth of the mulberry everywhere available, as expected by Dr.

Real causes of want of success.

Anderson. The first note of warning not to expect success everywhere was raised from the same quarter. The Chief and Council say: "in our opinion little or no advantage is to be expected from the propagation of the mulberry and silk-worm on this part of the coast, as the soil around Masulipatam is exceedingly sterile, and the price of labour very high. We conceive that if any advantage to the commerce or revenue of the country is to be derived from what is proposed, this can only be expected to arrive from the industry of individuals," and "it cannot be expected they would be adverse if they perceived any probability of its turning out to their advantage."

The Chief and Council at Masulipatam not sanguine as to the success of attempted introduction of silk-culture by Government.

More favorable reports from elsewhere.

19. From many places, however, more favorable reports were received.

Despatch from England recording appreciation of what had been achieved by Dr. Anderson, and approving the measures taken by Government for furtherance of his object.

20. In a general letter, dated London, 19th September 1792, the Court of Directors record their approval of what had been done, and their confidence in the future success of the enterprise. After recording their appreciation of Dr. Anderson's zeal and endeavours towards an object which must be considered as of great public utility, they desire to have his opinion as to the best way in which an undertaking apparently so beneficial can be aided from England. "In the only "country where, according to Dr. Anderson's representations, the insect con- "tinues in full perfection throughout the year as well as the tree on which it is "fed, it is natural to form sanguine expectations of the ultimate success of a "plan which will not only be productive of great commercial advantages, but "which is to give employment to the inferior classes of natives and thus "increase the population of the several districts under your Government.

Report on samples of silk sent to England very favourable.

"A very favourable report has been made upon two samples of silk "transmitted by the *Leopard* man-of-war, and we "wish to receive an account of the number and extent "of plantations already made, and the quantity of silk produced." They conclude by expressing an opinion that "every reasonable "degree of encouragement should certainly be given to a project pregnant "with so many advantages."

A certain misapprehension of Dr. Anderson as to the superiority of the climate of the Peninsula over that of Bengal and other countries noticed.

21. It may be remarked that Dr. Anderson was soon shewn to have been mistaken as to the advantages of the climate south of the Kistna being so superior to that of Bengal as to admit of the breeding of the silkworm throughout the year—an advantage which he thought the more northern parts of India did not possess owing to the coldness of their winter months. During these months, as was stated by the Superintendent of Bengal Silk Factories, all the operations of breeding, spinning, and reeling, were carried on in full vigour.*

A. D. 1793.

Further favorable report on silk sent to England in 1792.

22. In a subsequent letter dated London, 3rd July 1793, the Court of Directors, after referring to the extract above quoted, state, that "from the sample of silk lately transmitted "to us by the *Dutton*, which has been reported to us "as being equal in quality to China silk, and from a "perusal of Mr. Robert Spencer Corbett's observations, whose diligence in "procuring information upon this subject in Bengal is highly commendable, "we have been led to form more sanguine expectations of the undertaking; "we therefore direct that you take the propositions contained in Mr. Corbett's "letters † of the 9th May last, together with Dr. "Anderson's proposals of the 25th July 1792, into your "immediate consideration, and that after every neces- "sary previous inquiry and the maturest deliberation, "you adopt the plan that shall appear most likely to "answer the beneficial purposes intended."

The Governor in Council directed to take into immediate consideration Dr. Anderson's recommendation for fixed filatures, near those plantations which may be most conveniently situated as regards wood and water.

---

* In fact the cold weather "bunds" are the best.—J. G.

† Mr. Corbett died in September 1792.

At the same time they forwarded, for information and guidance, copy of some general remarks on the establishment of Italian filatures on the coast by Mr. Wiss,* their Inspector of Silk in England.

Another 100 skeins of silk forwarded by Dr. Anderson, reeled after the Bengal filature plan.

23. On the 21st January of this year, Dr. Anderson sent another 100 skeins of silk of the last month's crop reeled after the Bengal filature plan, with explanation of some improvements made by him in the Bengal machinery.

Dr. Anderson's endeavours recognised by the Court of Directors.

Dated London, 21st May 1794, Revenue Department, paragraphs 53 & 54.

24. That Dr. Anderson's endeavours were fully appreciated both by the Madras Government and by the Honourable Court of Directors is evident. In their letter referred to in the margin, they say that their earnest desire to afford every reasonable encouragement to Dr. Anderson's endeavours has already been evinced: "we shall cheerfully consent to your rendering such pecuniary assistance to the undertaking as shall give it a fair chance of success. With respect to the charges already incurred by Dr. Anderson * * * * we can only say that we are not only willing to discharge the amount, but shall have great satisfaction in giving him a more substantial proof of the sense we entertain of his zeal and ability.

Further report on silk sent to England.

"Of the samples of silk received by the contractor the following report has been made to us, that it is of good quality, and was admirably well wound; and, if it is procurable, at a rate of cost equal to what the article is afforded for at Bengal, it would answer for sale in this country."

Disappointment of Dr. Anderson at failure in the introduction of silk-culture among the people.

25. It was about this time that Dr. Anderson began to find that this culture did not make so much progress as he had anticipated. This he accounts for in part by the want of co-operation on the part of the Board of Revenue and the Collectors, and partly by the inducements held out to the natives to undertake the culture of the mulberry and silkworms not being sufficient.

Further inducements to be held out to the people to cultivate the mulberry plant, suggested by Dr. Anderson.

And carried out by the Board of Revenue.

Further privileges to be conceded to renters who will grow mulberries.

In his letter of the 21st January 1793, the Physician-General complains that "so little attention has been paid to the planting of mulberries for near two years, that I have not been able, notwithstanding I have been at the expense of collecting all the leaves for one hundred miles around, to supply the worms in my bungalow with a sufficiency of food; let this not however be imputed to the soil or climate." He then suggests rewards being given to natives who shall have shown enterprise and successful results in growing mulberries. The result of this recommendation was that in the following July gold earrings were presented to certain inhabitants of the neighbourhood of Madras at the desire of Government, and the Board of Revenue trusted that this encouragement might tend to increase the cultivation of the plant. More than this, when Dr. Anderson recommended that no grant or agreement should be entered into with any renters of villages unless they agreed to lay out and plant with mulberries a certain proportion of ground to be determined by the size of the village, the Board expressed their cordial concurrence, adding, in regard to some strictures passed by Dr. Anderson, that "they would be careful to discriminate those Collectors who shall be found to have paid proper attention to the plantations under their charge, and to extending the cultivation of the mulberry."

Account of the various modes in which artificial encouragement was given to the silk-industry.

And the result thereof.

26. The following account will shew that neither the Government nor the Board can fairly be accused of withholding encouragement, either direct or indirect, from this industry, and though their efforts did not in all cases keep pace with Dr. Anderson's wishes, the event showed that no amount of artificial encouragement was sufficient to establish silk-culture as a national industry on a large scale in the Peninsula.

* This is not forthcoming.

27. More ground was given to Dr. Anderson near the Company's Nopalry,* and eventually all the land in Dr. Anderson's occupation was exempted from quit-rent, and up to the end of 1796, Government had paid him Rs. 58,744 on account of expenses incurred by him.

Direct assistance to Dr. Anderson.

28. Early in 1793, the establishments mantained by Government on the plantations in the different Collectorates and Circars were doubled at Dr. Anderson's suggestion; and several applications for the rent or lease of waste lands in villages for the alleged purpose of the cultivation of the mulberry and silkworm were received and favorably considered by the Board; but there is little doubt that the caution exercised by that authority in granting leases was not uncalled for, as they suspected (not without cause apparently) that the real object of the would-be renters was simply to obtain leases of lands, and whole villages, on more favourable terms than they otherwise would have done for general cultivation. The most noticeable of these applications was from one Chinnatumbi Mudelly who was supported with funds supplied by some English gentlemen, and there seems no reason to doubt that this application was *bonâ fide* for the purposes set forth. They wished to take all the villages in the Ponnur (Porrur? west of Madras) Maganum (Division), in the Chingleput Jaghire on a lease for twenty-one years for the establishment of a silk factory. This application was complied with, but the result is not recorded; nothing appears to have come of the enterprise. Other applications were made by Perumal, a renter, who had tried a plantation near Chikareecottah (Sriharicota), in the Nellore District, which had failed owing to the sandiness of the soil; he now asked for three villages in the Ponnery Talook (Chingleput Jaghire), on rent for ten years retaining only the land not required for general cultivation on which to plant mulberries. Another application was made by Nattum Villayya to rent the Pakum Division in Poonamallee, and to erect a filature. Another applicant wished to rent the villages of Adyar, Codur, and Venkatapuram, in the vicinity of Madras. Mambalum (or Marmalong) near Sydapett was also thought to be a good spot for the culture of the mulberry.

The establishment on mulberry plantations supported by Government doubled.

Applications for rent or lease of waste lands for cultivation of that plant.

29. It became necessary for the Board to call for reports as to the extent of waste lands available for the purpose. It was ascertained that owing to famine and the late wars, the extent of waste was excessive, and the following is an abstract of the rules drawn up by the Board for the disposal of these lands. The land was divided into four classes, and the persons to whom it was to be granted into three classes:

Reports called for as to the extent, &c., of waste lands available.

The extent excessive, owing to causes stated.

Rules for the disposal of waste lands for special purposes, including cultivation of mulberry and erection of silk factories.

1*st Class*.—Natives of the country. The terms offered to these being less favourable, in order to prevent them throwing up their cultivated lands, and cultivating waste to the detriment of the revenue.

2*nd Class*.—Natives, but aliens or strangers, with a view to induce them to settle.

3*rd Class*.—Planters, including Natives, aliens, and Europeans, for the cultivation of special products as mulberry, coffee, cotton, black pepper.

To these the terms offered were the most favourable, namely, rent-free occupation for seven years on condition of cultivation from the eighth year, subject to the fixed quit-rent calculated on what the ground would yield, if cultivated with ordinary products. It is clear, therefore, that all obstacles in the way of expenses of cultivation of the mulberry and erection of silk factories were removed as far as possible; but nothing more is heard of the opportunities afforded being successfully made use of.

* Garden for cultivation of the Cochineal plant and insect.

The above rules approved by Government who suggest further encouragement to persons willing to erect filatures.

30. These rules for the disposal of waste lands were approved by Government who further suggested that the plantations already made at the Company's expense should be offered to such Natives as might be willing to erect filatures on them for the Company, it not being the intention of Government to establish any filatures on a large scale on the Company's account. There is little reason to suppose that the desired object would have been attained if Dr. Anderson's still further proposal had been acted upon that Collectors should grant off-hand on application without fee, reward, tax, or any duty, any waste and unoccupied land whatever for not less than 21 years for this special purpose—a proposal to which the Board could not consent.

Letter from Dr. Anderson to the Board, 27th December. 1793.

An account of this will be given below, para. 40.

Stipulation to be entered in future leases that mulberry leaves shall be received and paid for by Government at a fixed rate.

31. Still further to assure renters of some return for their expenditure, and thinking that "the rearing of worms may be too great a stretch of an idea to many," Dr. Anderson recommends that "the cowles in all future leases shall express the immediate payment for leaves brought to the Superintendent of the Honourable Company's filature at a reasonable valuation." To this proposal the Board assented, and it was ultimately agreed that the price to be paid for mulberry leaves should be 1 Rupee for 300 hands-full, 20 leaves in each hand-full.

General want of success of these measures.

32. No success appears to have attended these measures for the culture of the mulberry and the silkworm, except in the plantations and establishments under direct management, and the expenses of which were defrayed by Government.

Dr. Anderson resigns all direct interest and management in the experiment on behalf of Government.

33. In February 1794, Dr. Anderson declined any longer to superintend the Company's filature at Vellout, apparently dissatisfied with the complete control given to the immediate Superintendent of that establishment, who was paid by the Company; and in the following month expressed his intention of having no more to do with the culture at all, except on his own account. No particular reason was assigned, but it was implied that the want of success was due to want of proper encouragement and to the non-adoption of all his proposals.

The Board of Revenue entrusted with the general management of the enterprise.

34. On this the Government entrusted to the Board of Revenue the promotion, by every reasonable means, of the industry from which Dr. Anderson had withdrawn his support, especially by inducing the Natives to take advantage of the waste land rules above given.

General expression of opinion on the part of the Board and Government as to the proper manner of furthering silk-culture in the countries under their management.

Essentials to suitability of localities for mulberry plantations and silk factories not available, except in a few places on the East Coast.

35. In communicating the results of their endeavours, and noticing Dr. Anderson's relinquishment of his interest in the matter, the Government state to the Court of Directors that "they had always thought it more likely that the industry would succeed by favouring the exertions of private interest than by conducting it upon the Company's account." Silk of superior quality, they thought, could be made, "but there are very few places where mulberry plantations and silk factories can be maintained without heavy expense;" only on the banks of rivers which are not dried up in the hot weather, with water carriage for firewood, and for purposes of irrigation, could such plantations be profitably maintained, and of such spots there were not many on the East Coast.

Want of success recorded.

Certain plantations given up.

36. There is no success to record in the endeavours of the Government to induce the Natives to take up the industry on their own account. Towards the end of 1795, the Board had to report that no applications had been received for cuttings, nor for lands for the purpose of silk-culture in the Circars; and they, therefore, recommended that the Company's plantations at Masulipatam, Chicacole, Vizagapatam, and Guntoor, should be given up, especially as a filature* was to be erected at Ganjam. This was approved by

* Of this more below, paragraphs 38, 39, 47.

Government, the Board observing in a later letter that "as the plant was now cultivated in almost every garden throughout the Circars, as well as in the Botanical Gardens in the Masulipatam District, there will be no difficulty in obtaining cuttings, should it at any time become an object with individuals."

37. Early in the following year the Board recorded their opinion that the whole process of keeping up plantations, rearing the worms, &c., could not be carried on either by an individual, or by the Company with advantage, or even to reimburse expenses, as experience had sufficiently shown; and further, that upon the introduction of the growth of the mulberry and rearing the worms amongst the inhabitants its success must solely depend, and that either of these must be matter of time, and not likely to be taken up before the people were convinced of its success. In this the Government concurred, and towards the close of 1797, the Court of Directors ordered that no further expense should be incurred for this purpose on the Company's account, since "there seemed little probability of the manufacture of silk becoming an article of profitable export from the Coast of Coromandel; at the same time it does not appear that either you or the Board of Revenue have been backward in affording every reasonable encouragement towards its success." It is added that the Company had already expended nearly £20,000 in the furtherance of this object with scarcely any prospect of its attainment.

The Board record an opinion adverse to any further expenditure on the part of Government on account of silk-culture.

The above opinion concurred in by Government.

No further expense to be incurred on this account by the Company's Government in Madras.

Reasons for this resolution given by the Court of Directors.

The total expenditure incurred by the Company up to this time.

"It is stated that the texture of the silk from Madras being only similar to that from Bengal, it would be unnecessary, even if it were practicable to cultivate it for export to this country, as Bengal is capable of affording the commodity in larger proportions than the present state of the market requires."

38. The plantations at the various stations were accordingly on the 18th June 1798 advertised for sale, but no offers were made: that at Ganjam was eventually made over to the officer in charge of the Company's Breeding Stud, in 1799.

Plantations offered for sale and otherwise disposed of.

That at Waltair near Vizagapatam could not be disposed of even on an easy quit-rent, and it (and presumably the others) was finally incorporated again with Government lands.

39. It would be of little use to give in detail the results of the plantations at the various stations specified in paragraphs 9 and 11. Some success attended the planting of cuttings at some stations. That at Guntoor had within nine months supplied 10,000 cuttings; at Gudur near Masulipatam 6,800 young plants were flourishing, besides 400 Opuntia of the Kew and China species.

Short notice of plantations in various parts of the country.

Trivellore, some thirty miles from Madras, appears to have been well suited to the plant, and a plantation was kept up here, and cocoons raised till the end of the century, as it was near and apparently under the Superintendent of the Filature at Vellout.

More generally, however, the results were not encouraging, and the Collectors called on to report on the plantations in 1795 could not recommend that those at Masulipatam, Vizagapatam (Waltair), and Guntoor, should be kept up. From Cuddalore, too, the report was very discouraging.

At Ganjam, where favourably situated land was found, and where about 50 acres were planted, and a filature established, more success seems to have been obtained; but for a total expenditure of Rs. 10,066 up to the end of 1799, the only recorded return is "some silk (quantity not stated) sent to England in 1796."

The plantations started by the Company at Nellore, Ongole, Madura, Tiagur (in South Arcot District), and Arnee appear to have been entirely neglected after the country was restored to the Nawab (letter from Dr. Anderson, dated 26th April 1793).

Account of the Company's filature at Vellout, (Vellavedu) near Madras.

40. It remains to give an account of the Company's filature which was established at Vellout Choultry (or, as it is more properly spelled at the present time, Vellavedu), some four or four and a half miles from Trivellore, which is about twenty-five or thirty miles west of Madras on the line of rail. There was then stationed at Vellavedu a Cavalry regiment, and it seems to have been a place of some importance. The idea of establishing a filature on the Company's account appears to have originated with Government, very soon after the subject of silk-culture was brought to their notice. In April 1793, Dr. Anderson informed the Government that the Collector of the district had found about 200 acres for a plantation near Vellavedu, and urged the Board to spare no expense in sinking wells, fencing, and planting a nursery to supply the whole Jaghire.

The Board forwarded this recommendation to Government, advising that a special Superintendent should be employed, and, as the plantation would soon be advanced enough for the commencement of the manufacture, recommended preparation of plans and estimates for buildings for a filature, and that other similar establishments should afterwards be started in the Circars. With the approval of Government 300 tank-diggers, carts, bullocks, and ploughs were obtained, and a house was built for the Superintendent. In July arrangements were made for building a village for the accommodation of the people employed in the manufactory.

Early in 1794, Dr. Anderson was so well satisfied with the progress made in planting mulberries, that he considered the only object to be attended to was the perfection of the filature and production of silk of better quality than that produced in Bengal, and that to ensure this it was only necessary to carry out his instructions, and to import the China mulberry.

Native silk-weavers, ("cattanies,") from Bengal.

41. The Board recommended that an establishment of cattanies or native weavers of silk should be procured from Bengal to instruct the people, and that a European Superintendent should be engaged for the Company's filatures on the Coast.

The Company's filature at Vellout.

42. Notwithstanding Dr. Anderson's withdrawal from the pursuit of this industry (which has been described in paragraph 33) the Government sanctioned the completion of the filature at Vellavedu. In July 1794 seven men skilled in silk manufacture arrived from Bengal and were provided with accommodation at Vellavedu. The silk bungalow was completed in September following, and in February 1795, Mr. Parkinson, the paid Superintendent, who seems to have been a man of much zeal, industry, and good sense, reported that, although it had not been possible to rear the worms during the monsoon, he was able to send a small bale of silk containing various sorts of silk, and waste or refuse from the cocoons, all reeled between October 1794 and the end of January 1795. Silk 34 lbs. 2 ozs; waste silk 88 lbs. 14 ozs. The eggs had been supplied by Dr. Anderson, who appears again to have interested himself to a certain extent in the matter.

There were at this time enclosed 379 acres, exclusive of the village for the people employed in the works; 214 acres were planted, and 127 dug for planting; but difficulty was found in procuring labour, though higher rates than ordinary were offered. Already the Superintendent speaks of the difficulty in *forcing* into general adoption in this country any improvement, however beneficial it may be theoretically, when no immediate advantage is apparent.

The silk was highly approved by the Board, who authorised the employment of six Apprentices from the Male Orphan Asylum, and the sale of cocoons at 700 per fanam.* Thinking it indispensable, too, to get the cultivation of the mulberry and the rearing of the worm into the hands of the natives, and finding little response on their part, it was notified that the Superintendent would supply leaves and all the material to any one applying, the price to be deducted from the sale of the cocoons.

* Rupee 0-1-3.

There was great mortality among the worms from February to May 1798, when silk was again obtained from worms procured from Chittoor, and by June 61 lbs. of very superior silk was obtained, showing an increase of produce of 12 per cent. in quantity, and 28 per cent. in quality. The best silk it was thought would fetch Rupees 49 per 25 lbs.

Further experience only confirmed the impression that the rearing of worms by people on monthly pay could only be a dead loss, and every attempt was made to induce the Natives to embark in the business, but without success.

The quantity of silk made up to October 1795.

43. Up to the end of September 1795, 460 lbs. of filature silk and 550 of waste had been made at Vellavedu, but after the beginning of 1796, the Board having come to the conclusion recorded in paragraph 37, that it was hopeless to expect the Natives to take up the industry on their own account—a conclusion in which Mr. Parkinson concurred—nothing more was done after this time than to keep up the plantation.

Expenditure on the Vellout filature.

44. The total expenditure on the filature at Vellavedu and plantation at Trivellore up to the end of March 1797, amounted to Rs. 78,736.

45. The efforts of the Superintendent had not, however, been relaxed, and in January 1797 he was able to report that the worms had been kept healthy through the trying rainy season, producing large and hard cocoons. It was, however, found that the yellow worm was so inferior to the white, that the former would have been given up were it not that the yellow worm throve so much better in the damp. Mr. Parkinson had also got some Natives to engage in the care of part of the plantation on their own account, on condition of producing silk at so much a pound, and between January and March 1797, 169 lbs. of silk, and 135 lbs. of waste silk had been produced at Vellavedu.

The filature closed.

46. These results did not encourage the Government to pursue the experiment further, and the Bengal "cattanies" were sent back, or took engagement elsewhere, at Chittoor and Parrawak in Chingleput Jaghire on their own account; and in September 1798, the buildings and land at Vellavedu were made over to the Barrack Master, the plant being sent to Madras for disposal by auction.

The filature at Ganjam. Total expenditure on, and result.

47. The sum of Rs. 10,066 had been expended on the filature at Ganjam which consisted of about 50 acres, with buildings, cocoonery, etc. The manner in which this filature was disposed of has been described in paragraph 38, and no further information has been met with as to the results of the expenditure incurred there.

Statement of cost at which the silk produced was placed in the market, not obtainable.

48. It has not been found possible, as may be inferred from the above data, to state at what cost silk, fitted for the English market, was produced; but the following quotation from a letter from the Board of Revenue to Government, dated 10th December 1795, will show that the Board were not wrong in not speaking in more sanguine terms than they did of the results of the experiment as a commercial success. "The total expenditure in the Company's possessions and in the territories formerly under management, but restored to the Nawab, is Rs. 1,05,717½ exclusive of Contractor's bills for buildings at Vellout. The quantity of good silk produced on the plantation from the 6th October 1794 to the 1st October 1795, is only about 460 lbs. and the refuse about 551 lbs. The value of the former is about Rs. 147 per maund of 25 lbs. The staple of the latter is, however, said to be superior to that of Bengal, and* *if the Superintendent succeeds in introducing the care of the worm amongst the people, and cocoons can be procured at the rate of* 300 *per fanam, the prime cost of the article will not much exceed that of Bengal silk.*"

Conclusion of account of silk-culture on account of the East India Company prior to the commencement of the nineteenth century.

This concludes the account of the measures adopted by the Madras Government on behalf of the Honourable East India Company for the promotion of silk-culture during the last ten years of the last century.

* The italics are not in the original.

A. D. 1822.
The Government decline to take any direct share in assisting an Armenian gentleman in the culture of silk near Madras.

49. In 1822 a Mr. Narcis, an Armenian "of great respectability, but reduced circumstances," having produced some raw silk in his own enclosure in the Black Town of Madras, applied to the Board of Revenue to obtain for him on favourable tenure some land in the vicinity of Madras, for carrying on more extended operations. At Vulloor near Madras, he found large buildings well suited for the purpose which had been erected by Mr. Popham (of whom mention is made in paragraph 9) at great expense, for works in connection with his farm on which he, too, had cultivated silk in 1791. Mr. Narcis, therefore, proposed to rent the village. The Board had satisfied themselves of the probable success of Mr. Narcis, and recommended that he should be allowed to rent the village at 25 per cent. below the average actual collections of the last ten years. The Government, however, were of opinion that it might be productive of embarrassment to them to take any share in the undertaking; besides that the scheme did not appear in any way to be dependent on assistance from Government 'as it appeared Mr. Narcis could rent the village at full assessment', and, therefore, the Government left that gentleman to make his own arrangements with the villagers. The Collector was, however, instructed to afford him all fitting encouragement.

A. D. 1833.
A French gentleman allowed to live and establish a silk factory in the Malabar District.

50. The next mention of this subject occurs in 1833. Monsieur De Larme, a Frenchman, who had arrived at Mahé two years previously, had, with the support of the French Government, established a plantation and silk factory, the silk manufactured at which was represented to be of superior quality. Being desirous of establishing a separate manufacture of his own in the Cartenaud Talook (Malabar District), permission to reside in the district and to establish a silk factory was accorded.

No record of the results.

Nothing further is recorded of the results of this experiment or that of Mr. Narcis.

A. D. 1839.
Measures taken by the Madras Government for the introduction of the Philippine mulberry (Morus Multicaulis).

51. The next notice of matters connected with sericulture is contained in a despatch from the Honourable Company to Fort St. George in 1839, in which they forward a letter from Lieutenant-Colonel Sykes, bringing to notice a book entitled "the Silk Culturist's Manual, &c.," addressed to the farmers and planters of the United States: "By John D'Homergue, published and for sale at 30, North Fourth Street, Philadelphia." The purport of this communication has been already given in the chapter on Silk in Bengal.

The Government communicated the above letter to the Board of Revenue, the Horticultural Society of Madras, and Surgeon Wight, and the letter was also published into the *Fort St. George Gazette*.

The Board were of opinion that it was of great importance that the Philippine mulberry should be introduced into the Peninsula.

A. D. 1842.

52. The Madras Government appear to have done little towards obtaining cuttings of this plant till 1842 when they were instructed to apply to the Bengal and Bombay Governments by whom some experiments had been made; in the latter Presidency with but little success as is stated. It was, however, thought that the failure at Daporee and the nursery gardens at Nerjoree might have been due to want of knowledge of the habits and requirements of the plants, and the Madras Government were requested to proceed as they proposed in 1839-40.

In forwarding copy of the above instructions, the Government state that they understand the Philippine mulberry may be obtained from Pondicherry where there is a silk factory and plantation.

The Agri-Horticultural Society of Madras already in possession of the Philippine mulberry, which throve well both on the plains and on the hills.

53. The Agri-Horticultural Society replied that they were already in possession of this plant which was growing luxuriantly in their garden from cuttings presented by Mr. Groves of Chittoor. Several hundred cuttings had already been distributed to enterprising persons on the Nilgiri Hills and in Mysore. The Society undertook to supply 10,000 more cuttings by the next April or May if pecuniary

assistance were given. The plant was said to grow extremely well, the soil and climate being evidently well suited to it, and it was believed it would do equally well in most parts of the Presidency.

Government then called on all Collectors to report their demands for cuttings.

Reports of Collectors as to demand for cuttings of the Philippine mulberry.

54. The Collector of Salem applied for as many cuttings as could be spared; the silk manufacture having been introduced into the Denkanikotta Talook* for some six or eight years, and a few families being employed in rearing silk-worms in the Oossoor Talook also. The Collector of Coimbatore wished for as many cuttings as he could have, and the Collector of Bellary proposed to try the experiment in the Government plantations which were enclosed and provided with wells and gardeners.

The Collector of Rajahmundry asked for a few cuttings for distribution, as did the Collector of Nellore, who reported that the Native mulberry throve well in some parts of the district. In Cuddapah the ryots were said to be ready to receive any number of mulberry trees, specimens of which had been pretty generally introduced from Mysore into the Pullivendlah Talook; it is added that the Philippine mulberry had already thriven in Mysore. In Malabar there had been only one application, though the Collector had no doubt the district was well adapted to the culture of this plant. The Collector of Trichinopoly also applied for some.

The Commissioner of Kurnool was unable to say decidedly whether the cultivation was likely to be undertaken in that district.

The Collector of Tinnevelly applied for some model machinery for winding silk thread.

In June 1843, the Commissioner of Kurnool applied for some cuttings, and suggested the establishment of a plantation and maintenance of silkworms and machinery for winding silk at Kurnool and Nundial, on a small scale, at the expense of Government. This proposal was not approved by the Board, on the ground that neither place was considered very favourable for the purpose, and it was negatived by Government.

Notice of silk-culture in the Travancore State discontinued in 1840.

55. It appears that some experiments had been made in the rearing of silkworms and manufacture of silk in the Travancore State, which were discontinued by the Dewan in 1840—on what ground it was not known—probably to reduce expenditure, and also, it was believed, because the Rajah objected to such experiments in the Capital.

Silk Factory at Courtallum.

56. The Collector of Tinnevelly therefore proposed to buy two silk-winding machines of the latest and most improved pattern, one from the Travancore Sircar, the other from a private person at Billikal, with a view to improving the process of silk manufacture carried on by an enterprising Native at Courtallum (Tinnevelly District).

Report on silk produced in the Madras Presidency very favourable.

57. In 1845 the Committee of the Madras Agri-Horticultural Society made the following report on the competition for prizes for silk offered by Government according to Notification in the *Fort St. George Gazette* of the 29th January 1845:

"The competition for the prizes for raw silk, the Committee are happy to be able to report, has been more brisk [than for cotton]. The specimens offered by Mr. Groves† and Major Minchin‡ are very creditable to both gentlemen;

* Dr. Balfour, in the Supplement to the Cyclopædia of Southern India, published in 1862, says that the breeding of silkworms was then carried on in Denkencottah in the Salem district, there being 41 persons of all castes, who bred the worm. The annual value of the silk produced was about Rs. 1,000, fetching about 6 rupees per seer of 80 tolahs. The eggs took 10 to 14 days to hatch, the existence of the worm was 40 days and the pupa stage lasted from 10 to 15 days. Fresh mulberry leaves were supplied seven times a day. But no less than one half the worms were said to perish from "extremes of heat and cold." 1,000 cocoons were estimated to yield the *weight* of from 2 to 6 rupees in raw silk. The mulberries were planted both in black and red soils; but required continuous moisture. With care they lasted 10 years, yielding fresh leaves six times a year, the stems being periodically cut down. Thus it is clear that ehe Bengal or bush system was adopted to meet the wants of the worms, which were multivoltines, yielding 6 crops annually. The net profit per acre is calculated at Rs. 27-4-0.—J. G.

† Of Chittoor.

‡ An Invalid Officer on the Nilgiris who took up silk culture two or three years before apparently.

the degree to which they have succeeded in the short time they have turned their attention to the subject gives promise of still greater improvement."

* * * * *

"Major Minchin has transmitted the produce of only one species of silk-worm and that raised on the Nilgiris; Mr. Groves has transmitted specimens of both the country and the Italian worm reared both on the Hills and in the Carnatic."

* * * * *

"The competitors for the second prize for silk were Mahomed Cassim and Padsha Sahib. To Mahomed Cassim we award the prize of Rs. 150, as he has produced the quantity of silk stipulated for, although it is inferior to Padsha Sahib's; it is the produce of the indigenous worm of Mysore, while Padsha Sahib's is from the Italian worm procured by the late Secretary, Major Reid. In both these silks there is great room for improvement in reeling. The parties, however, say that there is no demand for finer silk among the Native manufacturers." Padsha Sahib was the first person who attempted the culture of silk in Madras on a supply of Italian eggs having been procured by the Society from Bombay.

Prizes offered by Government.

58. For the years 1844-45 and 1845-46 the following prizes were offered by Government for silk :—

					lbs.	Rs.
1844-45	(1)	For the best sample of raw silk, not less than		...	20	300
	(2)	For the second best	do.	do. ...	20	150
1845-46	(1)	For the best	do.	do. ...	40	300
	(2)	For the second best	do.	do. ...	40	200

Silver medals were also offered to Native and East Indian competitors only, for the best specimens of the above as well as of other articles of Indian produce.

The result is not given in the papers collected.

Extract from Report of the Jury on silk in 1857.

59. The following selection from the report of the Jury on silk and velvet appears worthy of transcription :—"The display of silk is such as to give the greatest reason for hoping that in every important silk-producing district in this Presidency the manufacture is in a state of improvement and needs but care in several localities to secure a great extension of trade.

"The richness and beauty in colour of some of the Hyderabad silks, the useful character and cheapness of those of Mysore, and the evident desire for improvement in the already good quality of those of Tanjore, shown by a departure from the old patterns," is noticed.

"With the exception of those from Mysore the silks cannot be styled cheap.

"The colours of most of the silks are such as to call for unqualified praise, but the range of colour is very limited. The blacks are in all cases bad.

"The Jury would direct the attention of producers to the manufacture of plain white silks for export to Europe, similar but superior to those manufactured in Bengal under the name of corahs.* * * * The cheap rate at which it is evident that Mysore can put out its manufactures seems to show that it can enter into successful competition with the Bengal weavers.

"It will be observed that the attention of the Jury has been given to the extension of the silk manufacture for European use; it is probable that for Native use the supply already equals the demand."

The Jury also recommended that samples of silk of the manufacture of France, England, Bengal, and China be obtained and exhibited in the various districts, with an estimate of the prices which such silks were likely to secure.

Application was accordingly made by Government to the Honourable Court of Directors, and in accordance with a suggestion of the Jury a collection which should fairly represent the products of the country was ordered to be deposited in the Madras Central Museum, and part sent to the Museum at the India House, London.

Notice of silk in reports of district agricultural exhibitions.

60. The reports of the district agricultural exhibitions for the years 1856-59, shew that in some districts small prizes were offered for, and won by, manufactured silk, but no special notice is taken of the industry. Most encouragement seems to have been offered in Ganjam, where, however, the silk exhibited was probably tusser silk either from the Khond jungles, or imported from the Central Provinces. In 1855, Madras appears to have exported by sea 1,666 lbs. of raw silk, valued at Rs. 6,569. In 1859, Tinnevelly was reported to produce a bad silk "to a very limited extent." This silk was reported to fetch Rs. 5$\frac{1}{3}$ to 7$\frac{1}{3}$ per seer of 80 tolahs, and was mostly exported to Madura and Tanjore. These two districts seem also to have absorbed most of the Mysore silk; the carpets and fringes of Tanjore having some reputation; while in the Madura district there appears still to exist a settlement of Suratee silk-weavers called Pattu-nul-kárans. These are described in the "Manual of the Madura country" as preserving their native language and keeping separate from the indigenous inhabitants. They are said to be skilful and industrious workmen.

Recent revival of the question of the possibility of establishing the silk industry in Madras.

61. In February 1868, Messrs. Dymes and Company announced to the Madras Board of Revenue, that they had bought a small experimental silk farm at Oossoor. In September 1869, Messrs. de'Vecchj and Pater addressed the Government of Madras on the subject of sericulture. They averred that both the Hindoo and Mahomedan population evinced a strong interest in the silk trade, and that the only way to meet the epizoic which had attacked existing stocks was to import fresh seed. This accordingly they intended to do from "Italy, the Punjab, Cashmere, China and Japan," and in the distribution of the eggs they asked the aid of Government. They did not ask for pecuniary assistance, till their success should be proved, and they offered to supply Government with silkworm's eggs and cuttings of the China, Japan and Persian mulberries which they had imported. Signor de'Vecchj expressed a decided opinion that "the whole of the Coimbatore plateau, the Cauvery valley and the slopes of the Nilgiris and Shervaroys up to 35,000 feet" were well fitted for silkworm breeding from climate, soil and cheapness of labour.

Instructions issued to the Board of Revenue.

62. The Board was directed to afford every assistance both to Messrs. Dymes and Company and to Messrs. de'Vecchj and Pater, and to report as to the advisability of establishing a small silkworm breeding establishment. The possibility of extending sericulture to the districts described by Signor de'Vecchj was also to be enquired into.

Offer of Messrs. de'Vecchj and Pater in 1870.

63. In February 1870, Messrs. de'Vecchj and Pater made the Government of Madras a definite offer to introduce 500 cartoons of the best seed from Italy, China, Japan and elsewhere, and to undertake their distribution to selected cultivators and others, on the condition that Government should pay them Rs. 10,000 if the eggs germinated successfully. They urged the commencement of the trial in the talooks of Collegal and Oossoor where silk was already cultivated; but drew attention also to Tinnevelly. The Board considered this proposal with the replies of Collectors on the subject of silk before them. From these it appeared, that though in most districts silkworm cultivation had been tried at some time or other, yet it had died away in all but Coimbatore, Salem, Cuddapah, North Arcot, Tinnevelly and South Canara, prevailing only in the first two to any great extent. The Board concluded that so far from the prevalent disease arising from the introduction of foreign seed, as believed by the ryots of Coimbatore, its only probable remedy was the introduction of foreign stock. They, therefore, recommended that the offer of Messrs. de'Vecchj and Pater should be accepted. The Government, however, postponed the question till the close of the current official year, *i. e.*, till March 1871.

Report on silk in Tinnevelly.

64. An interesting report on silk in Tenkasi, a talook of Tinnevelly, was submitted by a tehsildar under date 15th March 1870. The following is a brief abstract of it.

The mulberry on which the worms are fed is called by the natives "Kumbly Cheddy" (meaning woolly shrub) and is perhaps of the Philippine kind.

It is a perennial plant and would grow into a tree, but is kept down to the height of 4 or 5 feet by pruning. It grows well in "high nunjah land," but would thrive on punjah land if watered by picottahs. It prefers a mixture of black and red soil. It is propagated by cuttings which are put down in the month of June. The plant is said to have been introduced about 1830 by a Mr. Hughes. Up to the year 1250 Fuslee, it was cultivated in 25 villages to the extent of upwards of 200 (Madras) kottahs, but the area had diminished to some 24 kottahs in 4 villages. The mulberry requires hoeing monthly, and is manured with ashes, cowdung or sheepdung, once, if not twice, a year. Irrigation is essential to supply healthy feeding for the worms. A high, but not uniformly high, rate of assessment is laid on mulberry, and this, with the fall in the price of silk, and the rise in that of paddy, had, in the tehsildar's opinion, reduced the cultivation.

The tehsildar calculates that one seed kottah of land (=1·62 acres) will support worms enough to yield 22½ seers (Government) of cocoons, or 3¾ lbs. of silk. At eight crops a year this would give 30 lbs., or, at Rs. 6 a lb., Rs. 180. The cost of cultivation, on the other hand, is estimated at about Rs. 105.

The worms "are supposed to be of the sub-species Tussek Muttar," whatever that may mean. They are a domestic breed and reared in the house throughout. For the first ten days they are fed on chopped tender leaves six times a day. The caterpillars reach maturity in from 33 to 35 days, and are then placed in circular trays divided by concentric partitions, which again are sub-divided into suitable spaces for the spinning of their light yellow cocoons. The total cycle is placed by the tehsildar at 55 days. This would give about *six* 'bunds.' "The cocoons of the rainy season are sometimes smaller in size as well as in capability for silk. Five or six filaments are united to form one thread. A couple or two of such threads are then twisted together by the silk weaver to form a thread of the silk cloth manufactured at Combaconum."

"The Tenkasi rearers are no capitalists." No epizoic is reported in Tinnevelly, though two diseases are mentioned as attacking the worm, one in the rains, the other in the dry weather. The reeling is rude, and the tehsildar advocates the attempt to introduce better machines.

Orders of Government thereon.

65. Upon this report, which was accompanied by specimens of the cocoons and silk, the Government of Madras addressed the Secretary of State, sending cocoons, silk, and a Tinnevelly silk-reeling machine, with a request that he would ascertain whether it was probable that India-grown silk would fetch a better price in the European than in the Indian market, and would obtain competent advice as to the best mode of improving the machinery.

The Secretary of State consulted the Silk Supply Association, who gave it as their opinion, that attention should be rather paid to improvement of the worm than of reeling machines. The Madras Government, however, still pressed for a reeling machine; but also thought it would be well to get some seed from Natal.

Mr. Sullivan's report and orders thereon.

66. Meanwhile Mr. Sullivan had reported on the Kingheri filature (see the section on Silk in Mysore), and, in order to extend the industry to Coimbatore, made certain definite proposals, *viz.*, (1) that two Europeans employed in the district should be allowed to cultivate a small extent of land with mulberry, with a view to introducing improved breeds of silkworm; (2) that favourable terms should be allowed ryots taking up land for mulberry cultivation; and (3) that a filature and worm-rearing house should be established in the Coimbatore Jail.

These proposals were sanctioned by the local Government. The experiment in the Jail is said to have proved "quite successful;" 19,450 cocoons produced weighed 27 lbs. 14 ozs., yielding 3 lbs. 4 ozs. of reeled silk.

Views of Madras Board of Revenue as to what should be done.

67. I extract in full the views of the Board of Revenue, Madras, as to the action which Government should now take. The subject is reported to be now (February 1872) under consideration:—

"27. The Board have no intention and no wish to understate the difficulties attendant on any attempt to revive the culture of silk on a large scale.

"Introduced originally, as there is little doubt, with the assistance of State aid, brought at one time to a pitch of considerable excellence, and carried on, on an extended scale, silk culture in Southern India now scarcely carries on a languishing existence. Failure attended the attempts of the East India Company in the early years of the century; failure has quite lately been only too uniform in the efforts made by the Mysore administration.

"By the French Government in India silk culture has been entirely given up, as it would not cover one quarter of its expenses.

"28. But in spite of many adverse circumstances, falling prices, the result of competition among purchasers, and the rapacity of middle-men, through whom alone the poorer classes (into whose hands this production had fallen) could reach the markets; in spite of ignorance on the part of the growers, want of enterprise, and of means to restore by selection and importation the vitality of the worm, and to provide proper and sufficient food, this culture has not altogether died out. This shows that the industry has existed and can exist, notwithstanding neglect and under unfavourable conditions. The Board have little doubt that not a few parts of Southern India are well adapted to the growth of the mulberry and the culture of the silk-worm, (notably parts of the Coimbatore District, Courtallum in Tinnevelly, parts of Mysore and Madanapally in the Cuddapah District), and that, with the assistance of the State, the culture may be revived and successfully carried on—a source of profit both to the people and to the State.

"29. But they are convinced that it is only with aid from the State that this can be done; that if any assistance is to be given by the State, now is the time; and that no success can be looked for unless considerable expenditure and exertion be incurred, and the experiment carried out on a systematic and well-considered plan. If Government trusts simply to availing itself of the assistance of desultory efforts on the part of individuals, whether official or non-official, who may have a taste for this interesting and delicate culture, the result cannot but be a failure however well-intentioned, intelligent, and even successful the experimenters may individually be.

"30. Government have already sanctioned the measures which diminish or remove any obstacles which may have heretofore operated to discourage the growth of the mulberry tree, and have shown their readiness to encourage attempts to revive sericulture. It only remains to go further, to systematise future efforts and to provide those engaged in this industry with the means of contending against the difficulties with which it is at present oppressed by importing for distribution the best breeds of worm procurable.

"31. Trusting that Government will concur in the above views, and are prepared to incur the necessary outlay, the Board will, to the best of their ability, state the causes which have led to the degeneracy of the breed of silkworms and consequent decay of the trade.

"32. They have no doubt whatever that the real efficient cause of this is *starvation* of the worm. This cannot be too strongly put or too often insisted upon. On this subject the Board beg to refer Government to a valuable memorandum by the Superintendent of the Government Farm, which is appended to these Proceedings. Either as the natural result of ignoring the principles of agricultural economy, the consequence of which is a general exhaustion of the soil, which for ages has had increasing calls made upon it by cultivation, with hardly any attempt to restore to it those chemical properties necessary to fertility, or in consequence of inferiority of the trees selected for the food of the worm, or both, the worms have been starved; moreover, the food supplied has not been sufficient in quantity. And here it may be observed that whatever be the causes, whether it be that the localities in which this people are chiefly found were peculiarly suited to this culture, or whether by special encouragement on the part of their own rulers, or by a more natural aptitude on the part of this race, the industry is now confined almost exclusively to the Mussulman part of the population, and to the *lower* and poorer classes of that people, who, though in many ways well adapted for carrying on an industry requiring little physical exertion, much patience and delicate handling, are only too deficient both in scientific knowledge and enterprise, being unable or unwilling to incur present expenditure for future and not immediate profits.

"33. The necessary consequence of starvation has been degeneracy of the worm, a delicate exotic, which, even in countries most adapted to it, requires the finest and best nourishment to maintain it in that excellence which is essential to its being worth keeping alive at all, and there is no doubt that in a tropical climate, the worm is especially liable to deteriorate owing to its tendency here to generate much more rapidly than in more temperate climes, and to its being here especially liable to canker and disease.

"34. It only remains to state the measures which the Board consider best adapted for removing the prime cause of degeneration and decay in the worms, *viz.*, starvation, and for renovating and improving the breed.

"35. The Board would at first limit the cultivation of silkworms exclusively to those localities in which it is still carried on with fair success, and where it is best understood (see paragraph 28); adding only the Ganjam and Vizagapatam Districts, where, they have little doubt, localities very suitable for the culture can be found.

"36. Next, in addition to the measures already sanctioned by Government for encouraging the growth of the mulberry, it should be ascertained by experiment, and by reference to those who have a special knowledge of the subject, what kinds of soil and manures are best suited for the growth of the mulberry, and what kinds of mulberry are found to be best adapted to the nature of the silk-worm, with reference to the localities in which the culture is now carried out. To this end they would suggest a scientific chemical analysis of the leaves of the mulberry, for it is evident, as shown in the Silk Supply Journal (Vol. I, No. 9, page 163), that certain soils and climates develope bad qualities, such as wateriness in the leaf, which becomes deficient in gluten, and too full of acid, a result injurious to the worms. The Board would distribute seed of the kinds ascertained to be best to growers gratis.

" 37. To introduce, on a large scale, the best and most expensive kinds of foreign worms without providing beforehand proper nutriment, and depôts for receiving and hatching the eggs and distributing the seed, can only end in failure. The next step, therefore, is to start nurseries at well-selected centres, where the seed may be received and hatched, and the species kept up and improved by breeding and selection, and distributed at first gratis; it might eventually be sold and made to pay expenses.

" 38. The Government Farm affords facilities for starting a mulberry plantation on a considerable scale, and some of the farm buildings might easily be made available for a nursery.

" A note by the Superintendent of the Farm on this subject, which is appended, has been before referred to.

" 39. Constant renewal of the seed and careful selection will be the best restorative, and the Board would not delay arrangements for the importation of a *moderate quantity* of the best breeds procurable from Japan, China, Natal, and perhaps Egyptian, and Kangra varieties. Japan is undoubtedly the source of the best seed; it is the origin of most of the other kinds above specified, and also of the finest Italian species.

" 40. But the Board, as now advised, would not accept in its entirety Messrs. de'Vecchj and Pater's offer. Either half the quantity should be taken at half the cost now asked, or the firm should be requested to import 500 cartoons of the finest breeds in equal instalments for three years' payment of £1,000, being guaranteed proportionately for each year, on condition of a certain fixed quantity of the seed germinating successfully.

" The offer of this firm has this advantage, that they undertake the hatching and distribution of the seed imported.

" For that of other seeds, Government would, no doubt, have to make their own arrangements.

" 41. Natal seed should, however, be obtained at once; direct, if possible, if not, through the Secretary of State for India.

" 42. For carrying out the proposals of the Board, diligent and intelligent, indeed scientific, attention will be required, and considerable expense, as before remarked, must be incurred to prevent total failure. The Board think that a special officer with a small establishment ought to be appointed to superintend and ensure uniformity in the operations in the several districts where the culture is to be taken in hand. It does not seem necessary to enter more into detail on this point at present until the views of Government are ascertained.

" 43. The Board advise that at first, at all events, operations should not be extended to reeling silk."

Silk manufactures in Madras.

68. The above account contains some casual notices of manufactured silks. I have not been able to obtain any definite information on the subject, though the use of silk in either pure or mixed fabrics seems common in many districts. Thus, Dr Forbes Watson's list contains gold and silver embroidery on silk from Tanjore and Trichinopoly; silk sarees from Ganjam, Tanjore, and Combaconum; silk piece goods from Tanjore and Trichinopoly; silk and cotton turbans from Ganjam and Coimbatore; silk and cotton sarees from Ganjam, Tanjore, Trichinopoly, Madras, Combaconum, Ventapollum, Cuddalore, and South Canara; cotton and silk "loongees" from Conjeveram, Salem, Madura, Rajahmundry, and " Woozzoor" (? Oosoor;) and cotton and silk piece goods from Tanjore, Trichinopoly and Madras. Cotton "body-cloths" with mungá (? tusser) borders from Ganjam are also mentioned.

SECTION IV.

SILK IN THE PUNJAB.

Experiments in Umbala, Loodhiana, Bunnoo, and Hooshyarpore districts.

In 1836, Dr. Gordon, then Assistant to the Political Agent on the North-Western Frontier, conceived the idea that silk might be cultivated with success and profit at Umbala. He planted mulberry trees, which still existed in 1858, and built a filature, obtaining eggs of both annual and multivoltine kinds from Berhampore. The experiment was carried on for three years, and in the third year he obtained a marked improvement in his silk, and was sanguine of success. Some of the produce was sent either to Bombay or Europe, "but what became of it ultimately, and what was the issue of the speculation, or the attempt rather, cannot be discovered." Dr. Jameson, who succeeded Dr. Gordon, declares that the experiment would, if it had received proper attention, have been a most successful one. The small quantity of silk made was pronounced by competent judges to be of good quality, the mulberry throve, and the worms were healthy. But Dr. Gordon, on his departure, made the experiment over to a person who took little interest in its success, and the result was failure. Also in 1836, Colonel Sir C. Wade at Loodianah, having obtained some silkworms' eggs from Ladak, commenced experiments in sericulture, and carried them on for two years, when he was called on duty to Cabul. He is said to have produced some 10 seers of silk, but nothing is on record as to its quality. The worm, from its source, must have been an annual. In Bunnoo, Colonel Herbert Edwardes was taking steps to introduce silk cultivation when the second Sikh war broke out. In Hooshyarpore, Colonel S. Abbott, Deputy Commissioner, in 1854 obtained $1\frac{1}{4}$ seers of eggs, from the hills, and commenced experiments in the jail on a somewhat extensive scale. The first yield was 56 seers of unbaked cocoons. Twenty-four seers were set aside for seed (of which they are said to have yielded 3 seers), and from the rest 8 seers of coarse silk were wound. The experiment was repeated the next year, but, in consequence of Colonel Abbott's departure, it then fell to the ground. The influence of the hot weather on the cocoons produced was prominently noticed.

In Kangra, Mundee, Goordaspore, Umritsur, and Goojrat.

2. In Kangra, Mr. E. C. Bayley, when Deputy Commissioner, made an attempt to introduce silkworms, but from some cause, which he could not explain, the worms all died four days after hatching. In Mundee silk was successfully made in 1848 or 1849, but the Cashmeeree who was entrusted with the charge of the experiment absconded, with an advance of money, and "so the thing fell to the ground." In Goordaspore, about 1854, the rearing of worms seems to have been begun, on a small scale, by one Jaffir Ali, and with some success. He received a reward of Rs. 50 from the Punjab Government, and a silver medal from the Lahore Agri-Horticultural Society. The industry seems to have taken root in the district. In 1854, too, some fine cocoons are said to have been produced, and at Soojanpore, near Pathankote, for some years previous to 1858, there had been a Mussulman colony of silkworm-rearers. In Umritsur, some coarse silk had been manufactured by Sirdar Dessa Singh, father of Lehna Singh, from eggs obtained from Cabul. In Goojrat, an attempt was made, but without the least grain of perseverance.

In Rawul Pindee and Peshawur.

3. In Rawul Pindee, Mr. Cope, in 1858, reports that a small, but successful, factory had been kept up for some years at a village named Saiudpore at the base of the Hazara Hills; the source of the eggs having been Kandahar. The yield was stated at but five or six seers annually, fetching, however, no less than 18 to 20 rupees per seer. Many of the mulberries were said to have been brought from Kandahar. In Peshawur, silk seems, at one time, to have formed a staple; but under the Sikh Government the culture gradually died out.

Experiment at Lahore.

4. But the most important experiment in the Punjab was made at Lahore under the direct orders of the Government of India. The subject of silk cultivation was taken up by the local Agri-Horticultural Society in 1852, and eggs obtained from Bengal. Lord Dalhousie too supported the project, and sent up an efficient silk-reeling establishment from Bengal to aid the Society. In September 1854, the Society addressed the Chief Commissioner, Mr. (now Lord) Lawrence. It was represented that it had been shewn* that the silkworm could stand the climate of the Punjab; that the common mulberry was abundant, while the finer species (*M. multicaulis* and *M. sinensis*) were cultivable, and had thriven in the Society's garden; that the establishment sent up from Bengal had commenced to work, and had produced silk superior to that imported from Bokhara and Khorasan, and favourably pronounced upon by the Bengal Chamber of Commerce, and that a portion of it had been worked up by the Lahore silk-weavers.

Proposals of the Agri-Horticultural Society of the Punjab for 1855;

5. The Society, therefore, proposed that Government should offer graduated rewards for the production of cocoons by the people themselves, on the following scale:—

First Prize Rs. 250, for the largest quantity of dried merchantable cocoons exceeding 100 seers, that may be produced in the Punjab. Government to purchase the cocoons, on behalf of the Society, at Re. 1 per seer.

Second Prize Rs. 200, for the next largest quantity, not less than 75 seers.

Third Prize Rs. 150, for any quantity not less than 50 seers.

That Rs. 250 should be expended in the purchase of eggs at Moorshedabad, to be forwarded to the Punjab for distribution among local applicants.

These measures for the year 1855.

and 1856.

6. For 1856 the Society proposed prizes of Rs. 500, 350, and 200, respectively, for the encouragement of the cultivation of *morus multicaulis*, and in the meantime asked to be allowed to appropriate some 90 or 100 beegahs of land, near their garden, for the cultivation of the same plant.

Scheme sanctioned.

7. The Chief Commissioner supported these proposals, which were, with one exception, sanctioned by Lord Dalhousie. The exception was the proposal to annex to the Society's garden about 100 beegahs for the growth of mulberry, a proposal which was considered likely to cost more than its object was worth. This view came to be acquiesced in by the Society itself, and early in 1855 the Chief Commissioner applied definitely for the assignment of Rs. 17,000 for the experiment. This was calculated as follows:—

Spent in 1853 and 1854	...	...	... Rs. 5,279
Estimate for 1855	...	...	... „ 5,620
„ „ 1856	...	...	... „ 5,960
		TOTAL	...Rs. 16,859

"Already," writes Mr. (Sir R.) Temple, "a skilled and practical European Superintendent has been secured, and some silk-winders from Bengal have been employed, and furnaces and other apparatus constructed. There is a good stock of seed in store, and further quantities have been obtained from Cashmere and Bengal. It will be expedient to employ more winders in order to give the Superintendent full occupation and to initiate Punjabees into the art. With the same view also the apparatus will need enlargement.

"On the supposition, then, that the object is not to establish a large silk-factory as a Government concern, but to make an experiment on a moderate scale to test the practicability of producing indigenous silk, and, in the event of success, to induce natives of the Punjab to engage in the production, the Chief Commissioner would recommend that the Society be permitted to carry on their silk operations for two more years, *i. e.,* to the close of 1856, at a cost not exceeding Rs. 17,000, but it may be proper, perhaps, to render the above limits quite absolute, and to explain to the Society that they are on no account to be exceeded. Before the expiry of the above period, it will be clearly seen whether Punjabees, generally, will

* The Calcutta Agri-Horticultural Society had reported favourably on the silk in August 1854.

undertake the rearing of worms and the preparation of silk. If they do, then an important product will have been introduced at a cost not excessive. If they do not, still the amount expended will at least show that no reasonable effort has been spared for this object."

Progress of the experiment in 1855;

8. Accordingly, a sum of Rs. 17,000 in all was sanctioned, on the "distinct understanding that no further assistance would be given by Government." The progress of the experiment in 1855 is thus described:—

"During the season of 1855 the experiment was vigorously carried on. There was as Superintendent a gentleman of much practical skill, and a staff of eleven silk-winders from Bengal. The worms were also, for the most part, of the Bengal species. At first the generation of the worms was very successful. The insects came forth in surprising abundance; they throve on the mulberry leaves that were given them, and at first began to spin excellent cocoons. Everything prospered until the weather became hot and the atmosphere dry, but as the spring advanced towards summer, the food became deteriorated by the shrivelling up of the leaves, the worms grew sickly, and the cocoons fell off. The early promise was fair, but the ultimate result was almost *nil*. Some 94lbs. of silk were produced, valued at Rs. 500, where some 800lbs. had been expected, valued at Rs. 6,000, and there only remained these scanty proceeds to set down against an expenditure of Rs. 12,000. After this season the European Superintendent abandoned the undertaking, but the silk-winders remained.

"Perceiving this state of things, the Chief Commissioner, at the commencement of 1856, directed the Council of the Society to deliberate on the further continuance of the experiment," and "it was then decided to continue the experiment during the season of 1856 by means of Cashmere silkworms, as there appeared a hope that, perhaps, this species would prove more hardy than the Bengal species, which had failed in 1855."

and 1856.
The experiment pronounced a failure.

9. But the same fate befel the Cashmere worms, and from the same cause, and the Society "pronounced the Lahore silk experiment to have failed *in toto*." The establishments were accordingly discharged, and the concern wound up at a net loss to Government of Rs. 9,469. The Chief Commissioner concluded that though possibly in the sub-montane districts silkworms might thrive, and in some of those districts it was said that experiments had been "occasionally conducted with a certain measure of success," yet in the Central Punjab, the climate would not permit of the establishment of sericulture. A few pounds of marketable raw silk might be produced as samples, but no considerable quantities could be raised. The prizes for mulberry and cocoons found, it is manifest, no competitors.

The following extract from the report of the Society's Secretary gives a fuller account of the second year's experiment:—

"For the first three weeks after hatching, nothing could be more promising than the appearance of the worms. At the commencement they were fed on the leaves of the *morus multicaulis* and *sinensis* from the plantations in the Society's gardens, the common mulberry of the country not having come into leaf for a fortnight later, the number of worms daily increasing until the beginning of April, when their daily supply reached 80 to 100 maunds of leaves. They were consequently very indifferently fed, and only twice a day, and from the want of rain, and the drying winds which prevailed, notwithstanding every precaution was taken to keep the houses moist and cold, the leaves arrived in a dried shrivelled-up state, the worms began to fall off, and to spin very poor unhealthy cocoons much before the proper time. The earlier cocoons were shown at a meeting of the Society held on the 8th of April, and were remarkably fine, indeed quite equal to some samples of Hatian cocoons exhibited with them. At that time 950 cocoons went to a seer; but latterly, when they fell off, it took upwards of 3,000 to make up a seer. Ten maunds of cocoons have been produced, which have yielded 79¾lbs. of clean silk."

This experiment not held conclusive by some.

10. Some of those, however, who at first accepted the failure of these experiments as conclusive, saw reason afterwards to change their opinion. For instance, Mr. (now Sir Donald) McLeod, who, as a member of the local Agricultural and Horticultural Society, had taken a strong interest in the attempt to establish sericulture in the Punjab, wrote to the Chief Commissioner in September 1858, saying,—

"I now believe that two fundamental errors were commited, which mainly led to failure. One, that no mulberry plantation was previously established of sufficient extent to feed the very large quantity of worms raised, which led to their being latterly insufficiently fed, and on leaves which having been collected at heavy expense, from distant localities, wherever mulberries could be found, were dried up before they reached the worm-sheds, and were no longer fitted for the purpose. The other, that the worms continued to be reared, as long as eggs were hatched, so that a large portion did not reach maturity until the weather became too hot and dry to admit of their maintaining a healthy existence." And Mr. McLeod believed that if these two errors were avoided, "it would yet be found possible to produce silk at a remunerative cost in the plains of the Punjab."

Mr. McLeod's views.

11. At the same time the Financial Commissioner admitted that the "hill and sub-montane tracts were better adapted for rearing silkworms than the dry hot plains of the Central Punjab," and stated that "the matter was being taken up in earnest, and with every prospect of success by the Cashmeerees inhabiting the former localities." He also drew attention to the *bombyx Huttoni* and the tusser moth, and pointed out the existence of feeding-grounds of wild mulberry and *ber*, respectively suited to these two species. The letter concluded thus :—"It is not probable that Government will at present itself renew the experiment lately abandoned, but I believe that experiment, though in one sense a failure, to have been productive of very important advantages, fully commensurate with the outlay incurred, both by pointing out the errors to be avoided, and the localities best suited for the purpose, and by arousing enquiry, and exciting an interest in the subject. I shall continue to afford all the aid and encouragement in my power to all who may engage in the undertaking by affording such information as may be available, and endeavouring to interest local officers in the promotion of this new and important article of export, and I feel assured that the Chief Commissioner and the Government will gladly lend their countenance to all well-judged efforts directed to this end." In furtherance of these views, the Financial Commissioner forwarded to all local officers copies of the paper by Mr. Cope, from which the above narrative has been largely borrowed, and also of one by the same author on the silk *manufactures* of the Punjab—manufactures in which the material was of necessity for the time of foreign origin, being, to a large extent, imported through Afghanistan from Khorasan and Bokhara.

Mr. Cope's further experiments.

12. Mr. Cope, too, who had taken the leading part in the experiments of 1854—1856, was not discouraged, and in 1859 commenced another attempt to rear the Cashmere worm at Umritsur, where an abundance of leaves of the *standard* mulberry was to be had. A small number of cocoons were sent down to the Agri-Horticultural Society, and most favourably reported on by Count Fieschi, Mr. C. E. Blechynden, and Mr. Turnbull, of Ghattal Factory. Count Fieschi wrote :—"The cocoons are very beautiful, both for the shape and colour, and if they were more 'étoffés,' I should not find any difference between them and the finest of my country." Mr. Blechynden declared the cocoons superior to any he had seen reared in the country. "They would probably," he wrote, "be equal to Italian, if, as I suspect, the worms, at the time they were attaining maturity, and about to spin, had not experienced a sudden change of temperature,"—a suspicion confirmed by Mr. Cope. Mr. Turnbull, who reeled 100 of the cocoons, reported that they were twice as heavy as the cocoons of the Bengal annual (bara palu); that 5½ tolahs of cocoons yielded 9½ annas of silk, or 10·84 per cent., "which is something unknown." "Another great advantage is that 5 chittacks of fine silk could be reeled in a day, whilst I reel 3½ chittacks. The silk, I have no hesitation in saying, ought to sell higher than any of the Bengal mark, with careful reeling, and not be far off the Italian silk. I consider it, I may say, to be faultless, having a good colour, gloss, and mellow, taking into consideration its fibre; but there is one thing wanting: it has little or no elasticity." Mr. Turnbull was so pleased with the cocoons, that he ordered 100 rupees' worth of eggs, to try how they would thrive in Bengal, "as the boro poloo is degenerating fast." The silk was valued by a silk-broker in Calcutta at 22 to 23 shillings per pound.

Perseverance of Jaffir Ali.

13. Mr. Cope also writes :—"Jaffir's small establishment at Dheria has done remarkably well this season (1859), and he talks of retaining 3 seers of eggs for next year's operations. His stock, of which I have seen large portions, is perfectly healthy, and I hope to see a new silk colony rising in that neighbourhood in the course of a few years."

Mr. Cope's operations in 1860.

14. Mr. Cope continued the experiment on a larger scale in 1860. He gives the following account of his proceedings:—"I commenced with eggs of three different stocks: the first and largest, the produce of worms of my own rearing in 1859, preserved in a tahkhana; the second, obtained direct from Cashmere; and the third, a small part of a supply received from Bokhara by Lieutenant Powlett, Assistant Commissioner of Peshawur," who alone among district officers seemed to be taking much interest in the question of sericulture. "The acclimated eggs were the first to hatch; beginning on 21st February. The numbers continued to increase rapidly, until many thousands were hatched per day, and the whole batch ultimately filled 700 baskets in various stages of their existence, exhibiting to the very last day, with the exception of a very few baskets carelessly neglected by the Cashmeeree in charge, that unmistakeably healthy appearance that distinguishes the sound from the unsound worm. The Bokhara eggs were the next to hatch, beginning on the 24th February and coming on most freely, while the eggs from Cashmere did not evince any symptoms of vitality till the 2nd (? 22nd) March, or more than a month later than the acclimated, when they began to hatch very freely, and continued to do so till 6th April. Am I far wrong in assuming the dates of first hatching, as degrees of the barometer (? thermometer) and that the Bokhara silkworm temperature is consequently intimately related to that of Umritsur, the difference in the hatching of the respective eggs being only three days? The various periods at which the worms came into life afforded, moreover, useful indications for the future, and though I should always introduce a small fresh stock from Cashmere every year, in the event of the cultivation being largely extended, I should most certainly trust to the acclimated eggs for the bulk of my rearing, seeing how much earlier they hatch, giving the worms the very material advantage of a considerably lower temperature throughout the course of their brief existence (about 38 days) than could be afforded by the later period at which the Cashmere worms come forward. It was my desire to have ascertained, by keeping them separate throughout, whether there was any difference between the acclimated, the Bokhara, and the Cashmere worms; but through the further carelessness of the man in charge, the two latter were mixed up with the acclimated stock at the time of moving them from one house to the other, and could not subsequently be distinguished. Up to the time of their being moved, however, there was no perceptible difference between the three broods. The temperature in my office, where the main body of the worms was located, never rose above 78°, up to the date of the spinning of the last cocoon: whereas Signor Mutti found that in the Deccan they could bear a heat of 83°, but not more, 75° being the temperature under the influence of which they throve to the best advantage. In a rearing-house properly constructed, I make no doubt that the temperature could be kept to that point, or even lower, up to the middle of April, when all operations with acclimated eggs would cease; with the bulk, days before." The greater part of the cocoons had to be sent down to Bengal for reeling, and suffered on the journey. Nevertheless Mr. Turnbull, of Ghattal, reeled off some silk which was "greatly admired and again valued above Bengal silk." Some of the silk was sent to England, and was very favourably reported on, being valued at 25 shillings per lb.

Acknowledgment of Mr. Cope's efforts.

15. For his exertions in the matter of silk, as well as in connexion with the general improvement of the staples of the Punjab, Mr. Cope was given a grant of 100 acres of good land, near Umritsur, rent-free in perpetuity.

Mr. Cope's operations in 1861.

16. In 1861, Mr. Cope reared only a small number of worms as compared with the previous year, and though his manager had gone to Cashmere and he had to "put up with a dissipated Bengali," having himself little leisure to attend to the worms, he obtained a "considerable quantity of very fair cocoons," which when reeled by Jaffir Ali of Dehria "after his coarse fashion," yielded a silk which sold readily, at Umritsur, for Rs. 14-8 the seer, or Rs. 2 above the price of Bokhara silk.

Mr. Cope on the mulberry.

17. Mr. Cope expressed his intention of devoting the next season (1862) to experiments with the different kinds of mulberry. He described the existing species as four in number:—

(1.) "The common standard mulberry tree, apparently the *morus nigra*." The great objection to this was that it was "mostly fruit-bearing, and that in such masses, that the removal of the unripe fruit from among the leaves occupies much time and involves much trouble," while the male plant does not propagate with facility from cuttings.

(2.) "The shah-tút or royal mulberry, with long, white, sweet fruit, introduced, it is said, from Cashmere, grafted on the indigenous stock, and so much prized for its fruit, that it would be difficult to induce the proprietors to part with the leaves, as they say the stripping them off would injure the tree." Otherwise Mr. Cope considered the plant well suited for feeding worms and promised to try to propagate the male by cuttings.

(3.) The Philippine mulberry or *morus multicaulis*, a most prolific plant, first introduced into the Punjab from Saharunpore in 1853. "The growth," says Mr. Cope, "is sometimes astonishing. Cuttings put down in February 1861 have shot up into plants now (October), all more than six feet high, while many are eight, nine and ten, and some as high as twelve feet, covered from top to bottom of their numerous, wide-spreading stems with fine healthy leaves; while such is the power of reproduction of this species that I am within bounds when I assert that 95 per cent. of cuttings put down in February will thrive if treated with the most ordinary care, and watered to a reasonable extent. The more it is cut, the greater number of stems, and, as a matter of course, of leaves does it produce. Its roots strike deeply, and if, on taking up any plant, parts of the root are left in the ground, any where near the surface, they throw new stems in a very short time."

(4.) The Chinese mulberry or *morus sinensis* obtained from Saharunpore at the same time as the *M. multicaulis*. "It is propagated with equal facility with the *M. multicaulis*, but though the leaves are very much larger (some full 12 inches from the stalk to the apex and 9 inches broad), I do not think the crop, in weight of leaves, on an average number of plants of each kind of the same age, would be found so great." * * * "The plants are on the whole taller than those of *M. multicaulis*. My present impression is that the latter will be found best suited for cultivation and for feeding the worms." Mr. Cope, in the same paper, reported that in other directions measures were being taken towards the encouragement of sericulture. For instance, the irrigation officers were planting out mulberry along the canals; the Raja of Kupoorthulla was commencing plantations in the Jullundhur Doab; Jaffir Ali of Dehria was endeavouring to extend his cultivation, and people were stirring in the matter "about Soojanpore and Pathankote;" Kareem Khan of Tiloknath had been employed, besides carrying on his own small filature, by a planter in the Kangra valley; the better kinds of mulberry shrubs had been planted at Dhurmsala, and were said to be thriving, and some of the tea-planters, in the Kangra valley, had expressed their full determination to graft silk cultivation on their own immediate pursuit. One had planted mulberry largely; another had applied for cuttings, and the overseer of the Government tea plantation at Holta, who had a quantity of Philippine and Chinese mulberry at his disposal, had reared silkworms, and 28 seers of his cocoons were being wound at Umritsur.

Mr. Cope's operations in 1862; and further proposals.

18. In 1862, Mr. Cope continued his experiments, but not seemingly with much success, a result which he attributed to want of proper accommodation for the worms. But in May of that year he addressed the Financial Commissioner of the Punjab, urging that Government should again carry out an experiment on a considerable scale. He observed:—"The chief requirements to the successful rearing of the silkworm, are food of a good kind and in abundance, and suitable accommodation. The former is now available at Umritsur. In the public gardens there are 500 well-grown foreign mulberry plants, 18,000 of from 6 to 10 feet high, and about 100,000 plants which, in March next year, will be 6 to 8 feet high, yielding an abundance of leaves. There are about

1,000 country plants well grown, and a large number of trees alongside the roads, which, judiciously trimmed, would afford a large amount of food without suffering any damage. I have seven beegahs of land thickly planted, the produce of which I should be happy to make available for the year 1863, and if it should be necessary to purchase, there are abundance of trees in private gardens, the leaves of which the owners would sell; and, finally, I should be happy to give my small services for superintendence, of course, free of all remuneration." For the preparation of a proper rearing-house and establishment, Mr. Cope proposed an expenditure of about Rs. 3,000.

Orders of the Lieutenant-Governor.

19. The Financial Commissioner strongly supported the proposal, and in confirmation of the view that worms could be successfully reared in the Punjab, forwarded copy of a report on the native establishment of Jaffir Ali in Goordaspore, and added that five other natives had, during the year, raised silk in that and the Umritsur district. The proposal of the Financial Commissioner to grant Mr. Cope a sum of Rs. 2,000, was sanctioned by the Lieutenant-Governor of the Punjab, who also authorized a sum of Rs. 500 being presented to Jaffir Ali "to reward him for his past exertions and to enable him to extend his operations," and His Honor observed:—"It is of great importance that Jaffir, and others who follow his example, should meet with every encouragement from the local authorities, and that the cultivation of the mulberry should be extended. If then, with this object in view, you think it proper to make any proposals for remitting the revenue on lands planted with mulberries *bonâ fide* for the purpose of feeding silkworms, His Honor will be prepared to consider them favourably, and to sanction the bestowal annually of khilats on those who undertake to rear worms, and are successful." And a further report was called for as to operations at Peshawur, while an annual general report was also requested. Mr. Cope's experiments in 1863 proved, on his own admission, "a total failure." In 1864 he prosecuted the attempt at his own expense, entrusting a large quantity of Cashmere and indigenous eggs to a son of Jaffir Ali, and bidding him to follow out his own method of raising and feeding the worms. The result was "a magnificent crop of some eight maunds of cocoons"; and this was not a final report on the outturn of the season, Mr. Cope expecting when he wrote, 2 or 3 maunds more.

Account of Jaffir Ali's filature.

20. Lieutenant Powlett's account of Jaffir Ali's establishment, referred to above, is as follows:—

Conformably with Mr. McLeod's wishes, I proceed to give as good an account as I can of Jaffir's silk-raising establishment at Durreah Pattun in Goordaspore, which I visited in order to get some hints on the subject of silk-culture in the plains.

On my way to Durreah Pattun, I ascertained that considerable interest is felt by the neighbourhood in Jaffir's proceedings, increased no doubt by the jealousy he displays lest any one, unconnected with himself, should attempt silk cultivation, which he would fain keep as a monopoly in his own family. I was told that many would be glad of eggs, but Jaffir had refused to part with any; and indeed would allow no one near his worms, not even his own son! His objection to allow any one to approach the worms does not arise so much from jealousy as from a superstitious fear of the evil eye, to which fatal sickness among silkworms is, I believe, attributed all over Asia.* Jaffir told me that English gentlemen were alone permitted to see them.

On my reaching Durreah Pattun, the first thing Jaffir insisted on shewing me was the medal obtained for him by Mr. Cope from the Agri-Horticultural Society. He carries it about him, and seems not a little proud of it. He told me that he had been established at Durreah Pattun some twenty years, and that he originally learnt silk-rearing at Peshawur, where formerly valuable silk was raised; there were two establishments for the purpose when he was there.

I particularly questioned him regarding his stock of eggs, and measures for preserving them during the heat; as I was anxious to ascertain whether there was any trace of deterioration in the worms from plain-raised eggs, or whether renewal from the hills was beneficial. He assured me that, so far from deteriorating, acclimatised eggs were far better than hill-raised, as the

* The same prejudice exists on the part of the men (usually of the bearer or Kahar caste) who tend the tusser or wild silk. From the time when the worms are hatched and placed upon the trees in the forest, which they have previously prepared for their reception, they watch carefully that nothing from without may come near them, keeping themselves at the same time most punctiliously apart from all that might render them ceremonially impure.

latter produced in the plains sickly worms, many of which died in skin-casting, and on his commencing business, he found it necessary to procure eggs from Peshawur, as the Cashmere stock he had was unprofitable, and ever since, that is, for 20 years and upwards, he has raised his own eggs, keeping them during the hot weather in a "tahkhanah" at Majeetha in the Umritsur district. This method of preserving them is not, however, satisfactory, as from a fourth to a third is always destroyed by the heat. Jaffir shewed a quantity so destroyed, for the most part the heat had dried up the eggs, without hatching the worms. Those that survive the heat are not injured, but produce as healthy and fine worms as if the eggs had been kept in a cool climate. This the state of Jaffir's own worms clearly demonstrated, but it will undoubtedly be a great advantage to establish (when silk cultivation has extended itself) a depôt in the hills, where eggs may be kept during the hot weather. The carriage backward and forward would probably not cost 2 annas a seer, whereas loss by keeping them in "tahkhanahs" in the plains is (reckoning their value at 16 rupees a seer), 4 or 5 rupees a seer. Out of "tahkhanahs," the eggs cannot be preserved in the plains at all.

None of Jaffir's worms had commenced spinning when I saw them (April 7th); they were of various ages, some would begin in 4 days, some in 6, some not for 10, 12, or even 15 days; these last three sets were not of much value.

As I was under the impression that the silkworm was very delicate, I was much surprised to find Jaffir's, though under such poor shelter and so crowded, looking so fine and well. Two old pauls and five or six sheds, both very low, and the latter ill-ventilated, contain the whole of his stock. A hovel 30 feet, and scarcely high enough to allow a man to stand upright, held sufficient to produce three seers of silk; there was nothing to keep them off the ground beyond the accumulation of mulberry branches, which were removed but once in eight days; they occupied the whole of the ground of the shed with exception of a passage, 1½ feet wide, down the centre. In the pauls the worms lay as in the sheds; there was nothing, beyond a single fly, to keep out the rays of the sun, for such trees as there were near the pauls gave little shade. The worms, nevertheless, looked as well as could be wished. Jaffir said he certainly should be glad to give his worms change of air and position oftener than he could afford to do with the space at his command, but he laughed at any elaborate sanitary arrangements, and said it would never do for any but amateurs to adopt them.

In answer to my queries about the value of the silk he produced, Jaffir told me that last year he sold it at Rs. 15-8 a seer, and this seemed the average rate. As I happen to have made notes of the value at Peshawur of the different descriptions of imported silk, I can assert that the above is a higher price than is there obtained for the common Kokan, Bokhara, and Khulm silk, and within a few annas of the value of that called "lab-i-abee," which is raised on the banks of the Oxus, where the best Central Asian silk is, I believe, produced. Jaffir himself admitted that his profits were amply remunerative, and the impression in the vicinity is that he is wealthy, and that too in the face of considerable disadvantages. The greater portion of his mulberry leaves have to be brought two or three kos from the villages round, and as he has no trees of his own, he is at the mercy of the villagers, who, of course, endeavour to get as much as possible for their leaves. He was complaining bitterly of the owners of some, four kos off, for unconscionably raising the price of leaves, and thus depriving him of the supply, which he had always had until the present year. In addition to the price of the leaves, he has of course to pay for their conveyance, which costs no inconsiderable sum, as he is obliged to employ 12 men for the purpose. His out-turn averages 20 seers a year, and to supply his worms he requires 600 small mulberry trees. He has lately taken 5 acres of land, on lease, and planted some 1,500 trees on it, and is making a well. He is trying the Chinese and Philippine mulberry, having procured a number of cuttings from Mr. Cope, of Umritsur.

Jaffir informed me that a seer of good seed (eggs) should produce 21 seers of silk, or if the silk is sacrificed, the same weight of eggs; for it is said that the amount of seed produced by a given number of worms is equal to the amount of silk which would be yielded by an equal number, and this the price of seed (Rs. 16 a seer) in Cashmere bears out. The amount of silk that a certain number of cocoons will yield varies very much. Jaffir told me he had sometimes not two seers of silk out of 11 seers of (dried) cocoons, sometimes not one seer; the best cocoons should yield one seer for five. He knew nothing of cross-breeding, never having tried it. He raises silk but once a year. I believe it is possible to have a second crop, but Jaffir said that it could never pay, as the leaves lose their nourishing properties in the heats of summer; he seemed to think, too, the young tender leaves were necessary for the young worms. I should think Jaffir was right on this point, with reference to silk culture in the dry plains, though in the hills it may be different. He feeds his worms morning and evening. The leaves should be as fresh as possible, but are dangerous if given wet.

Jaffir winds his own silk; he said that he could wind four seers a month, working up to 12 o'clock in the day, which over a fire in the hot weather is as much as he can comfortably manage. If hard put to it, he would wind six seers a month. When winding, three assistants are necessary, to keep up the fire, &c. The dry branches of the mulberries, from which the leaves have been stripped, are sufficient to keep the pot that holds the cocoons boiling, so he is put to no further expense for firewood. The cocoons from which moths have been produced are worth two rupees a seer, being many times lighter than cocoons containing chrysalises. The latter cocoons, when dried, vary in value from eight annas to one rupee a seer.

Jaffir's success convinces me that there is no real obstacle to the unlimited extension of silk cultivation in the plains. The difficulties that have deterred the people are probably—

1st.—The necessity of investing a little capital at commencement; *2nd,* the want of immediate success that attends attempts with unacclimated seed; *3rd,* the utter ruin that the destruction of the mulberry trees entails, and this, in the time of the Sikhs, was pretty sure to occur whenever troops passed near them.

In districts where mulberry trees are plentiful (as in Peshawur, where silk culture was re-introduced three years ago by Captain Graham, and is now, I believe, promising well) but little encouragement will, most likely, be necessary. The plains on the salt range at Choya Sydan Shah*, and elsewhere, are celebrated for their mulberry trees, where they have the advantage of being watered by perennial streams, and, possibly, such places would be very suitable for extensive farms. In other districts the plan which is now being tried at Goojranwalla would probably be successful, *viz.*, a mulberry plantation will be established at the sudder station sufficiently large to make it worth the while of an experienced Cashmere silk-raiser to settle there and take charge of it. The plantation will soon become profitable to Government, and repay any advances that at first may be necessary for seed and sheds; the villages round will be encouraged to plant mulberry trees and keep worms, the management of which is simple enough, and the Cashmeeree would gladly purchase the cocoons from them at very remunerative rates.

The situation of the manufactory at the sudder station would render it easy to introduce improvements in the rearing, and winding of the silk, as information on the subject was collected.

I am aware that much that I have mentioned has been before stated by Mr. Cope, whose pamphlet on silk cultivation first gave me an interest in the matter, but perhaps information received from a successful silk-raiser may not be, at the present, uninteresting, although it is for the most part but repetition.

Experiment in the Peshawur Valley in 1863-64.

21. Mr. Scarlett, under date 11th July 1863, gives an account of a silk experiment at Peshawur. The trial was begun with about 4½ lbs. of eggs obtained;—

35 tolahs from Jelalabad.
16 tolahs from Bokhara.
14 „ acclimatized.
120 „ from Jaffir Ali of Goordaspore.

Three places were selected, Peshawur itself, the village of Khajána, in the Dáoodzai Pergunnah, and Charsadda, beyond the Kábul river. The experiment at the last place failed altogether, the eggs (Bokhara and acclimatized) not hatching. The Jelalabad eggs were tried at Khajána and with success. The eggs obtained from Jaffir Ali were reserved for the Peshawur "silkery." The eggs were left to hatch in an open basket on the sunny side of a room with an average temperature of 76°. They hatched irregularly. The young worms were fed with tender leaves stripped from the branches, but as they grew stronger the branches themselves were strewn over them. The consumption of leaves rose from 2 to 50 loads a day; the supply, chiefly of *morus alba,* was obtained from trees growing along the roads, or on Government lands. Lettuce was used with a few worms which hatched prematurely, and to all appearance with success. The average period of existence, in the worm stage, was 50 days, and 48 hours the average time spent in spinning the cocoon. The worms were, on the whole, healthy, but some presented a jaundiced appearance and were removed. "All diseases are ascribed to either (1) the use of damp floors or leaves, electrical state of the atmosphere, overcrowding, want of ventilation, insufficiency of nourishment; and these ascriptions have been corroborated by European experience; (2) the presence of evil spirits and of unclean persons. I need hardly add that these subtle enemies of the worm have, as yet, evaded the closest European scrutiny. It is a lamentable fact that the diseased worm cannot be doctored; so in the absence of cure, certain preventives are adopted, such as ventilation, cleanliness, and fumigation. The first two call for no particular remark, the third is a simple process. Earthen stoves, lighted in different parts of the silkery, are occasionally sprinkled with 'isfand' (or 'harmal,' *peganum harmala,* the wild rue of botanists, abundant on waste grounds in the Punjab), a grain to which native superstition ascribes the virtue of scaring evil spirits. I am at present unable to say whether it possesses any

* The arable lands on the salt range are situated in valleys of very considerable elevation and great beauty, enjoying a climate very much milder than that of the plains, and exceedingly salubrious. Choya Sydan Shah is situated in one of these valleys, which possesses an abundant supply of running water, and, in consequence, most luxuriant vegetation; but this is by no means generally the case, a want of water being seriously felt in most parts.

value as a disinfectant. Rats, mice, and birds also committed some havoc. The cocoons varied in size and colour. The largest weighed, deducting floss silk and worms, about 5 grains, the smallest, scarcely a grain, the average, 2 grains; most were of a light yellow colour, while the rest were either straw-coloured or white. The first are said to yield the finest silk."

Twelve seers of cocoons were set apart for seed and allowed to eat out, which they did in about a week, and yielded 115 tolahs of eggs. The rest were killed by exposure to the sun for a few hours on three consecutive days. The silk was then reeled in the rude native fashion, two men working at each reel. The average number of filaments composing the Peshawur (double) thread is stated to have been eighty. This is, perhaps, a misprint for *eighteen*. The total quantity of silk was 25 lbs. with 10 lbs. of "sarmakh" or coarse ends, 8 lbs. of punctured cocoons, and 52 lbs. of refuse (floss silk, &c).

	ozs.	lb.	ozs.
1,000 cocoons weighed		1	0
Floss silk and impurities	6		
Worms and glutinous matter	8		
	—	0	14
Balance of silk ...		0	2

Specimens of the filaments were measured and found to vary from $\frac{9}{4500}$ to $\frac{38}{4500}$ of an inch in diameter.

The silk, though uneven, was valued at Rs. 16 per seer of 104 tolahs, or about Rs. 12-5 per ordinary seer. The Vardanzai, or best Bokhara silk, is put down at Rs. 17 per seer of 104 tolahs.

"Pursuant to this experiment," continues Mr. Scarlett, "a meeting of the principal members of the commercial community was called, and the whole subject discussed, and it was resolved that a commercial company should be formed.

"A paper embodying the following propositions was drawn up and signed:—

1. That a company be formed consisting of 20 shareholders, paying Rs. 50 each;
2. That members possessing land cultivate as many acres as they can spare with mulberry, on the condition of being remunerated;
3. That the Paráchá members arrange to procure a supply of eggs from Bokhara and elsewhere;
4. That three or four families of silk-rearers be invited over from the nearest silk-growing districts and encouraged to settle at Peshawur.

"Active measures are on foot to ensure the success of this object. The supply of eggs for the ensuing season will probably be—

	115	tolahs accumulated at Peshawur.
	160	,, from Jaffir Ali.
	360	,, ,, Bokhara.
Total ...	635	tolahs or nearly 16 lbs.

"The silkeries are intended to be as numerous, and as widely scattered in the district, as the agency at command shall admit of. About 32 acres of fresh land are being planted with mulberry. It was intended to introduce the large-leaved species *M. multicaulis*, but the latest trials in Italy have shewn that it is not suited for the silkworm. An invitation has been sent to some families of silk-rearers to emigrate from Kajja, a district near Jelalabad; I am assured there will be no difficulty in effecting this. The families thus obtained, with those already in the valley, will afford all the necessary subordinate agency, while the members of the company now formed will undertake the direction and supervision."

The Government of the Punjab, in March 1864, sanctioned the expenditure of Rs. 550 in prizes and rewards to those engaged in the experiment, and placed a further sum of Rs. 500 at Mr. Scarlett's disposal for the then current year. That gentleman went to England before the operations of the year were concluded; but they were so successful that the participators in the scheme realized a profit of 42 per cent. Nevertheless the company dissolved, and gradually the whole experiment seems to have followed its fate.

22. **A trial was made in Googaira in 1863, of which the following is a narrative by Mr. Peake :—**

Experiment at Googaira in 1863.

Five tolahs of eggs were received from Peshawur in a closed tin-case. The box was opened about the 8th of March, and the hatching was found to have commenced. The young worms were first fed on tender leaves; and then gradually, as they grew in size and strength, allowed small sprigs and larger branches.

Two rooms were used, one $10 \times 14 \times 11$ feet in size; the windows were allowed to be kept open till the second week in April, when they were closed during the heat of the day. Charpoys were employed to form terraces or shelves upon; they were placed in an inclined position. Across these beds strings were carried, 2 feet apart, and the same distance above the bed; the stems of the branches rested on the beds and the tops on the cross strings.

The advantages of the plan were threefold—(1) the air circulated freely from all sides of the branches; (2) the excrements dropped on the bed and rolled down, and were thus easily swept away twice a day; (3), the branches were replenished with ease, as well as removed, without disturbing the worms in the least. It was amusing to observe how quickly they moved on to the fresh branches as soon as they were laid on. The room was on the south-east corner of the house, where light and air could be freely admitted. The temperature averaged about 75°, extremes being 62° and 80°. The second room was on a second floor with a door and two windows; the temperature was two degrees higher, and a greater amount of light and air was available. The maximum quantity of leaves, I think, never amounted to more than three loads per day for each room. This was supplied from trees growing in gardens and those on the road-side. The mulberry leaves used were of the white kind (*Morus alba*) only; these trees grow very luxuriantly at this station. The first cocoon appeared on the 35th day, but they began to increase in number, perceptibly, about the 42nd day, and on the 52nd day they were gathered. The worms appeared healthy throughout the time occupied in the formation of the cocoons. As soon as the cocoons began to appear, light bundles of brushwood were placed on the four sides of the charpoys, which were quickly occupied; very soon after, the worms began to spin, and in from forty-six to forty-eight hours the cocoons were quite formed. Of the remaining one-third of the eggs, the hatching was not attended to for ten days, the eggs being kept in the tin-box, yet they succeeded pretty fairly, only a few of the worms having died.

From 2,250 cocoons 35 tolahs of eggs were produced. The total yield of the two places was as follows :—

Rooms.	Eggs.	Cocoons in number.	Cocoons in weight.
	Tolahs.		Tolahs.
1st ...	9¾	3,587	574
2nd ...	3¼	6,122	950
Total ...	13	9,709	1,524

The various colors of the above, bore the following proportions :—

Rooms.	Yellow.	Straw.	White.	Total.
1st ...	850	550	2,187	3,587
2nd ...	1,701	1,223	3,198	6,122
Total ...	2,551	1,773	5,385	9,709

Mr. Cope pronounced the cocoons very good. I shall here quote from his letter :—"All I can say of the cocoons is that they are remarkably fine, and if you can rear any quantity of the same quality, the credit of Googaira, as a silk-rearing locality, would be at a very high figure."

There are about 600 mulberry trees in this station. The area of alluvial land which is available for the cultivation of these trees is extensive, and if the civil station is eventually removed to Sahiewal, this place would make a capital locality for sericulture, and the abandoned buildings would afford good breeding quarters, and the gardens any amount of leaves. I have ordered a rood or more to be planted with cuttings at every well.

23. **Dr. Henderson, the Civil Surgeon, gives the following account of an experiment at Shahpoor :—**

At Shahpoor in 1864.

In February 1864, an experiment, on a small scale, was commenced at Shahpoor under rather unfavourable circumstances, owing to the paucity of mulberry trees in the station, and the necessity of bringing leaves from a distance, and paying highly for them.

The result of the experiment shows how very profitable silk culture will be in the Punjab, in more suitable localities than Shahpoor. During half the time the experiment was going on, I was absent from the station on duty. The worms were all along attended to by coolies, who collected the mulberry leaves—many of whom had never before even seen silkworms.

Two tolahs of eggs were obtained on 10th February from Umritsur, and on the 1st of March, 15 tolahs more came from Peshawur, which were hatched in successive portions artificially; up to March 12th, the hatching was effected as usual by putting the eggs in a flannel bag, and getting a man to carry them close to his chest for about 70 hours. Putting the eggs below a hen might succeed.

On the 22nd March, the worms consumed 6 seers of leaves a day, and one coolie was sufficient to attend on them. On the 24th, an extra man had to be entertained. On April 6th, five men had hard work to bring enough leaves; and before the first cocoon was commenced on April 12th, nine men were employed. On the 17th April, most of the worms were ready to spin, or had completed their cocoons, and by the 1st May, there were 78lbs. of dried cocoons, and 10lbs. not dried, but kept to give eggs. The greatest space occupied by the worms was 800 square feet, but they were crowded.

Two weavers were sent to Goojranwalla to learn to reel; they returned and commenced operations in June. At first they made very coarse silk, but the last seer reeled fetched Rs. 18 at Mooltan. The following is a statement of the actual cost of the experiment:—

	Rs.	A.	P.
Cost of 17 tolahs of eggs	5	0	0
Coolies for collecting leaves and attending the worms at Rs. 5 per mensem	39	0	0
Leaves purchased	9	0	0
Two weavers sent for a month to Goojranwalla	12	0	0
Iron pan used in reeling	5	0	0
Reeling apparatus	1	8	0
Cost of reeling, being the wages of two reelers at Rs. 6 a month	25	0	0
TOTAL ...	96	8	0
The proceeds of the experiment were 16lbs. of reeled silk, sold at Mooltan	117	0	0
35 tolahs of eggs, valued at	8	0	0
Value of iron pan and reel	4	12	0
TOTAL ...	129	12	0

The actual profit was Rs. 33-4, but had there been no need of purchasing reeling apparatus and leaves, then Rs. 40-8 might be deducted, being a net cost of Rs. 56 and a profit of Rs. 73-12.

These 35 tolahs of eggs obtained were divided into three portions; one was sent up to Sakesar, 5,000 feet; one was sent to a lower locality, called Sodhi valley; and the third was put in an earthen jar, covered with paper, and kept in a bath-room at Shahpoor; the two former portions were spoiled during the rains, but the third portion being kept in the coolest part of the house, were found in February 1865 to be in good condition, and are now being reared at Sahiewal. The climate of the salt range is much milder than that of the plains, and wild mulberry trees are abundant: also there is a wild species of silkworm indigenous, which feeds on the camel-thorn (*Alhagi maurorum*).

The following observations on the silk at Shahpoor may be found interesting. About one-fourth of the worms were black, and all the rest white. Three days before commencing to spin, the average length of each worm was 3 inches. One hundred of the largest black worms then weighed 8 ounces and 360 grains, or about 42 grains each; the cocoons they produced weighed 6 ounces and 220 grains, and these yielded 30 grains less than an ounce of eggs. One hundred of the largest white worms, selected at the same time, weighed 10 ounces and 420 grains, or about 52 grains each. They gave of cocoons 7 ounces and 220 grains, and gave 1 ounce and 70 grains of eggs; 4lbs. of the best cocoons produced by black worms gave 250 grains less than 7 ounces of eggs; 4 lbs. of white worms cocoons gave 160 grains less than 11 ounces of eggs: 18 lbs. of average cocoons yielded nearly 4¾lbs. reeled silk.

Want of record of result.

24. Some experiments were also made at Siyalkot. But I have not been able to trace the details. The record even of the Umritsur and Peshawur experiments is very defective. The Punjab Government has given a categorical "no" in answer to the enquiry whether further information exists. Indeed that Government did not even receive a report from Mr. Cope of the results of the renewed experiments in 1862-63.

Present state of silk production in the Punjab.

25. In Goordaspore the industry seems still to survive. Lieutenant Hutchinson, Assistant Commissioner of that district, writes in 1869 of two kinds of worms being reared, one yielding white and the other yellow silk; the latter valued at Rs. 18 or 19 the seer, the former about one rupee higher. As to the amount of silk manufactured, he does not give particulars. But I believe it is not large,* the manufacture is probably much as it was when described by Lieutenant Powlett in Jaffir's hands.

Silk manufactures in the Punjab.

26. But though the Punjab has not yet succeeded in producing raw silk to any great extent, its silk manufactures form an important sphere of industry. The chief seats of the manufacture are Umritsur, Lahore, Mooltan, Bhawulpore, and Jullundhur. Delhi, too, uses some silk in its embroideries.

Sources of supply of raw silk.

27. The sources of supply are thus enumerated by Mr. Davies (Report on Trade of Central Asia): "Kokand, Bokhara, Balkh, Khulm, Akcha, Shibberghaum, Andkho, Cashmere, Bengal, and China *viâ* Bombay." No silk had, when Mr. Davies wrote, been for four or five years imported from Khoten. Mr. Cope, writing in 1852, gives, from "a good authority," the following account of the kinds of silk imported from the westward.

There are three kinds of silk imported:—

(1) Called *Verdan*, from Rs. 9 to 16 the seer of 101 tolahs: present price Rs. 11-12.

(2) *Busheree*, from Rs. 8-12 to 15: present price Rs. 10-12.

(3) *Nuwabee*, from Rs. 8-8 to 15: present price Rs. 10.

These all come from Khorasan, and are first-rate silks.

There are other sorts, *e. g.*:—

(4) *Chirkhee*, from Rs. 8-12 to 13-8: present price Rs. 8-12.

(5) *Phohen*, from Rs. 6 to 8-12: present price Rs. 7.

(6) *Tenee* a "prepared silk," from Rs. 10 to 19: present price Rs. 12;— besides twelve kinds of silk imported from Bengal, and varying in price from Rs. 2-8 to Rs 5 the seer. It is clear from this that only the worst kind of Bengal silk is imported, and to judge from what Mr. Cope says, the same is true of the imports of China silk. The Bokhara silk fetches, according to that authority, from 100 to 200 per cent. more than the China sorts used. But Khanikoff expressly declares the Bokhara silk inferior to that of China both in colour and softness.

Amount imported.

28. The following figures purport to give the importations into the Punjab in maunds of 100 lbs:—

Sumbut year.	Khorasan.	Bengal.	Total.
(1841) 1899	709	1,615	2,324
1900	1,825	926	2,751
1901	1,090	973	2,063
1902	66	700	766†
1903	980	667	1,647
1904	701	304	1,005
1905	..	232	232‡

A statement of the raw silk imports of the Punjab in 1852 gives the following figures:—

		lbs.
From China	...	2,466,605
" Bengal	...	1,335,951
" Other Countries	...	3,445,448
TOTAL	...	7,248,024

* Mr. Cope, in a letter to the Silk Supply Association, dated 1st February 1870, says the yield was 800lbs. in 1869, "the produce commanding a better price at Umritsur than the best Bokhara silk." In the same letter he says that several Mahommedan families of Pathankote and Soojanpur had taken up the industry independently of Jaffir Ali, and he maintains that "taking Deenanuggur as a base of operations, and proceeding north and north-east by Pathankote across the Chuckee towards Noorpore, very large plantations might be established and great silk operations carried on, if land could be procured on reasonable terms." This was the difficulty, according to Mr. Cope, which principally beset Jaffir Ali.

† First Punjab War. ‡ Second Punjab War.

But there is evidently some radical error in these figures. Mr. Davies values the silk trade at £200,000. This is of course the sum of the estimated exports and imports, and yet falls very far short of the value of the imports alone according to the figures quoted, even taking such a moderate average price for the silk as Rs. 3 per lb. Mr. Davies' estimate, on the other hand, may be too low, but not to such an extent as to allow of the discrepancy being reconciled.

Estimated value of manufactures.

29. In the Punjab Administration Reports for 1868-69 and 1869-70, the value of the silk *manufactures* of the province is set down at 13½ lakhs in the former, and 18¼ lakhs in the latter year. In the report for 1870-71, it is put down at 10½ lakhs.

Statistics of silk traffic at frontier fairs.

30. At the Palumpore fair of 1868, one merchant brought silks from Yarkand; the amount is not stated. Silk, both raw and manufactured, was also among the goods taken to the fair by merchants of Hooshyarpore, Mundee, Umritsur, and Noorpore. At the fair of November 1869, raw silk to the value of Rs. 14,860, and silk piece-goods to the value of Rs. 9,511 appear in the list of merchandise from Central Asia. The trade in this article at Palumpore seems to have fallen off the following year, for only Rs. 2,500 worth of raw silk was brought, and that does not seem to have been sold. And in the account of the fair of last November silk disappears from the narrative altogether.

At the Peshawur fair of 1869, 50 maunds 6 seers, brought by Cabul merchants, was sold for a total sum of Rs. 33,642, at Rs. 12, 16, and 21 per seer. Kincobs and embroidered silks to the value of Rs. 11,165 were, on the same occasion, sold by merchants of the Punjab for export. In the following year, however, only Rs. 4,609 worth of silk appears to have been sold at the Peshawur fair.

Railway imports and exports.

31. In the year ending 30th June 1871 the imports by rail from Bombay, *i. e.*, of *Chinese* raw silk, were (according to Mr. Rivett-Carnac's memorandum on the interchange of traffic between the Great Indian Peninsular and East Indian Railways) as follows :—

	lbs.
To Umritsur	35,424
„ Jullundhur	25,584
„ Delhi	4,674
„ Lahore	574
„ Mooltan	328
TOTAL ...	66,584

On the other hand, Umritsur sent to Bombay during the same year 21,156 lbs., and Mooltan sent 574 lbs. of raw silk, presumably imported from Turkistan or Afghanistan.

Imports by the Western passes.

32. Most of the western silk used in the Punjab is imported by the Khyber and other northern passes. But there is also a considerable import to Shikarpore in Sind, by the western passes, notably the Bolan; and Mooltan obtains a portion of its supply in this way. Mr. Cope in 1852 writes that Shikarpore imported 120 maunds annually from Bokhara and Khorasan* besides 131 maunds of China silk from Bombay *viâ* Kurrachee. And in 1840 Rohree on the Indus imported enough silk by way of Cabul to employ 160 looms. Dr. Forbes Watson mentions "Narrapore," "Runeepore," and Hyderabad in Sind as having sent specimens of mixed silk and cotton "loongees." Mr. Baden Powell (in his "Punjab Products") gives the following description of the kinds of raw silk imported into

* From recent correspondence it appears that silk has been successfully grown at Khelat in Beloochistan also. Captain Harrison, the Political Agent, says that two men have taken up the industry, and are encouraged by the Khan. The silk produced, however, is coarse: "similar to the inferior sort of China silk usually imported from Bombay," says the Kurrachee Chamber of Commerce. According to Captain Harrison, the two silk rearers clear Rs. 8,000 a year. There are "endless mulberry trees" in Khelat, Mustoong, and other valleys.

Shikarpore with their prices, after payment of import duty at Re. 1-6 per maund :—

1. Kokani, from Bokhara (produced in Turkistan), Rs. 4·42 per lb.
2. Tuni, from Herat, Rs. 6·08 per lb.
3. Shal-bafi, from Herat, Rs. 6·91 per lb.
4. Nawabi, from Bokhara, Rs. 6·52 per lb.
5. Gheilani, from Kirman and Yezd,* Rs. 4 per lb.
6. Kaluchir, from Herat, Rs. 4 per lb.

The annual value is said to be about Rs. 50,000.

Nos. 1, 2, 5, and 6 are prepared for weaving and dyed at Shikarpore; the Shal-bafi and Nawabi are manufactured at Rohree into a coarse silk fabric known as daryai.

Manufacture at Lahore;

33. Mr. Cope gives the following particulars as to silk manufacture at Lahore. In 1851, 229 Company's maunds of silk paid octroi duty. The price ranged during 1851-1855 from Rs. 11 to Rs. 13 per seer, having formerly been as high as Rs. 18 and Rs. 20; the seer being, in this case, a weight of 105 nanukshahee rupees = $\frac{17 \cdot 25 \times 105}{18 \times 80}$ = (about) 1¼ of a Company's seer. The range of price per pound would therefore be from Rs. 8·8 to Rs. 10·2. Mr. Cope calculates the value of silk manufactured from 229 maunds of raw produce at upwards of 2 lakhs of rupees, the number of persons employed in the industry being estimated at 935.

at Umritsur;

34. At Umritsur, according to the same authority, the import of Bokhara silk in 1851 amounted to 625 maunds, of which, however, 250 maunds were re-exported. The local manufacture employed 2,205 persons, and yielded goods valued at nearly 3½ lakhs. The same city also imported 1,148 maunds of Bengal silk at Rs. 1-8 to Rs. 2-8 the *seer*, all but 80 maunds being worked up in the city. The value of the fabrics produced from this silk Mr. Cope estimates at nearly 4 lakhs of rupees. Mr. Davies says:—"Raw silk is sent from Umritsur to all parts of the Punjab for manufacture. Silk fabrics to the value of 3 lakhs are manufactured at Umritsur. Those imported from Europe, Lahore, Bokhara, Bengal, and Benares are rated at £4,000, £3,500, £80,500, and £2,500 respectively." And the same authority gives the following figures as the value in rupees of the silk trade of Umritsur :—

	Annual value.	Jummoo and Cashmere.		Afghanistan and Countries Westward.	
		Exported to.	Imported from.	Exported to.	Imported from.
Raw silk	14,73,950	...	2,800	...	12,36,750
Silk fabrics	4,8600 0	62,000	...	10,500	1,000

From the statistics of the railway traffic it appears that Umritsur is the chief entrepôt for the Bokhara raw silk, not only for the rest of the Punjab, but for general exportation.

at Jullundhur;

35. Mr. Cope makes Jullundhur import 800 maunds nearly, of which 75 maunds were woven on the spot, the rest being only converted into thread and dyed, and in that form re-exported to Jummoo, Wazeerabad, Sealkote, and other places. Of the total supply ⅝ths were said to come from China *viá* Bombay, 2/8ths from Bengal, and ⅛th from the westward.

36. Mooltan in 1851, according to Mr. Cope, imported 370 maunds of Bokhara silk, the manufacture of which, *minus* 100 maunds re-exported, gave work to 811 persons. Mooltan also imported 60 maunds from Bombay.

at Mooltan;

The following account of silk at the same place by Lieutenant Corbyn, Assistant Commissioner, is cited by Mr. Baden Powell :—

"It has been ascertained from the best and most reliable sources that about 300 packages of 1st, 2nd, and 3rd quality raw silk, weighing in all 750 maunds, the price of which averages

* Or probably, as the name imports, from *Ghilán*.

Rs. 3,75,000, are imported annually into Mooltan from Kabul, Bokhara, Khorasan and Herat. Of this, 225 maunds, worth Rs. 1,12,500, are exported to the following places, *viz.*, Bhawulpore, Kurrachee, Bombay, Dera Ghazee Khan, Shikarpore, Sukkur, Hyderabad, Suratbundur, Delhi, Furruckabad, Bikaneer, Sirsa, Ajmere, Benares, Lahore, and Umritsur, &c.; 225 maunds of cleaned silk, after being dyed various colours, valued at Rs. 1,12,500, are also exported to Jhung, Kurrachee, Pindibhuttian, Chiniot, Bunnoo, Dera Ghazi Khan, Dera Ismail Khan, Leia, and Sukkur.

The remaining 300 maunds of silk at Rs. 1,50,000, after undergoing the process of cleaning, are applied in the manufacture of the following description of fabrics, *viz.*, dopatta, daryai, gulbadan, susi, mashree, and lunghi, which are partly used here and partly exported to Shikarpore, Hyderabad, Sukkur, Kurrachee, Dera Ghazi Khan, Dera Ismail Khan, Leia, Jhung, Chiniot, Kamaliya, Lahore, and Umritsur.

The following is an account of the approximate cost of dyeing :—

Kirmji, or crimson ...	Rs. 2	0	0	per every seer of silk.	
Sabz, or green ...	„ 1	0	0	„	„
Siyah, or black ...	„ 1	0	0	„	„
Zard, or yellow ...	„ 1	0	0	„	„
Gul-i-anar (*i. e.*, scarlet) ...	„ 0	8	0	„	„
Safed, or white ...	„ 0	6	0	„	„

Nature of stuffs manufactured.

37. The silks generally manufactured in the Punjab are classed by Mr. Cope under two heads; (1), "gulbadan," very stout and mostly broad and of high price; (2), "daryai," of a lighter texture and to be had both plain and shot. Mooltan also produced two other kinds, *viz.*, "khes" and "eklal," both very broad and much higher priced than anything made in Lahore. Dr. Forbes Watson's book on Indian textile fabrics gives several specimens of Punjab silk manufacture. From *Lahore* come "loongees" of cotton with silk ends or borders, or silk and cotton mixed; rich "loongees" all silk, and piece-goods of pure silk or mixed cotton and silk. *Kohat*, *Leia*, and *Pind Dadun Khan* produce "loongees" in which silk and cotton are used in conjunction; *Dera Ismail Khan* sends all silk piece-goods; *Jhelum* "loongees," either all silk, or silk and cotton; *Bhawulpore* contributes rich silk "loongees" and silk piece-goods; *Goordaspore* and *Rawul Pindee* also appear among the silk-*weaving* districts, sending silk "loongees." "*Rutul Mudpore*" (*sic*) is also mentioned as a Punjab silk centre, but I have not identified the place. *Bunnoo* is said to produce mixed cotton and silk loongees.

Silk in Cashmere;

38. I may, perhaps, be allowed to introduce here such scanty accounts as I have been able to glean about silk in Cashmere and Central Asia. The following paper relating to Cashmere is from "Punjab Products" :—

In Cashmere the houses where the silkworms are kept do not differ from the dwelling-places of the inhabitants; indeed, in many instances, the raisers and their families live under the same roof with the worms. The single spacious loft which ordinarily constitutes the upper storey of the houses occupied by the lower orders in the valley is generally the principal breeding room. The silk raisers (called "kirmkash") do not confine themselves to the production of silk, but are either agriculturists or shawl-weavers besides. One individual has not usually charge of more worms than are sufficient to produce 30 seers of silk. The eggs begin to hatch about the middle of April, and during the first few weeks of the worm's existence an untimely fall of snow frequently injures the owner's prospects. This year a fall in May did much mischief. Drought, as it affects the yield of mulberry leaves, is no less baneful. It is satisfactory to know that the interest of the Punjab silk-raiser can never suffer from unseasonable cold, and he will thus have an advantage over his brother of Cashmere.

I was informed that for some years past there have been unfavourable seasons in Cashmere, but I could not discover there was any known disease among the worms; undue cold or drought and the difficulty of procuring coolies to collect leaves were the causes assigned. Paucity of laborers is a serious obstacle to silk cultivation in Cashmere; in addition to causing the worms to be insufficiently fed, it must occasion a want of proper cleanliness. The importance of this last, however, is not fully appreciated by the raisers.

In the plains the worms exist for 38 or 40 days only before they begin to spin; but in Cashmere, owing to the comparative coldness of the climate, they live nearly twice as long. This then is a third advantage over Cashmere that the Punjab possesses, for the expense of attendance will of course be in proportion to the length of the worm's life, and I presume the same is true of the quantity of food consumed. Round Srinugger the spinning seemed to be at its height at the beginning of July.

A fourth advantage the Punjab may have will be superior winding (the Peshawur and Bokhara winding even is far better than the Cashmere); and a fifth and the greatest of all will be an immunity from an oppressive silk duty and a harassing interference on the part of the Government.

No particular precautions against cold are necessary for preserving the eggs during the winter; they are usually kept in an earthen vessel with the mouth of it secured (of course the vessel must not be placed anywhere near a fire, otherwise the eggs will hatch). I do not speak confidently, but as far as I can make out, excepting that mulberry leaves are procurable free of cost (a boon equivalent to less than half the amount of tax exacted), a greater facility in preserving the eggs is the only decided advantage which Cashmere, as a silk-raising country, has over parts of the Punjab plains; and this is not a considerable one, for eggs will probably be conveyed to and from the hills for less than one per cent. of their value.

I heard of several attempts in Cashmere to raise a second crop of silk during the year, but none had been successful. The failure was attributed to the unfitness of the old mulberry leaf for the young worms. I imagine that the leaf loses its nourishing properties as the season advances.

The male or fruitless mulberry (khassee) is in Cashmere the kind most valued for its leaf, which, as has been remarked by Mr. Cope, is due to the leaf's obtaining the share of nourishment which in other varieties is diverted to the fruit. The leaves of the "Shah tut" (not the Punjab "Shah tut," but the large crimson fruit-bearing English mulberry) are said to be bitter and almost useless for silk-worms, though many of us in our younger days have fed a few upon them. The other three kinds (the small black, white, and purple fruit-bearing "Siyah tut," "Chitta tut," and "Bara tut") are equally valuable, I believe, but inferior to "khassee." In Kotihar, the south-eastern part of the valley, I saw a plantation of grafted purple mulberries, the leaves of which were very fine. It had originally been planted for fruit; there was no lack of trees for leaves in the neighbourhood, but the owner told me that he found silkworms benefited much by a few feeds from these grafted trees just before spinning. When the worms are young he thought these leaves would be too strong for them, but he had evidently never made experiments with any care. Probably, the worms would be strong enough to thrive on the grafted leaf after their first casting, and up to that period they would consume but a small amount of food. As the leaf of the grafted trees is more substantial and apparently more nourishing than that of the ungrafted, it will perhaps become the most important.

I imagine the small "khassee" would be the description selected for grafting on well-grown seedlings, as that would add the peculiar virtue of the "khassee" to the benefit of grafting.

Travellers' works on Cashmere state the best silk is raised in the pergunnah Kotihar, and I was desirous of ascertaining the reasons, but I could not discover any difference, as far as appearance went, between the cocoons produced there and those of other places, and the general opinion seemed to be that Kotihar silk was no better in quality than that raised elsewhere; no other pergunnah, however, produces so large a quantity. The three adjacent pergunnahs, on the right bank of the Jhelum, separated from Kotihar by Martund, are the principal localities for silk; but it is produced more or less in most parts of the valley. I understood that 100 maunds was considered a very large outturn, but that must be below the capabilities of the valley, if all the available mulberry trees were turned to account. Under the depressing revenue system pursued by the Government, it would be strange if the cultivation did not languish; indeed, its existence at all, considering the difficulties it has to struggle with, gives one a great idea of its vitality when once fairly established. The Maharaja (who, however, cannot be considered to blame for the system which has been long in vogue) is the sole master-raiser and manufacturer. He has a darogha to superintend the silk operations throughout the valley, to whom is known the quantity produced.

From a recent letter it appears that the Chief Justice of Cashmere, (a Bengalee gentleman, by name Baboo Neelambur Mookerjee) is, under the orders of the Maháraja, taking up the subject of silk. Some promising specimens of wound silk have been received and are about to be forwarded to London for valuation.

39. With regard to Bokhara, I take the following account by Khanikoff, at second hand from Mr. Cope's pamphlet:

and in Central Asia.

"Among the fruit-trees cultivated with great care, although not grown in orchards, we may notice the *tut* or mulberry tree.

The *tut* are of two sorts:—

(1) The *donedar*, which is properly the Bokharian *tut*; and

(2) The *tut balkhi*, translated from Balkh.

The grafting of the one on the other gives a third sort called *khaseki*, the fruit of which is sweeter and more savoury than that from the former. The *tut* tree blossoms usually ten days after the vernal equinox, but the year we were at Bokhara it happened at the close of that month. The fruit of the *tut* is used in two ways, to make syrup and wine.

But the mulberry tree is principally used for feeding the silkworms with its leaves.

The education of the worm by the Bokharians offers some peculiarities and differs in certain respects from the mode used by Europeans. About ten days or a fortnight after the mulberry trees put forth their leaves, the eggs of the silkworms are removed from the place where they have been preserved during winter, and being wrapped in a cloth, are carried against the naked breast* or still oftener under the armpit. Three to five days are quite sufficient for the silk insects to be hatched. They are then placed in a vessel and fed with the leaves gathered from the *tut*; after ten days the worms, according to the expression of the Bokharians, fall into their first sleep or trance, *i. e.*, they take no nourishment three days running, repeating the same process every ten days until the time it begins to spin the cocoon. When these are finished, the worm inside is destroyed by exposing the cocoon to the heat of the sun. That done, the Bokharians proceed to reel off the silk threads.

"It may be mentioned that the quality of the silk of Bokhara is much inferior to that of China and even to the French and Lombard silks, as well in colour as in the softness of the thread."

Cope calculates that the price assigned by Khanikoff to the raw silk at Bokhara is equivalent to Rs. 9 the seer.

Captain Kostenko, as quoted by Mr. Michell in a pamphlet on Russian Trade, dated May 1871, places raw and waste silk among the imports from the Khanates into Russia. The value of such silk imported (free of duty, it is to be observed), is given by him for eleven years as follows :—

Year.	Value in roubles.
1857	75,643
1858	68,901
1859	93,520
1860	82,053
1861	149,969
1862	156,148
1863	51,779
1864	45,699
1865	35,534
1866	146,209
1867	1,273,088

The enormous increase in 1867 is noteworthy. Of the imports of that year, Captain Kostenko gives the following further particulars. The weight of raw silk imported was 7,822 poods,† the sources of which were as follows :—

From the	Kirghiz steppe	23 poods.
,,	Khiva...	336 ,,
,,	Bokhara	6,566 ,,
,,	Tashkend	2,887 ,,

In addition to the raw silk, silk fabrics to the value of 48,818 roubles were imported. The points of entry were mainly, Orenburg, Orsk, and Troitsk.

Manufactured silk appears as follows among the exports from Russia to the Khanates :—

Year.	Value in roubles.
1857	17,338
1858	32,209
1859	54,332
1860	45,381
1861	40,103
1862	50,494
1863	58,358
1864	72,267
1865	33,076
1866	71,011
1867	98,138

Of the exports of 1867, 45,246 roubles worth was destined for the Kirghiz steppe, while the value of exports to Khiva was 3,850 roubles.
,, ,, ,, ,, Bokhara ,, 10,902 ,,
,, ,, ,, ,, Tashkend,, 38,410 ,,

In 1867, moreover, 24 poods of *raw silk*, valued at 236 roubles, were exported to the steppe. The route of export was by way either of Orenburg or Petropavlovsk.

---

* Compare Vida *apud* "Prout's Reliques" :—
———Conde sinu velamine tecta,
Nec pudeat rosens inter fovisse papillas.

† 1 pood = 36 lbs. English.

SECTION V.

SILK IN THE NORTH-WESTERN PROVINCES.

Proposals of Capt. Hutton in 1856;

In February 1856, Captain Hutton, of Mussooree, represented to the Government of the North-Western Provinces the existence in the Himalayas and Dehra Doon of certain wild silk-spinning insects, and suggested that he should be employed in conducting an enquiry into the possibility of utilizing these insects.

"The object," he wrote, "should be, in the first instance, to ascertain what number of species our forests afford; the quantity and quality of the silk procurable from each; the practicability of transplanting them to Europe; and whether they will submit to domestication like *Bombyx mori*, or whether they require to be left to nature in suitable localities where they can be watched."

After obtaining the opinion of the Agri-Horticultural Society on Captain Hutton's views, the Government of the North-Western Provinces proposed that he should be allowed to undertake the experiment of forming a plantation of mulberry trees near Mussooree for rearing hill silkworms; and that, while so employed, he should be allowed a salary of Rs. 200 a month, and be permitted to incur an annual outlay of Rs. 3,000 for three years, when a full report was to be submitted. And in June 1858, the Government of India sanctioned this scheme. On 3rd November 1859, however, Captain Hutton reported that the experiment did not promise success. He founded this opinion on the following grounds:—

1*st*.—That the wild mulberry tree, when propagated by cuttings, was found of slow growth, and would require double, if not treble, the time allowed, to bring it to a size large enough to nourish a sufficient number of worms to ensure a tolerable return in silk; while the quick-growing China plant was not so well liked by the *Bombyx Huttoni* (the subject of the experiment). 2*nd*.—That the worms of this species were irreclaimably wild, though yielding good silk; nay, that even when a cross was made with Cashmere stock (*Bombyx mori*), the progeny, when there was any (for most of the eggs proved unprolific), retained the intractable habits of the wild parent. Captain Hutton "considered therefore that, both as regards the tree and the insect, the experiment had failed."

At the same time Captain Hutton contended, on the grounds set forth in fuller detail in his paper published by the Agri-Horticultural Society of Bengal, that Mussooree was an excellent place for further experiments with other silk-producing moths, and advocated further attempts. The Government of the North-Western Provinces, however, directed immediate discontinuance of the experiment, and, notwithstanding a remonstrance from Captain Hutton, the Government of India took decisively the same view.

and in 1863.

2. With a letter, dated 12th September 1863, the North-Western Provinces' Government forwarded certain "remarks on the best method of restoring the silkworm to health," by Captain Hutton. He therein maintains that the disease prevalent among worms of the species *Bombyx mori* in France and Italy is only one result of a general enfeeblement of constitution manifested by all the domesticated species. Captain Hutton states that a comparison of the pale domesticated worm with the strongly coloured wild *Bombyces* led him to conjecture that the *Bombyx mori*, too, was originally more strikingly marked. He therefore made experiments* by selecting the worms marked with a darker colour for purposes of breeding, and though his experiments were only carried through two generations, he traced signs of a stronger constitution in the insects, as indicated by larger size of the larva, the adherence of the eggs to the substance on which they were laid, and the greater liveliness of the moths. Captain Hutton asked the Government of the North-Western Provinces for assistance in continuing his experiments, which, he maintained, had a very great practical importance. The Lieutenant-Governor, in reply, expressed his opinion that the most appropriate way of encouraging the object Captain Hutton had in view was to offer,

* A fuller account of these experiments will be found below.

on the occasion of the agricultural exhibitions about to be held, a high prize for any process which should show a result superior to that ordinarily obtainable. Taking into consideration the magnitude of the interests at stake, and the fact that experiments on the largest scale in the breeding and cross-breeding of the worms, and in the management of their food and produce, had of late years been scientifically carried out in Europe, Mr. Drummond was disposed to think that either Captain Hutton's experiments had been anticipated, or that they did not at that stage call for any unusual action on the part of Government. The correspondence was published in the *Calcutta Gazette*.

Silk in small quantities actually produced in the North-Western Provinces.

3. In the Moradabad district some very fine silk was reeled by Captain White, and exhibited at the Roorkee Agricultural Show in 1864; and at Mussooree* some fine silk has been prepared by Captains Hutton and Murray.

At the Agra Exhibition of 1867, there was a very poor display of raw silk—only nine specimens in all, of which one only came from the North-Western Provinces, being contributed apparently by Bustee. Of the manufactured silks shewn the jury speak highly, but except the Kincobs from Benares, none of great merit seem to have come from the North-Western Provinces, though Azimgurh, Bijnour, and Agra also competed.

Experiments in the Dehra Doon.

4. Some papers recently received from the Government of the North-Western Provinces and a private letter enables me to give a somewhat fuller account of recent attempts at sericulture in the Doon. It seems that the *Morus sinensis* was introduced at Saharunpoor in 1850, and thence spread to the Doon, where it throve luxuriantly. Captain Murray appears to have commenced experiments in 1867 with seed obtained from Bengal, and in that year 350lbs. of dried cocoons were obtained and about 6lbs. of eggs. Want of reelers, however, prevented the conversion of the cocoons into silk. In 1868 4lbs. of seed were hatched, but the result was only 20lbs. of silk. The failure is attributed partly to want of supervision, partly to drought, and partly to the very late period at which the eggs hatched. Since 1868 much does not appear to have been done beyond keeping up the breed. The cocoons so far from degenerating are said to increase in size. It is stated that Captain Murray obtained 400grs. of silk from 300 dried cocoons weighing 1,740 grains. If these figures are not vitiated by error, the yield is almost unprecedented. As to the quality of the silk, it was valued in Calcutta at Rs. 18 and 19 the factory seer. The colour and quality were pronounced good, the *cocoons* being considered "very superior." But the thread was dirty and uneven. A report by M. Guérin de Méneville is much to the same effect. He declares the silk of second quality in the market, but that it would have ranked in the first class if reeled in France. Within the last year, a lady resident in the Doon (Mrs. Reilly) states that she has reared a small number of worms of Cashmere stock.

Tusser in the North-Western Provinces.

5. The tusser appears at one time to have been largely manufactured in the south-east corner of the tract now embraced in the North-Western Provinces. In an abstract of the results of the survey and settlement of Azimgurh in 1837, Mr. (now Sir R.) Montgomery estimates the quantity of tusser annually manufactured in that district at 318,772 pieces (of a size not stated), and large quantities both of cloth of pure tusser and of a cloth called soosee ("being a cotton dosootee cloth with a stripe of coloured silk through it"), used to be made at Ahrowrah in the Mirzapore district. English piece-goods, however, seem to have nearly driven these fabrics out of the market, though the price has fallen 50 per cent. The worm is still bred in the jungle tracts of Mirzapore, and the yield of the season 1870-71 is said to have been 1,500,000 cocoons. The silk is valued at Rs. 4 per seer, but the price has fallen, for it used to be as much as Rs. 7 a seer. Both cocoons and raw silk are exported; silk to Azimgurh and Benares, and both cocoons and silk to the Central Provinces. The Sanitary Commissioner of the North-Western Provinces in the report of his last tour mentions a town in Azimgurh as the seat of a mixed cotton and tusser manufacture, the fabrics being exported and getting even as far as Bombay.

---

* Extract from letter from Dr. Jameson, to Government, North-Western Provinces, No. 124, dated 26th January 1870.

Note to para. 5.—A letter received since the above was in type shews that in the Azimgurh district tusser cloth means a mixture of cotton and silk of a domesticated bombyx. This use of the term appears peculiar to the district, and has misled both Dr. Royle (from whose "Resources of India" a portion of the above is borrowed) and myself.

Captain Hutton's papers.

6. The history of silk in the North-Western Provinces being so brief, this may be the proper place for introducing, at considerable length, the views of Captain Hutton, a resident of those provinces, and one who has devoted a life-time to the question of silk in India.

Captain Hutton's general views on this question are fully set forth in the following extracts from a paper by him, dated November 1859, and published by the Agri-Horticultural Society of India. After describing the situation and climate of Mussooree and Dehra Doon, Captain Hutton goes on thus :—

With such diversity of elevation and temperature, it is but natural and reasonable to expect a corresponding diversity in the natural productions of the district ; and accordingly we find an intermixture, not only of Indian and Chinese, but likewise of European forms.

In the insect world more especially, the entomologist will recognise not only the swallow-tail and painted lady butterflies together with the common cabbage butterfly of Europe,* but he will likewise, of Chinese forms, meet with both *Erebus macrops* and *Crepuscularis, Nymphalis jacintha, Cynthia Œnone, Almana,* and *Crithyia, Limenitis leucothoe,* and a host of other Lepidoptera ; among the hard-winged beetles he will find the beautiful *Buprestis bicolor, Copris Midas, Molossus* and *Bucephalus ;* while if China can boast of its Atlas moth, its silk-yielding Bombyces, its Tusser, and Eria moths, and its oak-feeding Saturnia (*Antheræa pernyi),* Mussooree can likewise produce their analogues in its own Atlas (*Attacus Edwardsianus*), its *Bombyx Huttoni,* its Tusser, Eria and oak-feeding Saturnia (*Antheræa roylei*).

The fact that so many forms are common to both Mussooree and to China, and that the tea-plant of the latter country thrives well both in the hills and in the Doon, would lead at once, even in the absence of indigenous silk-spinners, to the conclusion that silk also might be extensively cultivated at suitable elevations along the lower ranges of the outer Himalaya, where the temperature, like that of the best tea-growing districts of China, may be about 73° of Fahrenheit ; but when we find not only a true mulberry-feeding Bombyx, a Tusser, an Eria, an Atlas, and four or five other wild species, all occurring in different portions of the same district, we are surely not expecting too much when we venture to believe that, with proper care bestowed upon the insects, Mussooree will at no distant date prove to be one of the most productive and best silk-yielding districts in India.

Experiments already tried with the domesticated Chinese *Bombyx mori* of Cashmere, and with the Madrassee *vel* Nistry (*B. cræsi* nob.) of Bengal, have proved beyond a doubt, not only that the worms thrive well in this climate, but that there is also a ready and remunerative market for their silk, while, strange to say, the Bengal annual silkworm, known as the *Boro poloo* of the natives, yields at Mussooree a second crop also.

Another circumstance calculated to add weight to the opinion that Mussooree will prove to be a good silk-yielding district is to be found in its temperate climate, for notwithstanding all that prejudice, ignorance, theory, and self-interest have hitherto asserted in regard to a high temperature being necessary for the production of that article, it is nevertheless a well-established fact that in a hot climate the domesticated worms become feeble, degenerate, and languish, and the silk is in consequence deteriorated in quality. The superiority of silk grown in northern climates has been well established by experiments long since instituted in Northern Europe, where, notwithstanding Count Dandolo's erroneous idea that the silk-worm is indigenous to the southern provinces of China, and therefore requires a high temperature to bring it to perfection, it was found that the silk produced in Sweden was far superior to the best Italian produce, and the same was likewise the case in Bavaria ; nay, we need scarcely travel so far from our own doors in order to prove that temperate regions are more favourable to the worm than tropical ones, since we have the fact prominently displayed in the superiority of the Cashmere stock over that of Bengal, the silk of the former being recently valued at Rupees 24 per seer in Calcutta, while that of the Madrassee worm reared in Bengal is reported at Rupees 14 only, thus showing a difference of Rupees 10 a seer in favour of the up-country produce.

Next to that of Cashmere, therefore, (if indeed it be not superior,) the climate of the lower ranges of the Himalaya lying between the Sutlej and the Ganges, will probably become the most productive, provided always that proper care and attention are bestowed upon the management of the insects, for even the much-belauded Punjab, although infinitely better than Bengal for silkworm cultivation, is yet, in my opinion, far too hot to preserve it long in perfect health ;† and with a better system of cultivation than that which is practised in Cashmere, or indeed than any native cultivators are likely to bestow, the probabilities are greatly in favour of our hill districts eventually being made to "bear the bell."

With regard to the treatment of the worms in more modern times, theory appears to have done its best to render them weak and sickly, by asserting that a high temperature was necessary for the successful rearing of the insects; whereas the truth is, that a temperate climate is by far the most suitable to it. A native of the northern provinces of China, it is

* *Papilio Machaon. Cynthia Cardui* and *Pontia Brassica.*

† Captain Hollings, too, long since attributed his failure in the Punjab to the heat of the climate.

but reasonable to suppose that the heat of such countries as India, Persia, or Syria would act injuriously upon its constitution, and render great precautions necessary in its management; and under any circumstances a temperate climate has, as M. Boitard justly observes, a great advantage over hot countries, in the fact that it is easy to raise the temperature of the rearing-houses by artificial means, whereas it is always difficult, and sometimes even impossible, to lower it. Besides which, experience has fully proved, both in India and in Italy, that a moderate and equal temperature is the best, since in the former country it is admitted that the winter or spring crop is the most successful, while in the latter a mild spring invariably produces better results than when the temperature is higher, and indeed it not unfrequently happens that in a hot spring the crop has nearly altogether failed; hence it is not the heat, but the northern position of Italy which has rendered its silks so famous. Self-interest, to say nothing of ignorance of the requirements of the insect, will doubtless point to the satisfactory results obtained in France, in Sicily, Italy, Piedmont, Spain, and even in India, and all will be attributed to the warmth of their several climates; but the question is, do those results claim precedence over what has been effected in colder climates, or are we to forget that Italy, France, and Spain are considerably to the northward of the latitude of the silk districts of China? If we can rely upon the published statements, the results hitherto obtained in elevated temperatures are far inferior to those obtained in northern latitudes. The best silk of China is produced in the northern provinces of the Empire, and in India the finest species of *Bombyx* under cultivation is that of Cashmere; while in Europe, we learn that "some years back silk was grown in Prussia of a quality which was considered superior to that even of Italy"—a fact that gives strength to an observation contained in a paragraph in the *Stockholm Journal* for March 1824, and reprinted in the *Bulletin Universel* of April 1825. After detailing the introduction of several plants lately raised in Sweden, it adds,—"that similar motives have instigated the encouragement of the growth of silk in this country; the idea, indeed, is not new, and experiments made long ago presented encouraging results. Experiments made in 1823 in Stockholm for the purpose of discovering some indigenous tree capable of nourishing the silkworm, have procured silk of very fine quality. The culture of the mulberry tree is extending itself in the provinces, and important communications on the most convenient mode of rearing the worm have been generally promulgated. The silk so produced in Sweden has confirmed in the amplest manner the remark formerly made on the superior fineness and solidity of silk grown in the north, compared with that from more temperate climes—a fact that has received the unanimous sanction of the members of the Royal Society of Commerce, as well as of many silk manufacturers. It supports the ordinary preparation and dye equally with the best Indian silk, possessing the same brilliancy and the same softness. The silk also that has been grown for the last few years in Bavaria is superior to that produced in Italy."

It has even been stated that "this branch of commerce has been established in Russia for several years in a latitude as far north as 54°, and with such success as to warrant the establishment of manufactories for working the silk, in the hope that a few years would render that country independent of Persia for the supply of this valuable produce;" and indeed no longer ago than the 20th of August 1859, it was stated in the pages of the *Illustrated London News* that "an attempt is about to be made on a scale of some importance to introduce the growth of silk into Holstein as a staple article of commerce. The mulberry trees which have been planted for some time on the shores of the Baltic near Heiligenhafen have thriven well, and an abundant supply of cocoons has been received, to the future produce of which those who are engaged in the enterprize look forward with confidence for a profitable result."

But after all, where is the difficulty in rearing the worms in northern latitudes, provided the trees themselves will grow there? In his report on the Paris Universal Exhibition, Dr. Royle has informed us that silk-worms were "early introduced into India from China, where it flourishes chiefly about Nankin, *or in 32° of north latitude;* but in India none of the old silk filatures extend to beyond 26° of north latitude," and this he very justly ascribes "to the excessive heat and dryness of the North-Western Provinces of India," which are unsuitable to the constitution of the animal. Nankin, therefore, where silk flourishes abundantly, is nearly two degrees further north than Mussooree, or about the latitude of Upper Kunawur, a district to the north of Simla, where the worm, being beyond the influence of the wet monsoon, would no doubt be cultivated with great success.

But if we can succeed, through the exercise of a little common sense and skill in rearing exotic plants, why can we not in like manner rear the insects which feed upon them? All that is necessary are properly constructed houses in which the required degree of warmth and shelter can be produced, so that provided the trees would grow, the insect might be cultivated in almost every part of Europe.

In regard to the mulberry itself, trees grown in stiff wheat lands are sure to produce leaves that are totally unsuited to the production of good silk, the necessary ingredients, or components from which silk gum is secreted, being either wholly wanting, or present in very small quantities; and yet so little is generally known upon these subjects, that the failure of experiments made in England with such leaves was attributed to *an excess,* instead of to *a deficiency* of nourishing properties, the truth being that the leaf abounds in water, while the saccharine and resinous matters are nearly altogether absent.

Nearly the same result will be insured by rearing trees in too rich a soil: if fine fruit be the object, such treatment may be well enough; but for healthy and nutritious leaves, the system is fully as bad as the former, inasmuch as the tree is forced, artificial, and incapable of producing leaves possessed of the requisite qualities.

It is true that the mulberry will grow, and, as to external appearances, thrive well in almost any soil, but that which is the best adapted for enabling the tree to produce the particular kind of leaf that furnishes the best silk is what may be termed a good *tea-soil*, composed of certain proportions intimately blended of *silica, clay*, and *carbonate of lime* with a little vegetable matter, the silica and lime predominating over the other constituents.

In a very hot climate, like that of the Doon or the plains of India, such a soil will require occasional irrigation in the summer months, as otherwise its light and porous nature would cause it to separate from the roots, which run chiefly near the surface horizontally, and so insure the destruction of the tree; but in a climate not subject to such high temperature, the trees after the two first years may be safely left to nature.

In a country which, like India, is subject to long continued periodical rains, the nutritive particles in a light and porous soil would soon be carried down beyond the reach of the roots, so that a top-dressing of suitable materials will be occasionally required to renew the soil, and the same rule will apply when surface irrigation is resorted to.

In a mountainous district like Mussooree, which is occasionally subject to strong winds, it would be as well to have here and there, on the borders of the plantation, a few large trees capable of resisting a gale and affording shelter to the tender wood of the mulberry trees, which, without such precaution, would be constantly liable to injury in the loss of branches, and there are few trees less able to bear such mutilation, or even injudicious pruning, than the mulberry.

At the same time great care must be taken that the mulberry plants are not placed too much under the shade of the protecting trees, and on no account ought they to be so near as to allow the rain-drops from the one to fall upon the other: all that is required is so to arrange that the indigenous forest trees may be so situated with respect to the plantation as to break the force of the gales which may sweep over it.

Let no one run away with the idea that a plantation is easily formed, and that there are no difficulties to contend with, for although it has been stated that no insect save the silkworm (*Bombyx Mori*) will feed upon the mulberry leaf or attack the tree, any one who may attempt to form a plantation in the mountain tracts of India will soon be convinced to the contrary, and find that the theories of closet naturalists are not always to be received as gospel truths. The name of the pests which destroy the trees is in fact legion.

At Mussooree not only are many young plants and cuttings destroyed by grubs gnawing away the roots, but much and very serious damage is occasioned during the night by the barking deer (*Cervulus moschatus*, DeBlain.), and another closely allied species (*C. apicalis*, nob.) which not only eat off the leaves and shoots within their reach, but cut through the stems of young trees which have attained to the height of six and eight feet, thus prematurely dwarfing them and converting them into mere bushes, often to the number of 20 or 30 in a single night, besides which, unless well watched, cattle, goats, and sheep will eagerly devour them during the day.

Of caterpillars, which are apt to destroy the foliage, there are at Mussooree at least three species, and so destructive is one of these that a large tree is sometimes half denuded in the course of a few days from the numbers of these pests which usually appear in the latter end of summer; while another, which is a *Geometra*, attacks the young buds early in the spring.

Besides these there is likewise a species of *Lamia* which, if the young trees are not narrowly examined, will cause much damage, its larvæ being nourished within the trunk and rendering the tree weak and sickly, while the mature beetle gnaws the green bark from the tender branches.

On visiting a nursery plot one morning in the beginning of September, I found to my great annoyance that five fine young trees, about seven feet in height, and with stems the thickness of a man's little finger, had, during the night, been cut off at about three feet from the summit As no barking deer could have reached so high, I was at first sight, from the cleanliness and evenness of the cut, inclined to regard it as the work of some mischievous person, but on closely examining the summit of the stump, I discovered in every instance just below the top a small longitudinal incision and intumescence at the side, and I was then at once convinced that a beetle had caused the damage, and after a short search, a female *Lamia* was discovered gnawing the bark of another young tree.

Cutting off the tops of the stumps just below the puncture, and laying bare the swollen part, I discovered a long groove in the wood, in which, as in a coffin, was snugly deposited a good-sized egg of about ⅝ths of an inch in length.

But why, it may be asked, did the female, after depositing her ova, cut off the summit of the stem? Instinct evidently taught her to act in this manner for the preservation of the grub which in due time would be disclosed from her egg, for the upper portion of the young stem being green, succulent, and deficient in the proper nutritive juices and woody fibre, besides being very liable to be nipped off by the frosts of winter, would insure the destruction of the grub if it took the upward direction. In order effectually to prevent this and compel the larva to descend into the thicker and more woody parts of the tree, the female beetle saws off the green summit at about three to four feet from the top, and thus by cutting off all upward progress clearly indicates the direction in which her offspring is to proceed; and that this decollation of the young shoot is made for the express purpose of preventing the grub from taking an upward course seems further proved by the fact that the head of the egg, or that part from which the grub would issue, is invariably placed pointing downwards, as if for the express purpose of indicating the direction in which its welfare behoves it to travel; besides which, were the upward direction the proper one, the egg would be inserted head upwards and at the root or base of the stem, as is the case with the *Lucanidæ** with a long line of nourishment before it. By the present wise arrangement, however, not only is the young grub prevented from taking a wrong direction, but as its size and voracity increase and its bulb expands, it meets, as it descends, with a correspondingly increasing supply of proper nourishment, with ample space in the additional thickness of the stem.

Having, in spite of all drawbacks, at length succeeded in forming a plantation, or rather in having produced the trees, great care should be bestowed in removing them from the nurseries to the open grounds, in order to preserve the roots from injury; for this purpose I should recommend that cuttings planted in February and well watered until the setting in of the monsoon be at that season removed from the nursery, as the roots being short would be less liable to injury, and indeed with ordinary care should meet with none; whereas if left until the following spring, the roots will have attained to so large a size, and have become so thoroughly interlaced, as to render it impossible to remove the tree without denuding them of earth and breaking away the larger ones, an injury that will materially retard the growth and affect the future healthiness of the tree. Standard trees should certainly not be planted closer than from 16 to 20 feet apart, while, if intended to be allowed to grow to a large size, even 36 feet apart will not be found too much.

In the feeding of the worms great attention will be required, and no leaves gathered from shrubs and immature trees should on any account be administered, and no tree under four or even five years can be considered sufficiently mature.

Standard trees are preferable to all others, and if these are grown in a suitable soil, such as I have above pointed out, the leaves will, as a general rule, be found to possess all those qualities which will enable the worm, by preserving it in health, to secrete good silk in proper quantity; and it may be said that the older is the tree, within certain limits, the better will become the leaf.

The theory laid down by Count Dandolo, which restricts the supply of leaves to four times during the day and giving none at night, is a pure absurdity, and calculated only to insure the starvation of the insects; neither is the Chinese method of repeatedly feeding the young worms and decreasing the quantity as they grow older to be attended to. Nature is the best and only guide that the cultivator should imitate, and as she has always ready at hand a fresh and abundant supply, whenever the worm is inclined to feed, so ought the leaves to be supplied at short intervals, both during the day and during the night, renewing them, in fact, whenever the previous supply has become withered and unfit for use. To lessen the quantity and frequency of supply as the worm increases in size and voracity is so obviously contrary to common sense that no one, I imagine, who is not incurably wedded to a theory, would be tempted to follow such a system; and even if the worms should not consume all the leaves, the waste should not be grudged, since it will certainly be more than compensated for in the superior health of the insect, and consequent increase in the quantity and quality of the silk produced. Surely, far better is it to waste a few leaves than, by practising too niggard an economy, secure the semi-starvation of the worm and insure a deficiency of silk; besides which a little practice will soon teach the feeders so to regulate the quantity to the number of worms as that there shall no waste ensue.

To the necessity of supplying the worms with food throughout the night, as well as by day, I would, as a naturalist, earnestly call the attention of the cultivator, for not only are all the *Bombycidæ* true night-feeders, but I have proved by repeated experiments that worms thus treated grow twice as rapidly as those which are fed by day only, and although it may be said that such a method will materially increase the trouble and expense of rearing, yet such trouble will be fully compensated by the increased vigour and well-being of the insect, as well as by the rapidity with which it will necessarily undergo its allotted changes; not, however, as now by being artificially forced onwards by extreme heat, but by a more natural and healthy system of feeding. Besides which, if good silk is required, no trouble or expense ought to be grumbled at so long as the desired end is attained, and the easiest and in fact the only way to insure good silk is to insure likewise the general health and welfare of the insect which is to produce it; and, consequently, it is but a false economy to pursue an injudicious system merely for the sake of avoiding a little additional labour and outlay, which would necessarily produce more lucrative returns.

It is to be observed, however, that by 'night-feeding,' I do not mean merely to advocate the system pursued in the Deccan by Signor Mutti, of *"gathering leaves in the afternoon for use during the night,"* since such a system I should regard as a patent method of slow poisoning, no matter in what climate or country pursued, but in a temperature ranging from 85° to 92°, such as the Signor acknowledges to have prevailed in his rearing-houses, the juices of the leaves reserved for night use must either be more or less in a state of fermentation before they reach the worms, or the fibre of the leaf will have become hard and dry.

* The larvæ of the stag beetles remain generally in the thickest part of the trunk of oaks, &c.

By night-feeding, I mean that the leaves must be gathered fresh, and during the night, and given to the worms in that condition at stated and proper intervals. The same system must, likewise, be pursued by day, since it is utterly impossible to keep leaves properly and naturally fresh for any time after they are gathered from the trees; and yet Signor Mutti advises that "the leaves, except in the hot season, should not be given during the day, immediately after being gathered, *but kept for a few hours!*" He does not explain why he thinks this necessary, nor indeed does it seem possible to assign a valid reason for acting in a manner so thoroughly opposed to nature and to common sense, for how do the wild worms manage in this respect? They feed upon the leaf in all its freshness, no matter whether heated by the sun or moistened by the rains and dews of heaven. It is, in my opinion, this very system of withholding the leaf until incipient fermentation has set in that has, in a great measure, tended to induce the present state of unhealthiness to which the worms of every country, where such artificial systems are maintained, have been reduced.

It appears, moreover, by underrating the strength of the insect's constitution, to be quite possible to fall into the error of over-pampering it, and inducing debility; such error, indeed, has undoubtedly been committed, and from the idea which most people entertain of the great susceptibility and sensitiveness of the worm, it has hitherto been too much the fashion to bake the insects in rooms which are almost hermetically-sealed against every breath of fresh air; true, they have lived, or rather languished through the ordeal and have produced what has been considered a valuable crop of silk, but the question is, would they not have been in a better condition as to health and have produced a far better crop under more judicious treatment?

That they do not require to be thus sealed up has been proved by some experiments lately instituted in France, and which I shall presently notice, as well as by others tried by myself at Mussooree in 1859, with a view to ascertain what degree of exposure they could actually bear. The worms selected were a cross between the Cashmere stock (*Bombyx mori*) and the Nistry, or Madrassee of Bengal (*B. Crœsi*, nob.); they were under the cover of a roof, it is true, so that neither the rays of the sun, nor rain, could directly fall upon them, but with this exception they were as much exposed as if they had been in the open air. The experiment was tried in the very height of the wet monsoon, and as every door and window, eight in number, were purposely left open on all sides, the dense damp mist, in which the hills are at that season enveloped, floated freely over the worms by day and by night, often rendering the trays, the leaves, and the insects themselves, as wet as if they had been exposed to a shower of rain. Many of course died, but this might have happened even under better treatment; the majority, however, struggled through every disadvantage, and at length spun yellow cocoons resembling those of the Madrassee, but exceeding them in size, and containing one-half more silk, giving great satisfaction to experienced judges in Calcutta to whose inspection they were submitted, and thus, notwithstanding the trying treatment they had undergone, beating the best Bengal Bombyx. All this time the thermometer was ranging up and down *ad libitum* between 62° and 78°, the changes being often sudden from bright sunshine to dense damp mist.

Finding that, notwithstanding the frequent saturation of the trays and leaves, the worms still lived on, I was induced to try further experiments by feeding other worms upon wet leaves for the purpose of testing the truth of the prevalent theory that "wet leaves invariably cause sickness and death." The theory is true only to a certain extent and under particular circumstances; for instance, were the leaves kept for some hours, as Signor Mutti recommends, and in that state given wet to the worms, the effect would, no doubt, be deadly, from the simple fact that the gases exhaled or thrown off by the process of fermentation are partially taken up by the moisture on the surface of the leaves and form acids which destroy the worm; but, on the other hand, so long as the leaf is fresh and free from the putrefactive process, the moisture on its surface is perfectly innocuous, precisely as is the case with the wet leaves growing on the trees which are eaten by the wild worms with perfect impunity.

The range of temperature allowed by M. Boitard in his work "on the cultivation of the mulberry tree and silkworm," is from 66° to 70° Faht., and beyond that, or from 86° to 95° Faht., he says the worm will produce little silk, and even that of a coarse quality. The reason for this he finds in the fact that by a high temperature the worm is so rapidly forced to a false or *premature* maturity that the secreting organs have not time themselves to come to perfection; and these views are sufficiently borne out by actual experience, since nearly all competent observers have remarked that the longer the worm takes to come to maturity the better will be the cocoon. Mr. Speed, among others, remarking in the 3rd volume of the *Transactions of the Agri-Horticultural Society of India*, when speaking of the desee worm, that according to the length of time "is the quality of the cocoon, the longest period producing the best;" and the longest period is moreover found to be that which is occupied by the November *bund*, or crop; thus showing that the less the worm is *forced*, and the cooler the season becomes, the more healthy and vigorous is the worm, and consequently the better also is the silk; while, again, in regard to temperature, Signor Mutti has remarked in the 6th volume of the same Transactions that "during the heat of the day, I keep all the doors and windows shut, and open the whole of them as soon as the heat declines. By these means I am able to keep the temperature at from 35° to 92°. This very extraordinary year (1837), on account of the heat, cold and rain, I have been unable to equalize the temperature so much. For some days the thermometer in the rooms rose to 98°, *and this was attended with a loss of about* 15 *per cent. of the worms. The survivors made but small cocoons.*"

Here, then, we have a practical proof of the truth of M. Boitard's remarks, and we see at once that the high temperature to which the worms are subject in the Deccan and other parts of the plains of India must tend rapidly to render them of less value than those which are cultivated in more temperate climates. Even the temperature of the Dehra Doon and of the Punjab must far exceed the limit beyond which the worm becomes unhealthy.

We have, likewise, a further practical proof of the advantage of a well-aired room over one that is kept shut and at a high temperature, in the fact that—"Madame Pirodou at Versoud, near Grenoble, has recently informed the French Academy of Sciences that she has caused silk-worms to be reared from the egg in rooms with windows open, but supplied with curtains to prevent currents of air from coming on the worms, and also, *in warm rooms with closed windows.* The worms reared in the former *produced the best silk of the year;* the silk of the worms in the latter *was nearly unsaleable.*"*

It becomes, then, quite obvious that the worms thrive better, and, as a natural consequence, produce a more valuable silk in a temperate than in a hot tropical climate, and hence the almost certainty of arriving at more satisfactory results at Mussooree and similar elevations in the lower Himalaya than in the Punjab and plains of India, for, besides all the facts above adduced, it was long since shown in the pages of the *Transactions of the Horticultural Society of India* that "the climate best adapted for the cultivation of the worm is the borders of a mountainous or high country where the air is warm, yet temperate and regular. Thus, the best cultivated in Europe, is in Piedmont, the Milanese, and the Tyrol, which countries border on the Alps; and indeed the silk produced in all parts of the north of Italy, which are mountainous, is good, for there the sky is clear, and the air warm, yet temperate and pure. *The worm cultivated in the valleys, where the warmth is great, exudes a looser and more irregular fibre, and thread formed from it becomes rather harsh and sticky.*"†

This, I think, is precisely what might have been expected when we reflect that the worms are from the mountainous tracts of the northern parts of China, and there is still more hope for Mussooree as a silk-producing district to be found in the fact that there is little difference in point of latitude between it and Tche-kiang in China, the province in which silk was first cultivated, Mussooree being situated in north latitude 30° 27′ 33″, and the Province of Tche-kiang in from 29° to about 30° 20′ north latitude, the district being described as comprehending "the south-eastern corner of the plain, and northern portion of the mountainous country extending along the sea. It produces more green tea than other provinces, and also silk, rice, grain, and pulse in abundance. Its principal port is Ningpo."‡

Although, as M. Boitard observes, the worms thrive well in a temperature of from 66° to 70°, yet I am inclined to regard such range as too confined, since I have found that they thrive healthily and as well as one could possibly wish in a temperature ranging from 62° to 78°; but beyond 80° Fahr., I confess I should look for nothing but debility and sickness.

As all climates out of China, and assuredly the entire system now termed *cultivation,* must be to a great extent purely artificial, I should recommend in the treatment of the silk-worm the adoption of the same principles as those by which we are guided in the rearing and cultivation of exotic plants.

Having formed a plantation of standard trees, no matter whether the fruit be black or white,§ the speculators should then erect suitable rearing-houses for the worm either within the plantation, or as near to it as possible, so that the leaves when gathered would have but a short distance to travel, and these should be gathered fresh and fresh at certain intervals, and be at once given to the worms; if they do not require them, the leaves will be wasted,—what then? Experience and attention will soon teach the feeder the exact length of time which must elapse before the worm will feed again, and he will regulate the supply accordingly. If the worms are in good health, they will be ready to feed again by the time the second supply can be gathered and brought in. But I again repeat that a little waste of leaves at the outset is not to be considered as a loss, if in the end a better crop of silk can be obtained. It will be observed, however, that I am speaking of a case in which the plantation is the property of the cultivator and reeler, and I maintain that such a plan will always be found in the end to be the cheapest and most productive, because the worms having been well fed and attended to under his own immediate superintendence, will produce a better return than can reasonably be expected, where one party sells damaged and immature leaves to another, whose object is merely to turn out the largest possible number of cocoons without caring for their quality. On the other hand, where everything is under the eye and management of a competent superintendent, not only are the worms carefully attended to, but none but the healthiest leaves are given to them, and the natural consequence is a better supply of cocoons.

Under the present system in Bengal the worms are never properly attended to, and the reeler at the filature must take what he can get or go without.

---

* Comptes Rendus, as quoted by the *Illustrated London News* of 13th August 1859, p. 161.
† Report of Messrs. Dover and Norton, Vol. 2, Agri. Trans., p. 152.
‡ Art. China, p. 79. *Penny Cyclopædia.*
§ More stress has been laid upon the alleged fact that the worm thrives best upon the white mulberry than was at all necessary; wherever silk is cultivated, both species are used.

The rearing-house should be so constructed as freely to admit the light on all sides, and be furnished with glazed doors and windows; stoves or fire-places are likewise necessary for the purpose of raising the temperature when required, and of evaporating all damp from whatever cause arising.

In fine calm weather the windows during the heat of the day should, provided that the cultivation be carried on in a temperate climate, be left partially open for the purpose of ventilating the room and giving the insects the benefit of the pure fresh air; but on any change, or threatened change of weather without, the windows should be immediately closed and an equable temperature preserved. In the hot plains of India the rooms must of course be kept closed during the heat of the day, and thus the worms must to a great extent suffer, clearly showing that such climates are quite unadapted to the permanent health and welfare of the insect; while reared in native huts amidst darkness, malaria, smoke and dirt, what wonder that the worm degenerates and dies?

Cleanliness, a thing unknown to the natives in the proper sense of the word, is of the utmost importance, as the effluvium arising from an accumulation of the excrement and remains of leaves, to say nothing of the abominable odour from a few dead worms, is sure to generate malaria and so kills or weakens the insects. On this account all wastage, refuse, &c., should be carefully removed daily, and of such consequence to the health of the silk-worm do I consider this operation, that I am surprised to find so experienced a cultivator as Signor Mutti advocating the cleansing of the feeding trays only once *in four days*, and that, too, in the hot climate of the Deccan, where putrefaction and fermentation must be much more rapid than in temperate climates. Nature, moreover, speaks an unmistakeable language on this subject, when she not only provides fresh food and pure air, but casts all impurities to the ground, where they are either absorbed, or their deleterious gases are dissipated into the ever-changing air.

While the worms are moulting they should be left quite quiet and undisturbed, and even loud and sudden noises should be avoided, as well as the shaking of the trays upon which they rest, for even the violent vibration of the air will cause them to start suddenly up as if frightened, which is injurious to them; of course during this time no food is required. On no account should a worm, when in its semi-lethargic state previous to the moult, be removed from the leaf, or spot whereon it stands, for by so doing the hinder feet become detached from the silken web which bound them to it, and the insect is often thus rendered unable entirely to cast off the old skin, from the loss of the hold of the anal feet upon the leaf, and which hold enables it as it were to crawl out of the skin, which remains behind firmly fixed to the spot occupied by these hinder feet.

In the hatching of the worms, if the eggs are attached to paper, cloth, or other substance, there is no difficulty whatever experienced in effecting the exit, except sometimes when they are too closely deposited; but when, as is the case with the Cashmere stock *(B. mori)*, the eggs are loose and unattached, unless the young brood is narrowly watched, many will be unable to cast off the egg-shell from the anal and penultimate segments, and in such case they will die from the constriction of the hinder part. In order to guard against this accident, which is very frequent, the French ingeniously make use of a card or sheet of stiff paper pierced with numerous holes of sufficient size to allow the young worm to pass through, but not large enough to admit the egg-shell, which is consequently thus scraped off as the worm passes through to the light, the cards being placed over the mouth of the vessels in which they are hatched.

On this point, then, a question arises as to why the eggs of *Bombyx mori* are loose, while those of the *Madrassee*, the *Dasee*, and the Bengal annual (*Boro poloo*) are all firmly attached to the cloth or paper upon which they may be deposited?

It is very clear that in its original state of freedom the moth must have attached the eggs, like other species of the genus, to the leaf or to the bark of the tree, for if scattered about broadcast, as they now are, without adhering at all, they would have fallen to the ground and been lost.

Can this be another system of disease? I am strongly inclined to regard it as such for the two reasons that to be unattached is *unnatural*, and because that, although the vast majority of the eggs are loosely scattered, a few will invariably be found adhering, though with no great force, to the cloth, or paper; proving, I think, thereby that they ought all to be thus attached, and that the reason why they are not is to be traced to the fact of weakness in the insect which has not the power to secrete the gum necessary to cause adhesion.

If it be urged against this view that in the Bengal annual (*B. textor*, nob.), the eggs, even when greatly diseased, will still adhere to the cloth, I reply that this does not by any means prove the Cashmere stock to be sound, but simply that disease is situated in some other organ. In the *Boro poloo* of the Bengalis it is *the egg itself* which is diseased, as shown in the variety of colours, in the irregularity of hatching, moulting, &c., but in the Cashmere stock it is seated in some particular gland *in the moth*, which fails to produce the gum by which the egg should become attached; and that this non-attachment of the egg is the fruit of disease is seen in the fact that the worm often experiences the greatest difficulty in freeing itself from the egg-shell, and indeed often dies through its inability to do so; and hence the necessity of resorting to the artificial process of placing over the eggs papers pierced with holes for the avowed purpose of assisting Nature, who, in the absence of disease, requires no aid whatever.

It is, indeed, scarcely to be wondered at that insects exported from their native land and climate, and reared through a long course of years in an artificial, and in many respects highly injudicious, manner should, sooner or later, betray symptoms of weakness and disease. The marvel is, that we have so long been able to preserve any stock whatever, rather than that we should now be compelled to inquire into the means by which it may be saved from utter ruin. It is not in the worm alone that disease is apparent, nor is it exhibited under one phase only, but appears to be as various as the causes which have tended to produce it. There is disease in *the egg*, disease in *the larva*, and disease in *the moth*, affecting one or more of the secretive organs, as shown in the different results produced.

In the egg, disease is shown in its discoloration; the natural colour being a pearlish grey or slate, any marked deviation from the type must be regarded as unhealthy and unnatural. This variation from the typical colour is chiefly seen in green, brown, and vinous red tints, the worms produced from which being often of a sickly yellowish green colour like that which is sometimes apparent on very damp walls, and there is generally great difficulty experienced in casting off the old skin at the moulting periods, the penultimate and anal segments remaining hampered and tightly bound up by the entire skin, which, having forced back so far, the worm cannot disengage from the anal extremity, and consequently, unless assisted, dies. Others exhibit a black spot or spots at the junction of two of the segments or annulations of the body, and die suddenly at different stages of growth, emitting almost immediately after death the most offensive odour.

Some, again, arrive at maturity, but instead of spinning the cocoon, become of a bright turmeric yellow, as if attacked by jaundice, leaving a watery yellow trail behind them; these also die. Others will spin a tolerable cocoon and die within it, spoiling the silk by their putridity; and many spin merely a thin cocoon containing but little silk.

This paucity of silk has, however, in some quarters been attributed, not to disease in the worm, but to a sudden change of temperature at the time when it began to spin. This view of the case is most decidedly erroneous, since if change of temperature caused the worm to cease spinning, death would be the inevitable consequence, and instead of a chrysalis or pupa, the worm itself would be found in the cocoon with its silk reservoirs still unexhausted.

* * * * *

Again, in the moth disease is shown in the unproductiveness of the eggs even after coupling has been effected; it is shown likewise in black spots appearing at the junction of the annulations of the body, which are indications of a malady which prevents the insect from depositing or relieving itself of the ova with which its body is sometimes greatly distended and so causes death; in others, the organs which secrete the gum by which the eggs are glued to the substance upon which they are deposited, are unable to perform their office, and the eggs are consequently loosely scattered in the trays, giving rise, as previously observed, to a difficulty in casting off the egg-shell at the time when the young worms comes forth. The eggs, moreover, being themselves unhealthy, as shown in the variety of their colours, proves likewise that the moth which deposited them must be unhealthy too.

If the ova are healthy, those which were deposited on the same day ought also to produce worms on the same day; diseased eggs are very irregular in this respect, and cause an immense deal of trouble.

A batch of diseased eggs which were deposited in Bengal on the 21st and 22nd of March, began at Mussooree to hatch for a second crop on the 1st of September, but instead of all hatching on the 1st and 2nd of that month, as they would have done had they been healthy, they continued to come forth daily in small numbers until the end of November, so that, although deposited in two days, they actually occupied three whole months in hatching!

This inconvenience was attended with another, for those which were hatched together on the same day did not all moult together, and consequently gave additional trouble in feeding, as they had constantly to be separated; and finally, instead of spinning together, they did so by twos and threes at a time, so as to render it difficult to obtain seed for the ensuing season. The cocoons were generally small, ill formed, and varied in colour, many of them being of a sickly yellow instead of pure white, and others of a beautiful pale green.

All these ailments are undoubtedly to be traced to improper feeding, unsuitable climate, and the long-continued artificial system to which the insect has been subjected, and the only remedies that can effectually restore it to health must, in my opinion, proceed partly from the introduction of a more careful and natural system of rearing, and partly from the periodical infusion of fresh stamina derived from moths produced from eggs imported from the northern provinces of China, to which the insects are indigenous. By these means fresh strength and vigour may be imparted to the constitutions of our present worn-out and debilitated stock, the trouble and the expense incurred being amply compensated for by the improvement which must take place both in the quantity and quality of the silk; and, indeed, I shall presently show that without travelling to China for fresh supplies, it appears quite possible, with common prudence, to produce a natural stock both in Europe and in the Himalaya.

That sickness has been induced by an improper system of rearing is likewise the opinion of Count Dandolo, while M. Boitard finds the origin of some maladies to proceed, he thinks, from an imperfect fecundation of the egg, which occurs, he says, when the moths have been kept in too high a temperature, which he would restrict to between 68° and 75°, because in a greater heat the coupling proceeds too rapidly, and the eggs are in consequence imperfectly fecundated. But it may fairly be questioned, I think, whether eggs *imperfectly fecundated* will produce any worms at all, and it seems like something bordering on a contradiction to say that they will. If fecundation is imperfect, the eggs cannot have been impregnated, and therefore will be unproductive; imperfect fecundation is imperfect impregnation, and imperfect impregnation is no impregnation at all; consequently, on the principle of *ex nihilo nihil fit*, no offspring is to be expected from a non-pregnant female. A moth may be only *partially* impregnated, and will in such case not yield the proper number of prolific eggs, but at the same time all that have been fecundated will produce worms; they may be healthy or sickly according to the condition of the moths, but their being hatched proves that the egg was fecundated. I should feel more inclined to attribute disease to sudden transitions of temperature, whether from heat to cold or from cold to heat; to impurity of air arising from the fermentation of excrement and decaying leaves; to too close an atmosphere; to feeding upon leaves of bad quality, whether proceeding from a defect in the quality of the leaf itself, or from their being faded, sodden, and in a state of incipient fermentation; to want of proper ventilation, want of light, excessive heat and various other causes, among which I would certainly include the custom of chopping up the leaves for young worms; starvation during the night; keeping the leaves for hours after they have been plucked before giving them to the worms; and last, though perhaps not least, feeding them upon shrubs and immature leaves instead of from old standard trees; yet at the same time I shall not expect much improvement in the present state of things, until the entire process of feeding and reeling is supervised by the master's eye, the plantation and the worm being the property of the same individual, so that the whole process of cultivation shall be under the superintendence of one responsible head.

For the purpose of endeavouring in some measure to restore the health of the insects, by obtaining eggs from moths reared in a natural way, I have more than once advocated the experiment of feeding the worms upon trees in the open air; and it is therefore gratifying to observe that while in India ignorance and prejudice were endeavouring to bring ridicule upon the proposition, at that very time, as it now appears, the experiment was actually being made in France with signal success, "M. Thannaron, President of the Société d'Agriculture de la Drôme, having recently experimented with great success on the rearing of silkworms in the open air, and likewise in rooms not warmed. The worms in the house made their cocoons five days earlier than those in the garden, but of about 650 cocoons formed in the house, 42 contained a dead black worm, which was not the case in any of the cocoons formed in the garden, though they were exposed to wind and rain."*

Similar experiments tried by me at Mussooree, both in 1858 and 1859, although not carried so far as to obtain cocoons, were sufficiently successful to prove that the worms will thus thrive better than when fed in the room, and the reason for this is, I think, to be found in the fact that the insect is always supplied with an abundance of good fresh food both by night and by day.

What could be easier, however, than in the large and well-regulated green-houses of Europe to obtain annually a supply of eggs from insects reared in the natural way on dwarf trees, growing, not in tubs, but through the floor? Surely, in those countries in which silk has become so important an article of commerce, it would be worth while to erect large green-houses for this express purpose, and so insure a constant supply of healthy seed to renovate the present debilitated stock.

When the young worm has left the egg and shows, by its manner of raising up the head and forepart of the body, that it is in search of food, the youngest and tenderest leaves, selected from the ends of the branches, should be gently placed over them, and upon which they will speedily crawl upwards to the light and riddle them with holes, and as the leaves become sufficiently covered they should be removed into the feeding-trays; chopped leaves, however time-honored the custom may be, ought on no account to be given, as this method of mincing them is by no means necessary, and is only a patent way of inducing the juices to ferment more rapidly than they ordinarily will do. Common sense ought to point out that nature is the best judge of what is necessary for the welfare of her productions, and as she does not appoint a leaf-cutter to attend upon young caterpillars when in a state of freedom, it is clearly because they are quite capable of cutting the leaf for themselves, having been furnished with strong horny mandibles for this very purpose. For thirty years past I have been in the habit of feeding and rearing caterpillars of various species, and never yet experienced the slightest difficulty in inducing them to cut the leaf for themselves. I can only regard the custom of leaf-chopping as one of those "old wives' fables" which originated doubtless with some tender-hearted ancient spinster, who, having lost her own teeth, considered *minced meat* the most wholesome diet; unless, indeed, our silk cultivators, taking into consideration the fact that human infants are born *without teeth*, have in their wisdom determined that young caterpillars must be equally helpless! The custom, in short, is pretty much allied in point of wisdom and utility to the superstition which in Assam gravely prohibits the individual appointed to put the caterpillars of the Moogah moth upon the trees from using "*his razor for 45 days and from eating fish, milk, and the sweet torie*."†

* *Comptes Rendus* as quoted by the "*Illustrated London News*," August 13th, 1859.

† "Transactions, Agricultural Society of India," Vol. 7, p. 99.

As the worms increase in age and size, so must maturer leaves be given to them, the best being obtained from old trees. The large and succulent leaves of young shoots ought on no account to be given, as they contain an excess of water and consequent deficiency of other more nutritive materials, such as saccharine and resinous matter. The small, hard, rough, and crisp leaf of a mature tree, with the green colouring matter equally diffused and of tolerable and uniform intensity, is by far the best adapted for preserving the worm in health and enabling it to elaborate a full supply of serviceable silk; where the colour of the leaf is of unequal intensity, appearing paler in some parts than in others, it is a sign that the juices are not in a wholesome state, and such leaves are to be avoided; they have this appearance most frequently after long continued rain and want of sun, and likewise towards the approach of autumn; it is induced, likewise, by too much moisture in the soil, which ought consequently to be drained off by trenches.

The leaves of trees growing in moist situations and stiff soils are never good; they are readily eaten by the worms, but contain an excess of water, and the silk obtained is of an inferior quality and deficient in quantity.

Care should be taken, as the worms increase in size, that they are not too much crowded in the trays, so that they may benefit by a free circulation of air and receive their proper supply of nourishment, since without this precaution the stronger ones will suffocate or starve the smaller and weaker. They should, in fact, be classed according to the time of hatching, each day's batch being kept separate from the others, otherwise it would be impossible to avoid disturbing those which, being hatched earlier, will also moult earlier. If the eggs are healthy, however, there ought to be little or no difference in the time of hatching.

Healthy worms are readily known by their plump appearance and hardness when touched, whereas unhealthy ones are soft and sluggish in manner.

When mature and ready to spin, small bundles of dry sticks should be supplied, among which the cocoons will be fixed; and here again attention must be paid to prevent undue crowding, or else two worms will spin together, forming a double cocoon which, from the interlacing of the threads, cannot be unwound.

The Bombyces have the power of producing a silken thread from the very moment of their exclusion from the egg, and even before they have taken any vegetable nourishment whatever—a circumstance which furnishes decisive proof that silk is purely an animal secretion, and at once refutes an absurd opinion which is current in some quarters, that this substance resides in the mulberry tree on which the insect feeds; it would be quite as reasonable to assert that human saliva resides in a leg of mutton.

The mulberry leaf, by nourishing the worm, imparts a healthy vigour to the natural functions of its system, and thereby affects the secretions to the extent of sustaining and strengthening the action of the glands by which these secretions are produced; but that the silk thus secreted does not reside *as such* in the leaf or tree, is proved, I repeat, by the fact that the insect possesses it at the very moment of its birth, and that *as silk* it has no existence until the glands of the worms have elaborated it out of the substance upon which it feeds, or rather, until it has passed through the spinneret; since previous to that the secretion is simply a viscid gum, which has the property of hardening into an elastic silken thread or fibre the moment it becomes exposed to the action of the air.

"As soon as it leaves the spinneret," says Kirby, "it becomes the thread we call silk, which being drawn through *two orifices* is necessarily *double* through its whole length."

By the aid of this thread the young caterpillar possesses the means, when disturbed, of effecting a rapid descent from leaf to leaf in order to avoid a threatened danger, or when in search of more palatable food.

In regard now to the cultivation of silkworms at Mussooree, experiments tried upon the wild *Bombyx Huttoni* have elicited the fact that apparently little is to be expected from its cultivation, as all attempts to domesticate it have hitherto proved ineffectual; the only mode of rearing it would consequently be upon the trees in the open air and left entirely to nature.

This mode of cultivation, if such it can be called, would, however, be always uncertain in its results, since the insects have so many enemies to contend against, such as birds, wasps, and ichneumons; silk could no doubt be produced, although scarcely in sufficient quantities, to render it a lucrative speculation. Little could be gained from crosses with the Chinese species, because the wild worm being inferior to them would return nothing equal to what could be obtained from them alone, and the time and trouble expended upon the cross would, consequently, be thrown away.

It may be as well, however, to state the reasons which induce me to think that success is unattainable, and this I shall do as briefly as possible, at the same time premising that I do not yet intend entirely to abandon all attempts to reclaim the species.

My opinion, then, is found upon the fact that the experiment, now carried on for about eighteen months, has shown—

First, that the wild mulberry tree when reared from cuttings is found to be of very slow growth, and would require at least from five to six years in order to bring it to a size capable of nourishing a sufficient number of worms to insure a tolerable return in silk. It is true that the insect could be reared upon the Chinese mulberry which is of rapid growth, but still it appears to prefer its own forest tree to any other and thrives better upon it; and indeed, while the wild tree is almost sure to have a brood of worms every year, the Chinese mulberry, unless far away from the other, will have none. Trees of the wild species, which are estimated by the hill-men to be five or six years old, are not large enough to feed more than a dozen worms; in many of the nursery beds, which contained say 2,000 cuttings, not more than half a dozen have germinated: while the beds of the Chinese species with the same soil, and entirely under the same influences, have nearly all sprung up into healthy trees of from six to twelve feet in height in less than a year.

Secondly, as regards the worm, the silk produced by it is decidedly good, and produced in considerable quantities would undoubtedly be valuable, a ready market being available at twenty-five rupees per seer. The worm, however, has hitherto proved so intractable that it cannot be reared in the ordinary way in the house, and thrives only on the trees from which, for the reasons above given, no certain crop could be obtained. With a view to curb its restless wandering propensity, I with some trouble effected a cross between it and the *Bombyx mori* from Cashmere, but in every instance, with very few exceptions, the eggs thus obtained proved unprolific, and the worms retained all the intractable habits of the wild species. Further crossing might probably correct this, but would the results obtained be worth the trouble which the experiment would entail? I doubt it.

This failure, however, if such it should eventually prove to be, detracts nothing from the value of Mussooree as a silk-producing district, since all the Chinese species thrive better in its climate than in any other part of India; while besides these we have several indigenous species of other genera which are as yet untried, to wit *Attacus Edwardsianus*, commonly known as the Atlas moth, but distinct from that of China, and which can be easily reared in a state of domestication, producing a large cocoon well stored with a fine yet strong silk of a greyish colour: the plants upon which it feeds are indigenous and abundant, namely, *Falconeria insignis* and *Bradleia ovata*.

Actias selene and *Antheræa roylei* are likewise far from scarce and are easily domesticated, the former being almost omnivorous, and the latter feeding on the common Himalayan oak (*Quercus incana*).

Added to these we have a true species of tussur found sparingly in the Deyrah Doon, and which I have provisionally named *Antheræa sivalensis;* and a very abundant species of eriah moth, which can be reared to any extent and is named *Attacus Canningi*. (nob.)

The introduction of *Bombyx Huttoni* into Great Britain might possibly be attended with more favorable results than can be attained at Mussooree, as the pests which destroy the worms would be left behind in India; and I accordingly intend to forward eggs to several persons interested in such matters, as likewise cocoons of *Actias selene* and *Antheræa roylei*, as the former thrives well both upon the cherry tree and walnut, while the latter may possibly be reared upon the British oak.

Although, therefore, little is to be expected from the wild Himalayan Bombyx, yet with so many untried species in this country, several of which might doubtless be rendered useful to commerce, it would be an undertaking alike honorable to and worthy of the Government to sanction experiments with one and all.

The same views were enforced in a paper contributed by Captain Hutton to the Agricultural Society in the following year (1860).

Experiments in the selection of "*vers tigrés et zébrés.*"

Captain Hutton, in two papers read before the Entomological Society in 1864, maintains that the *B. mori*, whether found in China, Cashmere, Europe or elsewhere, is degenerated by a long course of domestication. He holds that one of the signs of this degeneracy is the colour, and that the worms in a thoroughly vigorous state would be black. He, to test this theory in one year (year not stated), "picked out all the dark-coloured worms (a variety which generally occurs in each brood) and reared them separately, allowing the moths to couple only *inter se*, and the same course was pursued with the white worms. In the following spring the one batch of eggs produced nearly all dark-brindled worms, while the other produced white ones, sparingly interspersed, as before, with an occasional dark one. These latter were removed into the dark batch, which was at the same time weeded of its pale worms. In the third year the worms were still darker than before, and were always larger and more vigorous than the pale ones, giving likewise larger and better stuffed cocoons." Unfortunately, the eggs of the third year were literally scattered to the winds.

In 1862, however, Captain Hutton obtained from Mr. Cope, of Umritsur, a stock of eggs alleged to have been brought straight from Cashmere, but suspected by Captain Hutton to have been acclimatised Punjab worms. They were, according to Captain Hutton, largely diseased, as shown by microscopic examination of the eggs, by the appearance of the worms before spinning, and by the flimsy nature of the cocoons. Nevertheless, the few dark worms picked out " escaped disease altogether, though reared in the same manner, in the same room, in the same temperature, on the same quality of food, and in close contiguity to the others. These dark ones in due time spun cocoons and produced moths which, *inter se*, deposited a fair stock of eggs, with which the experiment was again carried on in the spring of 1863. I may here observe that it is a well-known fact that the more numerous are these dark-coloured worms in any brood the healthier it is considered to be, and *vice versa*." The eggs hatched in 1863 showed a decided improvement. There was still an undue number of white worms, but they did not show any symptoms of disease, and none died. They were, moreover, 3¼ inches long, their predecessors having only measured 3 inches. The cocoons were larger, but still deficient in silk, and the moths, though shewing signs of disease in the malformation and dark spottings of their wings, laid good-sized eggs, great numbers of which adhered firmly to the paper on which they were deposited—"a thing," says Captain Hutton, " I never witnessed before nor ever heard of in regard to *B. mori*." Another sign of vigour was that many male moths of the black stock would fly off their trays to seek females in other parts of the room.

"But still more extraordinary appears the fact, that some of the eggs of *B. mori* of the spring crop of 1863 began to hatch *again for a second crop* on 7th August of the same year They were all from the dark stock, and the circumstance arises, I am inclined to think, from an accession of strength acquired by reversion to a state approaching more nearly to the original constitution. * * * * *

* * The worms now hatched continued to grow and thrive, and spun good cocoons superior in size to those of spring crop, the worms attaining $3\frac{4}{10}$ inches in length. In due time the moths appeared, and were fully twice as large as those of spring, depositing large well-formed eggs." The spring-laid eggs went on hatching even in December. " All these worms were of the dark kind." The eggs laid in the spring and autumn of 1863 both began to hatch at the same time in March 1864. All were decidedly unhealthy; those from the autumn batch, however, much less so than those from the spring-laid eggs, which were so badly jaundiced that Captain Hutton had to throw them away. "The worms from the autumnal batch went on well enough and spun good cocoons, the moths from which deposited a goodly number of eggs in the end of May, and then began to hatch for a second crop in September 1864." These were " apparently healthy," and Captain Hutton contemplated carrying on the experiment for amusement with some of their eggs. "But," he writes, " I feel fully persuaded now, after several years of observation, that the constitution of the worm has been so thoroughly undermined that, although we may be able to restore it to its natural appearance, it will never be able thoroughly to shake off the various diseases to which it has so long been subject. The only way open to the sericulturist, therefore, is to re-seek in the original habitat in China, for the wild worms in their natural state of freedom on the trees, and, should any of them be procurable, then may the stock in Europe be gradually renewed, and the present impending ruin be averted."

Captain Hutton further argues that the dark colour is the natural one from comparison with the wild races of India, and from the analogy of the changes of colour in other domesticated animals, *e. g.*, rabbits, pigeons, &c., and horses, citing in respect to the last from General Daumas' " Horses of the Sahara." That the black worm met with in France should be unknown in Italy, Captain Hutton considers a sign of the more congenial climate of France. Again, he thinks that the white cocoons are symptoms of degeneracy, and that the greater number of white cocoons in Lombardy, as compared with France, shews the superiority of the latter. The same thing, he observes, occurs in regard to the Bara palu (*B. textor*) and *B. mori* at Mussooree, where they spin yellow cocoons.

Captain Hutton on the mulberry.

The following, on the mulberry, is from a paper by Captain Hutton, dated July 1870:

"The only point upon which I do not agree with Dr. Wallace in regard to the food of *B. mori* is his strong advocacy of the *Morus alba*, which he pronounces to be 'the only proper kind for mulberry silk culture'; whereas I have found that seeds, although all gathered from the same tree, will often produce several varieties, and I have not only obtained a *Morus alba* from the seeds of the black or deep purple *Morus nigra* and *M. sinensis*, but three trees of reputed *M. alba* from Cashmere yielded white fruit for four years, and then became purple-fruited. The cause of this may probably have arisen from the roots then striking into a different kind of soil; but this variation would seem to prove that both black and white-fruited trees were still identical as species. It may possibly be that there exists a true white species also; but this is a question for the botanist to decide, and I do no more than record the facts which have come under my own observation; although Count Dandolo seems to agree with me, when he tells us there are four wild varieties of the mulberry tree, one with white, one with red, and two with black fruit, the red apparently proving a connecting link between the others. I have, however, reared silk from *B. mori*, when fed exclusively upon the dark-fruited trees, which was valued at 25 shillings per lb.; and I strongly suspect that if two skeins of silk, the one from *M. alba*, and the other from *M. sinensis* or *M. nigra*, were placed side by side, it would sadly puzzle Dr. Wallace, or the best judge of silk, to say which was which. * * * * I have already spoken of *M. alba* as being so highly extolled by Dr. Wallace in England, and I know also that it is held in great estimation on the continent of Europe, in Cashmere, and in Afghanistan; and yet, for all that, I never found silkworms at Mussooree to thrive so well upon it as upon dark-fruited trees, of which the leaves are considerably coarser. And in this respect nature, by furnishing the indigenous *B. Huttoni* with very coarse leaves, appears to point out that northern worms in northern climates require the more abundant nourishment afforded by such leaves. I always found the foliage of my supposed *M. alba* to be both too small and too thin, and deficient in supplies of that milky, viscous juice so necessary to enable the worms to secrete an abundant supply of good silk-gum in their reservoirs. The same fault was found with the small, thin-leaved *M. multicaulis*, and the large, but thin, cup-shaped leaf of *M. cucullata*. Still it by no means follows that these trees, although found to be useless at Mussooree in the north, may not prove of some use in the hotter climate of the Colonies."

SECTION VI.

SILK IN MYSORE.

THE following on silk cultivation in Mysore by Surgeon Smith, of the 50th Regiment Native Infantry, brings the history of the attempts made in that province down to July 1857 :—

Silk in Mysore down to 1857.

The cultivation of silk is supposed to have been introduced into Mysore by Tippoo Sultan,* but although the climate is evidently well calculated both for the growth of the mulberry and the development of the silkworm, the cultivation does not appear to have made any great progress until after the government of the country fell into the hands of the British in 1832.

2. The Mahomedans adopted the feeding and management of the worms, and the reeling of the silk, as one of the few modes of gaining a livelihood to which they were not averse, purchasing the mulberry leaves from the cultivators; and the Commissioner gladly encouraged the growth of silk in every possible way, with a view of developing habits of industry among a class of men generally opposed to labour of any kind, unconnected with a military life.

3. The open parts of the country alone seem to suit this cultivation, such as the Bangalore, Chittledroog, and open parts of the Astagram Divisions. None is grown in the Nuggur, or in the Munjerabad sections of the Astagram Division; the climate is too damp in these last named districts. Most of the silk was formerly exported to Coimbatore and Tanjore, and a smaller portion found its way to Bellary and Dharwar, for consumption in native manufactories. At this time there was a considerable consumption of the raw material in Bangalore and Mysore in the manufacture of silk : shawls, handkerchiefs, and native cloths, &c.

4. In 1841, four specimens of silk grown in Mysore were sent to Bengal; two of the specimens were purchased in the bazar, and two were from cocoons purchased in the bazar, and privately and carefully reeled, the objects being to find out the defects in the Mysore silk, and to know if it would be valuable as an export in the state in which it was sold by the natives. The following are extracts from the report :—" One of the most apparent faults of this silk is its bad color; this arises from the circumstance of the cocoons having been boiled in copper pans instead of earthenware, and I should imagine that at the time of reeling the silk, the water in which the cocoons were placed was not changed often, as should be done. This latter precaution would not only have assisted to give the silk a better colour, but would have freed it somewhat from the gum, the superabundance of which renders these specimens harsh and hard."

It appeared from the above extract that the faults of the Mysore silk lay not so much in the article itself as in its mode of preparation.

5. A garden, originally planted as a private speculation, was taken by the Mysore Government in 1842, with a view to try how far Signor Mutti's proposal of growing silk from standard mulberry trees was likely to succeed in Mysore, and benefit the country. The larger and upper portion of the ground was planted with cuttings of the St. Helena mulberry, and a few China ones; the lower and wet part with Philippine; both grew well, and for the first few years promised well. Eggs were obtained from Mr. Groves' establishments at Chittoor; from an establishment in the Nilgherries; and some of the annual March bund from Mr. Blechynden's establishments in Bengal; these latter, being annual worms, it was hoped would have proved a valuable auxiliary to the Mysore breed, and enabled us to feed from the standard trees; but in spite of every care and precaution, they hatched on the 11th day as in Mysore, and from that time regularly produced their crops every 50 days. † The silk was certainly a great improvement on that of Mysore, but the worms were delicate, and required more care and attention, so that I much doubt if they were ever extensively used by the natives.

6. The Sub-Peshkar of Bangalore, a man familiar with the country method of reeling silk, was sent to Chittoor, and placed under the tuition of Mr. Groves, who had an extensive plantation of mulberries, and experienced reelers. The man returned to Mysore, well qualified for his post of superintendent of the Government garden. Reels of the best construction were made by Colonel Green, and so expert did the natives become, that in 1846, the Calcutta Chamber of Commerce and Agri-Horticultural Society, both reported most favorably on the cleanness, evenness, roundness, and good colour of certain specimens of Mysore raw silk submitted to them : the only objection made being to the excessive fineness in the reeling and want of sufficient twist.

7. The brokers, Messrs. Norton, Thilburn and Co., of St. Mary Axe, London, reported, of some samples of the silk sent them in 1850, as follows :—" This silk, with care in the getting up, would prove a valuable substitute for many other classes, and from its intrinsic qualities

---

* The mulberry introduced is said to have been the common mulberry of the Deccan, and the worm the *Bombyx synensis*.

† If the eggs sent were really eggs of the *Bombyx textor*, this is a very curious fact. But I suspect the eggs belonged to one of the Bengal multivoltines. The March bund *includes* multivoltines.

would find a ready sale in this market." These extracts prove the capability of Mysore to produce silk of first-rate quality. But until filatures, conducted by Europeans, are established, as in Bengal, but little of the silk will ever find its way to the English market. At present the natives find a ready sale in India for all they can produce, and it answers their purpose better to reel it roughly, and sell it as they do; for although clean reeling will produce a greatly enhanced price, the proceeds of the silk will be much less, and the sale of the raw material not so certain as it is now. Since 1846 the average annual produce of Mysore has been about 10,000 maunds of 24lbs., or 240,000lbs. weight—a quantity sufficiently large to attract attention to its cultivation.

The standard mode of cultivation failed for reasons explained in the following extract from a letter to the Commissioner, dated 11th August 1849:—"When we consider the incessant demand for leaves made on the standard trees, in consequence of the bi-monthly crops of silk which alone grown in Mysore, the cause of failure will at once be evident. The leaves of a plant are organs of respiration, digestion, and nutrition; a tree cannot be made to yield five or six crops annually without seriously impairing its vitality. If the leaves are stripped off a plant before the fruit has commenced ripening, the fruit will fall off, and not ripen. If a branch is deprived of leaves for a whole summer, it will die, and not increase in size perceptibly; and this is exactly what has taken place with the standard trees in the silk garden; they have aged, become woody, and throw out nothing but fruit, unless pruned back to the stems, when an entirely new set of branches is thrown out with an abundant crop of fine leaves; these branches, by the loss of their leaves, age and die within the year, and the same process has to be renewed; latterly, the only mode of obtaining good leaves from the standards has been by cutting them down to the ground; the roots then throw up abundant fine shoots, a proceeding which, in effect, is returning to the bush system. * * * * *

"In this country 6½ crops are the utmost ever obtained; each crop occupies 56 days—33 in the worm, 12 in the cocoon, 11 in the egg; the insect requires food for 198 days in each year, when the succession is regularly kept up. The cultivation by standard trees is obviously not adapted to meet such incessant demand.

"More than one private speculation with standard trees failed at Chittoor and Coonoor, under energetic and intelligent European superintendence. I have no reason to think that the experiment failed from any want of care or attention on the part of the attendants; they have done their best, and if the Commissioner will refer to the report of the Bengal Horticultural Society on the specimens of silk sent to Bengal in 1846, he will see there that the qualifications of the reeler at the garden are first-rate, I have lately found, when obliged to hire reelers to wind off a large crop, that it was not difficult to get very good reelers among the natives; and the reason why the natives do not practise reeling their own silk cleanly and fit for the European market, is, that it is not saleable in this country; and there is a demand for all that can be produced reeled in the country fashion; independently of which, the increased value of the silk, cleanly reeled, will not compensate for the loss of weight and increased time and expenses of reeling.

"The standard trees are all worn out and useless; they require to be replanted, and, if replaced by young trees, not a leaf should be taken from them for the next five years. A large portion of the garden is laid down with the common country bush mulberry cuttings; the St. Helena for standards are planted at distances of 20 or 30 yards from each other among the bushes, and this, I think, is the proper way of growing standard trees, which, thus planted, in no way interfere with the bush system, and at the same time afford food in season, when from want of water or other causes, the bushes fail. The Philippine, planted as bushes, has not answered; though the leaf is large and nutritious, it is said by the natives not to yield an equal weight of food on the same space of ground.

"I beg respectfully to suggest to the Commissioner, either that the entire garden be laid down in the country fashion, with standard trees at intervals as above described, or else, that it be let out to natives to be cultivated in their own way, keeping up the present breed of worms, which are very superior to their own in the bright colour of the silk."

8. At present the cultivation of silk is carried on by the natives in their own way, and by the bush system which they have found practically the best.

Silk cultivation in the hands of natives.

2. The cultivation continued to be carried on principally in the Bangalore District, and in 1859-60, the yield of raw silk was estimated at 350,928lbs. The quality had meanwhile much fallen off, for, in 1866, Signor De'Vecchj described the native reeled silk as the worst he had ever seen, the thread being bad in colour, "irregular, flat, knotted and dirty," and worth in Europe not more than 13 or 14 shillings per lb. The method of rearing followed by the natives was much the same as that pursued in Madras, and described by the Tinnevelly tehsildar. The method of reeling practised by the natives is thus described by Mr. H. E. Sullivan, Acting

Collector of Coimbatore, in a report addressed to the Madras Board of Revenue after visiting Kingheri near Bangalore :—"The native reeling apparatus consists of a small axis working in bearings on two uprights, the motion being communicated from the hand by a winch-handle. Radiating from the axis at each end, within the uprights are four or six arms of either wood or metal (stiff hoop iron is sometimes used), which are connected at the upper extremities by bars of smooth polished wood or bamboo. This forms the reel. At the opposite end of the axis to that where the winch-handle is fixed, a pulley is attached, which, communicating by a band with a rough eccentric,

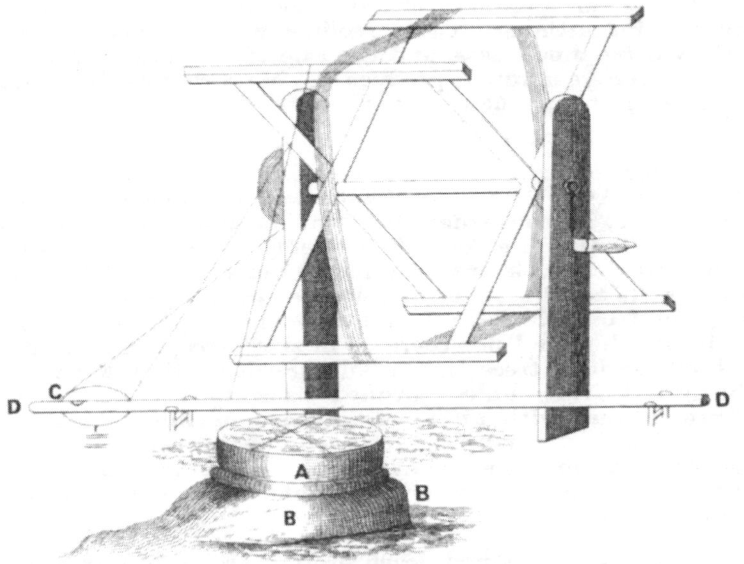

marked C in the enclosed sketch, gives a lateral motion to the bar D D. In the centre of this bar, and immediately in front of the basin where the cocoons are steeped, two holes are punched, through each of which a filament ofs ilk, (the two crossing each other below), is led on to the reel. The object of the crossing is to free the filaments from the gummy substance present in the cocoon, and to give the silk a roundness, and the lateral movement of the bar distributes the silk evenly on the reel. It also, I imagine, serves to detach some of the gummy substance above referred to; but in this essential part of the process, the country apparatus is certainly very defective. Hence the harsh coarse feeling of country-wound silk, which, combined with other defects, renders it of little value in comparison with the material reeled in the European manner." In 1866, a disease broke out among the silkworms (described by the Chief Commissioner as "a sort of atrophy") which much discouraged the cultivators.

Advent of Signor de'Vecchj.

3. European enterprise had meanwhile entered Mysore in this branch. In 1865 Signor de'Vecchj obtained some land for mulberry cultivation, and established a small filature at Kingheri, near Bangalore, and laid himself out to purchase cocoons largely. He also took great trouble and spared no expense to improve the native worm, and to introduce superior mulberry.* In July 1866, he supplied the Commissioner for the affairs of Mysore with a number of cartoons of eggs produced by a cross of the native worm with Japanese and Italian stock. These eggs were distributed to men carefully selected from among the garden-holders of the Closepet and Hosakote talooks; but several heavy rain-falls retarded the opening of the eggs, and the first attempt was unsuccessful. In 1867, however, another experiment was tried, and 196 cartoons of eggs obtained from Signor de'Vecchj were distributed among the cultivators of nine talooks of the Astagram and Bangalore Divisions. But the experiment failed again, the worms dying of the disease which had appeared among the native worms. The few survivors spun very superior cocoons. Again the experiment was tried, and 375 cartoons of Japanese eggs were purchased at a cost of Rs. 7,161, and distributed gratuitously. But some of the eggs failed to hatch, and when they did hatch, the worms died. In 1869 the experiment was repeated on a still larger scale, the Chief Commissioner sanctioning the expenditure of Rs. 9,000 on 500 cartoons of eggs supplied by Signor de'Vecchj.

---

* He mentions having introduced the "*Morus sinensis, M. Japanensis*, and *M. Perottetæa*."

Mr. Fretwell's account of the state of things in 1869.

4. The following extract from a memorandum by Mr. Fretwell, who was deputed by the Bombay Government to study "among others" the subject of silk cultivation in Mysore, will show what was the state of things in that province in 1869:—

The objects of my recent journey, as laid down in my instructions, were—

1st.—That I should make myself practically acquainted with the details of the various processes involved in raising silk, and preparing it for the market.

2nd.—That I should ascertain the most suitable season for commencing the experiment in Khandeish, and bring with me a supply of eggs for the purpose of introducing the culture, or, should it turn out that the season was not the right one, I should make arrangements for procuring a supply when wanted.

With regard to the first object of my journey, I have been able (notwithstanding the untoward circumstance of a complete failure in the crop,) to fulfil it completely, and trust that I shall be able to produce, by a slight and inexpensive improvement on the ordinary native apparatus, a machine, which in native hands will be as effective as is the expensive and beautiful machinery at Kingheri. The second object has not been so satisfactorily carried out, owing to the complete and through deterioration in the breed of worms throughout Mysore (both native and imported species). The insect has, in fact, exhausted its vital energy, and dies off just when the spinning process ought to commence. To have commenced an experiment with eggs from such a breed would, in my opinion, have been highly injudicious, as the inevitable failure of the crop would have been probably attributed to some defect of the climate, or to carelessness in the manipulation of the insects, instead of to the actual cause, *i. e.*, the want of vitality in the worms themselves. Dr. de'Vecchj de'Piccioli would not, even after a microscopic examination of the cartoons just arrived from Japan, guarantee that they were good, and I judged it better, therefore, to await the result of their development at Kingheri than to bring any with me, more especially as it was apparent that many of the eggs would have been hatched before I could reach Khandeish, and would consequently have been lost.

Dr. de'Vecchj de'Piccioli has promised to send us any quantity of seed which we may require on ascertaining their healthy condition (but nothing can be possibly done in the matter till after the monsoon). The supply just now is very limited, owing to the original stock, as well as the imported species, having become almost extinct in Mysore; and whatever seed is available for a first crop this year has been purchased by the Mysore Government, and distributed to the impoverished cultivators. The natives attribute the loss of their silk crops to the introduction of the Japanese worm, the crossing of the breeds, and the extended culture of the *Japanese** mulberry, but there can be no actual foundation for this belief. My own opinion (which, however, I offer with much diffidence) is that the culture of both the plant and the insect has been too much forced. Nowhere in the world are so many consecutive crops of silk produced in one season as in the silk districts of Mysore. The mulberry is cultivated under irrigation, and never allowed to attain any size, or to become a strong hardy plant. It is kept down to the size of a shrub by cutting down alternate stems every year, whilst the growth of the leaves is forced by constant irrigation; and the result will naturally be that leaves produced under such conditions will contain a much larger proportion of watery matter than when the plant is allowed a more natural growth. Such food will, doubtless, be consumed in larger quantities by the insects, and will stimulate their growth, and produce in them an earlier maturity, and a consequent more frequent succession of generations; but in the course of a season or two, it must impair the vital energy of the insect. This is of course only a theory, but it is, I submit, a most reasonable one, and though Dr. de'Vecchj de'Piccioli will not accept it, he has no other to suggest. He simply says the insects are dying of "atrophy," and that he is unable to account for it. The mulberry and silk culture is only carried on in four districts in the Mysore territories, and the quantity of land occupied as mulberry gardens is about as follows, *viz.*:—

Mysore District	... ...	11,013 acres.
Bangalore "	... ...	6,150 "
Colar "	... ...	1,215 "
Hussun "	... ...	45 "

So there is a total of 18,443 acres altogether,† which pays a higher average assessment than even sugar-cane land. The profitable nature of the culture is well demonstrated by the fact, that with such heavy assessments, and after the loss of three years' crops in the Bangalore District, and of two in each of the others, there has as yet been no manifestation of any wish to give up the culture throughout the four districts on the part of any single individual. The Messrs. de'Vecchj had not a single worm or cocoon of their own in existence; but whilst I was there, some small parcels of native-raised cocoons came in from Madoor and Closepet, and afforded me the opportunity of seeing the Kingheri machinery in active operation for a short time. On subsequently visiting Madoor, Closepet, Chinapatam, and Mysore, I had the opportunity of observing the native method of reeling the silk and tending the worms. Everything was as rough and untidy as it is possible to imagine, but with a very little painstaking and a slight

* This seems an error; Mr. Fretwell perhaps means the St. Helena mulberry.

† These figures are, however, fallacious, for Colonel Meade states that by no means all the land entered as "mulberry garden" is cultivated with mulberry.

modification of the native apparatus, I am convinced that it could be made to perform its work (if not in so wholesale a manner) at least as perfectly as the most costly machinery.

From six to eight crops of silk per annum have been realised of late, the larger number being raised from the cross-breed insect resulting from the intermixture of the Japanese species with that previously existing in Mysore (which latter also appear to have been a cross between a native species and the Chinese worm introduced by Tippoo Sultan).

I understand that the failure originated three years ago at Kingheri, and has gradually extended to the districts occupied by native raisers alone. It has, during the past season, thoroughly exterminated the worms, except a few at Madoor and Chinapatam, which appear to belong to the old stock of the country, the cocoons of which are much larger than those raised in Europe, and nearly approach in size those of the silkworm indigenous in the Coorg forests (where there are no mulberries, the worm being found only on the *Ficus Elastica*, the *Ficus Religiosa*, and the *Isonandra Acuminata*). Much neglect and carelessness is apparent in the native silk-raisers' places. The worms are not fed at regular intervals of time. No attention seems to be paid to either temperature, ventilation, or cleanliness, and no separate apartments are given up to the insects, which are simply confined in large trays of split bamboo, and stowed away in any convenient corner. In the establishment of Messrs. de'Vecchj and Company at Kingheri, the temperature is carefully regulated, as is also the feeding day and night, and all refuse is carefully removed. The mulberry leaves are even chopped up by a sort of sausage machine when the worms are still young, though this is not continued afterwards. * * *

Above 600 cocoons go to the pound; out of this quantity de'Vecchj extracts one ounce of good reeled silk, whilst the natives get 1¼ ounce. The latter, however, is not so clean as a rule (Mr. Scarlett's memorandum on the subject states the average outturn from 1 ℔. of cocoons at Peshawur to be two ounces of good silk). The different results obtained by the natives and Dr. de'Vecchj are doubtless the result of greater cleanliness on the part of the latter, though I have seen a few specimens of native-wound silk which would lose nothing by comparison with the best produced at Kingheri. The natives inform me that with a mulberry garden 90′ × 20′ they can produce in the year the weight of 156 Company's Rupees in reeled silk, which, on an average, will sell for Rs. 36. The price of silk varies very considerably: the lowest price given by the Dharwar and Belgaum merchants who come to Mysore to buy the native silk is Rs. 4 per seer of 26 Rupees weight, and the highest price given in the district for the best reeled silk is Rs. 14 per seer. Dr. de'Vecchj tells me that it is useless to think of raising silk where the heat in the shade exceeds 80° Fahr., but I find, on referring to the registered thermometric readings for five consecutive years at Bangalore, that the mean monthly heat is above 80° for ten months in the year, at 80° for one month, and only below 80° during one month. This is, of course, the mean of greatest heat during the day and in the shade. No other place where silk is raised in Mysore is so cool as Bangalore, and at Mysore itself the heat is many degrees higher constantly; besides which, in the native huts, as I have said, there is neither ventilation nor cleanliness, and no apparent regard whatever to temperature. Should it be deemed advisable, I shall be able, through the Amildar of Closepet, to induce one or two families accustomed to raise and reel silk to emigrate to Khandeish. The price paid by the Messrs. de'Vecchj to the natives for cocoons is only Rs. 18 per maund, which leaves a very handsome profit to the factory for reeling it. The floss silk and surmukh is all sent home, where it is carded and treated similarly to cotton.

Mr. Sullivan's account of Kingheri filature.

5. The following extract from a letter by Mr. Sullivan, Collector for Coimbatore, describing the Kingheri filature, is also of interest:—

"In propagating and rearing the worm, so far as I was able to judge, there is very little difference between the system followed in Messrs. De'Vecchj's establishment and the mode adopted by the silk-producing ryots in Mysore and Kolligal. Two essential points are, however, carefully observed at the Kingheri Factory, which are entirely neglected by the ryots, namely, cleanliness, and giving the worms sufficient space. In the villages which I inspected, the trays were so closely packed that the worms could barely move, and when they did, they crawled over and fouled each other in a manner which made the inspection anything but a savoury task; and where they had the disease, I noticed the living and the dead worms lying together in the same tray. In the same way, when the worms are about to spin, they are placed so thickly together in the partitioned screens, that they have no space to develope the cocoon to its proper size. Now at Kingheri, all these matters are carefully attended to. Throughout the whole of the rearing-house there was nothing offensive, and ample space was afforded to the caterpillar in all its stages of growth. It must be remembered, however, that Messrs. De'Vecchj's operations are conducted in a building especially constructed for the purpose, whilst the ryot has to conduct his within the confined area of his dwelling-house, and these worm-trays and spinning screens take up a great deal of room, so that it can hardly be wondered at that the number of them is limited.

"4. From the rearing-house at Kingheri we were conducted to the room where the reeling apparatus is erected. Unfortunately, this beautiful machinery was not at work on the occasion of our visit, and I gathered from the attendant that no silk had been reeled there for upwards of a year for want of material, but as he only spoke Canarese, in which language I am not a proficient, I may have misunderstood him. Though not in motion, the machinery is so beautifully simple, that we had no difficulty in understanding the mode of working, and both Mr. Grimes and myself were struck by the facility with which it might be adapted for use in a jail, convict labor being substituted for steam as a motive power. It was curious to observe the similarity of design in these finished appliances to the rude apparatus used by the native silk reeler, the difference being that in one case the design had been worked out to perfection, in the other no attempt has been made to improve on the crude invention.

* * * * *

The paragraph describing the native apparatus has already been extracted.

"Without the aid of a sketch, which I am not able to make, it is rather difficult to give a description of the machinery used in Messrs. de'Vecchj's factory. As before stated, it is, in main points, very similar to the rude apparatus above referred to. It consists of a number of reels of the same sort as those above described, though of course highly finished. An equal number of light iron driving wheels set below the reels communicate motion to them by friction with a wooden cylinder set on the axis of the reel. These driving wheels have a common axle, to which motion is communicated from the shafting attached to a small steam engine, so that when steam is turned on, the whole apparatus moves simultaneously. As, however, the operation of reeling has to be stopped whenever a filament breaks, an arrangement is made for throwing each reel out of gear by means of a small tumbler lever within the reach of the operator handing the cocoons. In front of the reels is a long stand containing metal basins for steeping the cocoons in during the process of reeling, the water in them being heated by flues connected with the boiler of the engine which drives the machinery. The filaments, two in number, crossing each other, are led from the cocoons in the basin through holes in a metal bar to which lateral motion is communicated by an arrangement of cog-wheels; they are then again crossed and passed through two agate guides on to the reel, which being placed in gear, the operation of winding commences. The above is, I think, a tolerably accurate description of Messrs. de'Vecchj's machinery; but as it was not working when I saw it, and as there was no one present capable of explaining it to me, I may have left some important points unnoticed. There are, doubtless, other processes to which the raw material is subjected with which I am unacquainted, before the beautiful article which Messrs. deVecchj send into the market is produced."

Further attempts to revive the industry.

6. Colonel Meade, in two reports addressed to the Madras Board of Revenue, gives the following account of the attempts of 1870 and 1871:—

For the fourth time, in January 1870, a large quantity of newly imported Japanese cartoons was distributed in the Bangalore, Toomkoor and Kolar districts. The first results were favorable, and the demand for eggs was very large, but the worms did not seem to thrive in the second generation, and the foreign species became extinct. Again, in February 1871, 500 Japanese cartoons were distributed gratuitously; but proved a complete failure. In the Bengalore and Kolar districts a small number only of the eggs were hatched, and even in these cases the worms died within a few days. The symtoms preceding death appear to have been similar everywhere: the worms assumed a reddish colour, their heads became enlarged, and a greenish fluid exuded from the mouth. The ryots in the Toomkoor district seem to have given no attention to the matter, being apparently disheartened by former failures. The eggs distributed in the Mysore District are reported to have failed owing to climatic causes.

Conclusion.

7. The following extract from a letter from Colonel Meade, dated 21st August 1871, shews the present state of affairs and his opinion thereon:—

"Both Monsieur de'Vecchj and Dr. de'Vecchj (who succeeded to the charge of the Kingheri Factory), have now left the country, discouraged, it is believed, by the failure which, notwithstanding their own persevering efforts and the liberal aid of the Mysore State, has throughout attended the measures which have been adopted. The Chief Commissioner is thus debarred from obtaining, as he would desire to have done, the views of these gentlemen as to the causes of the failure that has occurred in the acclimatisation of the foreign, and especially the Japanese species, of silkworms. Colonel Meade is disposed to attribute that result to the climate of Mysore, to which the cartoons were brought direct from Japan, without undergoing any preparation for so marked a change, and he is of opinion that no advantage would arise from continuing the experiments with that species of worm. On the other hand, the China species has successfully established itself, having been cultivated in the province for very many years, and though deteriorated by close breeding, it is possible that the cause of the sickness and mortality to which it is now subject, and which threatens to extinguish the industry, may be removed by importing fresh seed from the south of China, the climate of which approaches more nearly than Japan to that of this plateau."

The Mysore Administration Report for 1870-71 states that 31 per cent. of the cultivated land was under mulberry, and the value of the silk produced in the province is estimated at 5½ lakhs of rupees. The Nundidroog division was said to have exported 4,610 maunds (Madras maunds probably).

SECTION VII.

SILK IN THE CENTRAL PROVINCES.

Attempt at Sericulture at Kamthee in 1827-31.

THE first attempt at rearing the domestic worm, in the territories now included in the Central Provinces, seems to have been that of Miss Calder in the years 1827-31. The experiment was entirely a dilettante one, and the silk was ill wound. The record in the transactions of the Agri-Horticultural Society is very brief.

At Nagpore.

2. In 1836, Mr. (now Sir D.) McLeod, writing from Seonee says:—"After repeated trials at Nagpore, the rearing of the genuine silkworm has hitherto been found impracticable."

Trials in the Seonee district.

3. About 1852, a private gentleman named Wood appears to have attempted to introduce the mulberry worm into Seonee: but no record of success attained exists. "A few mulberry trees are pointed out as having been planted by him, but no further trace of his operations is now visible."

Again, in 1863, preparations were made for an expriment; $2\frac{1}{2}$ acres being planted with mulberry cuttings, and the services of a silkworm rearer secured. But the authorities seem to have begun to build without counting the cost: "the local funds could not meet the expense, and the matter was then indefinitely postponed."

In 1869, Captain Saurin Brooke was appointed to the same district, and was permitted to make an experiment in naturalising the domestic worm. He planted some six acres with mulberry and obtained some cocoons, apparently of the nistree or *Bombyx Crœsi*, from Dr. Mackenzie, whose experiments at the Dharwar jail have been noticed in the Bombay section. The worms of the season 1869-70 were fed on the leaves of old existent mulberry trees, and the cocoons produced were pronounced good by Mr. Lotteri, silk broker, by Capt Hutton, and by the Bombay Chamber of Commerce. Captain Brooke obtained four crops of cocoons in the first season; "but here a totally unlooked for obstacle presented itself." The mulberry refused to grow in the black cotton soil, and the experiment had to be given up, as the worms could not be fed. Captain Brooke attributes the ill success of the mulberry to the excess of moisture in the soil, a view corroborated by the fact tbat the few isolated mulberries which have thriven, stand on spots exceptionally possessed of a perfect natural drainage. The inference Captain Brooke draws is, that in the Central Provinces an effort should be made to familiarize the markets of Europe with the tusser, of which more anon.

Silk manufacture in the Central Provinces.

4. Though not producing silk from domesticated worms, the Central Provinces *manufacture* fabrics in which such silk is used; the supply being obtained either from Bengal *viâ* Mirzapore, or from China, by way of Bombay. During the year 1867-68, the imports of silk were estimated at 228,862 lbs., of which nearly one half was Bengal silk,* about the same quantity from Bombay (*i. e.*, China silk), the remainder having been brought up from the coast into the eastern districts. The imported silk is worked up on the looms of the Nagpore, Bhundara and Chanda districts, either into fabrics entirely of silk, especially women's "sarees," or into handsome silk fringes for "dhotees" and "sarees" of cotton. These cloths with silk borders are largely manufactured at Nagpore, and find their way all over the Mahratta country.

The tusser traffic in the Central Provinces.

5. Side by side with the manufacture of fabrics from foreign silk, there exists an important industry, or group of industries, dependent on the produce of the indigenous tusser worm. This insect is utilised in the following districts, Raipore, Bilaspore, Sumbulpore, the Upper Godavery, Chanda, Bhundara, Nagpore,

---

* In the year ending 30th June 1871 some 94,000lbs. of raw silk seem to have passed Allahabad from the eastward, bound for stations on the Great Indian Peninsula Railway. Probably most of this quantity was destined for the Central Provinces.

Balaghat, Seonee, Chindwara, Betool and Nursinghpore, more especially in the four first mentioned. Figures are given of the number of cocoons used up annually in thread; but they are very inconsistent and admittedly untrustworthy, and it would be of little use to reproduce them in detail here. A few of the estimates may however be given. Sumbulpore is said to yield 3,500 seers of silk, Raipore 6,000, Bilaspore 900, and Chanda 22,500. This last is probably a very excessive estimate. Suffice it to say that the quantity used is very considerable, but varies greatly from year to year, the collection and rearing of the worms being pursued not steadily, but as an accessory to other employments. The tusser silk is, for the most part, woven up and used in the province. It seems to be chiefly employed for fringes, or for weaving with cotton into mixed fabrics, the woof being cotton and the warp silk; cloth all of tusser silk is rarely manufatured; in Seonee, according to Captain Brooke, only on the order of European residents. But, at any rate in some districts, muktas (garments worn by Brahmans after bathing), cholees (women's bodices), and doputtas and dorwas, seem to be made of pure tusser silk.

SECTION VIII.

SILK IN THE BERARS AND NIZAM'S COUNTRY.

Silk cultivation in Berar and His Highness the Nizam's territory.

THE following account has been supplied by the Resident at Hyderabad:—

The climate and soil of Berar are well adapted for the cultivation of the mulberry tree, it is believed; but as it was not indigenous, and as the breeding of silkworms for the purpose of trade was an unknown industry, application was made for encouragement and support by the Government, which resulted in a sum of Rs. 5,000 per annum being set aside for the object.

Before steps could be taken for utilising this grant, a general failure arose both in India* and Persia, owing to an epidemic among the silkworms.

Experiments were consequently deferred to a more favourable season.

A foundation, however, has been laid for future experiments by the cultivation of the mulberry tree in some of the nursery gardens in Berar, and by the distribution of young plants among the people.

Mr. P. Chamarette, of Yeotmahl, had a number of trees in his compound at Ellichpore with caterpillars and cocoons on them, with which it was his intention to have experimented, but his removal from that station prevented him from carrying out his designs.

The mulberry tree was extensively cultivated in the Nabob's gardens at Ellichpore.

Thirty years ago, Captains Fenwick and MacDonell, retired officers of His Highness the Nizam's service, had silk manufactories at Kunneer, with extensive mulberry plantations for rearing the various species of *Bombycidæ* yielding silk of superior quality. The remains of the factory and plantation may be now seen.

In the Woon district there are but few Mahomedans, and Captain Bushby doubts whether the "Koonbees" would forego the cultivation of cotton in order to propagate the silkworm.

The Deputy Commissioner of Akola writes that silk does not appear to have been cultivated in Berar, or labour spent in its experimental produce.

The Commissioner, West Berar, says that "there are a few silk-workers at Dewulgaon Raja, who import their supplies from Poona, Nuggur, Bombay, &c."

No mulberry cultivation exists or has existed in West Berar.

Tusser in the Nizam's country.

2. The manufacture of tusser seems to be carried on to some extent both in the Berars and in the Nizam's territories. The places named as seats of this industry are Ellichpore and Kunneer in the Berars, and Warrungal and Bhudrachellum in the Nizam's dominions. Ellichpore, however, where there are said to be 75 silk-workers, derives its tusser cocoons from the Baitool district of the Central Provinces, whence they are brought by the Dheemurs.

---

* It may be inferred from this that it was intended to introduce seed from Mysore. Epizoic disease has not appeared in Bengal. The narrative of a Russian silk merchant who had visited Khokand and Bokhara, recently quoted from the *Russian Messenger* in the *Pall Mall Gazette*, states also that the worm of the Khanates had escaped the disease, which has however reached Persia.

SECTION IX.

SILK IN OUDH.

THE following, on Sericulture in Oudh, is by Dr. Bonavia :—

About the beginning of 1847, Captain Hollings who had charge of the Chargebagh in Lucknow, introduced the large-leaved China mulberry plant into that garden; formed a small plantation, and tried some experiments with silkworms.* He quitted the station, and no one continued the experiment of rearing silkworms.

In 1863 † at the request of the Chief Commissioner of Oudh, I made extensive experiments with various kinds of silkworms, in order to ascertain whether they could be profitably reared in Oudh.

The kinds of worms tried were—

The China silkworms,
The "Desee" silkworms,
The "Boro Pooloo" silkworms,
The Madrasee silkworms,
The Cashmere silkworms, and
The Bokhara silkworms.

Of these the China silkworm could be reared from June to September, and the Boro Pooloo in February and March. All the other kinds were much less successfully reared. The former produces several crops in the year, the latter only one, in the winter. The experiments were continued through the years 1863 and 1864. In the hot weather of 1865 I was obliged to leave Lucknow for three months on account of ill health, and during my absence a large number of worms which I had left under the care of trained natives died. The experiment has never been resumed. The mulberry plants used were—

"Morus cucullata," with large and thin leaves, shaped more or less like a skull-cap.
"Morus alba," imported from Europe.
"Morus multicaulis," the small entire-leaved China mulberry.
"Desee Shatoot," which grows into a large tree with lobed leaves, &c.
"Bedana Shatoot," which grows into a small-sized spreading tree.

The leaves of all these were readily eaten by the silkworms, and they were all valuable, as their leaves sprouted at different times, some much earlier in the season than others.

In connection with the larger experiments in Lucknow, there were other smaller experiments, carried on in most of the districts of Oudh, and somewhat extensively in Seetapore. They were less successful than those in Lucknow. A reeler was brought from the silk-producing districts of Bengal; he taught some natives in Lucknow the Bengal mode of rearing worms and taught some of them to reel. Another reeler was brought also from Bengal by the Deputy Commissioner of Seetapore, and natives were also taught there.

---

* The silk, however, was not readily reeled, and was declared unmarketable.

† Experiments had, however, been made in the two previous years. The following account of a brood of worms in 1861 is taken from the Oudh Administration Report for 1861-62 :—

In February 1861, Colonel Clarke procured a small supply of Cashmere silkworm eggs from Mr. Cope of Umritsur, and made them over to Mr. P. Carnegy, who undertook the charge; the worms were kept in an empty room in his house, and the trays and baskets were of the same kind as used in Bengal. The following memorandum of his proceedings and the result was given by Mr. Carnegy :—

"On the 24th of February I received from the Commissioner a small box of silkworm eggs of the Cashmere variety. On that day a few of these eggs were hatched, and they continued hatching till the 3rd of April, after which date about a hundred eggs remained, which have showed no signs of vitality. The worms were at once supplied with mulberry leaves and fed well and regularly, except at the intervals of changing their skins. The worms continued very healthy until the 29th of March, when the first cocoons were spun. On the 10th of April there were fifteen hundred cocoons, and on the 27th of April, when the last cocoons were formed, the number amounted to three thousand one hundred. The cocoons first formed were very good, indeed superior to any I have ever seen, but as the heat increased the quality deteriorated much, till the last formed cocoons were not better than the common Bengal cocoons. Some of the last-hatched worms spun prematurely and went into the chrysalis state after surrounding themselves with a mere film of silk. From this it seems that it would be advisable to force the hatching, so that all the cocoons would be spun by the 1st of April. The irregularity of hatching has been the only drawback, and this, I think, would be remedied by exposing the eggs to a moderate heat about the middle of February. A plentiful supply of mulberry leaves was always procurable, and it has been fairly proved that the worms will thrive on them.

"Five hundred of the Cashmere cocoons have been sent to Bengal to be spun into silk and reported on. Nothing has been heard by me about the result as yet, but, judging from some silk wound off by myself in a rough manner, there is every reason to expect that it will be favorable."

Some of the cocoons were sent to Mr. Cope at Umritsur, who describes them as very beautiful and of excellent quality. The cocoons sent to Bengal were also favorably reported on. Mr. Turnbull, of the Ghattal establishment, writes—

"They are certainly very fine, and far superior to any thing of the kind in Lower Bengal. If they are from the Cashmere worm they have deteriorated about 56 per cent. and are much smaller, as 100 cocoons weigh $3\frac{1}{4}$ tolahs, while those sent by Mr. Cope from Cashmere, and which elicited such praise from Count Fieschi, weighed $5\frac{1}{4}$ tolahs. However strange it might appear, your cocoons have yielded more silk—400 cocoons producing $2\frac{3}{4}$ tolahs, while those from Cashmere $9\frac{1}{2}$ annas. I consider your silk as good as any I have reeled from Cashmere and elsewhere."

Specimens of the silk produced were sent to Calcutta for examination at different times. Some samples were favorably reported on; others unfavorably. Those favorably reported on were said to be not unlike Japan silk, and would be worth in the Calcutta market from Rs. 15 to 16 per seer. All the silk produced was sold in the Lucknow bazar for Rs. 16 per seer (Lucknow seer of 92 tolahs).

The result of these experiments was that silkworms could be reared in Oudh, and good silk might be produced, but that it would not remunerate any one to undertake the cultivation of the silkworm under the present condition of this province, and the reasons are the following:—

1st.—Silkworm rearing requires a great deal of careful labour, besides the occupation of a large space of ground grown with mulberry trees. The same space of ground grown with serial crops would require very much less labour, and would be proportionably more remunerative.

2nd.—The variations of temperature throughout the year are very great, the maximum in the shade for 1869 having been 118·9, the minimum 34·0, and the mean temperature 84·1. Therefore the worm could not be reared in sufficiently large numbers throughout the year, without very special arrangements. This circumstance would entail the discharging of a large portion of the skilled labour at certain times of the year, which would be found very inconvenient.

3rd.—In this province, the mulberry trees, in order that they might furnish a good supply of leaves, require to be often irrigated in the winter, and in the hot dry weather they would require *constant* irrigation. Frequent irrigation from wells by bullocks or other means is expensive, and therefore would make the enterprise unremunerative.

These are the main reasons for which, under existing circumstances, silkworm rearing in Oudh cannot be remunerative; whether, when irrigation is made easy by means of canals, and the climate of Oudh is also modified through the agency of canals, silkworm rearing would become remunerative is a problem yet to be solved.

With regard to wild silkworms there is one species in Oudh known by the name of "kooswaru" (*Phalæna Paphia*). It is said to feed on the "bair" (*Zizyphus Jujuba*), and also one "sal" (*Shorea Robusta*). Hardly any experiments have been made with it. In former times the cocoon used to be cut spirally into a thin strip, and used for tying the barrels of matchlocks to their stocks.

In 1869 the cultivation of silk in Oudh was reported to be "almost entirely abandoned."

SECTION X.

SILK IN BRITISH BURMA.

Scattered notices of the silk of Burmah.

In 1847, Major Bogle, Commissioner of Arracan, forwarded to the Agri-Horticultural Society specimens of silk in the raw and scoured state raised near Bassein. The report on this silk was to the effect that if more carefully reeled, it would meet with ready sale in England. As it was, it was uneven and abounded in 'gouts,' besides being harsh, from reeling at too high a temperature. In March 1850, Sir A. Phayre sent up further specimens both of the worms and the silk with a note on the subject by Lieutenant (now General) Fytche. It is there stated, that the worm is fed on the shrub mulberry and domesticated, having been introduced into Sandoway by immigrants from Burmah. The period given for the changes of this insect are—

Caterpillar	...	...	...	...	... 16 days.
Chrysalis	...	...	...	...	... 8 ,,
Moth	...	...	...	...	... 8 ,,
Egg	...	...	...	...	... Not stated.

The local price of the silk is given at from Rs. 4 to Rs. 5-4 per lb.

In 1855, Government forwarded to the Agri-Horticultural Society a specimen of silk from Prome, but it was pronounced unfit for the European market. It was said to sell in the town of Prome at Rs. 16 the viss (=$3\frac{1}{4}$lbs).

Note on silk by Lieutenant-Colonel H. Browne.

2. The following paper by Lieutenant-Colonel Horace Browne, dated 16th August 1870, was published in the Journal of the Agri-Horticultural Society, and contains most of the information available as to silk in Burmah. The notes are added by me.

Introduction of silkworms.

1. Concerning the period at which, and the country from which, the silkworm and mulberry were first introduced into Burmah, nothing certain can be ascertained from the traditions of the people themselves. From time immemorial the present silk-growers and their forefathers have been engaged in the manufacture. Neither the worm nor the mulberry is indigenous, *i. e.*, neither of them is found in a wild state. They appear, therefore, to have been imported, and I am inclined to agree with the prevailing belief that they were introduced by the valley of the Irrawaddy from Assam or China, and not across the mountains from India.

Occupation distasteful.

2. The occupation of manufacturing silk in British Burmah is a lucrative one, and many parts of the country are admirably adapted for it. That under these circumstances the occupation is not more extensively followed than it is, is due mainly to the Budhistic prejudice against the taking of life. The manufacture of raw silk of the best quality involves the death of the chrysalis in the cocoon, an act of impiety which is looked upon by orthodox Budhists with horror. The people who live by the commission of this sin, therefore, are considered by their neighbours as of "low caste," if such a term can be appropriately used with regard to a people who acknowledge no distinction of caste. The silk-growers live in villages by themselves, and hold but little social intercourse with their neighbours for fear of being taunted with allusions to the wickedness of their calling. In the Eastern Yoma range, these people, though of pure Burman descent, have come to be regarded as a distinct tribe and are called Yabaings or Zabaings.*

Cultivation of mulberry.

3. The Burman mulberry (*Morus Indica ?*), is a thin, lanky, shrub throwing out several vertical shoots from near the ground, and growing to a height of eight or ten feet. It has no flower or fruit, and is propagated by cuttings. After about three† years a plantation of mulberry trees ceases to produce good and succulent leaves, and is then uprooted or abandoned. The plant is grown chiefly on the slopes of hills, but a small quantity is likewise produced on alluvial soil by the margin of mountain streams, where it appears to thrive well, though the silk produced on such localities is inferior to that obtained on high land. The Burmans call it "Po-tsa-beng" (literally "silkworm's food trees"). I am not aware whether it differs from the *Morus Indica*, but have sent some plants to the Horticultural Society at Rangoon with the view of ascertaining its species.

---

* In Toungoo "a few Karens" engage in the industry, and even the Zabaings obtain the eggs they use from the Karens. Capt. Forbes (Tharrawaddy), says the best eggs are obtained from the Karens, but that the breed "deteriorates to the same standard as the local breed in a couple of years, owing to the warm temperature of the lower locality."

† In the Tharawaddy sub-division, according to Capt. Forbes, "fresh trees are planted every year, last year's trees being cut down in July, and cuttings planted out in fresh ground." In Prome, according to the Deputy Commissioner, they are cut down every *two* years.

If the mulberry leaves fail, the worms are fed on the leaves of the *Broussonetia papyrifera*, (Burmese Mahlaing-beng) a tree belonging to the mulberry family, from the bark of which the Burmans also make their coarse paper known as "*paraback*." The leaves of the above two trees are the only ones ever used to feed silkworms upon in British Burmah, or at least in this district.

Inferior quality of silk.

4. The silk produced in Burmah, though admirably adapted for the manufacture of the strong coarse silk so universally worn by the natives of the country, is of a very rough and inferior description, and would, it is believed, be almost unsaleable in Europe. The European value of a specimen of it was, in 1855, estimated by the Calcutta Chamber of Commerce at 5 shillings or 6 shillings a pound, or not much more than half the price which it fetches in the local market.*

Statistics of production.

5. In British Burmah the manufacture of silk is carried on in the districts of Prome, Thayet, Henzada, and Toungoo, and in the northern portion of the Rangoon District†. The mulberry is grown chiefly on the slopes of the Yoma Range—the watershed between the vallies of the Irrawaddy and Sittoung. A small quantity is grown on the eastern slopes of the Arracan Range, and a still smaller‡ quantity in the valley of the Pairee stream which rises on the Arracan Range. The silk produced here (on the Pairee), fetches a lower price than that grown on the high lands, but the people make a profit by the sale of the eggs which are taken across to the silk-growing localities on the east of the Irrawaddy and sold there. The whole of the silk produced is used in local manufactures.§ None of it, it is believed, finds its way to the Rangoon market.

From the information I have collected, the following appear to be the most prominent statistics connected with sericulture in the districts of Prome and Thayet, the two northernmost districts of Pegu extending on both sides of the Irrawaddy, from the Yoma Range on the east, to the Arracan Mountains on the west, covering an area of 5,500 square miles, and containing a population of 360,712 souls. The number of persons engaged in silk culture is 713, of whom 422 are men, and 291 women. The number of acres under mulberry cultivation is 452,|| and the average annual outturn of raw silk is 5,469 viss (1 viss=3·65 lbs.), or about 9 tons. The price of the raw silk when brought to the markets on the river bank varies between Rs. 15 and Rs. 24 a viss, and the average price is about Rs. 20. The value of the whole, at this rate, will be Rs. 1,09,380, or £10,938. The above statistics for Prome and Thayet may be depended upon as tolerably accurate, though, as the information is obtained from the silk-growers themselves, the outturn of silk is probably rather under than over the mark. I have no statistics to guide me in estimating the amount produced in the other districts, but I have travelled through them and believe that the following estimate is not far wrong.

Toungoo probably produces as much as Prome and Thayetmyo together,¶ and Rangoon and Tharrawaddy together about the same amount. This will make the total outturn of raw silk in Pegu amount to 16,400 viss, or about 27 tons, of the value of £32,800.

Silk is produced also along the Yoma Range beyond the British frontier in Burmah Proper.

Method of manufacture.

6. The method pursued by the manufacturers of raw silk in British Burmah is rude and careless in the extreme. All the processes are carried on in the ordinary bamboo dwelling-houses of the country, which are open to all the elements, and generally smoke-begrimed and dirty. The worms and cocoons share the accommodation with the family of the house-owner, and live and thrive in close proximity to the place where the culinary and other domestic operations of the household are carried on.

---

* In a supplementary paper Colonel Browne remarks: "since writing the above I have forwarded a specimen of the raw silk to Mr. Blechynden, Calcutta, who observes that the thread is much thicker than Bengal silk, being reeled with twice the number of cocoons; and that though there was no market for such silk in India, it would fetch in London from 10 to 11 shillings a pound."

† It is also cultivated in the Shwè-Gyeen district, "in portions of the Ananboh and Ramree circles, at the foot of, and on the lower slopes of the Eastern Yoma range."—*Report by Deputy Commissioner Shwè Gyeen deted 16th August* 1871. The Deputy Commissioner of Sandoway also reports a small cultivation of a multivoltine in the gorges of the hills of that district. The cultivation of the mulberry and the breeding of the worm is carried on altogether by the women. The silk is very badly reeled and is consumed in local manufacture. The Deputy Commissioner thinks the worm different from that in cultivation in Toungoo, which gives larger cocoons. In the Bassein district, too, silk is cultivated in a few villages on a small scale, and as a succedaneum to other means of livelihood.

‡ According to Captain Plant even this is diminishing in the Henzadah district.

§ In Shwè-Gyeen the Deputy Commissioner estimated that one-third of the outturn is locally manufactured, and the rest exported to Prome and Shwè-Doung. The Toungoo silk is said to be all exported into Independent Burmah, one circle of that district yielding a superior silk which "supplies the royal household at Mandalay with material for Putsoes, &c."

|| Captain Street, however, puts the mulberry cultivation of Prome alone at 1,853 acres, and the yield of silk at 6,600 viss. The number of persons engaged in silk-weaving in the same district he estimates at 800, and the value of the fabrics manufactured by them at 2¼ lakhs of rupees. The weavers of Prome use some imported silk, both Chinese and Siamese.

¶ The Deputy Commissioner of Toungoo, however, in a report dated 13th September 1871, estimates the outturn of his district at 2,500lbs. only, or about one-eighth of Colonel Browne's estimate. In Shwè-Gyeen the Deputy Commissioner calculates the yield at 2,500 viss, or about 9,000lbs.; but he admits it is only a "guess." The Deputy Commissioner of Henzadah puts down the number of silk-workers in his district at 800, and the mulberry cultivation at 600 acres. Assuming the quantity of silk produced by each worker at 9 viss valued at an average of Rs. 20 per viss, he estimates the annual production at Rs. 1,44,000. But he probably puts the production of a silk-worker much too high. His subordinate, Captain Forbes, calculates that a silk-working *family* only produces 6 viss of silk.

The Japanese silkworm is said to be of such delicate organisation as to be seriously affected by bad smells or tainted air. He certainly must be a much more sensitive insect than his Burman *congener*,* and his life in a Burman hut† would be a very brief one.

The plant of a Burmese silk filature is simple and inexpensive, consisting only of the following articles:—A number of circular flat trays with slightly raised edges. They are made of strips of bamboo, plaited—and are from 2 to 4 feet in diameter—some neatly made circlets of palm leaves three or four inches in diameter—some strips of coarse cotton cloth—a common cooking pot—a small bamboo reel—a round block of wood with handle and axis turning on wooden or bamboo supports—and a two-pronged fork.

The different processes commencing from the time when the eggs are laid are as follow:—

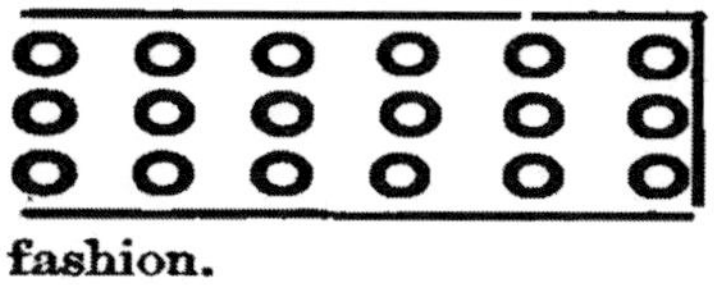

The males and females having completed the procreating process, the males are thrown away and the females placed within palm leaf circlets on a sheet of coarse cotton cloth, two or three feet square. The eggs are then deposited on the cloth, and as they adhere to it the cloth becomes covered with circular cartoons of eggs in this fashion.

These cartoons, when sold, are sold at the rate of about eight for a rupee.‡

The moths having completed the laying of their eggs which takes them about a day, they (the moths) are thrown away. The pieces of cloth with the eggs are wrapped up and left to themselves. About the eighth day the eggs are hatched: the cloths are then opened and worms begin to appear. As the worms, tiny little black specks, emerge, they are swept by a feather off the cloth on to a tray. The worms cling tenaciously to the cartoons and cannot be shaken off. The feather brushing operation, though rough, does not appear to hurt them. The produce of one circular cartoon will more than fill one large tray 2 or 3 feet in diameter with worms when full grown. The worms are hatched in the morning. In the afternoon they are fed with finely chopped up pieces of the tenderest mulberry leaves. This goes on for four or five days when the worms become torpid, sleep for 24 hours, and shed their skins. They then become voracious and require plenty of strong leaves. Beyond being plentifully supplied with food they receive but little care. Very little attention is paid to cleanliness. They live and thrive on heaps of *excreta* and refuse leaves, and they bear handling of the most rough and reckless description, being scraped up in handfuls and tossed about in a way which looks most dangerous to their delicate frames.

Their only enemy appears to be a kind of blue-bottle fly, which, when a tray is exposed, alights for a second, punctures and lays its eggs on the body of the worms. These worms become unhealthy and are generally picked out and thrown down through the bamboo flooring to the fowls which lie in wait for them below the house. If such worms are allowed to make cocoons, the fly eggs develope in the chrysalis and spoil the cocoons. To protect the worm from this fly, the trays are generally kept covered with a cloth.

The silkworm's existence lasts about 30 days, during which period he becomes torpid and moults four times. When "ripe," or ready to commence cocooning, their colour changes from a blueish to pinky white. The ripe ones are then picked out by the hand and thrown in heaps on to a small tray, in which they are conveyed to the cocoooning tray. This is a large-sized tray, 3 or 4 feet in diameter, within which a long ribbon of plaited bamboo, a couple of inches wide, is wound round with its edges on the flat of the tray in a helix or spiral. The worms are then taken up in handfuls and scattered with as little care as if they were so many grains of corn over the tray. They gradually find their places and then spin their cocoons, attaching them to the walls of the plaited bamboo.

Whilst this operation is going on, the trays are covered with a cloth. The cocoons are generally yellow; some few are pure white. In 24 hours the cocoons are completed. They are then torn away from the tray and placed in baskets. In two or three days those cocoons from which the best silk is to be reeled, are taken out and placed in a pot (the family cooking pot) of water, which is allowed to simmer over a slow fire. Above the pot is placed a pair of cross sticks from which a bamboo reel is suspended, and beside the pot, is a wooden cylinder turning on a trestle. Some filaments of silk are caught and drawn out of the pot, run over the bamboo reel, and fastened to the cylinder.

Then the reeler (generally a woman) with an iron fork in one hand and the handle of the cylinder in the other, keeps catching up the filaments in the pot with the fork and reeling them on to the cylinder. The thread produced is coarse and dirty, and brings with it from the pot bits of pupœ and other refuse, all of which goes with the silk on to the cylinder.

The silk in the pot having been exhausted, the denuded grubs are taken out and fried in oil; they form a savoury addition to the family dinner.

* The Deputy Commissioner of Shwè-Gyeen says:—"Five (? two) kinds appear to be kept mixed, a white and a yellow variety; the latter is the most common."

† The Deputy Commissioner of Toungoo, however, says: "the use of nga-pee or salt-fish in the villages during the three months (of silkworm rearing) is prohibited." And "when the grubs (? worms) sleep, the whole village remains quiet; no noise is allowed." The Deputy Commissioner of Bassein writes to the same effect, and Colonel Browne himself, in his attempt at rearing in the jail, had a proof of the sensitiveness of the worm to smells, though he adds—"to which he is not accustomed." The smell of tar carried off "all his little ones, at one fell swoop."

‡ 8 to 10 for fine silk, 10 to 15 for the coarser kind, according to Captain Forbes.

These cocoons which are left to produce moths are ready in about eight days. The moths are then formed. As they emerge, they are put into large trays and kept there for a day, during which time the coupling process goes on. The males having been thrown away, the females are arranged on a cloth as before described to lay their eggs.

A coarse and inferior kind of silk is reeled off the cocoons which have been allowed to come to maturity. This silk fetches only a third of the price obtained from those cocoons which are reeled whilst the chrysalis is still in them, but as, by this process, the sin of taking life is avoided, it is preferred by some who are more attentive to the duties of religion than their neighbours.

The length of the different stages making up the cycle of the Burman silkworm's existence is as follows:—

Eggs	...	8 days or 11 days in cold weather.
Worm	...	30 ,,
Cocoon	...	8 ,,
Moth	...	1 ,,
TOTAL		47 days.

From the completion of the cocoon to the appearance of the worm, therefore, there are only 17 days in the hot weather, and 20 days in the cold weather. This is altogether too short a time to allow of the Burman species being conveyed to Australia (by one stage at least) with any hope of success.*

7. The chief merit of the Burman silkworm appears to be its extreme hardiness as compared with other species. Whether the coarseness of its silk is inherent in the nature of the worm, or is due to the rough and careless manner in which it is treated, my limited knowledge of silk manufacture does not enable me to say. There certainly appears to be room for improvement, as far as concerns the manufacture of silk fitted for the European market. Whether the manufacture of such silk would pay the growers better than the manufacture of the coarse stuff they now produce, I can hardly say. But any recommendations for the improvement of the present system of silk culture, made by a person having a competent knowledge of the subject, would not be wasted on the Burman silk-growers, provided such recommendations were at all feasible.

Improvement of silk manufacture in British Burmah.

The silk-growers are quite ready to adopt any measures, whether by the introduction of new breeds of silkworms or the improvement of their machinery, which may be expected to be profitable.

3. Captain Hutton, in some brief remarks upon Colonel Browne's paper, expresses a doubt whether the mulberry tree of Burmah is really *Morus Indica*. He strongly condemns the method of treatment described, as in itself sufficient to account for the inferior quality of the silk produced. Captain Hutton believes the worm to be a species distinct from any of those domesticated in Bengal, and has called it *Bombyx Arracanensis*. He bases his belief in its distinct nature on the facts—(1) that the moth deposits its ova in rings, and (2) that it undergoes a change of colour from blueish to pinky white.

Captain Hutton's remarks on this paper.

4. The following is an extract from a letter addressed to the Chief Commissioner by the Honorary Secretary, Rangoon Agri-Horticultural Society, under date 18th August 1871:—

Contribution by the Rangoon Agri-Horticultural Society.

* * * *

3. Just as in the districts of Prome, Thayetmyo, Henzadah, and Toungoo, the silk-weavers live in small villages apart by themselves, so in the northern portion of the Rangoon districts, it happens that there are three or four small detached villages, where silk cultivation to a small extent is carried on for local consumption, the worm being the same as that bred in the Prome and Thayetmyo districts from whence no doubt it was brought. Colonel Browne has given "tolerably accurate" statistics of silk cultivation in the Prome and Thayetmyo districts in the paper above alluded to, but just as Colonel Browne has done, the Deputy Commissioners of Toungoo, Henzadah, and Rangoon can do for their districts.

4. The quality of the silk now produced in all these districts is of an inferior description, arising principally from the crude machinery used by the cultivators in silk filature. With a view to remedy this, I have sent drawings of improved machinery to Colonel Browne (as used in France), to see if, with a few modifications, it cannot be adopted by the weavers in his districts, and the ordinary Bengal machine has been sent for also for introduction into British Burmah.

5. There appears to be but one description of silkworm in Burmah, and an attempt made to transmit a batch of eggs to Bengal was described in my letter to your address, No. 96,

* It thus appears that the species is a multivoltine. In Shwè-gyeen and Toungoo, however, I gather from the account of the Deputy Commissioner, that the broods of the colder months, November to February, are alone used for silk.

dated 28th March; another attempt is to be made during the ensuing cold weather, it is to be hoped, with better success. Its scientific name is still unsettled. Captain Hutton in his "Remarks" on Colonel Browne's paper observes—"only procure it, and we will soon divulge his name and family."

6. The method of rearing the worms and reeling the silk are certainly open to very much improvement; they are the crudest imaginable. And the same gentleman pertinently observes, with regard to Colonel Browne's photographic description of the Burmese method of rearing the worms, that "no really good silk can be expected from Burmah, while the worms are subjected to such vile treatment."

7. The extent of European enterprise is simply *nil*; the same answer must also be given to the query—"quantity and value of silk exported." On the other hand, last year there was imported into Rangoon alone, 884 cwt. of raw silk from the Straits Settlements. The only fabrics woven on the spot consist of the well-known Thamiens, Loongyies, and Putsoes worn by the Burmese.

8. I have now growing with me (sent by Colonel Browne), a plant of the mulberry cultivated by the Burmese in the Prome and Thayetmyo districts, for the food of silkworms. From that gentleman's description of the plant, I informed him that it could not be (as he thought), the well known *Morus Indica* cultivated in Bengal for the same purpose. He then sent me a plant, and from its growth and the formation of the leaves, I remained of the same opinion; since which, however, Mr. Scott, the Curator of the Royal Botanical Gardens, has pronounced it to be a different plant. *Morus Indica* bears both flower and fruit, which the Burmese plant (according to Colonel Browne) does not. But be that as it may, a discovery of some importance has been made by Colonel Browne, *viz.*, that the Burmese silkworms are also fed on the leaves of the "*Broussonetia papyrifera*," a tree belonging to the same order as the mulberry "*Artocarpaceæ*." I have failed up to the present time in obtaining living specimens of this tree (several cuttings that were sent me having perished on the passage down), but I hope to do so very soon. At Colonel Browne's request a few are to be sent to Calcutta also, to Mr. Blychenden, the Secretary of the Agri-Horticultural Society of India.

Silk among the Shans.

5. Colonel Hannay in 1836 writes that "handsome pieces of silk, exceedingly rich, and of various check patterns, can be had from the Shan States, the art of dyeing being well understood." Bhamo imports both raw and manufactured silk from China.

SECTION XI.

WILD SILK-PRODUCERS.

The Tusser.

THE most important and most widely distributed of the wild silk-producers of India is the tusser (I suppose from तसर a shuttle). It is generally identified with *Antheræa Paphia,* but Captain Hutton has shewn that there are probably several species going under the name of tusser. At any rate the insect known by this name is found in the Sub-Himalayan tracts almost throughout the extent of the range, through the hills from Assam to Chittagong, in the Soonderbuns, everywhere in the great belt of hill and forest inhabited by the Sontal, the Kol, the Khond, and the Gond, in the western ghâts, and in portions of the Madras Presidency. The worm is multivoltine, but it is not very clear how many times in the year it goes through its transformations, or whether its periods of existence may not vary according to conditions of climate. But on the whole, it seems probable that the apparent discrepancy in this respect between various accounts arises from the fact that in different tracts different crops are gathered, the intermediate ones being neglected and the worm left to shift for itself. It feeds variously on the ber (*Zizyphus jujuba*) the country almond (*Terminalia Catappa*), the seemul (*Bombax heptaphyllum*), the asun (*Terminalia alata*), the saj (*T. Tomentosa*), the sal (*Shorea robusta*) and other trees. Mr. Fretwell, in his paper on silk in Mysore, mentions a wild worm spinning large cocoons found in the jungles of Coorg and feeding on the *ficus elastica, ficus religiosa* and *isonandra acuminata.* If this be a tusser, we have here an important addition to the list of trees on which it feeds. Dr. Henderson of Shahpoor also mentions a wild worm as occurring in the Panjáb salt range and feeding on the camel-thorn.

Notices of the tusser; in Bengal, by Michael Atkinson;

2. Though it seems probable that the utilization of the tusser dates from centuries ago, I have not found any very early notices of it. "Michael Atkinson of Jungypore," as cited by Dr. Roxburgh in the *Transactions of the Linnæan Society,* 1804, writes of the worm as a species that cannot be domesticated. He describes the hill people as tracing the young worms upon "byer and aseen trees," by their excrement beneath and cutting and carrying off the branches and distributing them in trees near their houses. According to the same authority the "natives cannot even retain any of the species for seed."

by Bengal Board of Trade;

This moth is noticed by the Bengal Board of Trade in a minute of 1819. It is said to be reared in all the western forests from Ramghur to Midnapore, the goottee or cocoon being of three* qualities, "mooga, teerah, and bonbunda." The mooga is the "most common and plentiful; the thread coarse, but winds easily:" the teerah is a "smaller goottee, said to be the male of the mooga;" the thread is finer, but not so easily wound; the bonbunda is the "largest of the wild silk-worms; being found in forests in its natural state" (as the name indicates), "and not stinted in its food, it attains a greater size than the mooga, which appears to be the only difference between them; but it is scarce. Thread coarser, but runs easily." These three kinds are bred in September. The mode of rearing is thus described: "The seed is purchased from the jungle people, and plots in the forest appropriated, where the ashun, sal, and sejah trees predominate, especially the first, which is the best food for the worm. * * * In all Baudoon (August—September) the grub eats out, and is immediately placed on the trees. * * * * When eggs are produced on the leaves, they are carefully folded into a kind of cup, and gently rubbed with turmeric. In a few days the young worms appear, and are removed to the trees in which they are to remain. The rearers keep guard with pellet-bows. * * * About the beginning of Assin (middle of September) the worms begin to spin, and by the end of that month the goottee is finished." The grubs are killed with boiling water. "The rearers have advances from the

* Colonel Rowlatt, Deputy Commissioner of Maunbhoom, in a brief notice of the tusser in the jungles of that district at the present day, speaks of three varieties of cocoons, one "raised in" Asarh called mooga, the second in Bhadro and Assin called daba, the third in Cheit called ampatee: besides these a considerable quantity of cocoons is gathered in the jungles; this last being evidently the Board's "bonbunda."

pykars in money, rice, salt, cloth, and other commodities. After the collection the price is settled, and the advances adjusted accordingly. The rearers are of no particular caste, but a superstition exists amongst them that one of the party should keep *neeaum* (a ceremony which enjoins daily ablutions and restrictions as to particular food, &c.), for the success of their operations." These cocoons, probably the cocoons of one species, are called "the rainy-weather sorts; but there are others of the dry months; the Cartic (in October) denominated the dabba and buggoy." The chrysalis of the dabba "begins to cut its way through the pod after the Roinse Caut (a period from 8th to 22nd Assar, end of June) and spin from the middle to the end of August."* "The buggoy is of a light drab colour, and gives a very fine thread," so much so as to be used in adulterating filature thread. "Seed procured in Baudoon (August—September) begins spinning in the middle of November, and completes by the end of the month. This superior tussah is chiefly reared in Singbhoom." Another "inferior sort of tussah" is mentioned, named "tarroy," gathered in December. "It is a small goottee, difficult to wind; thread harsh." It is not clear whether these three last sorts are other "bunds" of *Antheræa Paphia* or not. "The natives, in preparing this silk for use, first boil the cocoon in alkali till it shells off. The process is thus continued until the thread appears to separate, when they run it into *ulluah* in a wet but not hot state, mixing oil and filth to add to the weight, by which they are paid for the work done. The *ulluah* is given to other spinners, who twist it into thread called *packwaun*, adding, on their part, for the same reason, potato starch and more oil. The skeins are always tied up with some thick good-for-nothing *ulluah*, all of which is sold together by weight."

by Dr. Buchanan;

Dr. Buchanan gives the following account of the rearing of the tusser and the winding of the silk in Bhagulpoor:—

"The chief use to which the tree (*terminalia alata*) is, however, applied is to rear the tasar silk of which I shall here give some account. The tree abounds chiefly in the part of the district that is situated east from the Chandan, and between that and the Rajmahal hills, and there occupies as large a space as the bamboo does towards the west. The animal is reared by all castes who inhabit these parts, but in general by the armed men employed under ghatwals to preserve the peace of the country. With a view perhaps of securing the employment to themselves, they have established certain rules of purity, as they call it, which they allege are absolutely necessary, and they allege that any infringement would totally destroy the insect. Women, who are best fitted for such a work, are entirely excluded from it as totally impure, nor are they permitted to approach the place; and while employed in this work, the men totally abstain from the company of their wives. Again, most of the low vile castes are excluded by their appetites, abandoned to the gross impurity of animal food. The breeders eat sparingly once a day of rice cleaned without boiling, and seasoned only with vegetables. They are considered also to preserve their purity by never employing the washerman or barber.

"Concerning the method of procuring the seed cocoons, I found in the accounts of the natives the utmost difference. In Bangka it was stated that the only good seed was procured from the forests, from whence the spontaneous cocoons were brought by people of wild tribes, were purchased by merchants, and distributed among those who rear the worms. From these cocoons three successive broods are reared, but those reared from the wild cocoons (dhaba) are the best: the other, sarihan, jarhan, and langga, gradually degenerate. At Tarapur and Lakardewani it was stated that the kinds are quite distinct, that the good tasar (dhaba) is always reared from cultivated cocoons, some of which are preserved through the year for propagating the breed, and that the wild cocoons are only used for this purpose, when from accident and carelessness the proper seed is lost; and the tasar which these give is always of an inferior quality, but is of two kinds, sarihan and langga, the last of which is very inferior, and is seldom employed. Each kind, according to these people, breeds twice in the year. In Fyezullahganj, again, it was said, as in Bangka, that no seed was preserved through the year; that in the beginning of the season wild cocoons were procured, but that the silk which these gave was of inferior value, and that the cocoons of this brood were chiefly preserved for producing a second, of which the silk was of the best kind. These accounts are in direct opposition to each other, nor can I take upon myself to assert which is true, or whether any of them is false, although I am inclined to rely most on the account given in Lakardewani and Tarapur; but it may happen that such different practices really prevailed, and that the influence of them on the quality of the silk is quite imaginary, for I would observe that at Bhagalpur all the cocoons are usually sold indiscriminately as of the same value, and very often intermixed. The weavers, indeed, say that there is a difference in the quality of cocoons, and that one kind (dhaba) is more easily wound, and gives a larger quantity of silk, while the sarihan produces ¼ less, but

* It is not clear how this can be considered as belonging to the dry months. I have not been able to discover what "Roinse Caut" stands for. It is no doubt some native term eccentrically spelt.

is of a better quality. The merchants who deal with the simple breeders endeavour probably to keep up distinctions, of which they avail themselves. They pay in advance for the whole, and give a very low price; but they no doubt are often defrauded by people who never fulfil their engagements.

"Among other ridiculous imaginations concerning the insects, propagated, as I suppose, to impress the people with an idea of their purity, it is supposed that a tasar female moth will not admit the embraces of a male of the same paternal family with herself. The breeders, however, very judiciously leave the whole adjustment of this delicate point to the discretion of the females. The seed cocoons are placed on a large flat basket; and when the moths burst the cocoons, they are allowed to form such connections as they please. In from 15 to 20 hours afterwards the males are thrown away, and from 20 to 25 impregnated females are placed in a cylindrical basket with a narrow mouth, which is covered with leaves, and some leaves are laid on the bottom of the basket. In some places an earthen pot is preferred. On these leaves in the course of the day the females deposit their eggs, and are then thrown away, and the eggs are placed in small baskets made of the bhela leaves. On the ninth day afterwards, the eggs are hatched, and the baskets on which they are lying are put upon a tree, over the leaves of which the young insects immediately spread. When they have consumed these, the worms are removed to other trees, and in 36 days from being hatched they begin to spin. In 15 days this operation is completed, when all the young branches are cut, and the cocoons are thus collected with very little trouble. The only operation at all troublesome is the removing the worms from one tree to another, and this might probably be avoided by putting no more worms at first on each tree than it should be able to maintain. The worms, however, must be watched, as crows and other birds and hornets are apt to destroy them. The whole space of time occupied by the two crops may be about five months, beginning about the 1st of July, and ending about the last of November. A great number of the cocoons preserved for seed burst, and these can only be sold for about half price. Those originally intended for sale are killed by being put in boiling water, and then dried in the sun.

"In procuring food for these worms, the only trouble is to select a piece of ground on which the asan tree grows, intermixed with few others. These latter and all bushes ought to be removed, and all the large branches of the asan tree should be lopped near the stem, and young shoots permitted to grow, for those produce large succulent leaves fit for the worm. The worms are only applied to the same tree once in two years, a whole year being necessary to allow the new shoots to grow.

"A woman takes five pans of cocoons (405), and puts them in a large earthen pot with 600 sicca weight of water, a small mat being placed in the bottom to prevent the cocoons from being burned. A small quantity of potash, tied in a bit of cloth, is put into the pot, along with the cocoons, which are boiled about an European hour. They are then cooled, the water is changed, and they are again boiled. The water is poured off, and the cocoons are put into another pot, where they stand three days in the sun covered with a cloth to exclude insects. On the fourth day they are again boiled, with 200 sicca weight of water, for rather less than an hour, and then poured into a basket where they are allowed to cool, after which they are washed in cold water, and placed to dry on a layer of cow-dung ashes, where they remain spread and covered with a cloth for six hours. The woman then picks out such cocoons as are not quite ready for winding, and exposes them for a day to the sun, which completes the operation. The outer filaments of the cocoon are then picked off, and form a substance called jhuri, of which the potters make brushes used for applying a pigment to their vessels. The fibres from four to five cocoons are then wound off on a miserable conical reel, which is twirled round by one hand, while the thread is twisted on the thigh, the cocoons adjusted, and the broken fibres joined by the other. The cocoons while winding are not placed in water. This thread is called lak, and after the lak has been removed, there remains another inferior kind of filament, called also jhuri, which is wound off, and is purchased by those who knit strings. Even the cocoons that have been burst by the moth are wound off; but owing to the frequent joinings give a weaker silk. When the tasar is neither very high nor very low, that is, when 405 cocoons cost a rupee at Bhagulpoor, a woman boils and winds the number in ten days. At this rate she would wind 1,215 cocoons in the month; these would yield 2,257 lbs. of fine thread worth 5 rupees 6 annas, and 1½ annas worth of refuse (jhuri); but the cost of pots, firewood, &c., reduce the profit to Re. 1-8 to Re. 1-12 per mensem.

in the Soondurbuns by Mr. Homfray;

The gathering of the tusser in the Soondurbuns is thus described by Mr. Homfray, of Baroeepoor, in a paper dated March 1836, published in the Transactions of the Calcutta Agri-Horticultural Society. The cocoons are found on the khoura or wild plum-tree.* Each female lays about 150 eggs of a reddish colour; these eggs take from 9 to 14 days to hatch. The young worms are speedily removed to the tree, where they live at liberty, satisfying their voracious appetite till they become 3 or 4 inches long, and of a brilliant green colour, marked with golden spots. They spin on the trees, the period from hatching to completion of cocoons being about 50 days. The cocoons fetch Rs. 3 to Rs. 5 per kahan

* I have also seen a notice of "a tusser" feeding on the "plum-tree" in the jungles of the Attiah sub-division of the Mymensingh district.

(=16×80=1,280). If of good quality, ¼ kahan yields enough silk to manufacture a pair of dhotees, which sell for Rs. 4 to Rs. 5. The rearers squat on the edge of a jungle and camp there in gipsy fashion, the zemindar levying a cess of 1 rupee per party. "The result of their labours for upwards of two months is very precarious, sometimes yielding Rs. 30, sometimes barely 10. During this time they are obliged to submit to many restraints which an ignorant superstition has imposed on them, such as abstaining from eating fish, anointing their bodies with oil, which to natives are severe deprivations, and mentioning the names of certain things which are considered unclean."

in Chota Nagpore;

A paper in the Agri-Horticultural Society's Journal for 1861 describes the mode of rearing the tusser silk-worm in Palamow (Chota Nagpore) :—

"The worms are fed on the ásan or *terminalia tomentosa*. The moths emerge about the middle of June. The males are small with a large red dot on each wing; those of the other sex much larger, fuller made in the body, particularly the hinder parts. Some two or three hours after the moths have burst out of the cocoons they are mated for a half-hour; the males are then shut in a basket, and the females have their wings tied close to the shoulder, and put on a board or bamboo flooring, when they immediately commence laying. The wings are tied to prevent them flying away. The next day the eggs are collected from under them, and a few of their wings plucked, and gently rubbed in the hand to a powder. The eggs are put in this powder, and shaken till they separate. It is then put into a thin piece of cloth, tied and put carefully away, so that the ants do not get at them. This is continued daily, each moth laying for three or four days, when from exhaustion she dies. * * * On the eighth day the eggs are hatched, and the worms immediately taken to the jungle, and a nest formed on the tree by tying together a lot of growing leaves into the shape of a cup, in which the worms are placed. In four days they are an inch long, and are removed to other trees, and as they grow larger, are from time to time diffused over a large number of trees. * * * Boys are employed in scaring the birds. * * * The worms grow to the size of five to six inches long and one thick, when they commence to spin. After formation into cocoons, they are allowed to remain a week on the trees to harden them, taken down, attached to small twigs, and daily laid out in the air to dry. From the time the worms are put to the trees and the cocoons taken down occupies a month and a half, or till the end of July. A second crop commences about the latter end of August or beginning of September, and the yield is more full and larger. Purchasers come from Patna, Daoodnugger, and other large towns, buying cocoons at Rs. 3 to Rs. 6 per 'thousand' of 1,100—1,300. The burst cocoons also find ready market at Rs. 2-8 to Rs. 3 per thousand for June and July produce, and Rs. 4 for the October produce. The revenue or málguzári for a silk field is Rs. 3 for each cutter or full-grown man, who is expected to take the cocoons down; at an average there are three of these to a good-sized field covering some 30 beegahs of land."

Captain Hutton disputes the accuracy of that part of the description which assigns the Palamow moths a red spot on the wing. He considers them *antheræa paphia*, but the largest specimens he has seen. Dr. Boisduval in the *Annales de la Société Entomologique de France* for 1854 quotes an account by Captain Sherwill of the breeding of the worm in Hazareebagh. This account describes the process very much as the paper just quoted. Captain Sherwill adds that, on completion of the brood, the breeders cut down the trees to the height of about 3 feet, reducing them to a coppiced state.

in the Midnapore District;

The following memorandum on the tusser in the Midnapoor District is extracted from the Agri-Horticultural Society's Journal. It is by Mr. Charles Blechynden, Superintendent of the Radnagore Silk Factories :—

"Cocoons for seed are purchased in the month of Pous (December) and Maug (January) at 15 or 16 gundas per rupee; they are hung in a pot for four months or till about the 13th Bysack (April), when some of the moths come out of the cocoons and are removed into another pot, and kept there for a fortnight; during this period eggs are laid.

"These eggs are now put into saul leaf boxes for four days, at the end of which time they begin to hatch, and are placed on clumps of either assun or saul branches.

"After two or three days, the worms growing stronger, no very great care is requisite, vesa to remove them from one branch to another when they have eaten all the leaves of that which they are on; this is effected by cutting down the branch, and placing it against another. In three weeks these worms weigh 2 chittacks each; they cast their skins three times, after which they spin, and are brought home, when they undergo boiling, and are after that fit for sale. There are two bunds; first, in the month of Joisty (May); second, in the month of Srabun (July). The castes that follow the rearing of worms as a means of livelihood are Koormee, Bhoomij, Náik, and Manjhee.

"The price of the cocoons is never fixed; eight puns make one kahun* which sells for Rs. 3-8, rising sometimes to Rs. 4-8. To manufacture the cocoons into a thread, they are boiled in cow-dung and water, and drawn out into a fibre on a hand-reel."

in the Deccan;

3. I have found two papers on tusser in the Nizam's country, one by Dr. Walker of the Madras Army, in the Journal of the Asiatic Society for the second half of 1841, the other by Dr. Smith in the 11th volume of the Journal of the Agri-Horticultural Society.

According to Dr. Walker, the tusser breeders are mostly Teloogoos of low caste, or Gonds, and reside principally at Chilpoor, Madapoor, and Chinnore. As the rains commence they collect a few cocoons which their experience teaches them to be females, and place them in a box of teak leaves dried. When the moths eat out the males speadily approach; the eggs number about 60, and are hatched in 10 days. The small worms are fed on *careya sphærica*, and in six weeks begin to spin. The first crop of cocoons is preserved for seed, and the same process gone through, except that the second brood is fed on *pentaptera tomentosa*. The cocoons yielded by this brood are sold, the moth being killed by heat and the winding being "accomplished by boiling the cocoons and twisting 8 or 10 filaments from as many cocoons on the middle of the thigh with the left hand to be wound on a rude reel." Dr. Smith's account, obtained from the talookdar of Wurrangul, differs somewhat from the above. According to his account, the trees on which the worms are fed are *terminalia alata* and *zizyphus jujuba;* the male and female have generally to be approximated (a task requiring absolute ceremonial purity on the part of the person performing it); the number of eggs is much larger than given by Dr. Walker, and three broods are reared in the year. The wild cocoons too are said to be gathered in the mowah season, not in the rains. A mixture of "dhobee's earth" with alkaline ashes of the sesamum, castor oil plant, or *butea frondosa* is said to be used for boiling the cocoons.

in the Central Provinces;

4. As Buchanan complained of the discrepant accounts in Bhagulpoor, so it is very hard to reconcile the various statements received from the different districts of the Central Provinces. The best description of the insect is perhaps that given by Dr. Shortt of Madras, who had observed the insect in the jungles west of Orissa. He writes:—"The eggs are of the size of a split peppercorn; nine of them in line occupy the space of one inch in length. They are circular and bi-convex, with a light creamy colour. * * The worm is very small, scarcely perceptible when first hatched, but before it attains maturity it is from 3 to 4 inches long and from two to three lines in girth (? diameter). The larva is of a light green colour with a slightly yellowish streak on either side, and the 6th and 7th segments are marked with an oblong yellow spot, and on the back are several round darker-coloured spots surmounted with a few dark coarse hairs, while smaller ones are scattered all over the body. The larva is chiefly found on the *bher* or *zizyphus jujuba, asan* or *pentaptera tomentosa*, and the *teak* or *tectona grandis*. * * The larva when ready to undergo transformation forms a cord round a twig from a peculiar resinous substance it secretes, and with which it also encircles the selected part of the branch and then prolongs it to the extent of one or two inches. If the branch is thick, the cord is short and stout and about a line in girth, but if it be a twig, the cord is thin, from 3 to 4 inches long and fastened to an upper and thicker branch and prolonged to the end of the twig with several intermediate ties of the same material. From the end of the cord, which is solid, begins the expansion of the cocoons which is reticulated with fine fibres of the same stuff as the cord is made of on the outer surface, thus giving firmness and solidity to the cocoon, and as it approaches completion, a few of the leaves in the vicinity are drawn to line and conceal the cocoon externally, and thus to a certain extent mask it from observation; but this occurs only on the bher tree, for I have seen no such leaves attached to the cocoons found on other trees where the foliage is large and dense. The larva now imprisons itself within the cocoon, and the same secretion that forms the cord is freely applied to all parts to make it water-tight. Having done this,

* This seems a mistake; 16 puns make a kahun.

the transformation commences, and lasts nine months (?) before the moth is perfected, having its head at the upper part next to the cord, from whence it appears to discharge an acid secretion which readily dissolves the plastering from the cocoon, and the fibres of the silk giving way, the perfected moth emerges from its prison, as a rule, early in the morning about daybreak. That the secretion is an acid can be readily ascertained by examining an empty cocoon immediately after the moth has emerged; as the part being moist, it can be readily tested with litmus, when it is seen to give an acid re-action. This knowledge I have practically applied by adding diluted sulphuric acid in the water in which the cocoons are boiled to dissolve the gummy substance out and loosen the thread. and it can then be readily wound off on a hand-reel. The male and female moths differ in size, the male measuring from the tip of one wing to the other between four and five inches, whilst the female measures from six to seven inches in expanse of wing; both are of a uniform yellowish brown having a couple of lunated transparent talc-like spots* on each wing, and it is chiefly in the form of these spots that they differ from other moths of the same kind. * * * It takes from 10 to 12 days for the eggs to hatch and from 6 to 7 weeks from the extrusion of the young larva to the completion of the cocoon. * * * The cocoon is slightly rough, of a greyish white colour and slightly reticulated externally with an internal smooth varnished surface; is of an oval form, measuring one and a half inches in length and one inch in breadth; the average weight with the chrysalis is 150 grains, that of the chrysalis itself 130 grains, the empty cocoon 20 grains, and the prepared thread 12 grains. But the cocoons vary much in size."

The fullest account of the method of rearing the worms is given by Captain Brooke, Deputy Commissioner of Seonee, but the Chief Commissioner, Central Provinces, has also furnished accounts from Chanda and Sumbulpoor, and I have seen accounts in the settlement reports of Chanda and Bilaspoor. I extract Captain Brooke's account in full, adding in the form of notes such additions, corrections, or doubts as the other reports may suggest.*

Castes engaged in rearing the silk-producing worms.

3. The Dheemurs (fishermen) are the principal caste engaged in rearing the tasar moth,—as a rule, they add the production of tasar cocoons to their ordinary calling.

In the northern half of the district, I have not been able to learn that any other caste share the profits with the Dheemurs, but in the jungles of the central and southern parts Kumhars (manufacturers of earthern vessels), Bussores (bamboo-mat weavers), and a few Mohammadans are also engaged in the trade.

State of the industry.

4. In Seonee, the silk-producing worms may be said to be in a state of partial domestication, the rearers tending the insects through all their stages, but depending entirely on the wild cocoons for each year's stock.

In the Chhattisgarh Division it is said that rearing is not attempted,† the mere collection of the wild cocoons sufficing for the demands of the local market. Here, however, matters are different, as it does not appear that anywhere, either in this district or the adjoining tracts, are the wild cocoons so numerous as to make their collection and sale for the production of tasar silk a sufficiently remunerative undertaking; on the contrary, the price‡ paid for wild cocoons, *viz.*, 4 cowries for a male, and 8 or 10 cowries for a female cocoon, or on an average 750 cocoons per rupee, would seem to indicate that they occurred too rarely to be utilized directly as an article of commerce.

Instead then of depending on the natural occurrence of the cocoon, as is common elsewhere, we have, in this part of the country, a regularly organized and thoroughly understood industry, from the rearing of the insects to the weaving of the silk into cloth, with all its accompanying machinery of trade-guilds, money-lenders, &c.

This state of things is, in my opinion, no disadvantage, for in place of having to contend with the difficulties which in India always surround the introduction of anything new or unknown, the demand is all that is necessary to stimulate production to any extent required.

Nor is this a figure of speech, for the natural food of the tassâr worm is the leaves of the *saj*, *lendeya*, and *dhowra* trees, all of which are found in every part of this district, and are, I believe, common to the whole of Gondwana. These trees are besides propagated with facility, and as far as the requirement of the silk insects goes, are of rapid growth; hence, if the silk became more known and better valued, and the profits sufficiently attractive, we might

* Said by the natives to resemble Vishnu's "chakra" or discus, whence the sacredness of the insect.
† This does not seem to be borne out by the local accounts.
‡ In Chanda apparently much higher—"12 to 32 cowries each."

witness a development of the culture similar in kind to that which has of late years taken place in the case of cotton.

Supposing then a demand to spring up, I am of opinion that the supply would, in a very short time, amply meet it.

The nucleus of no inconsiderable trade now exists, and only awaits the stimulus of high prices. The primary question whether the product is, or may become, of such value as to occasion a large demand is one, perhaps, that more nearly concerns traders than Indian Administrations; still, so convinced am I of the value and beauty of the fabric that can be woven from well-reeled tasar, that I would venture to strongly urge Government action in introducing it to the markets of Europe.

5. In the months of May and June,* wood-cutters and graziers† find the wild cocoons on the saj *(pentaptera tomentosa)*, lendeya (*lagerstrœmia parviflora*), and dhowra (*conocarpus latifolia*).‡ These they collect and sell to the rearers at the rate of 4 cowries for a small, and 8 or 10 cowries for each, large cocoon; the small cocoons nearly always yield male moths, the larger female; the rule, however, is not without exception, although it generally holds good.§

Method of rearing the worms.

These wild cocoons, from which the stock of the rearers is invariably replenished, are called in the north of the district, where a pure Hindi dialect is spoken, "*ariya*," and in the south bordering on the Nagpur province "*ránwat*."‖ When the moths, "*phudi*," have cut their way through the cocoons, the males, "*gaura*," and females¶ "*kír*," are placed** together and allowed to remain so for nine or ten hours; they are then separated, and the wings of the female broken off; accepting this process as a hint that she is not to leave the place, she begins at once†† to deposit her ova, the larger and healthier insects continuing laying for about 12 hours. The eggs are then tied up in pieces of cloth and carefully opened on the same day in the ensuing week. The rearers have new little sacks made from one or two leaves of the tendoo (*diospyros melanoxylon*), which are apparently chosen for their toughness. In each of these packets, as soon as the worms begin to appear, which happens usually on the ninth day, from 50 to 100 eggs are placed, and the tendoo leaf sacks are then fastened to lendeya trees, upon the leaves of which the insects begin at once to feed. In a few days they are removed to saj trees, and are changed about according as they require fresh food. When the worms show signs of beginning to spin, they are known as "dunihaá." Some rearers at this time remove them from the saj to kowha trees (*pentaptera arjuna*), but this is not common; the bulk of the cocoons produced are spun on the saj.

During the feeding time the greatest care is necessary to preserve the worms from being destroyed by birds and ants.‡‡

The first crop of cocoons is produced in the month of *Bhadon* (August), and in consequence is known as "*Bhadeli*." These cocoons are carefully kept, and when the moths have eaten their way through, the empty cases are sold to the silk dealers at prices varying from 4 to 8 pice the hundred, equivalent to 1,600 and 800 for the rupee. The uncut cocoons of the bhadeli crop are never sold, except to rearers as seed, when they bring from Re. 1-8-0 to Rs. 2-0-0 per 100.

The moths produced from this crop are treated in precisely the same manner as already described; except that the young insects are not placed, in the first instance, on the lendeyá tree, but directly on the saj, the process in no way varies. The second crop of cocoons is ready in the month of Kartik (October—November) and is known as "*Katkáhai*." These are the most valued cocoons, and are purchased by the weavers at rates varying from Rs. 2 to Rs. 4 per 1,000. The highest price ever known was Rs. 8 per 1,000 which was realized five years ago. Although I said that the katkáhaí cocoons are the most valued, the weavers assure me that the cocoons of the other crops are just as good if they could procure them uncut.

In the north of the district cocoons are often sold in lots of 1,450 called a "kár," and in the south by the khundy of twenty hundreds.

There are two distinct computations used in the purchase and sale of cocoons, one method prevailing when the transaction is by the kár, another when by the 1,000. These are—

6 kosá = 1 gandá.
40 gandá = 1 kúrí.
6 kúrí = 1 kár.

* In Chanda "from middle of June to middle of February" according to Captain Lucie Smith; "in April" according to another account.

† Gandahs, Chumars, Gonds, Bijwars, and Bhoomiyas, and also to a certain extent Khewuts.

‡ In Chanda chiefly on the "en" tree, which is cut down into a coppiced state. In Sumbulpoor the sál (*Shorea robusta*) and Arjoona or Kowa (*Terminalia Arjuna*) are added to the list.

§ The Sumbulpoor account inverts the rule; wrongly it would appear.

‖ Or "rewat" in Chanda.

¶ "Pipolee" in Chanda.

** In Sumbulpoor the people say that males of the same batch fly away and that others come and impregnate the females. See also Buchanan's account above. However that may be, it appears that in Sumbulpoor the sexes are left to pair of their own accord and not artificially approximated.

†† "In about ten days" according to Captain Lucie Smith, but I doubt the accuracy of this statement.

‡‡ In Chanda fine nets are sometimes used for the purpose.

According to this calculation the kár would contain 1,440 kosa or cocoons, but the buyers always take 10 over and above to make up the 1,450.

When buying by the 1,000, the calculation is—

5 kosá (cocoons)	=	1 gandá.
40 gandá	=	1 kúrí.
5 kúrí	=	1,000.

In all other transactions the gandá is equal to four units, and there is no obvious reason why in buying and selling cocoons the gandá should contain in the one case 5, and in the other 6. Probably the system originally arose from the inequalities in the size of the cocoons, and the desire to obtain an average gandá equal to four large cocoons. The Koshtas or buying classes, however, confess with refreshing *näiveté* that it is an old device to cheat Dheemurs.

The rearing of the worms is attended by many ceremonial observances, which begin when the insect leaves the egg, and are not discontinued until the cocoons are gathered and taken to the rearer's house. During the feeding of the worm, the Dheemurs lead lives of the strictest abstinence, and are expressly forbidden to consort with their women. None of the sex are allowed within a considerable distance of the trees upon which the worms are feeding, and if by chance a woman or impure man passes near the feeding grounds, the trees and worms are sprinkled in the name of Jogní (an incarnation of the god Mahadeo, whom the worms are supposed to represent) with water taken, if procurable, from a running stream, and in which tulsí leaves have been steeped. During the same period the Dheemurs carefully abstain from flesh, fish, or haldí as their food, nor do they cut their hair or shave, and carefully deny themselves all ablution, even the ordinary one after performing the offices of nature. When the cocoons are all formed, they are collected into a heap, and a goat, pig, or fowl is sacrificed ot Mahadeo in his form Jogní, the blood is sprinkled over the cocoons, and after a bout of liquor, are taken home. On the third day following, the Dheemurs shave and resume their normal condition.

In the south of the district, and in the jungles bordering on the Nágpúr province, a part of the Katkáhí or Kártik crop is kept for seed, and a third* set of cocoons is reared; this is ready in the month of Mágh (January), and hence known as "Mághur." North of a line running east and west through Seoní this practice is unknown, the Dheemurs never attempting to rear the worms after the Kártik crop.

There does not appear to be any valid reason why the culture should not be kept up continuously throughout the year; what they say is, that the insects would not propagate owing to the weakness of the male. The female is, however, admitted both in October and January to be more than usually vigorous. The real cause of the cessation, in one case from January and February, and in the other, from October—November to May, is probably the dislike of the rearers to the life of abstinence which their religious views of the industry impose upon them. I have traced the rearing of the worms from the gathering of the wild cocoons early in May to the production of the crop in January and February. It will then be apparent that the tasar moth must mature the May cocoon in its wild state. This gives then four crops of cocoons during the year, which are known as—

1.—Aríyá or ranwat.
2.—Bhadelí.
3.—Katkahaí.
4.—Mághur.

I have mentioned that the worm seems to feed indifferently on the saj, lendeyá, and dowrá trees. The closest enquiry that I have been able to make does not indicate the fact that there is more than one variety of worm known†; at any rate, it does not, I think, admit of doubt that the same worm feeds with equal avidity on the three kinds of trees.

The worms, whose habitat are the ber trees and castor-oil plants, are unknown in this district, at least their silk if produced is never utilized.

When the crop is gathered, Koshtás‡, a weaving caste, visit the villages and buy the cocoons from the rearers. They are then, as soon as practicable, boiled in a lye made from the ashes of Jugní§ stalks, a plant grown for the oil expressed from its seed. This process|| effectually kills the chrysalis, at the same time dissolving the mucilage of the cocoon. The cocoons are then stored for use.

Method of reeling tasar silk.

6. The method of reeling is primitive in the extreme, and to its imperfections I solely attribute the scant attention this valuable and very beautiful silk has hitherto received.

A description of the process is as follows:—

The spinner, always a woman, sits on the ground, on her left is an earthen vessel with a thickish rim about 6 inches in diameter and 3 deep. The saucer is three parts filled with a mixture of potash and ashes patted down to a level surface and kept damp with water. Upon this the cocoons to be spun are placed, the outer portion of inferior and nearly useless silk

* Also the case in Chanda. But in Sumbulpoor the practice seems to agree with that in *North* Seonee.

† In Sumbulpoor the people say that there were two kinds; but that which spun the larger cocoons is nearly extinct. But such a statement has no scientific weight.

‡ In Chanda a Teloogoo tribe of weavers called Koskatis.

§ Or the Aghara, or the castor-oil plant.

|| According to most accounts they are first of all simply steamed to kill the grub.

having been first removed. The thread in ordinary use among the weavers is spun from seven cocoons*; these are all placed at the same time in the earthen saucer, a filament is then taken up from each cocoon, and being brought together, are rolled between the hand and left thigh of the spinner, which are kept damp by an acid solution of tamarind and water.

Here the first imperfection often creeps in, the spinners not being careful to prevent an unequal number of fibres coming off the same kernel, "*gabha*," the result being an uneven spinning which greatly detracts from the beauty of the silk.

In the right hand is the "*natwá*," a small roughly made triangle of wood with a thin handle passing from the apex through the hypothenuse. The silk passing from the left thigh of the spinner is wound round the arrow head of the "*natwá*." When a thousand cocoons are reeled off, the silk now known as tasar is slipped off the point of the *natwá* and placed on the "*parti*." This is simply a rod with two cross pieces of wood, the extremities of the cross pieces and the upright being connected by stays of soft cord. The sides of *natwá* being rigid, the silk was in a state of tension, but on the *partí* it is relaxed and easily wound off. When on the *partí*, the silk is known as *orí*. From the *partí* the *orí* is passed by a púnerá or hollow stick about 2¼ inches long, the object of which is to prevent the silk being injured by the hand, on to the *jalír* to prepare it for the loom; the process now differs in no way from ordinary weaving. In the mixed fabrics of cotton and tasar manufactured in this district, the silk always forms the *púriá*, *i. e.*, warp or length, of the piece, the binará, woof or breadth being cotton. The warp and woof are also known as tana and bana. When in the loom, the silk again changes its name from *orí* to *nár*.

The method of reeling, though extremely simple,† is ill-calculated to bring out the latent gloss and beauty of the fibre. The natural colour of the silk is a light brown, and often, notwithstanding its imperfect treatment, exhibits a richness and depth of colour quite its own.

In India the shade of the raw silk will be best understood when I say that it is a pure *khákí*.

Cloth woven from the undyed silk and unmixed with cotton is known as "*solá*."

I may mention that the outer covering of the cocoon, consisting of inferior silk removed by the Koshtas before spinning of the true tasar, is not lost, but sold to another class of weavers called *Patwá*. The silk bracelets and armlets worn by all classes among the Hindoos, in the month of Sáwan at the feast of "*rákhí bundún*," are made from this refuse. Its value, however, is very small, being sold for one rupee per seer.

It may be interesting to know that the perforated cocoons of the tasar—that is, the cocoons from which the moths have escaped—are quite capable of being reeled off, and a large loss of silk is thus obviated. No Koshta rejects a cocoon simply because the moth has eaten its way through it.

It sometimes, though rarely, happens that the perforated cocoon will reel off without a break, but, as a rule, the filament has to be joined several times. If the junction is neatly effected, and confined to a single fibre, it can hardly be detected, and, judging from the appearance of the reeled silk, I do not think its value would be seriously affected even in a European market; it certainly is, but in a minor degree, among the weaving classes of this part of the country.

* * * * * * * * * * *

In the North-West Provinces.

5. I have only found two brief notices of the breeding of tusser in the Mirzapoor jungles. They both agree in stating that the cocoons for seed are first collected in Aghun, but that the moths do not emerge till Asarh. The first crop of cocoons is obtained in Bhadoon, and this is considered the better crop; a second is obtained in Kartik. It is clear from this that the Mirzapoor insect is trivoltine, whereas in the Central Provinces the tusser seems to be quadrivoltine. The rearing of the worms is carried on by the Koles upon the asun tree. The cocoons are by them sold to beparees, who take the cocoons to the market at Ahrowrah and Kone. The cocoons are then boiled, and, when cool, an infusion of "reh," carefully strained, is poured over them to clean them and loosen the thread; they are then treated much as in the Central Provinces, except that the first thread is of five cocoons. The Nagpoor silk is said to be of better quality than that of Mirzapoor.

The tusser known elsewhere, but not used as a silk spinner.

6. In Upper Assam and the Punjab the tusser is found, but not utilized as a fibre-producer. In the former province it is known as the kutkuri. In the Punjab the cocoons, from their extreme toughness, are cut into strips, and used to bind the stocks of matchlocks. In Bombay and Madras, though found,

* Sometimes five or six only.

† The Chanda account describes also another method of reeling with an instrument held in the *left* hand and called "poonko:" also a rude but ingenious method of what is in fact silk *throwing*, whereby two or three "singles" are twisted into one thread.

the tusser does not seem to be utilized,* except, perhaps, in the jungles of Ganjam.

The following account of it is given by M. Perottet, of Pondicherry:—

It is generally found on the following trees :—

1. *Terminalia catappa* (best cocoons) 50 weighed " one French pound."
2. *Syzygium jambolanum.*
3. *Zizyphus jujuba.*
4. Less frequently on *Pentaptera coriacea.*

" These cocoons are exceedingly rich in silk ; they reel by means of an alkali, or any other solvent, with great facility, and to the very end. The silk they produce is very elastic, and of singular brilliancy."

M. Perottet distinctly states that he has bred this moth in a state of captivity. When he had an excess of females, he had only to tie them out at night to find them provided with mates in the morning. He had obtained four generations in the year, but only in years of abundant rains and a continued damp atmosphere.

At the Madras Exhibition of 1855 the Jurors in Class IV gave the following account of tusser silk:—

" Cocoons, from which this description of silk is obtained, were exhibited from several localities. They were formed by caterpillars of several species of moth, belonging to the genus *saturnia.* That which is most commonly met with in Southern India appears to be *S. paphia.* The caterpillar feeds on the leaves of the country almond tree (*terminalia catappa*), whence it is often called the almond moth. It is also found on the leaves of the ber tree, *(Zizyphus jujuba)*, the *casuarina,* &c. The cocoons are ingeniously attached to the twiggy branches of the ber by a long stalk, terminating in a ring, encircling the branch. In the thicker foliage of the *casuarina* the silk is woven among the leaves without the above provision. It does not appear that silk in any quantity has been obtained from this source in the Madras Presidency. Considerable quantities of the small silk cloth worn by the Brahmins at their meals are imported into the Northern Circars from Cuttack. The only use to which the cocoons appear to be turned is that of a ligature for native matchlocks. They are cut spirally into long narrow bands, with which the barrels are tied to the stock."

The tusser is also found in most parts of Bombay. Captain Coussmaker of the Revenue Survey states that he has found it in Tanna, Poona, Satara, and Kolhapoor. It feeds, according to the same authority, on the " nandrook or pimproon, the paeer or baseree (trees of the ficus kind) and on the bher, the karunda (canisar), the rameta (quidia) and in the ain (pentaptera)," the last probably the aseen or asun. The moth is said to emerge only " during the monsoon;" *i. e.*, from May to November. This would nearly correspond with the account in Mirzapoor.

The Moonga.

7. Next in importance to the tusser comes the moonga of Assam (Antheræa Assama), also found, but sparingly, in the Dehra Doon. The earliest notice I find of the moonga is given by Dr. Buchanan. "The silkworm," he writes, " produced on a species of *laurus* and called mugá, is the most common. The tree is planted and its branches are pruned, but the insect is fed on the tree as it grows. Some people who have seen the insect say that it is the same as the tasar of Bengal, but the silk is so different that I suppose they are mistaken. There are two crops, the silk procured in the beginning of the dry season (Kartik) is red, that which is cut in the end of spring (Jyaishtha,) is white, and is reckoned the best. The silk called medanggori is reared in Assam Proper on a tree that is cultivated, but of what kind I do not learn, nor could I procure the insect ; it is higherpriced than mugá." A fuller and more accurate account will be found in a paper by Captain (late General) Jenkins, read before the Agri-Horticultural Society of Calcutta, and dated 5th February 1833. I reproduce it *verbatim et literatim* :—

" Muneeram gives me the following account of the silk of Assam :—

" The worm that gives the common fawn-coloured moonga silk, when fed on the most common plants, gives a whitish silk when fed on the leaves of other trees. The plants it feeds on are named and estimated as follows :—

No. 1.—*Champa.*†—The silk produced from the worm feeding on this plant gives the finest and whitest silk, used only by the Rajahs and great people, and

---

* Colonel Sykes identifies the tusser with the kolisura of the Deccan ; this also he describes as used to bind matchlocks.

† *Michelia.*

is called *champa pattea moonga.* The thread is sold at from Rs. 11 to 12 a seer.

No. 2.—*Maizankurry** called also *Addakurry.*—The leaves of this tree also give a white silk, and is called *maizankurry moonga.* The old trees are cut down and the jungle about burnt, and the worms are fed upon the tender leaves of the offshoots for one year, when the leaves become too old and hard for the worms. Silk is sold at from Rs. 6 to 7 a seer.

No. 3.—*Soom.*†—This is the common tree of the vicinity ; the silk from the worms fed on this gives the finest sort of fawn-colored moonga. Silk is sold at Rs. 3½ to 4 per seer.

No. 4.—*Soonhalloo.*‡—This is also a brown silk of inferior quality. This plant is most common in Dhurumpore and about Russa chokey.

No. 5 —*Digluttee.*§—This is also a brown silk of inferior quality, but the worms fed on the leaves of this tree increase much in size.

No. 6.—*Pattee hoonda.*‖

The moonga worm gives broods five¶ times a year, and the cocoon is very large, but thin. I could only obtain silk, the produce of worms feeding on Nos. 3 and 4, and manufactured into cheap cloths for the lower classes."

Mr. Hugon, in the Asiatic Society's Journal, gives a fuller account of this moth and its treatment. To the list of trees on which the worm is reared he adds the "kontooloa," and the 4th and 6th in Captain Jenkins' list he calls the "sonhalloo" and "pattee shoonda." Moreover, according to Mr. Hugon, the "addakoory" is used till it is *four* years old, though the worms fed on leaves of the first year's growth produce the best silk ; the yield of the third year being "little, if at all, sup rior to the common moonga." The tending of the worms on this tree is more laborious, the plants having to be constantly renewed, and the smoothness of the bark rendering it necessary to help the worms in moving from branch to branch. The tree is said to be more abundant in Upper than in Lower Assam. Mr. Hugon puts the *mezankoree* silk on a par with the *champa* silk, and values each of them at 50 per cent. above the common fawn-coloured silk. According to the same authority the champa tree is not found in Lower Assam. As to the "kontooloa," he remarks : "This is a large tree found both in the hills and the plains, also a few in the villages. The leaves are too hard for young worms : they are reared on the soom till the third moulting, and then put on this tree, by which process the silk obtained is stronger than that from worms reared entirely on the soom." Of the "pattee shoonda," he writes : "Middle-sized tree, found principally in forests ; few to be met with in the villages of Lower Assam ; used when the leaves of No. 3 are done." The "sonhalloo" is thus described : "The sonhalloo is found in the forests of the hills and plains, where it attains a very large size. It is also found in the villages, where in six years it attains its full growth (30 feet) ; it is very abundant in the western portion of this district (Nowgong,) Rara, Jumna Mookh, Joyntea, and the valley of Dhurmpore. At the latter place, where the hill-tribes of Mikirs and Kacháris clear dense forests for the cultivation of rice and cotton, numbers of the plants spring up spontaneously. After three or four years, when the land getting poorer requires more tillage and the use of the plough, these tribes, who only use the *kar*, or hoe, remove to new forests, and leave behind them plantations of these trees, which they have used during the short period they have remained. To them the ryots of the more settled parts resort in the spring to rear up worms." Mr. Hugon puts the silk of the "sonhalloo" fed worms lowest in the scale. The "Jarooa" and "Jeytooa" are the best of the five annual crops.

---

* Perhaps of the laurel family ; looks marvellously like a willow, though it is probably not of that genus. *Tetranthera quadriflora ?* Major Sherer, or the authority on which he relies, says, that the chrysalis of the moonga fed on the Adakuri "loses its vitality." This is a curious fact, if authentic.

† A species of *tetranthera* or *laurus.*

‡ *Tetranthera macrophylla.*—Roxb.

§ A plant of the laurel tribe belonging to *tetranthera.* Hamilton calls it *tetranthera diglottica.*—W. Much the same quality of silk as the foregoing.

‖ *Laurus obtusifolia*—Roxb. W.

¶ Called from the seasons or months respectively :—
Jarooa in January and February.
Jeytooa in May and June.
Aharooa in June and July.
Bhodia in August and September.
Khotia in October and November. In Seebsaugor the Aharooa and Bhodia broods are generally neglected. The same seems to be the case in Durrung.

The rearing of the worms is thus described :—

The cocoons selected for breeding are taken from among those which have begun in the largest numbers on the same day. They are put in a closed basket, and suspended from the roof, the moths, as they come forth, having room to move about. After a day the females, known by their larger body, are taken out, and tied to small wisps of thatching grass, taken always from over the hearth, its darkened colour being thought more acceptable to the moth. If out of a batch there should be but few males, the wisps with females tied to them are exposed outside at night. The males thrown away in the neighbourhood find their way to them.* These wisps are hung on a string tied across the house to keep them from the lizards and rats. The eggs laid during the first three days, about 250,† are the only ones thought worth the keeping. Those laid on the two or three subsequent days are said to produce weak worms. The wisps are taken out morning and evening, and exposed to the side where the sun is shining. Ten days after the laying of the eggs a few of them are hatched. The wisps are then hung up to the tree, the young worms finding their way to the leaves. Care must be taken that the ants have been destroyed, their bite proving fatal to the worm in its early stages. To effect this, they rub the trunk of the tree with molasses, and tie to it fish and dead toads. When large numbers have been attracted to one place they destroy them with fire. This they do several times previously to the worms being put on. The ground under the trees must be kept clear of jungle, to make it easy to find the worms that fall down. Young trees are preferable until the second moulting. To prevent the worms coming to the ground, fresh plantain leaves are tied round the trunk, over the slippery surface of which they cannot crawl. They are removed to fresh trees on bamboo platters tied to long poles. Bats, owls, and rats are very destructive at night. In the day the worms require to be constantly watched, crows and other birds being so fond of them that they lie in wait in the neighbouring trees. An old lady's doze over her morning "kanee" (opium), however short, is sure to be fatal to several worms; the 'goolail,' which is always at hand, often punishes the thief; but the mischief is done. Numbers are destroyed in the more advanced stages by wasps and by the ichneumon. * * * The worms thrive best in dry weather, but a very hot day proves fatal to many at the time of moulting. At these periods rain is very favourable. Thunder-storms do not injure them as they do the mulberry worm. Continual heavy rains (which are rarer in Assam than in Bengal) are hurtful by throwing them down. Showers, however heavy, cause no great damage, they taking shelter under the leaves with perfect safety. The worms during their moultings remain on the branches; but when about to spin, they come down the trunk. The plantain leaves preventing their going further down, they are collected in baskets, which are afterwards put under branches of dry leaves suspended from the roof. They crawl up into these, and form their cocoons. As with the 'eria,' several are often joined together. The silk of these they spin instead of winding. Above the plantain leaf a roll of grass is tied for those that come down during the night, to begin spinning in. After four days the selection of cocoons for the next breed is made, and the rest wound off."

The cycle of the insect is thus given :—

From emergence from the egg to commencement of cocoon	30	days.
In the cocoon	20	,,
As a moth	6	,,
In the egg	10	,,
TOTAL ...	66	days.

The worm and the method of reeling are thus described by Mr. Hugon :—

"On being hatched, the worm is about ¼ inch long; it appears composed of alternate black and yellow rings. As it increases in size, the former are distinguished as six black moles, in regular lines, on each of the twelve rings which form its body. The colours gradually alter as it progresses, that of the body becoming lighter, the moles sky-blue, then red with a bright gold-coloured ring round each. When full-grown the worm is above 5 inches long; its colours are most brilliant and varied in shades; the body appears transparent, and is of a very light yellow or dark green colour, with a brown and a yellow streak at the sides; in the latter the breathing-holes are distinguished by a black speck; the moles are red and have each four sharp prickles and a few black hairs; the head and claws are of a light brown, the holders green and covered with short black hair: the last pair have a black ring on the outside. On being tapped with the finger, the body renders a hollow sound; by the sound it is ascertained whether they have come down for want of leaves on the tree, or from their having ceased feeding. The chrysalis not being soon killed by exposure to the sun, when they have many cocoons they put them on stages, cover them up with leaves, and burn grass under them. The cocoons are then boiled for about an hour in a solution of potash made from the dried stalks of rice; they are then taken out and laid in cloth folded over to keep them warm.

* Manirám Baruá, in a paper submitted by Captain Jenkins to the Agri-Horticultural Society adds: "After the males and females have been together for three days on the evening of the fourth day a small torch of fire is shown them, when the males separate and take their departure."

† An account by Major Sherer, Deputy Commissioner of Nowgong, says "about 120."

From this they are taken, as required, and thrown in hot water (not over the fire), after the floss* has been removed with the hand. The instrument used for winding off the silk is the coarsest imaginable. A thin bamboo, about three feet long, is split in two, and the pieces driven equally in the ground two feet apart; over the interior projection of one of the knots is laid a stick, to which is fixed, a little on one side, a round piece of plank about one foot in diameter. The rotary motion is given by jerking this axle, on which the thread rolls itself. In front of the vessel holding the cocoons a stick is fixed horizontally for the thread to travel upon. Two persons are employed, one attending to the cocoons, while the other jerks the axle with the right hand, and with the same hand directs the thread up the left fore-arm, so that it is twisted in coming down again towards the hand. The left hand directs the thread over the axle. Fifteen cocoons is the smallest number they can wind off in one thread; twenty is the number generally; even the last is often broken from the coarseness of the instrument used, although the fibre is much stouter than that of the mulberry silk. When nearly a quarter of a seer has accumulated on the axle, it is dried in the sun, and made into skeins of one or two rupees weight. This is done with a small bamboo frame, set in motion by the common spinning machine of the country."

The following table is given by Mr. Hugon, showing the nature and prices of the various kinds of cloth made from moonga silk:—

Name of Cloth.	Size in cubits.	Weight.		Price of Thread.			Cost of weaving.			Total.			REMARKS.
		Sr.	Chk.	Rs.	A.	P.	Rs.	A.	P.	Rs.	A.	P.	
Soorias ...	7 × 1½	0	6	1	14	0	0	3	0	2	1	0	Dhoties.
Ditto ...	16 × 2	1	0	5	0	0	0	8	0	5	8	0	
Mekla ...	5 × 1¾	0	4	1	4	0	0	2	0	1	6	0	Petticoats.
Rhia ...	12 × 1¼	0	8	2	8	0	0	4	0	2	12	0	Scarfs.
Gaursha ...	8 × 1	0	2	0	10	0	0	1	0	0	11	0	Worn as turbans or round the waist.
Joonta Bor Cappor	12 × 2½	1	0	2	0	0	0	6	0	2	6	0	Made of the floss, and worn in winter.

Manirám Baruá, however, says: "The price of the common moonga silk in thread is Rs. 3 to 4 per seer of 80 tolahs, but the mezankuri fetches Rs. 6 to 8 per seer."

Fifty thousand cocoons are estimated to yield upwards of 12 seers of silk, and Mr. Hugon puts the price at Rs. 5 per seer. It is considered a good yield for an acre of land to give 50,000 cocoons. From unknown causes the moonga occasionally fails completely in certain tracts. For instance, Mr. Hugon writes:—"This last season in our *Jumna Mookh (Cachar)* pergunnah the moonga was a complete failure; there are no worms on the trees now, from inability to procure cocoons, although there was a very abundant crop in two pergunnahs at the opposite end of the district."

The account given by Colonel Agnew in 1869 agrees, in the main, with Mr. Hugon's. The worm stage is, however, put by the former at "26 or 27 days," and it is stated that the total cycle varies, inversely as the temperature, from 42 to 84 days, the *average* being 66 days. The yield of each worm is estimated by Colonel Agnew at from $\frac{1}{4000}$ to $\frac{1}{5000}$ of a seer; the price of the silk at from Rs. 6 to 15. Breeding cocoons are said to fetch Rs. 2 per thousand. It is noteworthy that the breeders of Upper Assam annually import cocoons for breeding purposes from Kamroop. All attempts to perpetuate the race in Luckimpore and Seebsaugor are said to have failed.

The eria or arindy worm.

8. The eria or arindy worm (*Attacus* ricini) does not seem to have spread beyond the province of Assam, and a tract to the south-west of that province comprising the districts of Dinagepore, Rungpore, and perhaps parts of Bhaugulpore and Purneah. The earliest notice of the insect which I have found, is that already referred to above (p. 19). The passage in the Agent's diary is as follows: He had observed that the bags in which the merchants brought this silk to Cossimbazaar were of different stuff from any he had seen. He was informed "that 'twas called Arundee, made neither with cotton nor silke, but of a kind of Herba spun by a worme that feeds upon the leaves of a stalke or tree called Arundee, which bears a

* According to Major Sherer this floss, called "jotha," is utilised, being spun like eria. The eria has no "floss."

round prickly berry of which oyle is made; vast quantitys of this cloth is made in the country about Goora Ghaut beyond Seripore Mercha, where the wormes are kept as silk-wormes here: 'twill never come white, but will take any colour: 'twill not rott nor receive any damage by wet: it burns like hair, not in flame, nor keepes for long and wards (? wears) to admiration insomuch that when the cloth is first made 'tis given up and downe to poore people to weare and to lay in shops to be footed upon before 'tis fit to be sold."—(*Notes on and extracts from the Government Records in Fort St. George, Mardras, 2nd Series, p.* 58.)

Attention was drawn to it, as already observed, by Sir W. Jones in 1791, and by Dr. Roxburgh in 1804. It is thus noticed by Dr. Buchanan:—

"The Ricinus (Erondo of the natives) is raised in many part of this district, feeding a silk-worm, which I take to be the Phalæna Penelope. There are two kinds of the plant, the Ricinus Communis and R. Viridis of Willdenow. This excellent botanist has, with great propriety, changed the name given by Linnæus to the first species; but with regard to the last he has been uncommonly unfortunate, as the stem of the plant is of a bright red, and the leaves are stained with brown, so that it may be considered a very remarkable exception to the vegetable colour being green. Both plants seems to answer equally well; and those who rear the worm drop a few seeds round the fence that encloses their farm yard, or sow a small spot adjacent to their house. The seed is put in the ground about the beginning of November, and again about the beginning of May. Both plants are annuals, although they have strong woody stems, often 12 feet high, and they live about eight months, so that leaves are procurable at all seasons. The seed is sometimes made into oil for medicine, but is never used for the lamp as in many parts of India. The plant requires a mixed free soil. In some places one brood only of worms is reared, in others 12 broods spin silk in the course of the year. The cocoons preserved for breeding, having produced moths, which are very beautiful, the impregnated females cling to a small twig that is hung up near them, deposit their eggs round it in spiral rings, and then die clinging to the stick. These twigs are often sold at markets, and, with the dead moths hanging round, make a very curious appearance. A breeder having procured one of these twigs, scrapes the eggs into a piece of cloth, which he lays on a wide-mouthed basket, which is supported at some distance from the floor in one end of his hut. The eggs are soon hatched, and the worms are daily supplied with fresh leaves, and kept clean. The worm grows rapidly, and when ready to spin, some twigs are put into the basket to assist its operation. The cocoons, that are to be spun, are thrown into boiling water, and the threads of from five to six are wound into one by means of the common silk-reel of Bengal. This forms a coarse rough thread of a dirty white colour, and totally destitute of the silky lustre.

"A seer of 96 sicca weight ($2\frac{464}{1000}$ lbs.) of this thread is worth from annas 12 to Re. 1, but it is very seldom sold, and the people who keep the insect in general rear no more than is just sufficient to make cloths for their own family. The cloth lasts very long,* owing to which quality it is probable that some use might be found for this material in our manufactures at home."

In the same paper as quoted above, in regard to the moonga, Captain Jenkins gives, *teste* Manirám Baruá, the following particulars as to this worm, known in Assam as the eria:—

"The eria or eria pat is the produce of another worm, and very inferior in appearance to that of the other (moonga), though I believe it is equally lasting. The worms are fed in the houses, and entirely upon the leaves of the arund (castor-oil plant), if they are procurable, and if not, on other trees in the order following:—

1. The ricinus communis (green) or viridis (red)—v is a misnomer of Willd.
2. *Kisseroo*, a plant I know not as yet.
3. *Bengalee aloo*, a common plant; divided leaves like that of the papeeah. I know not its name as yet.
4. *Jatropha manihot*.
5. The common ber (*zizyphus jujuba*).
6. *Keora kaura*.† This I know not.
7. *Gooluncha phool*, Assamese name, the Bengalee *Bherondo* (*Jatropha curcas*).

This worm produces broods every month or every month and a half.

The cocoon is smaller than that of the moonga, weighing from 4 to 5 grains, or 1 grain less than the moonga cocoon. The silk is very warm and lasting, and is worth from Rs. 6 to 8 per seer."

Mr. Hugon writes to the following effect:—

"The broods number seven each year, in summer the cycle lasting from 43 to 47 days, and in winter two months. The summer crops yield a produce both greater and better. It is

* Mr. Michael Atkinson of Jungypore describes the eria cloth as "of incredible durability, the life of one person being seldom sufficient to wear out a garment made of it, so that the same piece descends from mother to daughter."
† *Sapini schiferum*. It would be *S. baccatum* if it were not for the glands on the leaves.—W.

fed principally on the hera or *palma christi (Ricinus communis)* leaf, but, failing this, is fed on other trees, *viz.*—

1. Koossool.
2. Hindoo grass.
3. Mukurdal.
4. Okonnee.
5. Gomarree.
6. Litta Pakoree.
7. Borzonolly.

"The worms thrive best on the castor-oil leaves.

"The cocoons to breed from are selected as in the case of the moonga, those containing males being distinguished by a more pointed end. These cocoons are put in a closed basket and hung up in the house out of reach of rats and insects; when the moths come forth, they are allowed to move about in the basket for four-and-twenty hours, after which the females, known only by the larger body, are tied to long reeds, or canes, 20 or 25 to each, and these are hung up in the house. The eggs that have been laid the first three days, amounting to about 200, are alone kept. They are tied in a piece of cloth, and suspended to the roof until a few begin to hatch. These eggs are white, and the size of turnip seed. When a few of the worms are hatched, the cloths are put on small bamboo platters hung up in the house, in which they are fed with tender leaves. After the second moulting they are removed to branches of leaves suspended above the ground. Under them, upon the ground, a mat is laid to receive them when they fall. When they have ceased feeding, they are thrown into baskets full of dry leaves, amongst which they form their cocoons, two or three being often found joined together. The caterpillar is at first about ¼ inch in length, and appears nearly black. As it increases in size, it becomes of an orange colour, with six black spots on each of the twelve rings which form its body. The head, claws, and holders are black. After the second moulting, they change to an orange colour; that of the body gradually becomes lighter, in some approaching to white, in others to green, and the black spots gradually become the colour of the body. After the fourth or last moulting, the colour is a dirty white or a dark green. The white caterpillars invariably spin red silk; the green ones white. On attaining its full size, the worm is about 3½ inches long. Unlike the moonga caterpillar its colours are uniform and dull. The breathing holes are marked by a black mark; the moles have become the colour of the body; they have increased to long fleshy points, without the sharp prickles the moonga has. The body has a few short hairs hardly perceptible. In four days the cocoons are complete. The chrysalis is killed by exposure to the sun. The hill tribes settled in the plains eat the chrysalis. To draw off the silk the cocoons are put over a slow fire in a solution of potash; when the silk comes easily off, they are taken out and the water slightly pressed. They are then taken one by one, loosened at one end, and the cocoon put over the thumb of the left hand; with the right they draw it out nearly the thickness of twine, reducing any inequality by rubbing it between the index and thumb.* In this way new cocoons are joined on. The thread is allowed to accumulate in heaps of a quarter of a seer. It is afterwards exposed to the sun or near the fire to dry; it is then made into skeins with two sticks tied at one end and opening like a pair of compasses. It is then ready to be wove, unless it has to be dyed. The dyes used are lac, munjeet, and indigo. * * * The thread is wove as cotton. The different prices of the cloth are as follow :—

Name of cloth.	Size in cubits.	Weight.	Price of thread.	Cost of weaving.	Total.	REMARKS.
		Srs. Ch.	Rs. A. P.	Rs. A. P.	Rs. A. P.	
Borkapor ...	16 by 3	1 8	3 0 0	0 8 0	3 8 0	Worn in winter. Used as a blanket, and also made into coats.
Mekla ...	5 by 2	0 6	0 12 0	0 2 0	0 14 0	Used only by the poorer classes.†
Rhia ...	10 by 1½	0 8	1 0 0	0 2 0	1 2 0	
Gaursha ...	8 by ½	0 4	0 8 0	0 2 0	0 10 0	

In a "letter from Mr. George Eveleigh, dated Calcutta, 8th February 1843," published in the 2nd volume of the Journal of the Agri-Horticultural

* It will, however, have been noticed that Dr. Buchanan in his account of the Arindy worm in Dinagepore distinctly says the silk is *wound* on a *reel* from several cocoons previously boiled.

† A paper recently received says that the eria is regarded as unclean and not as true silk. The prejudice is, however, said to be dying out.

Society of Calcutta, that gentleman states that he wound silk from eria cocoons by simply placing them in lukewarm water. This he attributes to his having fed the worms occasionally on mulberry leaves and given them leaves at all times in as moist a state as possible. "This," he says, "appears much to increase the growth of the worms, * * * and the silk appears greatly improved both in quantity and quality, and there appears to be less deposit of the resinous matter on the silk, which is therefore more easily wound off." If there was no mistake as to the identity of the worm, this is curious. If Mr. Eveleigh was not in error on this point, he was entitled to the prize offered by the Society. This worm was introduced into Malta, France, and Italy. In Malta, Signor Lotteri is said to have "unwound" the filament, but "declared that his fingers stuck together for a very long time afterwards, so gummy and resiny was the binding matrix of the silk." From this we may infer that he did not find any solvent, or he would have applied it to his own fingers; and indeed the Governor of Malta says, "we have gone through all the operations *as practised in Assam.*" It was tried also in Algeria and the Canaries. M. Guérin-Méneville, writing in 1860, maintained that its cultivation would not pay in France, because it continued to hatch all the year round, and it would be too expensive to grow ricinus under glass for it. The same authority attributes the impossibility of winding to the fact of the cocoon being open and filling with water, instead of floating as that of Bombyx mori.

Both in Malta and Piedmont the worms throve well on the castor-oil plant; in Piedmont actually on the growing plant and in the open air. It is probably to the Malta experiment that Captain Hutton alludes when he speaks dubiously of the filament having been wound in Italy. He himself could find no solvent.

Captain Jenkins, in conjunction with the Agri-Horticultural Society in 1839, offered Rs. 600 and a gold medal to the discoverer of an effectual and cheap solvent for the adhesive material which attaches to the cocoon. Though this prize was before the public for seven years, no claimant for it appeared, and the amount was diverted to another purpose.

The moonga and eria worms are said by Colonel Agnew to be chiefly bred by low caste Hindoos, Mikirs, and Cacharees; whereas the pât or B. textor is bred by the joogee caste. Colonel Agnew (writing in 1869) puts the price of the eria silk at from Rs. 2 to 3 the seer. Mr. Hugon puts it at Rs. 2. Captain Hutton says the Dinagepore and Rungpore cocoons are much smaller than those from Assam and Cachar, resembling too in *shape* the cocoons of the *A. Cynthia*. He seems to suspect that the Dinagepore worms may be distinct.

Attacus Cynthia.

9. Closely resembling, and nearly allied to the *Attacus Ricini*, is the *Attacus Cynthia*; indeed, I believe some naturalists hold the *Attacus Ricini* to be only a domesticated form of the latter. However, the wild *Attacus Cynthia* occurs throughout the greater part of the Himalaya, in the Dehra Doon, and in Assam and Cachar. It feeds on the *Xanthoxylon hostile*, the *Coriaria nipalensis* and some other indigenous shrubs, and will eat the castor-oil plant. In China, and in Europe, whither the worm has been transported from China, it is fed on *Ailanthus glandulosa*, and Dr. Bonavia, in an unsuccessful attempt to introduce it into Oudh, fed it on *A. excelsa*. In the wild state it is annual. Captain Hutton thinks by patience it might be domesticated. He has crossed it with *Attacus Ricini*. The cocoons are wrapped into a leaf, and present the same difficulty in reeling as the eria cocoons. The silk is at first glossy white and changes to dull sandy brown or grey. The *Attacus Cynthia* or Ailanthus worm was introduced into Europe in 1857 and tried in Piedmont, France, and Algiers. In 1860 Mr. Guérin-Méneville believed that he had proved that it could be profitably grown in the open air in the north of France, yielding two crops annually. His estimate indeed is too sanguine to be accepted as altogether accurate. I have not found how far the silk has established a market for itself. It does not yet seem to have been reeled, the thread breaking owing to the cocoon being spun with an opening at one end. M. Guérin-Méneville, however, from examination of the Chinese-made fabrics, maintains that the thread must have been in some cases *wound*.

M. DeSanley, who, in 1864-65 tried experiments with the ailanthus worm (which he admits were *tout à fait désastreux*), states that this insect has quite changed its period of existence in the course of acclimatization in France, and from a multivoltine become a uniovoltine.

Attacus Atlas.

10. *Attacus Atlas* is the largest of the group in India. It is found at Mussooree, and is abundant in Kumaon and eastwards to Cachar. At Mussooree it is found on the *Falconeria insignis, Bradleio ovata* and other plants; in Kumaon on the barberry. The silk is difficult to reel, though it yields partially if boiled in vinegar. The silk is said by Captain Hutton to be "decidedly good."

Antheræa Perotteti.

11. *Antheræa Perotteti* was found by M. Perottet of Pondicherry on the *Odina wodier*, Roxb. M. Perottet never could make it eat anything else. The silk is reported strong, wiry, and brilliant, but had to be carded.* The worm breeds in captivity, undergoes four moults, and yields four crops in the year. The chrysalis of the fourth generation remains in cocoon till the tree it feeds on (which is deciduous) is again in leaf.

A. Roylei.

12. *Antheræa Roylei* is found at Darjeeling and in the Himalayas from Kumaon to the Punjab, feeding on *Quercus incana.* It is properly an annual, but can be made to yield two or three crops. Its silk is favorably spoken of, but not abundant. The true cocoon is contained in a large closely-woven glazed case and enveloped on all sides by the leaves of the tree, the impression of the nervures being deeply imprinted on the glazed surface. It is like the tusser moth, but smaller. It can be domesticated.

Other Species.

13. Several other species of wild skill-spinners are known, *e. g.*, the *Bombyx Huttoni*, a bivoltine, feeding on the wild mulberry and ranging westward in the Himalayas from Kumaon. The *B. Bengalensis* is found near Calcutta on the *Artocarpus lacoocha*; this is apparently rare. Another species of *Bombyx* resembling the *B. Huttoni* was found in Ranchee, Chota Nagpore, also feeding on the *Artocarpus lacoocha*. The *Bombyx religiosæ* is found in Assam upon the pipal (*Ficus religiosa*). Dr. Hilfer identified this with Mr. Hugon's Deomoonga found on the *Ficus Indica*, and described as spinning a small cocoon, active, under 2½ inches long, slender, reddish in colour and glazed, the moth resembling the mulberry moth. The silk was declared a delicate white thread. Since 1839 no further information has been obtained as to this moth. Mr. Creighton of Maldah in 1839 mentions a wild cocoon on the mango tree; the silk was used to mix with that of the arindy worm. Mr. Hugon also mentions a worm called "haumpottonee." It forms an imperfect cocoon, feeds on "most leaves," is said to go through the same stages as other silkworms, is two inches long, brown and covered with hair. The moth is of the same color as the moonga, but only half the size. The cocoon is of a transparent yellow, with an opening at one end. The silk is capable of being spun like eria silk, but not used, because it excites severe itching. This is identified by Mr. Moore with the *Cricula trifenestrata* which Captain Haughton found also at Moulmein feeding on the cashewnut tree (*Aracardium Orientale*). Other species are *Antheræa Frithii, Saturnia Sylhetica, Actias Selene, Attacus Edwardsi,* and some kinds of *Ocinara*; but I have found nothing definite as to their value as silk-yielders. They will be found noticed in a paper* in the appendix with which Captain Hutton has favoured Government. I also reproduce in the appendix a paper† by Mr. Brownlow of Cachar on the open air rearing of undomesticated worms, published in the Journal of the Agri-Horticultural Society.

* See Appendix A.

† See Appendix B.

* Fishing lines are said to be made in Dinagepore from the silk of a worm feeding on Odina wodier. The food of the worm and the quality of the silk point to the identity of the insect with *A. Perotteti.*

APPENDIX A.

NOTES ON THE INDIAN BOMBYCIDÆ AS AT PRESENT KNOWN TO US:

BY CAPTAIN THOMAS HUTTON, F. G. S., C. M. Z. I., CORRESPONDING MEMBER OF THE AGRICULTURAL AND HORTICULTURAL SOCIETY OF INDIA,—DATED MUSSOORIE, THE 26TH JULY 1871.

BOMBYCIDÆ.

1. *Bombyx mori.*—(Lin.)—The largest of the domesticated Chinese Bombyces, originally from China, about North Latitude 32° to 34°. Also in Japan. This has been cultivated in Europe, especially in France and Italy, as well as in Syria, Egypt, Persia, Bokhara, Afghanistan, Cashmere, in one or two localities of the Northern Punjab near the hills, and thrives well at Mussoorie, everywhere feeding upon various species of mulberry and everywhere an annual, only *except* at Mussoorie, where I can obtain two crops. This is the worm that lately failed in France after centuries of domestication. It occurs *nowhere in the lowland Gangetic Provinces*, but its name is assigned, in ignorance, to *all* the under-mentioned species. "Where ignorance is bliss, 'tis folly to be wise," and after all, "what's in a name? a rose by any other name would smell as sweet!"

This species has been introduced into Australia, where it is said to thrive well, although Dr. Wallace of Colchester has lately informed me that Australian eggs do not hatch so kindly and regularly in England as English-bred eggs; instead of coming forth in a swarm, they appear daily in small quantities only. This I attribute to the high temperature of Australia having acted injuriously upon the constitution, which is debilitated.

The best silk of all is produced by this species, and readily sells with good reeling, at 25 shillings per lb. Mr. Cope sold some at that rate which he produced in the Punjab; and that reared at Mussoorie fetched the same price. A splendid silk is produced by crossing this species upon the smaller monthly worm known in Bengal as the *désee*, but the crossing requires great attention, and the out-turn after all may not be worth the trouble, for unless very closely watched and attended to, the worms will invariably revert to annuals. Silk—golden yellow when in health.

2. *Bombyx textor.*—Hutton.—This species is cultivated sparingly in several parts of India, but its constitution is thoroughly worn-out, and it ought to be sent to a hill climate. At Mussoorie it thrives well, and although like the last, an annual everywhere else, here it yields a second or autumnal crop also. It was originally brought from China, near Nankin, in North Latitude 32°, but is fast fading away from Bengal. It is cultivated in France and Italy and in China, as well as in Bengal, and in those countries generally produces a pure white silk; in Italy there are more white than yellow cocoons, but in France more yellow than white; this is dependent upon climate, as is well shown at Mussoorie where worms introduced from Bengal produce *white* cocoons for the first crop, but almost all yellow in the second crop. The worm being northern, is impatient of heat and suffers accordingly in constitution, the silk in consequence becoming white, which, as I have elsewhere pointed out, is generally a sign of loss of constitution, not only among silk-worms, but among animals still higher in the scale of nature; the natural color of the worm of *Bombyx mori* is nearly black-brindle, whereas the worms under domestication are of a sickly creamy white. So, then, the climate of France being more temperate than that of Italy, produces more yellow than white cocoons. This species is often termed the Milanese or Italian stock, and in Bengal is known as the Burra pooloo, because its cocoon is larger than those of the so-called *désee* worms or polyvoltines.

It is cultivated in Assam, and, according to Dr. Royle, is there and elsewhere called "*Pat* major," although it is invariably confounded with *B. mori*, than which it is at least an inch smaller, though in other respects closely resembling it. The cocoons are of a different texture, with more floss. The silk varies in price from 18 to 22 shillings per lb. Unless it be very soon transferred to the hills, this species will certainly die out; here I *could insure its life* without difficulty.

3. *Bombyx Crœsi.*—Hutton.—This is the largest of the monthly worms, and in Bengal passes under the Native name of the Madrassee or Nistry, and is as usual confounded by Europeans with *B. mori*, although the one passes as an annual, and the other as a monthly worm.

The silk is good, of a golden yellow, and the worms thrive best in a temperate climate; in Assam (*apud* Royle) it is known as "*Pat* minor." This species is cultivated in several parts of India, and thrives well at Mussoorie. It is to be particularly remarked, however, that none of the Chinese species, whether annual or monthly, have hitherto succeeded in the North-Western Provinces, Dr. Royle long since remarking that all the Old Company's Filatures did not extend higher up the country than about 26° of North Latitude, owing to the dry hot nature of the North-Western climates.

4. *Bombyx fortunatus.*—Hutton.—Known to the Bengalees as the *désee* worm, and like the others dignified by Europeans with the name of *B. mori*. Silk—golden yellow, distributed over Bengal and other parts of Southern India; but people know so little of the distinguishing characters of species, that it becomes very difficult to say what species is alluded to in magistrates' reports unless the native name is mentioned. This also is one of the polyvoltines. A sure mark of distinction between the worm of this species and that of any of the others exists in the fact that when near maturity, it becomes of a dull leaden blue color. This species thrives best in the cold weather. It is very small, but yields a good cocoon, although the returns of silk are said to be uncertain; there are no dark worms observable among them. The worm is figured in the second part of my paper "On the Reversion and Restoration of the Silk-worm," as published in "The Transactions of the Entomological Society of London"—(*quod vide*).

5. *Bombyx Sinensis.*—Hutton.—This is known as the "*Sina*" of Bengal, but, like the others, it originally came from China; it is very prolific, and even at Mussoorie goes on yielding crop after crop, up to the middle of December. The cocoons vary in color, some being white and others yellow, while others even have a beautiful faint greenish hue. These changes clearly show that the health of the worm is becoming impaired. There is a peculiarity about these also which may enable the tyro to distinguish them from any of the others; while all the other species hatch slowly during the morning, from six to twelve o'clock, the *Sina* worms come forth all in a batch, or continue hatching all day and all night.

6. *Bombyx Arracanensis.*—Hutton.—This I have only once been able to procure and the worms died off soon after hatching. The cocoon is said to be larger than those of the Bengal monthlies, but very little beyond the fact of its existence appears to be known, and people are so apathetic in these matters that letters, as a rule, remain unanswered. As the species is supposed to have been introduced from Burmah, it may probably turn out to be the same as that which was lately reported to exist in Burmah.

7. *Bombyx*———? I have heard of a species which in Central India is said to yield three crops of silk in the year, and that as soon as they are hatched, the worms are placed out upon mulberry trees and left there until they spin the cocoon. Some of the cocoons were kindly sent to me, but were so crushed in transit that they were destroyed; the cocoons were small, but silk good, of a pale color and something like those of *B. fortunatus*. I wrote for more cocoons and eggs, but my application has been unattended to, although my correspondent promised to assist me. I shall try again.

The following, with the exception of *B. Huttoni*, are little known. Mr. F. Moore wishes to place them in a separate genus under the name of "*Theophila*," one of his chief characters being the rows of spines on the larvæ; I object, however, to the establishment of this genus, because, in truth, we know little or nothing about them, and as to the spines, two species only are as yet known to possess them; nevertheless, they certainly do not stand properly under the genus *Bombyx*, but we must wait yet awhile in order to ascertain whether all can be included in the same genus.

8. *Bombyx* (Theophila) *Huttoni.*—Westwood.—This is a wild mountain species, feeding on the indigenous mulberry of Simla, Mussoorie, and Almorah. I first discovered it at Simla in 1837, and afterwards in great abundance at Mussoorie. In some years they swarm to such an extent, that by the end of May, the worms of the first, or spring brood, have thoroughly denuded even large forest trees, not leaving a single leaf. In this predicament they quit the tree in search of another which they generally find near at hand, and which is then soon thickly covered with cocoons spun in the leaves; but if, unfortunately, they fail to find a tree at hand, the whole brood perishes, the most forward worms spinning cocoons among shrubs and grass. The trees thus denuded instead of dying, are in another month once more in full leaf, as if nothing had happened.

It is a strong and hardy species, yielding a beautiful soft, whitish silk, and although the worm is too intractable and wandering to be treated in the usual manner in the house, yet I am by no means sure that it cannot be turned to good account by collecting the cocoons from the trees, as was evidently done in the outset by the Chinese with respect to *Bombyx mori*. For a full report I refer the reader to my paper Part II., "On the Reversion and Restoration of the Silk-worm," published in the "Transactions of the Entomological Society of London."

9. *Bombyx* (Theophila) *Bengalensis*—Hutton.—If the species discovered some years ago in Bengal by my friend A. Grote, Esq., is correctly figured in my paper No. 2, just alluded to, then that sent to me from Chota Nagpore in 1869, by Mr. King, must be distinct, for it is in all respects as to shape, colouring, markings, &c., a perfect miniature of *B. Huttoni*; that it is distinct, however, is shown in the smaller size both of larva and imago, as well as in its being a polyvoltine instead of a bivoltine like *B. Huttoni*. In Chota Nagpore the food was the leaf of *Artocarpus Lacoocha*, upon which tree likewise Mr. Grote found his specimens; but as the latter gentleman was in the habit of employing an accurate native delineator of insects, I much doubt any error

occurring in the figure kindly supplied by him to me, and therefore am inclined to regard Mr. King's species as distinct from Mr. Grote's, and would term the Chota Nagpore insect *Bombyx* (Theophila) *affinis*, (nob.) in reference to the remarkable affinity to *B. Huttoni*, in all its stages.

10. *B. affinis—Hutton.*—When the young worms hatched at Mussoorie, from eggs and cocoons sent from Chota Nagpore, I had no leaves of *Artocarpus* within some miles and was sadly puzzled to feed the worms; I tried, without success, the leaves of wild fig trees, *ficus venosa, morus nigra, morus sinensis, m. multicaulis, m. cucullata, m. serrata* (wild), but all to no purpose, and I had almost made up my mind to lose the species, when it suddenly occurred to me to try the leaves of *m. indica*. With these I succeeded, the young worms riddling the hard, coarse leaf into a perfect sieve in a few minutes. Like *B. Huttoni*, in the two first stages they were dreadfully troublesome, wandering down from the branches and spreading all over the table, but as they grew larger they became more tractable and remained tolerably quiet, eventually spinning their cocoons in the leaf like *B. Huttoni*.

When the moths appeared, there was equal difficulty in getting them to pair, and then even many of them laid no eggs; those that did so, deposited them in batches and then covered them over thickly with the brush or tuft of hair at the end of the abdomen; thus the eggs of *B. Huttoni* are pale straw colour, glued to the trunk or branches of the tree, and quite naked, whereas those of *B. affinis* are of an orange color and covered with dark hair. This renders it difficult to detect them on the bark, and the covering is probably used as a non-conductor of heat. The eggs of *B. Huttoni* are scattered along the under side of the small branches or over the bark of the trunk, whereas those of *B. affinis* are placed in patches or groups, and none of the eggs that remain without a coating of hair ever produce worms. I obtained four broods, the last being reared on the trees of *M. nigra* in the open air. I am sorry to add that none survived the winter, although the cocoons were kept in a room with fire; thus, after all my trouble, I lost the species. The silk resembles that of *B. Huttoni*, and is equally good, although from the smaller size of the cocoons there is less of it.

Mr. Grote kindly sent me a specimen of his moth which arrived, as usual by post, quite crushed; the specimen, however, as far as I can remember, was whitish and very much smaller than that of *B. affinis*.

11. *Bombyx* (Theophila) *subnotatus*.—Walker.—Nothing more is known of this species than is contained in Mr. Walker's description of the moth, and that it was procured from Singapore by Mr. R. A. Wallace; neither the larva nor its food is mentioned.—*Vide Proc. Linn. Soc. Lond. iii. Zool., p.* 188. (1859.)

Whether this be a true Theophila, we cannot tell.

12. *Bombyx* (Theophila) *Sherwilli*.—Moore.—This is closely allied to *B. Huttoni*, but the larva is unknown; all that has been ascertained is that the specimen was obtained from a collection made by the late Major J. L. Sherwill, but whether captured in the plains or at Darjeeling, no one knows. People who have often collected at Darjeeling assure me they never saw the species there; hence I incline to regard it as a lowlander, feeding on *Artocarpus* perhaps. All that Moore says of it that it is "allied to *B. Huttoni* and differs from it in being somewhat larger, and of a grayer color, the fore-wing having the apical patch, fuliginous instead of black, and it has only a single transverse discal streak (instead of the two as in *B. Huttoni*). A most prominent character is that the abdomen is tipt with black, as well as having the dark waistband."

13. *Bombyx* (*Ocinara*) *religiosæ*.—Helfer.—Although this stands as a Bombyx, the entire description as given by Dr. Helfer applies rather to a species of *Ocinara*. It is called the Joree silk-worm by Helfer, and the Deo-mooga silk-worm by Mr. Hugon. It is said to occur in Assam and Sylhet; but I have failed to elicit information from those localities. Bombyces are far less erratic than the allied genera of *Theophila* and *Ocinara*, and if indigenous in any district, there they will remain year after year, sometimes in greater, sometimes in lesser, numbers; but *Theophila* and *Ocinara* are both inconstant; plentiful one year, absent altogether the next, and with the latter sometimes for two or three years. Hence Grote for four or five years lost sight of *Theophila Bengalensis*, and no one seems to have seen Helfer's *B. religiosæ* since the time of its discovery.

14. *Ocinara Lida*.—Moore.—This species is found at Mussoorie where it feeds upon the leaves of *Ficus venosa*, the larva being very like that of a geometra, and spinning a small white cocoon on the leaf or against a stone beneath the tree. It is too small to be serviceable. I named it after Mr. F. Moore, but he tells me it is the same as the Javanese O. lida. It is a multivoltine. It feeds on the wild fig also.

15. *Ocinara lactea*.—Hutton.—This also occurs at Mussoorie, feeding on *Ficus venosa* and spins a curious little cocoon of a yellow color, within the leaf; over the cocoon is laid a net-work of yellow silk, too small to be of use. It has several broods during the summer. The larva is smooth, whereas that of the preceding is hairy.

16. *Ocinara comma.*—Hutton.—The moth of this is white, with a dark comma-shaped mark on the disc of the upper wings; hence the name. It occurs both in the Doon and at about 5,500 feet of elevation below Mussoorie.

17. *Trilocha varians.*—Moore.—Is a small species found in Canara; and again by Mr. Grote in Calcutta. As a silk-yielder, it is of no value.

For further remarks on these species, consult the second part of my paper "On the Reversion and Restoration of the Silk-worm."

18. *Cricula trifenestrata.*—This handsome and curious species is found in various parts of India, sometimes in such numbers in the larva state as to become a perfectly destructive pest; it denudes the mango trees of every leaf, destroys the foliage of the cashew-nut, and is even said to attack the tea plants. It occurs in Burmah, Assam Moulmein, and Chota Nagpore in Central India. The cocoons are formed in clusters, so closely interwoven, that they cannot be separated for reeling, which, indeed, their very texture prohibits; they are therefore carded, but are not much used; the cocoons are very irritating, from a number of minute bristly hairs from the caterpillars. I am inclined to think there are two species now standing under this name; as some cocoons are very much reticulated, while those from other localities are far more closely-woven and scarcely reticulated at all. This will never prove productive as a silk-yielder, unless the cocoons can be reduced to a gummy pulp, and used for some other purposes.

19. *Antheræa paphia.*—Linn.—This handsome species is distributed all over India from Burmah to Bombay; but it has to be observed that there are in this wide range several distinct species included under the name. To separate these effectually must be the work of time, and until it is done, there can no really good Tusseh silk be produced. That several of these species are capable of producing a very valuable article of commerce is an undoubted fact, and from its cheapness and durability it would be a boon to that class of the British population which cannot afford to indulge in expensive silks. There is a stupid outcry against Tusseh silk now raised at home by some of the would-be-knowing ones, who are quite ignorant of the fact that they are not sitting in judgment upon a genuine article, but upon one compounded by the natives by the mixture of the silks of three, if not four, distinct species whose fibres are of different thickness. Take the silk of any one uncrossed species and reel it as carefully as is done with the produce of the Chinese Bombyces, and these cavilling quidnuncs, who do not know one species from another, would soon sing to a different tune.

At present the native method is this: At the season when the cocoons have been formed, the jungles swarm with them, and men sally forth to pluck them from the trees. These jungles, however, contain several distinct species, a thing of which the natives are profoundly ignorant; these cocoons are all promiscuously huddled together, placed in hackeries, and carted off to the dealers. They are then sorted according to size, thickness, color, &c., and named accordingly as a kind of trade mark, but without any reference to species. The cocoons selected for reeling are treated in the roughest manner and all kinds spun off together; those that are kept for breeding are allowed to eat out of the cocoon, as it is termed, and to interbreed, still without reference to species; and as this has been going on from time immemorial, of course the species have become blended into a most confusing cross-breed. Hence it results that if a dozen cocoons are taken at random, no two moths will probably resemble each other.

The system of crossing is not confined to the Tusseh group. I have detected it more than once in what were termed Japan worms imported direct from that island; indeed, I have not only detected the cross, but I have succeeded in separating the species which composed it; in one instance, I found *Bombyx mori* crossed with *B. Sinensis*, and on another occasion *B. Textor* and *B. Sinensis* in the case of domesticated species there is no great difficulty to contend with, but with regard to the wild species the thing is very different, and, in short, I can scarcely yet say that I see my way at all clearly. In the Dehra Dhoon and extending up the hill side to about 4,500 feet, or perhaps more, we have two species of Tusseh, one of which is also found in Central India; what the other is, I am not yet prepared to say. Here, however, we have no artificial crossing, so that our species may be regarded as types. The difficulty is to get the sexes of two moths showing marks of relationship to come forth at the same time, so as to obtain a brood and compare the larvæ with others. To trust to the reports of the unscientific would only add to the confusion; a gentleman residing in one of these silk districts kindly furnished me with cocoons of what he declared to be distinct species, and furnished me with voluminous notes, but neither the one nor the other furnish the slightest data upon which I can work or depend; that a cross exists I can see, but my correspondent is not able to enter into my views and wishes. To visit the jungles myself at the season when the worms appear is out of the question, and the cocoons afford no information. Nevertheless, I shall continue to collect hints from all who may be kind enough to give them.

20. *Antheræa nebulosa.*—Hutton.—This is one of the species that has been crossed upon *A. Paphia,* and it seems to be not uncommon throughout Central India. It is a well marked species, and as specimens have been sent to England, we shall soon hear what the opinion is, provided the moths arrive in safety. The silk would probably rival that of *A. Paphia.*

21. *Antheræa*———?—I refrain from naming this until I can obtain more specimens; it is found in Central India and in the Dehra Dhoon. It is quite distinct from either of the foregoing.

22. *Antheræa Pernyi.*—Guér. Mén.—This species was discovered in Mantchouria to the north of China, where it feeds on the oak. According to Mr. Atkinson, of the Educational Department, Calcutta, he has captured two specimens of what he declares to be this species at Darjeeling; these flew to a light placed out in the evening, but nothing further was ascertained. The great difference between the climates of Darjeeling and Mantchouria calls especial attention to this discovery, and leads one to wonder that the species has not been detected at Mussoorie and Simla, both farther to the north. It would be as well if Mr. Atkinson would give his attention to the subject, and enable us to bring it under cultivation.

23. *Antheræa Yamamai.*—Guér. Mén.—This is a Japan species and is well thought of both in England and in France, where great efforts have been made to introduce it, but as yet with very indifferent success. Last year I received through the kind offices of Dr. Wallace an ounce of these eggs direct from Japan, and found them to thrive admirably on our hill oak; unfortunately my means were not adequate to the undertaking, as gauze covers were found to be indispensable in order to ward off the attacks of insects, such as bugs, the larvæ of coccinallæ, spiders, &c., and as some of the young trees were about six feet in height, the expense was greater than I cared to undertake, as I was certain of no reward. However, the experiment was suddenly cut short in one night when the worms were in the fourth stage, by the incursion from below of a swarm of large black ants which carried off every one, so that like Lord Ullin, "I was left lamenting." The species, however, is well worth another trial if only for my own amusement.

21. *Antheræa Assama.*—This is the Mooga or Moongah worm of Assam which produces a very excellent silk, which, if well reeled by skilful hands, instead of being carded, would be extremely valuable. I have found this species in the Dehra Doon feeding upon a tree known to the natives as "*Kirkee,*" but I only procured one male and have not since seen another. I am searching for it, as there must be more than one.

22. *Antheræa Perrottetti*—Guér. Mén.—Said to occur at Pondicherry, but although I long ago applied to the late Mr. Perrottet, he could not procure any specimen of it, although he sent *Antheræa Paphia* (vera) and Actias Selene.

I am half inclined to regard it as a mere variety of *A. Paphia.*

23. *Antheræa Helferi*—Is found at Darjeeling, the cocoon resembling that of the common Tusseh; but no one seems inclined to do more in those regions than collect the moths.

24. *Antheræa Frithi*—Is another Darjeeling species, of which we know no more than of the last. At that station, where species are abundant, no one ever does more than collect the imago.

25. *Antheræa Royle*—Moore—Is common at Simla, Mussoorie, Almorah, and, I think, Darjeeling. It feeds upon the common hill oak, spinning a large but thin cocoon between three or four leaves. I found it at Simla in the winter of 1836 by following a flock of tomtits, one of which, after a time, began tapping so loudly that I hastened to the spot and found the little fellow hard at work on the outer cocoon from which I drove him off and pocketed the prize. The outer coating is very strong, and I do not think it could be reeled; but within this case is the true cocoon, of an oval form and yielding a good silk. The worms are easily reared, and sometimes give two or three crops, but this is when treated in the house.

The males will couple with *Antheræa Paphia,* but the produce never comes to anything.

26. *Antheræa*———?—This is a species occurring near Bombay and discovered by the Messrs. Robertson, of the Civil Service, who regard it as allied to *A. Yamamai* of Japan. They have very kindly promised to send me cocoons as soon as procurable. From the rough sketch of the cocoons which Mr. E. P. Robertson sent me, it certainly appears to differ from *A. Paphia,* though I do not think it can possibly be *A. Yamamai.*

27. *Antheræa*———?—Nothing is known of this species, except that I possess a well formed (probably male) cocoon of about the size of one of the *Bombyx mori;* the peculiarity exists in there being no vestige of a pedicle or safety rope, the cocoon being equally perfect at both ends. Unfortunately, during repeated illnesses, the label has been lost, and I have not the least recollection of where it came from or who sent it, although I incline to think it came from Madras through the kind offices of Mr. A. H. Blechynden. I am particularly anxious to obtain living specimens of this which is not only an undescribed species, but promises to be a valuable silk-yielder.

These remarks will serve to show how much scientific work yet remains to be done in this single genus of *Antheræa*.

28. *Attacus Atlas.*—Linn.—This, the largest of the real silk-spinners, is common at 5,500 feet at Mussoorie and in the Dehra Doon; it is found also in some of the deep warm glens of the outer hills. It is also common at Almorah where the larva feeds almost exclusively upon the "*Kilmorah*" bush or *Berberis Asiatica;* while at Mussoorie it will not touch that plant but feeds exclusively upon the large milky leaves of *Falconeria insignis.* The worm is perhaps more easily reared than any other of the wild Bombycidæ, producing a very large and well-stuffed cocoon of a grey color and somewhat difficult to unwind; a strong ley of potash appears to be the best solvent. The species is also abundant in Cachar, Sylhet, and is found also at Akyab, in Arracan, as well as in China.

29. *Attacus Edwardsi.*—This species was discovered at Darjeeling and is much darker in color than the other, and rather smaller in size, but nothing seems to be known of its food and silk.

30. *Attacus Cynthia.*—Abundant at Mussoorie, feeding on various wild plants; common in China where it feeds on *Ailanthus glandulosa*; found in Assam, Cachar, Saugor. Although it is commonly reported to be under cultivation in different places (*vide* Colonel Agnew's Assam Report), yet such is not the case, the *Attacus ricini* being in India invariably mistaken for it. Indeed, until a few years ago, when I pointed out the fact, *Attacus Cynthia* was not known to occur in India, the other species passing under that name, as the silkworms did under that of *B. mori. Attacus Cynthia* has been imported into France and England and reared out in the open air on trees of *Ailanthus glandulosa*; it has likewise succeeded to some extent in Australia, and I believe they have it also at the Cape of Good Hope. There are difficulties attending the reeling of the silk as there is with all the *Attaci,* but nevertheless the French have succeeded in turning out some very good silk pieces. In England it is not quite so highly thought of as it once was. In Australia Mr. C. Brady has produced silk from it.

31. *Attacus Ricini.*—This is the worm that produces the silk known to the natives as the Arrindy silk; it is easily reared and feeds on the castor oil plant *Ricinus communis.* The silk is obtained by carding. The chief places of cultivation are Assam, Rungpore, and Dinagepore, in Eastern Bengal, *not at Dinapore,* as stated in one of Dr. Bennett's reports. It is also cultivated in smaller quantities in other places. The Mekirs to the eastward possess a very fine kind with white silk. *Attacus ricini* thrives well at Mussoorie, and has been introduced into France, Algeria, Malta, and other places.

32. *Attacus Guerini*—Moore—Is known only from a few specimens of the moth in some museum in England, and I am induced to regard it as no more than an ill-fed specimen of *A. Ricini.* I have failed to procure it from any part of the country, though I have seen an approach to it in ill-fed specimens of the former in my own trays. This under-feeding, or semi-starvation, is well exemplified in some very Lilliputian specimens of *Actias Selene,* received from a gentleman who reared it at Serampore, near Calcutta, where he only supplied the worms with food *twice a day*; the moths are only a quarter of the natural size.

33. *Actias Selene*—Very common in a wild state at Mussoorie, where it feeds on the wild cherry, wild pear, walnut, cedrela paniculata, coriaria nipalensis, and several other forest trees and shrubs. It occurs also at Almorah, Darjeeling, Assam, Cachar, Saugor, and at Serampore, near Calcutta. Mr. C. Turnbull failed to reel silk from the cocoons sent down from this, but it has been reeled, though there is not much of it.

34. *Actias Mœnas*—Doubleday—Occurs at Darjeeling and is a very large species, but nothing has been recorded of its habits, food, or produce.

35. *Actias Leto*—Is another Darjeeling species, the economy of which has yet to be ascertained.

36. *Saturnia pyretorum*—Occurs at Darjeeling and Cachar, but nothing more is known of it.

37. *Saturnia Grotei.*—Has been found at Darjeeling, and one or two specimens have been captured at Mussoorie, but collectors of moths make no inquiries as to economy, and for all practical purposes the species might as well remain unknown. I am inclined to think that the larva feeds on the wild pear tree (*Pyrus Kytul?*)

38. *Saturnia Lindia*—Moore.—Of this nothing more is known than that it occurred in a collection made by the late Captain James Lind Sherwill, and is supposed to be from Darjeeling or its neighbourhood. It is allied to *Saturnia Grotei.*

39. *Saturnia Cidosa*—Moore.—From Captain J. L. Sherwill's collection also, and from North-Eastern India, but we have no information regarding it. From its being closely allied to *Saturnia pyretorum,* I should be inclined to suppose it an inhabitant of Darjeeling or Cachar.

40. *Neoris Huttoni*—Moore.—Found by myself at Mussoorie at about 6,500 feet of elevation, feeding on the wild pear tree. The larvæ are to be found in April. The cocoon is an open net-work, and would produce no silk.

41. *Caligula Simla*—Occurs at Simla, Mussoorie, and in Kumaon, feeding on the walnut, salix Babylonica, wild pear tree, &c., but the cocoon is a mere coarse open net-work through which the pupa is visible, and yields no silk.

42. *Caligula Thibeta*—Occurs at Mussoorie, where I have taken it on andromeda ovalifolia, wild pear, and common quince. It occurs also in Kumaon, but the specific name is a misnomer, the insect never approaching Thibet. Specimens were taken out of a collection made in Kumaon, and because the collector travelled into Thibet it was ridiculously enough called a Thibetan collection, and the species named accordingly. The cocoon is a coarse open net-work through which the larva is visible, but there is no available silk.

43. *Loepa Katinka*.—West.—A very beautiful yellow moth discovered originally in Assam occurring also, according to my ideas, at Mussoorie. Mr. Moore, however, considers mine as distinct. I am not quite satisfied that the cocoon will not yield silk, but there is very little of it.

44. *Loepa Sivalica*.—Hutton.—Closely allied to the last, and found at Mussoorie at about 5,500 feet and lower. It will probably yield a small quantity of silk.

45. *Loepa Miranda*.—Atkinson.—Found by him at Darjeeling; a good and handsome species, but nothing more is recorded of it.

46. *Loepa Sikkimensis*.—Atkinson.—A very beautiful species found by Mr. Atkinson at Darjeeling. It may be known from the others, by the smaller size, and by the wings being clouded with maroon. Of its economy nothing is known.

Three or four other species of this family occur in Darjeeling and Sylhet, but beyond their existence, nothing is recorded.

Those species, which like *Actias selene* and *Antheræa paphia*, weave strong compact cocoons perfectly closed at both ends, are furnished on each shoulder with a hard wing spur for the purpose of separating the fibres when the moth is ready to come forth; it may be heard grating against the silk and the point may often be seen protruding. It is common to the genera *Actias* and *Antheræa*, and was discovered by myself.

In *Attacus*, *Neoris*, and *Loepa*, the upper end of the cocoon is left open, the fibres pointing forward closely arranged, like the fine wires of a mouse-trap. No spine is needed in these *genera*.

In *Bombyx* and others, although the cocoons are entire, the silk is loosely woven, and the fibres being moistened by an acid from the mouth, are then easily separated by the claws on the forefeet of the moths.

This is about the state and extent of our knowledge of the *Bombycidæ* of India; that there are many other species yet to be discovered, no naturalist will think of denying. Nature is the book through which the Almighty teaches man to look from earth to heaven, and as His works and knowledge are boundless, so has this beautifully illustrated book no end.

MUSSOORIE: *the 26th July* 1871. THOMAS HUTTON.

APPENDIX B.

REMARKS ON THE DISTRIBUTION OF SILK TREES.

"Before proceeding to describe the *modus operandi* in a piece of silk cultivation, it will be necessary to make a few remarks on the distribution of those silk trees which are most promising in respect of utility or abundance, or both.

"Any considerable portion of upland (1,000 acres for instance) that may be taken up in a block will be sure to consist of both upland and alluvial land, and of these the proportions vary, the alluvial in many places constitutes a half, sometimes a third, and seldom less than a quarter.

"If the grant should be situated in an uninundatable part of the country, the outlying portions of the alluvial land will generally consist of tree jungle containing a large proportion of silk trees, patches of from ten to fifteen large trees. In each patch will generally be found, called by the natives Chelitaoora, and consisting of *Dillenia Speciosa* alone, or with little intermixture; on this the Atlas worm feeds.

"The Juki or Ooriam (*Andrachne trifoliata*) one of the Mooga trees, will also be found pretty evenly sprinkled over such land at the rate of from two or three trees at least per acre, and more uniformly than *Dillenia Speciosa.*

"The Ficus Indica, Butt or Banian, the food of another species of Antheræa, also affects such lands, and may generally be found one to every ten or fifteen acres, and of a large size.

"The alluvial land lying within the borders of the upland, and divided and enclosed by it in strips of varying width and length (called by the natives "towars") is generally too defective in its drainage to admit of tree jungle, but here and there, intermixed with the null and ekur grasses, there may be found a swamp tree (Heejol) fed on by the tussur worm; this tree taken alone is too sparse, but might be made use of in cultivation in conjunction with other trees.

"Ascending the uplands we shall find, particularly in* secondary forest, the Soom (*Tetranthera lanciæfolia*) which scarcely occurs on alluvial land, in considerable numbers, averaging perhaps four or five fine trees to each acre besides saplings; this tree should be specially sought after, being one of those on which the Mooga worm feeds.

"In deserted 'jhooms' of ten or twelve years standing, large patches of fifty and sixty acres in extent will be found to consist almost entirely of koorkooree and *A Gordonia?* Wild tea never occurs in anything like the density and abundance of these plants, the land is occupied by them over large tracts quite as advantageously as it could be were they cultivated, and all that is required is, that they should be thinned out by the hand of man instead of being left to the natural process, which is tedious and irregular.

"Where these plants occur, so completely is the land shaded by their closeness and regularity, that weeds can gain very little ground, and are easily checked.

"Such patches as these would prove most valuable in a mixed system of cultivation, as both of the trees are fed on with avidity by the Atlas worm. Even allowing the necessity of carding the silk, and its consequently inferior value, these drawbacks would be compensated, in a great measure, by the yield that land so advantageously occupied would give, the facility of protection against birds, and the low cost or rather the small amount of labour,† by which the weeds might be kept down on the overshaded land, to say nothing of the advantage of having ready grown trees.

"Those can best appreciate the advantage of having their land in this overshaded state who have experienced the trouble and expense and the frequent failure sustained in getting their plants, whether of tea, coffee, fruit or any other objects of culture, into that advanced stage in which they overtop or overshade the weeds, and are in no further danger of check or destruction from that source.

"In such tracts of primitive forests as there may be in the grant, wild mango and black varnish trees will be sure to occur in considerable numbers, the foliage of which is convertible into cardable silk, through the medium of an abundant, social and very hardy silk-producing bearworm, *Cucula S. P.*, to be described hereafter. Thus, both upland as well as alluvial will be found to possess large numbers of silk trees, which it only requires the industry and intelligence of man to turn to a good advantage by availing himself of what nature has done for him and supplementing her deficiencies. Any one who attempts rearing silk-worms on jungle trees will not be long in finding out that the shape of these trees, as they exist wild, is by no means the most favourable possible. In the original forest they are by mutual influence drawn up with not long stems, and want of pruning has given them wide straggly heads; in these heads,

* By this I would be understood to mean that sort of forest not necessarily very recent or of small growth, which takes the place of the primitive forest, when that has been removed in Kookee or Bengali cultivation, and when at the same time, the land has not been too much scourged or interfered with by cattle-grazing, wood-cutting, &c.; for, in this case, as I have before had occasion to remark, instead of forest, bamboo weeds, scrub and grasses get the prevalence and hold it.

† Money by no means implies labour, especially in Cachar, where a planter may have his chest full of rupees and not a local labourer on the garden.

though there is no deficiency of foliage, it occupies more space in surface than in depth, and is in detached and disjointed portions.

"The difficulties presented by these defects, when it is attempted to rear worms on the trees, are by no means small; in the first place, the long bare stem is a disadvantage, when it is considered that the tree must be climbed, both to put the worms on it, as well as to move the produce; and the foliage being in detached masses, makes it necessary to apportion the worms not only to the whole foliage, but to every individual detached portion of it; besides this, the worms being unable to reach more food when they have consumed that they are on, without returning by the main stem, are liable to become restive.

"In gathering the cocoons also, the more straggly the head, the greater is the risk to life and limb from loss of footing and weak branches.

"On the other hand, there can be no doubt that if it be attempted to alter the shape of the tree, and to give it a shrub by habit, by cutting off the head together with more or less of the stem, the tree both sustains a great shock, from which it takes a considerable time to recover, and to reproduce a system of branches of equal extent with those it lost.

"When once, however, the tree had recovered its strength, and had formed a close and dense head of foliage not too high from the ground, both the apportioning the worm to the tree and removing the produce would be greatly facilitated. The work-people (who have generally an inveterate dislike to climbing, and no wonder) would easily be enabled to reach the larger boughs from the ground, and by means of them the very extremities of the smallest twigs, which might then by a regular system of pruning be easily kept within reach—and as all the extremities would anastomose—the worms would be enabled to move about freely in search of their food by the outside instead of the inside; and owing to the multitude of twigs would be little likely to disturb each other; the cocoons also would be more uniformly distributed over the tree, and could be easily got at and detached. Of trees, when pollarded, all are not alike in their reproductive power. Tea, for instance, suffers very little from the process, and has at the end of a year all its original foliage and more. *Andrachne trifoliata*, *T. lanciæfolia*, *D. speciosa*, are also, especially the first, quick reproducers; but this is not the case with *F. Indica*, *Nuclea Cadamba*, and one or two other silk trees, which should, therefore, be left in their original form.

"As to the length of stem which should be left to form the frame-work of a future tree, if the stump be too short, there will not be room for the simultaneous production of a sufficient number of boughs to support the full quantity of foliage the tree is capable of producing. From trials made, it would appear that in most cases, a stem of ten feet in height affords ample room for boughs to produce a fine and symmetrical head; a greater length of stem would therefore be unnecessary, and only throw difficulties in the way of climbing.

"The reduction of the tree to this height should be performed in two operations; the first at some height above the ten-foot point, in order to allow for lacerations, which will necessarily take place owing to the great weight of the upper portion of the tree, and its being generally more or less out of the perpendicular; the second operation should remove the lacerated portion with a sloping cut so as to avoid canker.

"Previous to reducing the trees to the shrubby form which would seem on the whole to be the most advantageous, the foliage already on the trees may or may not be converted into silk; if it should be decided to take off a crop, a sufficiency of worms should be placed on the boughs near their junctions, whence they will find their way to the extremities; the worms having consumed the leaf and spun, the entire boughs should be lopped down, at as near their junction with the main stem as possible; this is easily accomplished with a common dhaw, as the horizontality of the boughs greatly helps their breakage; the cocoons should then be gathered from the fallen boughs. The branchless trunk should now be reduced to the proper height, as previously directed; this being done in June and July, the trunks will give little or no leaf that year, all their energy being consumed in forming buds, but by the setting in of the rains in the following year, the trees, though they will not have attained the full development they are capable of, will yield a very fair crop of silk.

"The shrubs (for such they are now) should of course be pruned regularly at the commencement of the cold weather, a proper number of leading branches only being left, and the shoots not allowed to become straggly. The labour required to effect this is very insignificant. When once the shrubs have got back their full strength, they will bear being stripped of their leaves twice a year for many years in succession, provided they are allowed the six months from November to April to recruit.

"In forming a silk plantation, too much stress cannot be laid on the necessity of care being taken that the roots of the trees shall not be cut in hoeing.

"The roots of all jungle trees, and especially on uplands that have at all a steep pitch, are very superficial and easily injured, and if in the course of hoeing the plantation over all the roots met with at a depth of even six inches be cut indiscriminately, the trees will sustain irreparable damage; the damage may not show itself immediately, but will soon be perceived in the sickening of the trees, and their death perhaps as long as one or two years after.

"In a tea plantation, of course, injury to the roots of the forest trees is not avoided; on the contrary, it is rather an object, but in hoeing up the land for silk, something narrower and with a less extent of cutting edge than the common koddallie would be necessary. Having reduced to a proper shape all the trees available for silk that are already on the land, the next object of a silk cultivator will be to fill in the vacancies: to do this to the best advantage, it will be necessary to select from among the known silk trees one which at the same time that it yields a good unreelable silk, also strikes readily from cuttings, as the method by seedlings is generally tedious and uncertain.

"I know of no tree that unites in itself more of these desirable qualities than the Ooriam, *(Andrachne trifoliata)*. Large-sized boughs of this tree, placed in the ground and supported by a tripod of bamboos, become in the course of one year immoveable trees, and the worm that feeds on it is the mooga, than which none can be of a more desirable quality in every respect; besides these advantages, the tree is of sufficient abundance on low lands to afford an ample supply of large sized cuttings. None of the other mooga trees strike with sufficient readiness from cuttings; and the Soom (T'Lanciœfolia), though desirable in other respects, is a very slow grower when raised from seed. The cuttings should be planted at the time the natives choose to put in their plaintain and other fruit trees, and if possible not later than July.

"In this sort of cultivation, it would not be advisable to burn the jungle, as it lies on the land, as is done in forming a tea plantation, as the injury to the foliage and bark of the trees would be too great; all bamboos, therefore, and undergrowth, together with the trees that are not required for silk, should be either thrown off the land or else burnt in heaps at a proper distance from the trees that are to be preserved.

"The fruit-yielding power of the trees is much impaired after pollarding, and in most instances entirely suppressed; this is probably an advantage as far as the yield of leaf is concerned, and at any rate is no drawback.

"Having given some idea of the method of forming a plantation, it will next be necessary to point out the difficulties to be encountered in rearing worms in the open air.

"These are hail, wasps, ants, crows and other insect worms;—birds, lizards, ichneumon flies, and the unusual early setting in of cold. Mr. Hugon mentions in addition, bats and owls.

"The lizards and flies may almost be neglected. Crows and other insectivorous birds are easily deterred, and do by no means so much mischief as might be supposed; a boy with a good pellet-bow, going from tree to tree, might easily protect from six or ten acres of trees during the critical time, which, however, is not over a month.

"Wasps, large and small (particularly the large), are very destructive, as also a species of ferocious and venomous stinging ant (Duhya pipra), which exists in immense numbers in the hollows of all trees, and a single sting of which is death to the large worm. Unfortunately, too, they invariably use their stings for numbing their prey, if it should show signs of resistance, in the attempt to drag it away. Both this ant and the wasps kill much more than they actually want for food, and hence are serious evils, to be got rid of if possible.

"A fluffy net, placed over the tree, would keep out the wasps, but as this would scarcely be remunerative, a certain precentage (which at all events would not exceed five) must be allowed for their depredations; placing decaying fruit or goor near the trees, might possibly divert them from the worms. The ants can fortunately be got rid of to a great extent by a method adopted in Assam, *viz.*, putting a plate of decaying fish at the foot of the tree which will not fail to attract them in large number; as soon as the plate is full, boiling water is poured on, and this process is repeated until the diminishing numbers show that there are comparatively few left; in addition to this, boiling water might be poured into the hollows, and sulphur smoke injected with a pair of bellows would probably have an excellent effect. In shaping the trees, however, much may be done towards obviating the nuisance of ants by leaving no laceration, which might afterwards form cankers and give them a lodgment.

"Hailstorms, if severe, would certainly prove very destructive, but in most years the severest storms are over by the middle of April, *i. e.*, before the worms are hatched, and if the first crop or bund should be ruined by severe hail in May, such as we had in 1864, there would be the more leaf for the second brood in September, at which time hail has never been known to fall in this district. The second brood may, however, suffer from another cause; should the perfecting (or the ripening, as the Assamese call it) of part of the worms be protracted into November, and should there, at the same time, be an early setting in of cold, the worms become very uneasy, descend from the trees, and spin prematurely on whatever comes in their way. We lost a whole brood of Moogas in this way once, but the Atlas is more hardy and does not suffer so much from this cause.

"The next point to be considered is the raising of stock for the plantation; this part of the business will require great care and attention, as upon it depends the whole success of the speculation.

"Without actual experiment on a large scale, it is impossible to state exactly the course to be pursued in this department, as modifications might be necessary which it is impossible even to guess at without actual trial on such a scale. With our present experience, the following seems the best course to be pursued in obtaining a supply of eggs:—a sufficient number of healthy breeding cocoons should be set apart either from the plantation or the stock trees; in apportioning the sexes, the females can be distinguished from the males by the experienced eye, with a very small percentage of error, by their greater size.

"The equality of the sexes being observed, the cocoons should, when about to hatch, be hung on a tree (either that proper to them or any other), having a roomy and not very coarse net placed over the whole, so as to keep in the males; too great a number should not be placed under one net, or they might disturb one another. It may be asked why a large room should not answer as well; the reason is because the moths immediately find out they are not in a state of nature; hence they become alarmed and will not visit the female. The moths do not unite the same night they issue from the cocoons; they take the remainder of the night to develope their wings, and the female to reject a watery fluid with which the body is filled.

"The pairing does not take place till the next night, and the process of impregnation lasts the whole of this second night and the day succeeding, in the evening of which, as the process is nearly complete, the male should be driven away and the female shut into a basket to lay; if they be left, they will both take flight during the night; the female remains quiescent on the cocoon from the time of her issuing till when about to lay. She can with ordinary care be carried about without letting go of the cocoon, and as she never goes in search of the male she requires no tying, which process only irritates and disturbs her, though some seem to consider it necessary.

"The pairing off and laying of the whole batch should be finished in the course of a week, within which limits the bulk of a wild brood (if healthy) do not fail to appear. The manual approximation of the male and female moths, as practised by the Assamese with the more docile Eria and Mooga moths, would probably be unsuccessful with the wild Attacuses and Antheræas.

"In order to ensure success in all operations with the wild worms, it will be necessary to have a due regard to their habits, which are somewhat different from those of worms which have been cultivated through several generations; the former inherit a considerable share of wildness from the egg, and will not bear handling or moving about in the way cultivated worms will; any motion to which they have not been accustomed, such as a jar, will disturb them, and set them wandering, and the same remarks apply to the moths.

"The stock trees before mentioned are trees which it will be found necessary to have, in order to secure as large a supply of eggs as possible from the jungle cocoons with which the plantation is to be started. Of these trees, there should be one species (not necessarily more) answering to each species of worm. No dependence can be placed on procuring a sufficiently large supply of cocoons from the jungles to stock a plantation at the outset; on the contrary, so sparsely do they occur in their wild state, that after a diligent search the planter may be rewarded with perhaps a single female of a certain species: of this he must make the best, he will rarely fail to secure a mate by mere exposure; and in order that he may lose as few as possible of the progeny, he must resort to the stock trees before insisted on. These trees should be situated for convenience sake as near the houses as possible, and should be provided with a fine net, not necessarily as large as the propagating net, but having meshes of sufficient smallness to keep out the small wasps (bullahs), which are especially destructive to the young worms, and will scent out and attack them in a verandah or even inside the house; the stock tree should also be well purged of ants and other vermin.

"After frequent trials, we have found rearing the worms in-doors, whether on trays or on branches placed in bottles of water, to be very unsatisfactory; sooner or later it is necessary to disturb them to change the leaf, and this sets them wandering over the edges and underneath the tray, so that it is some time before they find their food again.

"Unlike the more docile Eria, the wild worms will not feed in close contiguity and appear to disturb each other. Whether any change will be brought about in the habits of the wild worms in this respect, it is for a lengthened course of experiments to decide.

"The wild Mooga of Cachar, which there can be little doubt is identical with the Antheræa Assama, or cultivated Assam Mooga,* shows in its wild state the same want of docility with all other *boná fide* wild worms; but we see the Assamese have in the course of time overcome this wildness, and induced the moths to pair readily in captivity, and the same result may therefore be looked for in the case of the Atlas; and of all the wild species that man should find it worth his while to domesticate or train.

"The climate of Cachar is favorable both to the growth of silk-worms as well as to quick reproduction: the warm and moist atmosphere which prevails from the setting in of the rains in April to somewhat beyond the autumnal equinox, affords a stimulus, and encourages quick development in all the stages of insect life; during none of the breeding months, and they comprise the hottest of the year, does the heat of the sun seem to check the growth of the worms or injure them, unless they happen to be exposed to its direct rays; protected by their

---

* If there should be any lingering doubt in the minds of naturalists as to the absolute identity of the cultivated Mooga of Assam with the wild worm of Cachar above referred to (which unfortunately has no native name here), it ought to be set at rest by the consideration that, besides the identity in appearance, which no authority has yet gainsaid that I am aware of, the worm of Cachar has been found to feed in a state of nature on two of the identical trees on which the Mooga is cultivated in Assam; and this in primeval forest and at a distance of a hundred miles from the nearest silk cultivation. Moreover, in Cachar, no other silk-yielder that could be mistaken for it has yet been found to feed on these trees. The inference is, that the Assamese (in the case of these two trees at least) have availed themselves of natural adaptation, and trained the worms on those trees on which, in the first instance, they found them wild; and this supposition is strengthened by the fact that the wild worm of Cachar is by no means a diffuse feeder like the Atlas, but feeds on a very limited number of trees, and those possessing for the most part aromatic leaves.

M. Periottet, Pondicherry, notes the exceptional occurrence of four generations of the Saturnia Mylitta feeding on the Zizyphus Jujuba: this worm is probably the same as the Cachar Tusser feeding on the same tree.

leafy covert, they endure even the broiling days of May without suffering in their health as is shown by the first brood being in no way inferior to that which, coming in in the latter part of October and commencement of November, enjoys a portion of cool weather; indeed, as has been before mentioned, in the case of the Mooga at any rate, I have observed cold check development and produce a decided injury to the health of the worms; there would seem, therefore, to be a strong reason for concluding (in opposition to ideas hitherto prevalent) that the moist and warm climate of Assam and Cachar, natural to the worms, is the best for them in every respect, so long as the natural conditions they exist under are not altered.

"Two broods at least of wild worms are comprised between April 15th and November 15th. The first brood attain maturity at the end of May and commencement of June, and the last at the end of October and during the first few days of November. Some irregularities are occasioned by the stragglers of each brood, of which there will be sure to be some even out of the same batch of eggs; though the irregularity in the hatching of the eggs seldom exceeds a day or two, there is room for, and in all probability does exist, a middle brood between the two before mentioned. We have met with full-grown worms late in August, it is very improbable that these should be stragglers of the first brood, and they in all probability belong to a distinct or middle one; of the existence of such a brood (though strongly suspecting it), I have not, however, been able to satisfy myself.

"The worms of the last brood, which, as before stated, spins in the latter end of October and beginning of November, lie dormant in the chrysalis state, through the whole of the cold weather, through the whole of the hot, though not moist month of March, and do not turn into moths until about the 15th April, thus again originating the cycle. Chrysalides of the Mooga and Tusser occasionally turn in January and February. The eggs take about eight days to hatch. Even if there should be three broods, it is doubtful if any advantage would accrue in a silk garden from making use of all three instead of two only, the first and last. The trees themselves would have to be considered as well as the worms; to strip them too frequently of their leaves would be like killing the goose that laid the golden eggs, and probably after all produce little extra gain to the cultivator beyond what would accrue if the plants were allowed plenty of time to put forth and ripen their foliage. There can be no doubt that crude unripened foliage both yield an inferior quantity, if not quality, of silk, and are also less wholesome food for the worms than foliage which has had a proper amount of sun and air.

"I now append a list of the forest trees fed on by those worms which are likely to be of practical utility in silk cultivation, and in order that the identification of the trees may be rendered easier, I have to the best of my ability delineated them. The native name has been given except when there was none, but it is not to be depended on, some names being purely local while others are common to Cachar, Assam, and indeed, the whole of Bengal, as the Baer, the Chelita and the Kadam. The trees given are those that have come under my own observation, but the list is probably far from exhausted, especially with regard to the Atlas, which seems more entitled to the term omnivorous* than any other. Probably, were proper search to be made, the list might be doubled if not quadrupled, and it yet remains to be ascertained how many trees there are on which the worm does not occur in a state of nature, but on which it would nevertheless be found to thrive, if, for instance, the "Ping," Inga species (Mymosœ), which is the food of a silk-producing sphinx, should be congenial to the Atlas, the percentage of Atlas trees would at once be greatly increased, this tree being one of the most common and generally distributed of any. As has been before stated, even if science should not succeed in overcoming the unreelableness of the Atlas cocoon, it would still be worth cultivating as a cardable silk, owing to the great abundance in which it might be grown; where the other silks could only be produced in seers, this might be obtained in maunds, and might even, under a proper system of culture, cost very little more to produce than the fine and long-stapled cotton. The Atlas trees are—

"1. *Phakeera*—Cinchonaceæ? Foliage slightly bitter, stature middling, tolerably abundant.

"2. No native name,—probably a laurel, foliage redolent of prussic acid, fruit like a plum, kernel containing a large proportion of oil, resembling that of bitter almonds; stature large, not very common.

"3. Could not find out any native name, but the tree may easily be identified by its resemblance to the China tea plant, and its frequent occurrence as a weed in tea gardens, where it is often left by the weeders by mistake for tea; stature middling, common in jhoom lands; less so in primitive forest.

"4. *Nagdana, Arternisia, s. p.?* An annual, and one of the most common of jhoom weeds; it may be known by the satiny pile on its leaves, which rubbed in the finger and smelt, cause sneezing; they possess a scent similar to lavender,—the Cachar name is quite local, and is probably given to it because of its fragrance. The true Nagdana is the *Boswellia thurifera;* this plant is too small in stature to be available as a silk tree, for which, in other respects, its abundance peculiarly fits it.

"5. *Monphul* (Cachar name), known in Dacca as the Myna kata, a thorny, rapid-growing fruit tree, not indigenous, but found in great quantities self-sown about the villages; the

* I once placed a female Atlas moth on a tree not selected on account of its being the food of the species, but simply the first that came to hand, some eggs happening to be on the tree. I found about a month after a fine brood of healthy worms on the tree.

fruit is somewhat smaller than an apple, but except in being yellow has a good deal of resemblance to that fruit; the fruit is cut up by the natives into slices, which are threaded on string and hung up in their houses to smoke and dry; stature middling.

"6. *Balos*, a rapid-growing weed, which affects new clearances, the deep green of the leaf with the elongated delicate red leaf stalks, enable it to be easily recognised; very common and of large stature, fed on also by *A. Canningi.*

" 7. *Koorkooree*, one of the commonest of "jhoom" weeds; it invades and monopolizes large tracts of land; exclusively or very nearly so grows to a middling stature, and, where abundant, shades the ground completely; this tree is one of the most eligible for training the Atlas on.

" 8. *Lutki (Osbeckia)*, the common conspicuous pink-flowering plant; it scarcely grows large enough to train silk on, but the silk off it is very white.

" 9. *Bon Chelita*, so called probably from a resemblance in the grouping of the leaves to the Chelita; a large, hardy, rapid-growing tree, sufficiently common for purposes of silk cultivation.

" 10. *Kadam (Nauclea)*. A common large-leaved, rapid-growing tree, especially on new clearings, where it soon, if allowed to grow, overshades the land; well adapted as a nurse for young tea or any delicate plants; the leaves become of great size when the plant is young, especially on rich hill lands; as the tree grows larger, they diminish in size; occurs mostly on hill lands, seldom on alluvial.

"11. *Chelita (Dillenia speciosa)*, a large-sized luxuriant tree, partial to alluvial lands, on which it may be found in clumps or groves; grows very well even in badly-drained soil and with water about the roots; owing to the large size of this tree, its growing in clusters and the large quantity and bushiness of its foliage, it is eminently adapted for training the Atlas worm on.

" 12. *Boidraj (Pedrelaceæ) ?* a large-sized and very common tree in old forests. Atlas silk off this is very dark. This tree is very common in the Sylhet District, and occurs all the way down to Dacca.

" 13. *Lood*, also a full-sized tree, may be known by its dark green shiny leaves, and its bark, which is thicker than that of probably any other tree; this tree is also fed on by the *A. Canningi.*

" *Attacus Canningi trees.*—Besides the two before mentioned, which are fed on by this worm, as well as by the Atlas, *viz.*, the Balos and the Lood, there are—

" 1. A small annual, apparently an Amaranth, which would not be available for cultivation.

" 2. The Honoor, a large-sized tree sufficiently common. On this tree I have in some seasons seen the worms so abundant naturally, as completely to strip it of foliage. I was unable to obtain a drawing of this tree.

Mooga or Antheraea Assama trees.

" 1. *Hooara or Booara.*—This is one of the trees on which the Mooga is cultivated in Assam, where the tree is, I believe, called Aownla or Awla; its leaves are somewhat aromatic, and are almost round, with their venation very much in relief. Great destruction of this tree takes place in Cachar for tea box wood; it might be turned to a more profitable use by rearing silk on it; it is very common both on low and up lands.

"2. A laurel, having a considerable resemblance, both as regards shape, aroma and flavour of the leaves, to the common cultivated bay; the foliage is, however, much larger and coarser, limited in quantity, but growing to a large size.

" 3. *Phooair, s. p.*—This tree, which is somewhat less common than the "Soom," hereafter to be mentioned, is nevertheless one on which the worm thrives very well; the leaves are aromatic, and in other respects it has a considerable resemblance to the laurels, and will probably be found to belong to that family.

" 4. *Cheng Phisol.*—This is the Cachar name; in Assam it goes by the name of "Soom," which is stated by masters to be the *Tetranthera lanciaefolia Lauraceæ.* I have in Cachar met with two varieties, one more aromatic than the other; it is found in the shape of large trees in primitive forest, but is much more common, though of a less size in relinquished Bengali and Kookee* jhooms on hill land. This tree presents in Cachar, as in Assam, great facilities for rearing the worms, as where it does occur it is in considerable numbers together; it is rapid-growing, soft-wooded, so as to make pruning easy, and when cut over, forms a fine bushy tree in a short time.

" 5. *Kanta Hingra, (Castanea, s. p. ?)*—This is an umbrageous tree, with plenty of dense foliage; the new growths are a fine velvety red; where the tree does occur, it generally may be found that there are more in the neighbourhood; four or five such trees well cultivated would occupy one acre of ground advantageously, and properly tended would yield no small return of a fine silvery silk. The other oaks, of which there are many, deserve trial to ascertain whether any of the known silk-yielders will feed on them, as they seem a likely class of trees.

---

* It may be mentioned once for all that a "jhoom" is a clearance made by either Kookees, Nagas or Bengalees for purposes of cultivation.

"6. *Butt (Ficus Indica).*—Every here and there, and especially on the low lands, one of these trees either standing alone or else in union with another tree, may be found, its wide-spreading head covering a great extent of ground. I do not think vicious pruning would answer for this tree, the silk from which would have to be procured by climbing, or else by causing the descent of the worms when about to spin, as is contrived by the Assamese.

"7. *Juki (Andrachne trifoliata).*—This tree is called Ooriam in Lower Bengal, and may be known by its triple serrated leaves, and its deep red short-grained wood, as has been mentioned before. This tree possesses great vitality, and strikes readily from cuttings of whatever size, and its general distribution on low lands makes it a very desirable tree, and one by no means to be omitted in an out-door silk cultivation.

"*Tusser and A. Frithii trees.*—The cocoons of these two species are very similar.

"The tusser occurs on—

"1. Ramdallah; this occurs in great numbers on deserted jhoom lands or old clearings: its appearance is very peculiar, owing to its fronds being upwards of six feet in length and all radiating from the main stem. I have also found on this tree cocoons resembling those of the mulberry worms, but never could procure the moth.

"2. Boice, Baer of Bengal (Zizyphus Jujuba), not indigenous, nor to be found in the jungles except in the vicinity of Kookee jhooms; abundant near the villages, where a large amount of silk might be procured off them, if the villages were supplied with seed, and the demand for cocoons was steady.

"3. *Heejol*, a swamp tree, occurring in great numbers along the bases of hills, and in the swampy low lands which intervene. Whether it would be worth while to embrace these trees in a system of culture remains for experiment to decide; but I do not think the obstacles presented by the swampy ground to communication between the trees are insuperable. There is one advantage, *viz.*, that the water in which the trees stand would keep away some depredators, such as lizards and owls.

"*A Frithii* feeds on—

"4. *Phooair, s. p.*—A common jungle as well as village tree, being probably sown from wild seed by the villagers for the sake of its oval sour fruit, the leaves become a bright red before they fall; common, and of pretty large stature.

"*Cucula trifenestrata.*—This hardy and abundant worm produces a silk, brilliant in appearance, but which can only be carded; we have found large quantities of its cocoons on several trees, but at present only remember—

"5. The Dolijam, or common indigenous tea;

"6. The Luckiam or wild mango, an abundant tree, and one growing to a large size;

"7. The Am Jhowa or black varnish tree; the one the foliage of which resembles that of the mango. The cucula silk is used in Assam for adulterating Eria, owing to the abundance in which it is procurable in the forest.

"Having thus pointed out a number of the trees which might be used for silk training, which number, I am convinced, might be greatly increased by further observation and experiment, it remains to point out a few of the advantages possessed by the cultivation of silk on full-grown trees over that of tea, coffee, or any other plant, even supposing the produce of each per acre to be of equal value—*1st*, then, in silk, that first and most laborious preparation of the land which is necessary in all other cultivation preparatory to putting in the seed or plants is dispensed with; *2ndly*, with other plants than those ready grown in the forest there is for one, two, three years and even more, a constant struggle against the weeds, and should these, owing to failure of labour or other unforeseen circumstances, which in practice do frequently occur, gain the mastery for any long time, the whole of the previous operations are rendered null; but in silk the trees have already, and while in the forest, grown to such a height as to be out of the reach of the smothering influence of weeds, so that these gaining the mastery, though it might for a time affect the yield of leaf, would not produce actual death. If a silk plantation should even be forsaken and ran up to jungle, the trees would survive, and it might again be resumed. *3rdly.*—In silk, weeding and other operations are rendered less expensive, because they require to be less frequently repeated, owing to the overshaded state of the land. *4thly.*—Whilst tea takes four years, and coffee five, to reach their prime, up to which time capital lies in the ground, a silk tree is capable of producing as much the first or at any rate the second year as at any subsequent time. *5thly.*—Not only in cultivation would the labour required in silk be less, but also in subsequent processes, and reeling, &c., employments, requiring no great effort but constant attention; are suitable to the nature of the Bengali; numbers of men, boys and women would also attend a silk filature who could not be induced to attend a tea or coffee plantation.

"I have thus pointed out as clearly as my limits would allow the advantages possessed by a system of silk cultivation by wild worms over that by domesticated worms; and, indeed, over any system in which it is necessary first to remove the original forest and then to wait for a long period for the returns.

"I do not pretend to have indicated the exact course to be pursued in practice, being too well aware of the difficulties to be encountered, which, although unforeseen, invariably present themselves in carrying out any scheme, particularly of an agricultural nature. I shall be satisfied if I have convinced such as are capable of taking an interest in the subject of the feasibility of the project; and that in the carrying out the details there are no obstacles which are insurmountable, with sufficient capital, patience, and—what is especially needed for the successful conducting of sericulture—intelligence.

"It is not to be excepted that merchants will risk capital in a path of speculation so perfectly new and untrodden as this. It is the function of Government to lead the way and show what can be done for the encouragement of future capitalists; this it has not been slow in doing in the case of tea and of cinchona, and the results speak for themselves; it is to be hoped, in a new branch of agriculture so promising as this, its encouragement will not be wanting. A lakh of rupees laid out in carrying out the experiment on a proper footing would be no great expenditure even if it should turn out fruitless. Considering the great results at stake, let Government address itself to procuring and perpetuating all the different species of wild silk-worms by means of an establishment as in pisciculture; let it also strive to increase the list of trees that are and may be made available; let it also publish its results, and speculators will not be long in coming forward, by whose agency Eastern Bengal may yet become a great silk, as it is becoming now a great tea, producing country."